ALSO BY JEFFREY BROWN

INCREDIBLE CHANGE-BOTS

CAT GETTING OUT OF A BAG & OTHER OBSERVATIONS

I AM GOING TO BE SMALL

EVERY GIRL IS THE END OF THE WORLD FOR ME

AEIOU: ANY EASY INTIMACY

MINISULK

BE A MAN

BIGHEAD

UNLIKELY

CLUMSY

LITTLE THINGS

A MEMOIR IN SLICES

JEFFREY BROWN

A TOUCHSTONE BOOK
PUBLISHED BY SIMON & SCHUSTER
NEW YORK · LONDON · TORONTO · SYDNEY

Touchstone
A Division of Simon & Schuster, Inc.
1230 Avenue of the Americas
New York, NY 10020

First Touchstone trade paperback edition April 2008

TOUCHSTONE and colophon are registered
trademarks of Simon & Schuster, Inc.

For information about special discounts for
bulk purchases, please contact Simon & Schuster
Special Sales at 1-800-456-6798 or
business@simonandschuster.com

Manufactured in the United States of America

10 9 8 7 6 5 4 3 2 1

Library of Congress Cataloging-in-Publication Data
is available.

ISBN-13: 978-1-4165-4946-8
ISBN-10:   1-4165-4946-3

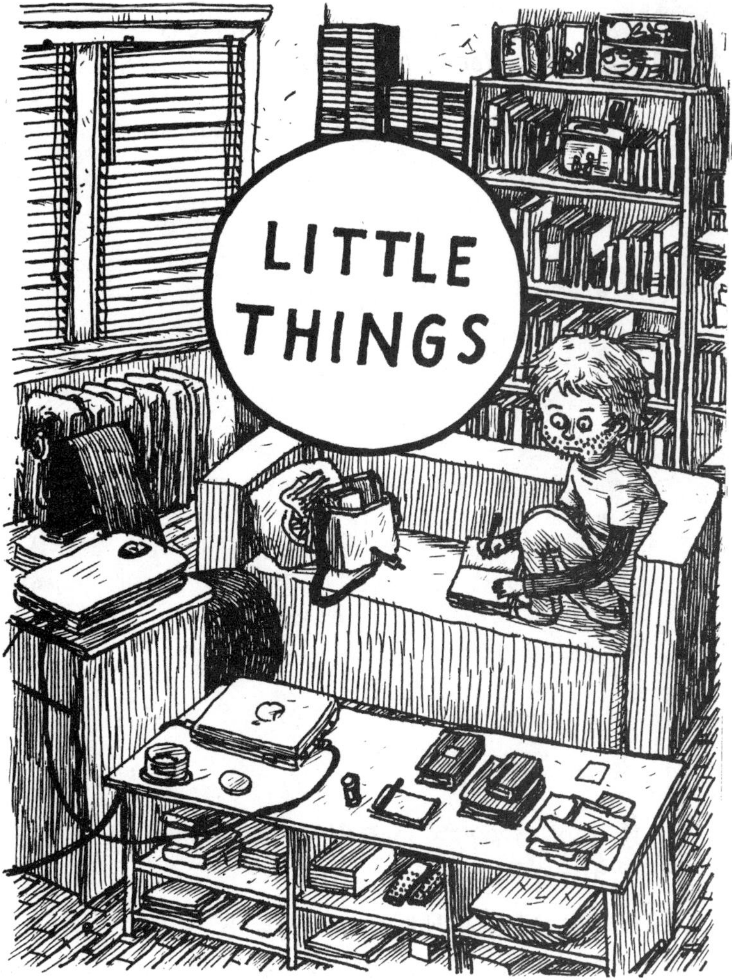
LITTLE
THINGS

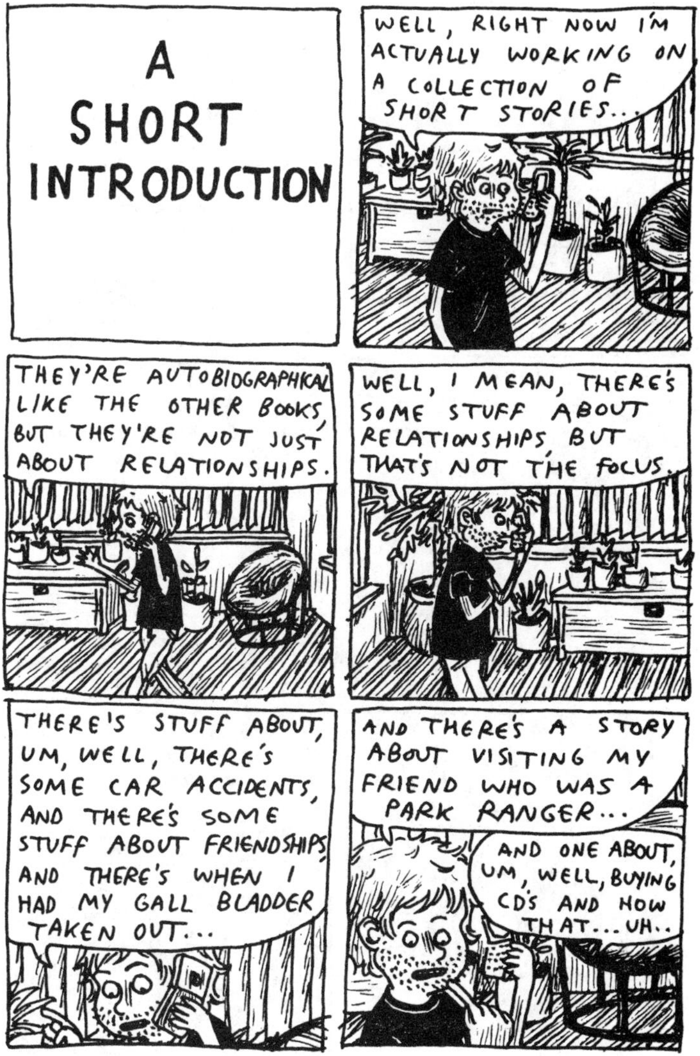
A SHORT INTRODUCTION
WELL, RIGHT NOW I'M ACTUALLY WORKING ON A COLLECTION OF SHORT STORIES...
THEY'RE AUTOBIOGRAPHICAL LIKE THE OTHER BOOKS, BUT THEY'RE NOT JUST ABOUT RELATIONSHIPS.
WELL, I MEAN, THERE'S SOME STUFF ABOUT RELATIONSHIPS, BUT THAT'S NOT THE FOCUS.
THERE'S STUFF ABOUT, UM, WELL, THERE'S SOME CAR ACCIDENTS, AND THERE'S SOME STUFF ABOUT FRIENDSHIPS, AND THERE'S WHEN I HAD MY GALL BLADDER TAKEN OUT...
AND THERE'S A STORY ABOUT VISITING MY FRIEND WHO WAS A PARK RANGER...
AND ONE ABOUT, UM, WELL, BUYING CD'S AND HOW THAT... UH..

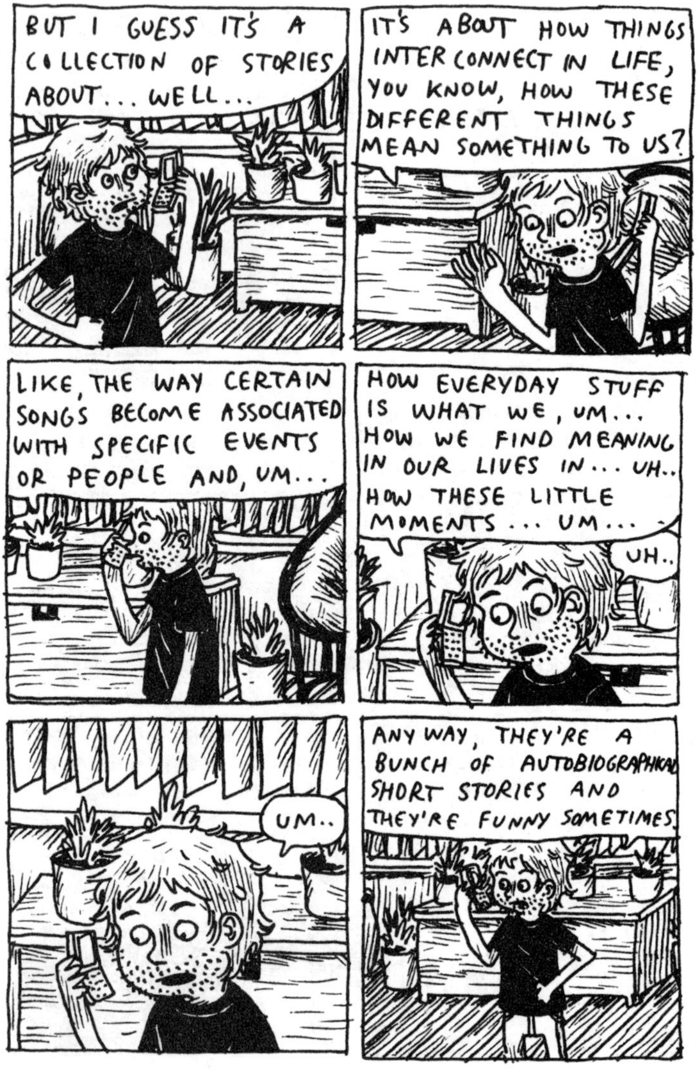
BUT I GUESS IT'S A COLLECTION OF STORIES ABOUT... WELL...
IT'S ABOUT HOW THINGS INTERCONNECT IN LIFE, YOU KNOW, HOW THESE DIFFERENT THINGS MEAN SOMETHING TO US?
LIKE, THE WAY CERTAIN SONGS BECOME ASSOCIATED WITH SPECIFIC EVENTS OR PEOPLE AND, UM...
HOW EVERYDAY STUFF IS WHAT WE, UM... HOW WE FIND MEANING IN OUR LIVES IN... UH.. HOW THESE LITTLE MOMENTS... UM...
UH..
UM..
ANYWAY, THEY'RE A BUNCH OF AUTOBIOGRAPHICAL SHORT STORIES AND THEY'RE FUNNY SOMETIMES.

THESE THINGS THESE THINGS

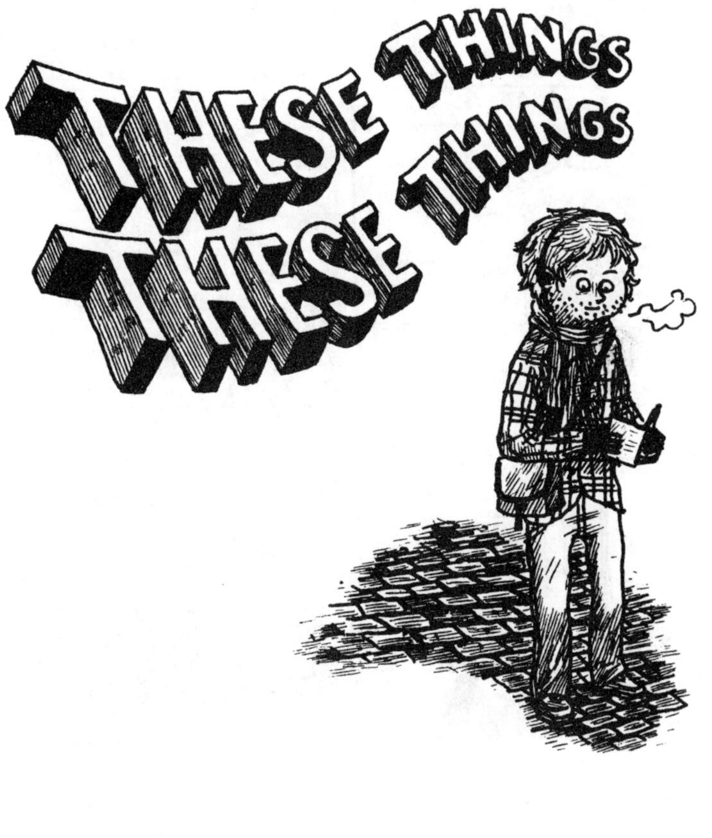

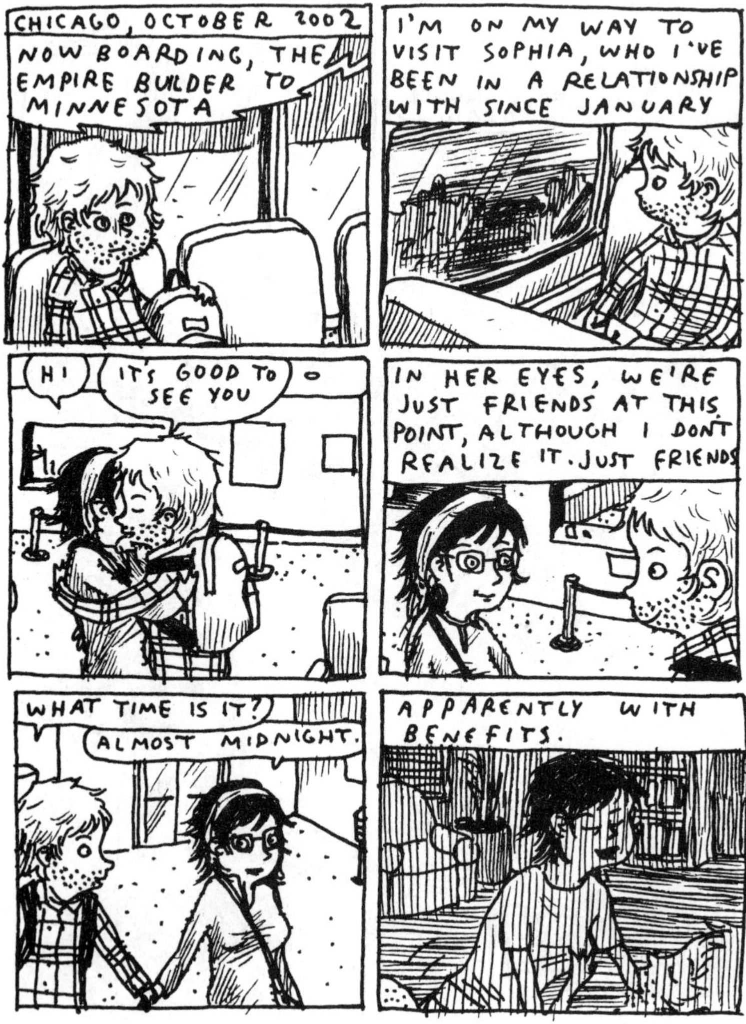
CHICAGO, OCTOBER 2002
NOW BOARDING, THE EMPIRE BUILDER TO MINNESOTA
I'M ON MY WAY TO VISIT SOPHIA, WHO I'VE BEEN IN A RELATIONSHIP WITH SINCE JANUARY
HI
IT'S GOOD TO SEE YOU
IN HER EYES, WE'RE JUST FRIENDS AT THIS POINT, ALTHOUGH I DON'T REALIZE IT. JUST FRIENDS
WHAT TIME IS IT?
ALMOST MIDNIGHT.
APPARENTLY WITH BENEFITS.

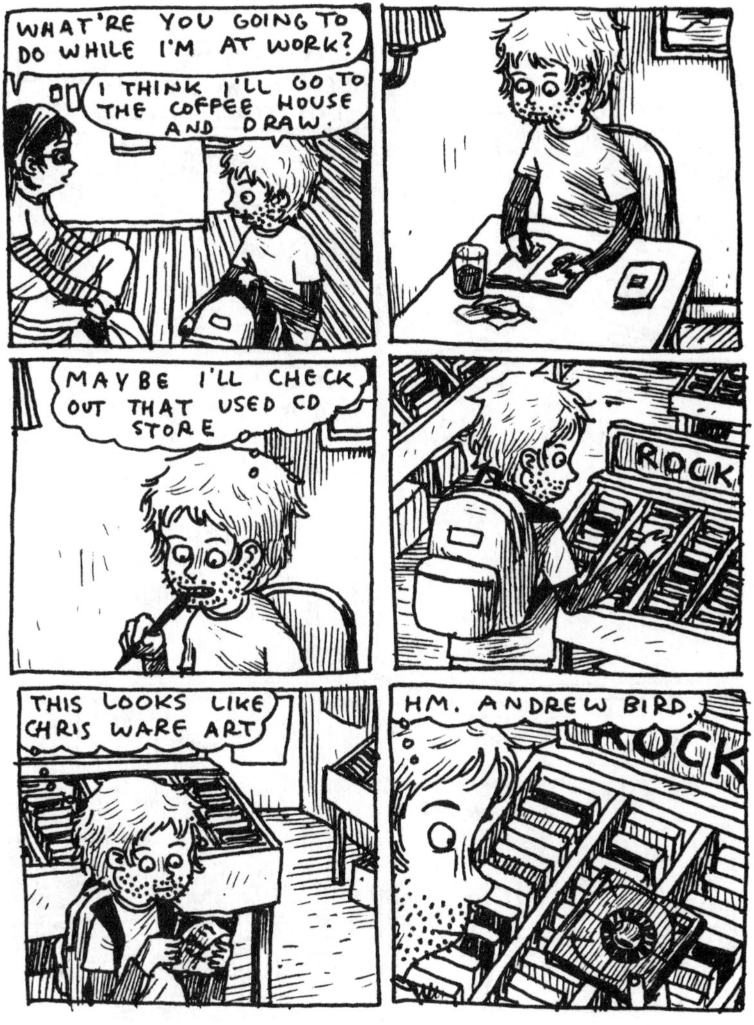
WHAT'RE YOU GOING TO DO WHILE I'M AT WORK?
I THINK I'LL GO TO THE COFFEE HOUSE AND DRAW.
MAYBE I'LL CHECK OUT THAT USED CD STORE
ROCK
THIS LOOKS LIKE CHRIS WARE ART
HM. ANDREW BIRD.
ROCK

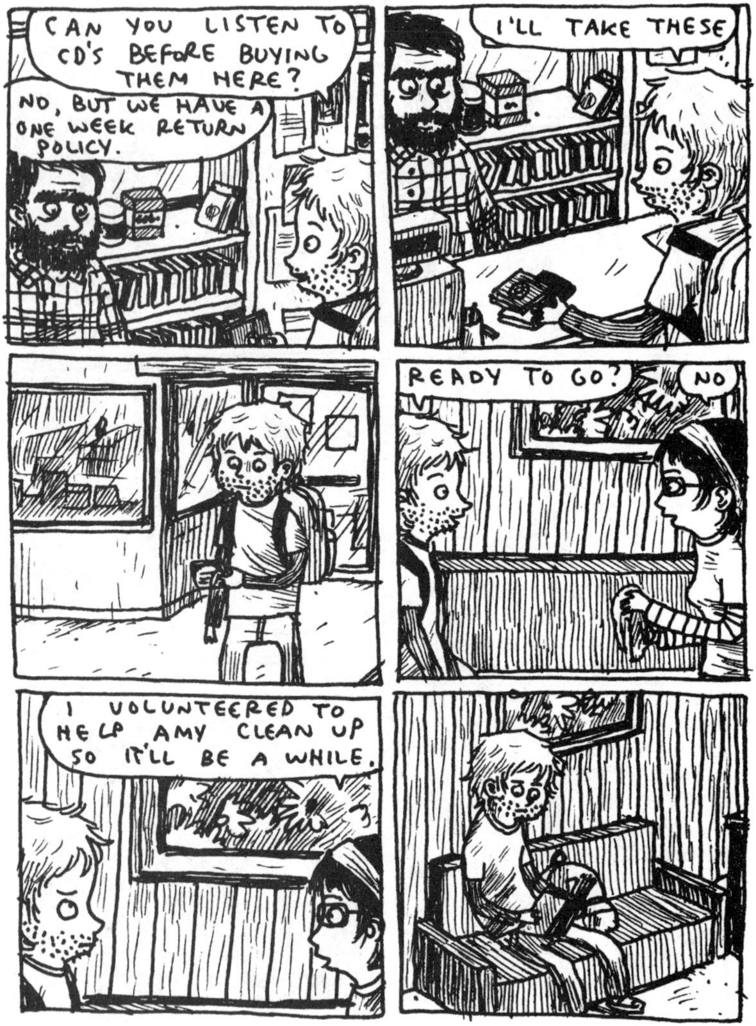
CAN YOU LISTEN TO CD'S BEFORE BUYING THEM HERE?
NO, BUT WE HAVE A ONE WEEK RETURN POLICY.
I'LL TAKE THESE
READY TO GO?
NO
I VOLUNTEERED TO HELP AMY CLEAN UP SO IT'LL BE A WHILE.

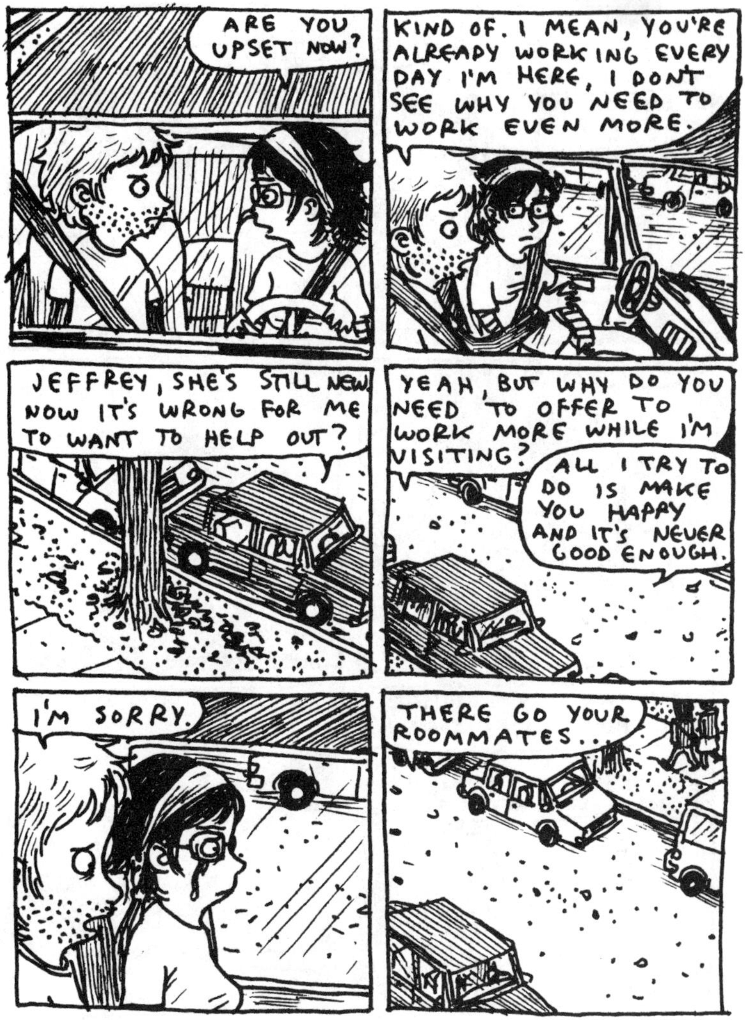
ARE YOU UPSET NOW?
KIND OF. I MEAN, YOU'RE ALREADY WORKING EVERY DAY I'M HERE, I DON'T SEE WHY YOU NEED TO WORK EVEN MORE.
JEFFREY, SHE'S STILL NEW. NOW IT'S WRONG FOR ME TO WANT TO HELP OUT?
YEAH, BUT WHY DO YOU NEED TO OFFER TO WORK MORE WHILE I'M VISITING?
ALL I TRY TO DO IS MAKE YOU HAPPY AND IT'S NEVER GOOD ENOUGH.
I'M SORRY.
THERE GO YOUR ROOMMATES...

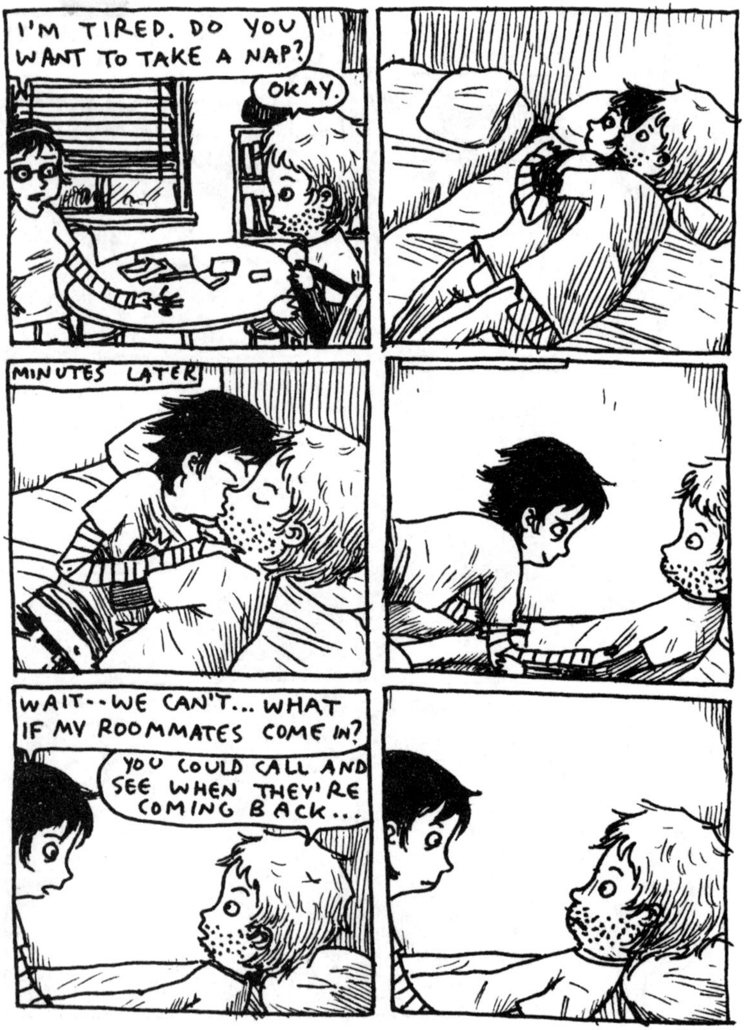
I'M TIRED. DO YOU WANT TO TAKE A NAP?
OKAY.
MINUTES LATER
WAIT--WE CAN'T... WHAT IF MY ROOMMATES COME IN?
YOU COULD CALL AND SEE WHEN THEY'RE COMING BACK...

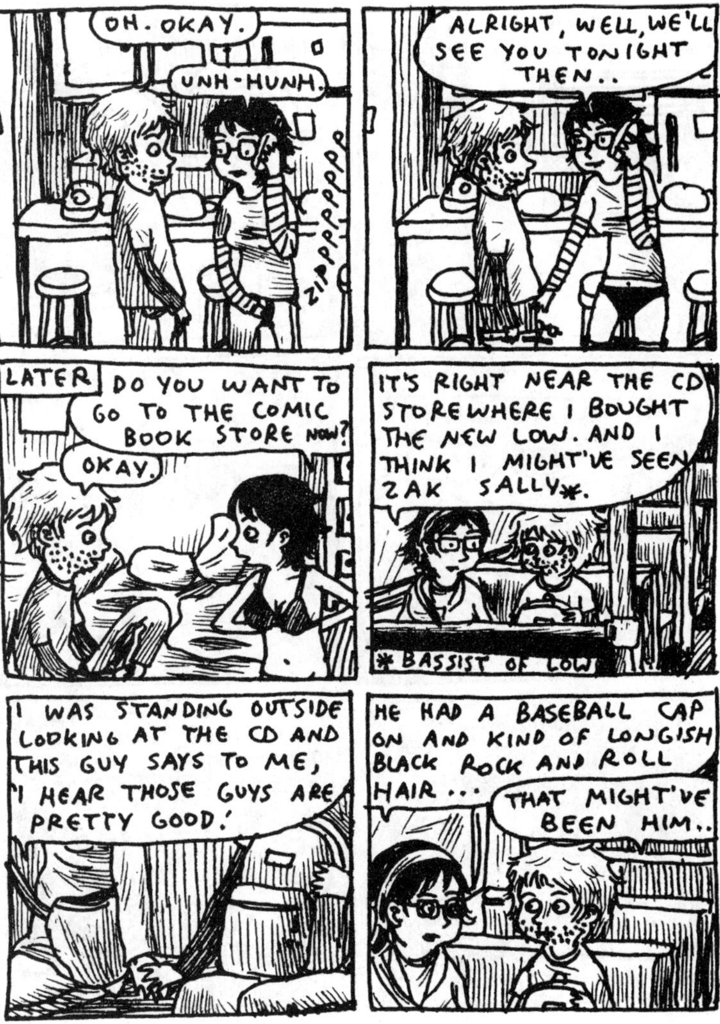
OH. OKAY.
UNH-HUNH.
ZIPPPPPPPP
ALRIGHT, WELL, WE'LL SEE YOU TONIGHT THEN..
LATER
DO YOU WANT TO GO TO THE COMIC BOOK STORE NOW?
OKAY.
IT'S RIGHT NEAR THE CD STORE WHERE I BOUGHT THE NEW LOW. AND I THINK I MIGHT'VE SEEN ZAK SALLY*.
* BASSIST OF LOW
I WAS STANDING OUTSIDE LOOKING AT THE CD AND THIS GUY SAYS TO ME, 'I HEAR THOSE GUYS ARE PRETTY GOOD.'
HE HAD A BASEBALL CAP ON AND KIND OF LONGISH BLACK ROCK AND ROLL HAIR...
THAT MIGHT'VE BEEN HIM..

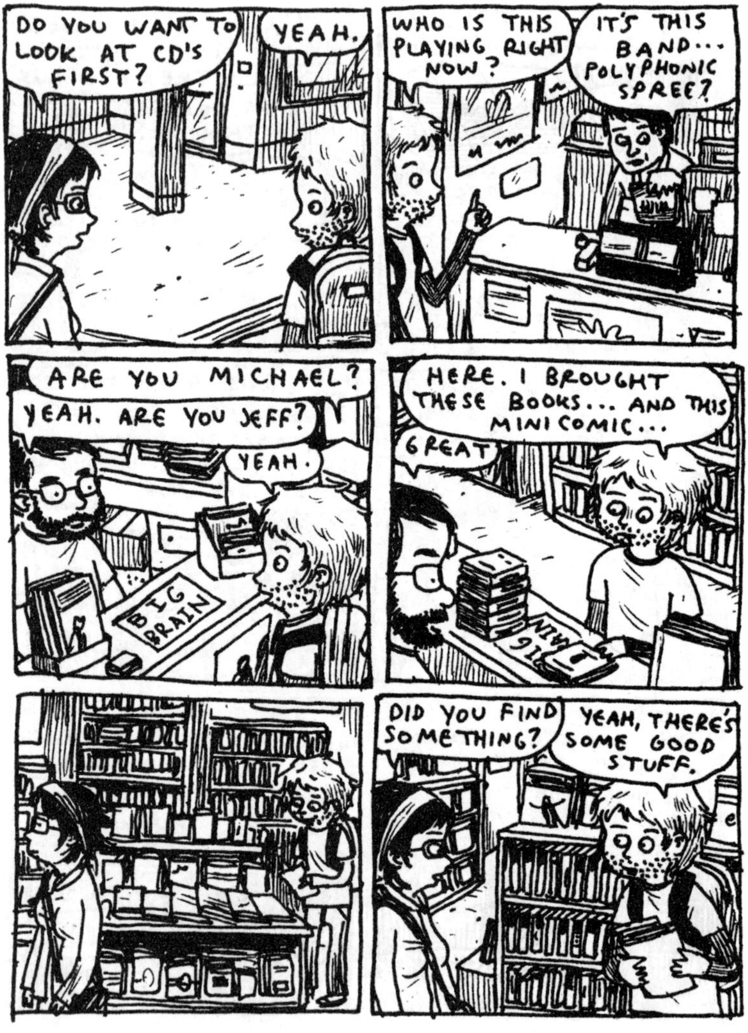
DO YOU WANT TO LOOK AT CD'S FIRST?
YEAH.
WHO IS THIS PLAYING RIGHT NOW?
IT'S THIS BAND... POLYPHONIC SPREE?
ARE YOU MICHAEL?
YEAH. ARE YOU JEFF?
YEAH.
BIG BRAIN
HERE. I BROUGHT THESE BOOKS... AND THIS MINICOMIC...
GREAT
DID YOU FIND SOMETHING?
YEAH, THERE'S SOME GOOD STUFF.

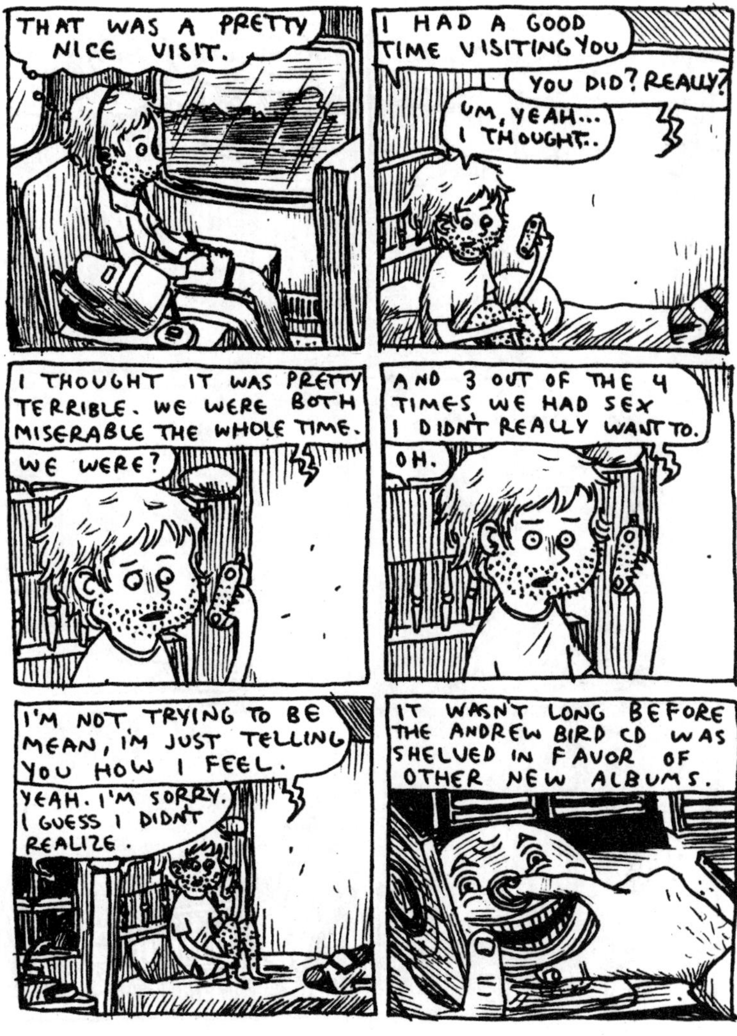
THAT WAS A PRETTY NICE VISIT.
I HAD A GOOD TIME VISITING YOU
YOU DID? REALLY?
UM, YEAH... I THOUGHT..
I THOUGHT IT WAS PRETTY TERRIBLE. WE WERE BOTH MISERABLE THE WHOLE TIME.
WE WERE?
AND 3 OUT OF THE 4 TIMES WE HAD SEX I DIDN'T REALLY WANT TO.
OH.
I'M NOT TRYING TO BE MEAN, I'M JUST TELLING YOU HOW I FEEL.
YEAH. I'M SORRY. I GUESS I DIDN'T REALIZE.
IT WASN'T LONG BEFORE THE ANDREW BIRD CD WAS SHELVED IN FAVOR OF OTHER NEW ALBUMS.

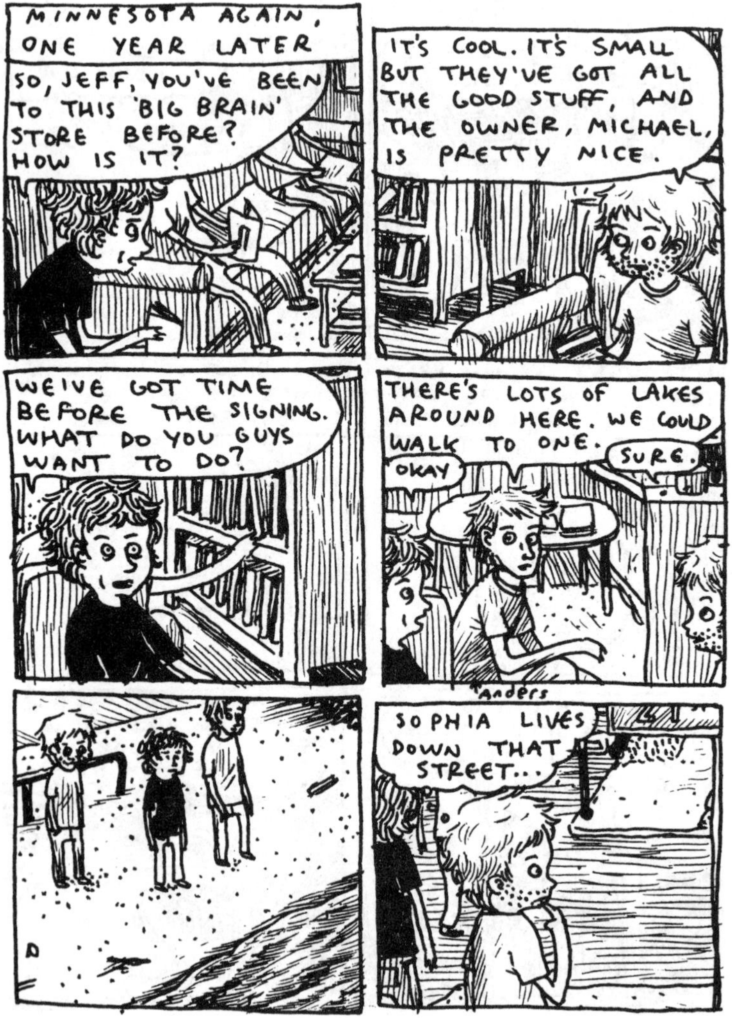
MINNESOTA AGAIN, ONE YEAR LATER
SO, JEFF, YOU'VE BEEN TO THIS 'BIG BRAIN' STORE BEFORE? HOW IS IT?
IT'S COOL. IT'S SMALL BUT THEY'VE GOT ALL THE GOOD STUFF, AND THE OWNER, MICHAEL, IS PRETTY NICE.
WE'VE GOT TIME BEFORE THE SIGNING. WHAT DO YOU GUYS WANT TO DO?
THERE'S LOTS OF LAKES AROUND HERE. WE COULD WALK TO ONE.
OKAY
SURE.
anders
SOPHIA LIVES DOWN THAT STREET...

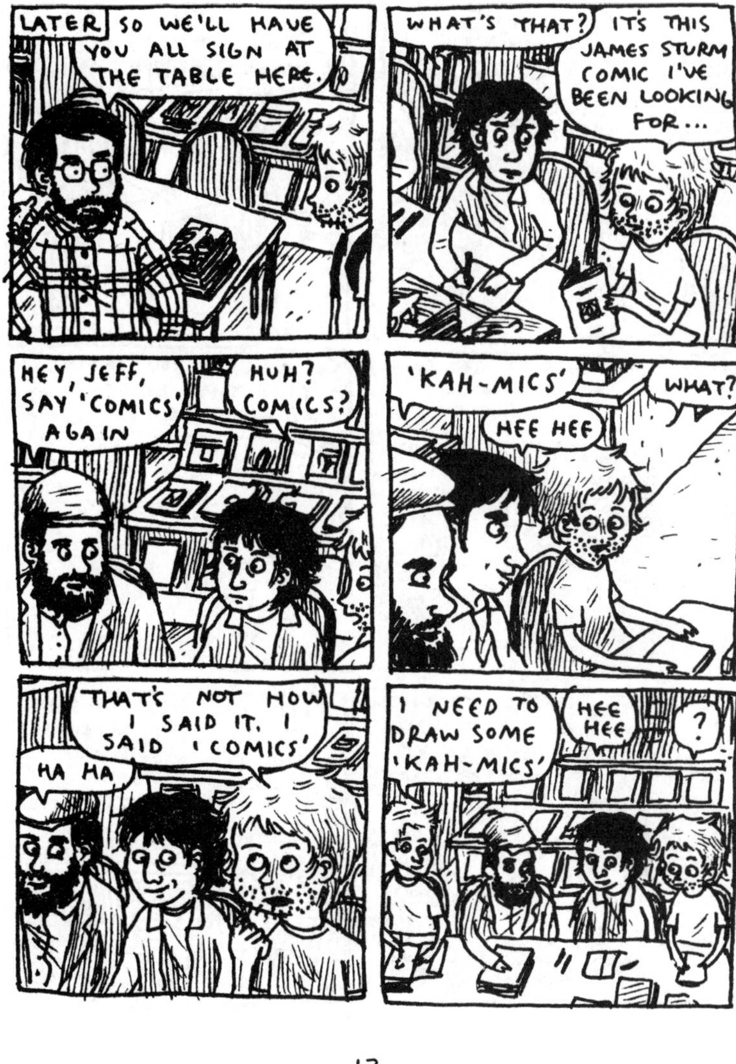
LATER
SO WE'LL HAVE YOU ALL SIGN AT THE TABLE HERE.
WHAT'S THAT?
IT'S THIS JAMES STURM COMIC I'VE BEEN LOOKING FOR...
HEY, JEFF, SAY 'COMICS' AGAIN
HUH? COMICS?
'KAH-MICS'
WHAT?
HEE HEE
THAT'S NOT HOW I SAID IT. I SAID 'COMICS'
HA HA
I NEED TO DRAW SOME 'KAH-MICS'
HEE HEE
?

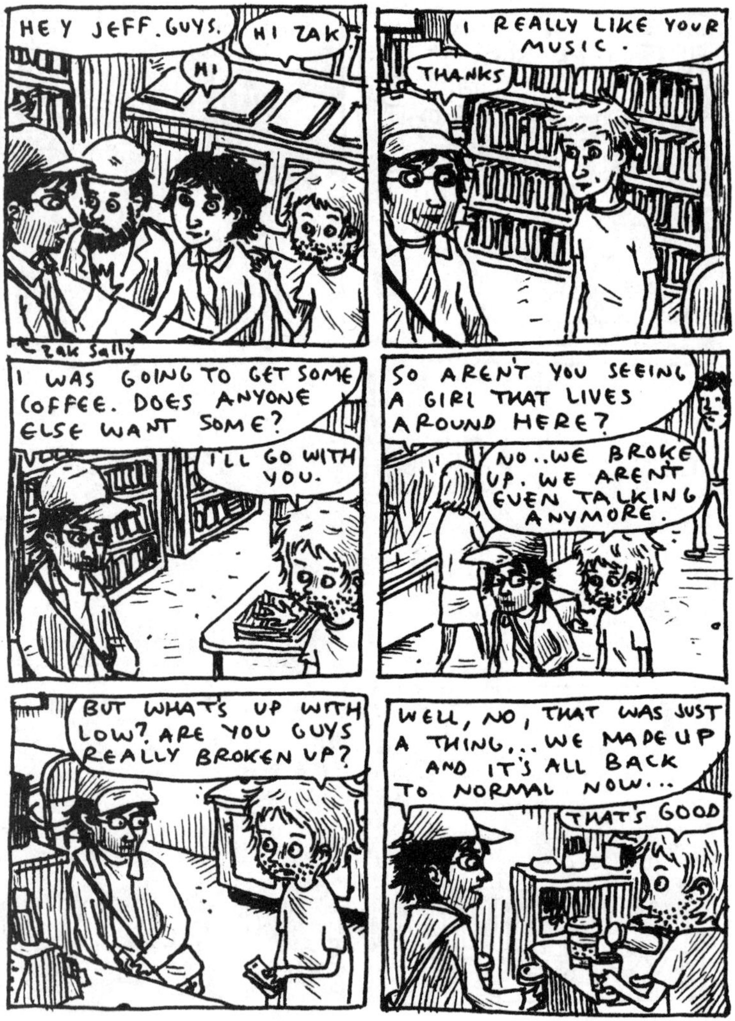
HEY JEFF. GUYS.
HI ZAK
HI
I REALLY LIKE YOUR MUSIC.
THANKS
Zak Sally
I WAS GOING TO GET SOME COFFEE. DOES ANYONE ELSE WANT SOME?
I'LL GO WITH YOU.
SO AREN'T YOU SEEING A GIRL THAT LIVES AROUND HERE?
NO.. WE BROKE UP. WE ARENT EVEN TALKING ANYMORE.
BUT WHAT'S UP WITH LOW? ARE YOU GUYS REALLY BROKEN UP?
WELL, NO, THAT WAS JUST A THING... WE MADE UP AND IT'S ALL BACK TO NORMAL NOW...
THAT'S GOOD

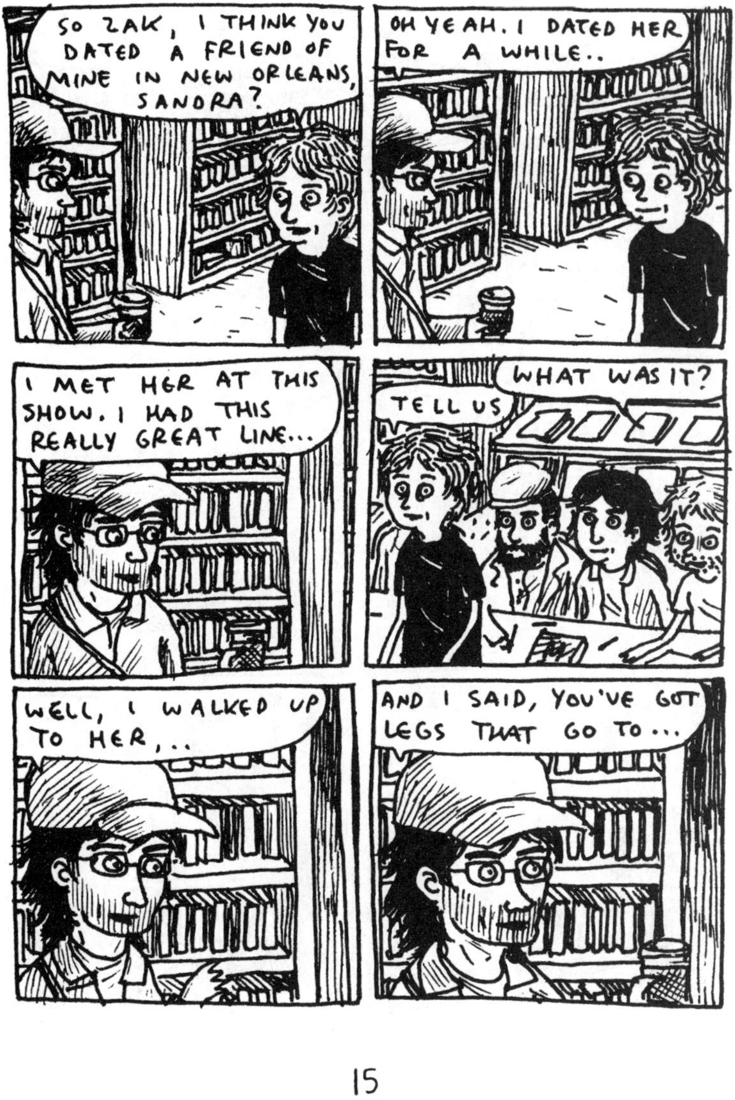
SO ZAK, I THINK YOU DATED A FRIEND OF MINE IN NEW ORLEANS, SANDRA?
OH YEAH. I DATED HER FOR A WHILE..
I MET HER AT THIS SHOW. I HAD THIS REALLY GREAT LINE...
WHAT WAS IT?
TELL US
WELL, I WALKED UP TO HER,..
AND I SAID, YOU'VE GOT LEGS THAT GO TO...

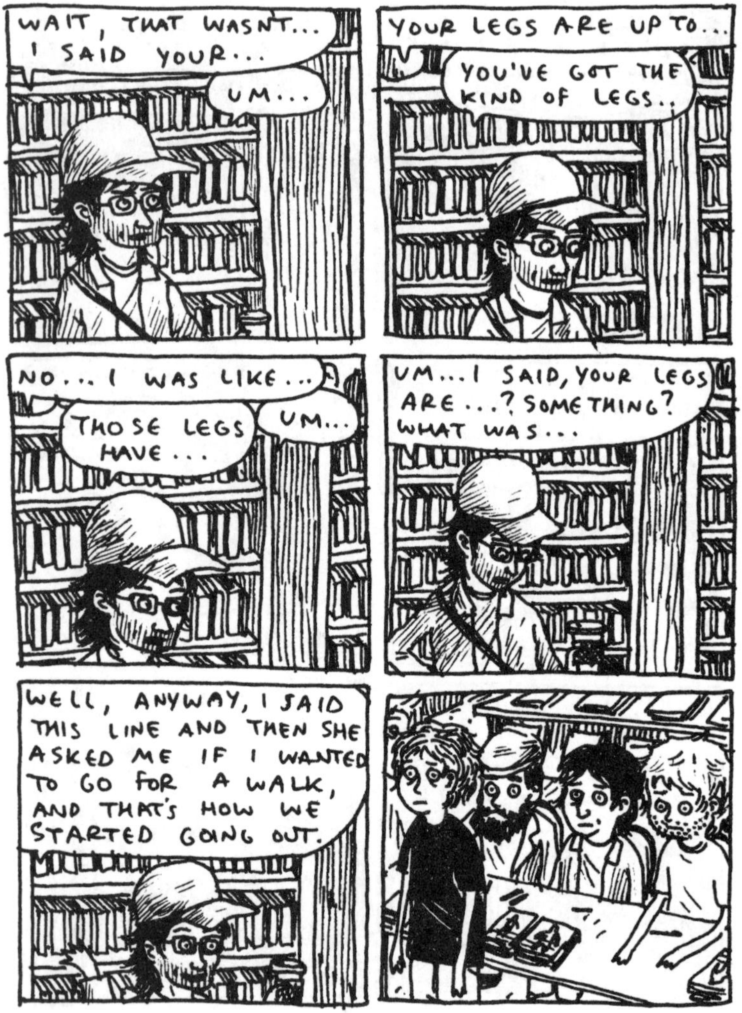
WAIT, THAT WASN'T... I SAID YOUR...
UM...
YOUR LEGS ARE UP TO...
YOU'VE GOT THE KIND OF LEGS...
NO... I WAS LIKE...
THOSE LEGS HAVE...
UM...
UM... I SAID, YOUR LEGS ARE...? SOMETHING? WHAT WAS...
WELL, ANYWAY, I SAID THIS LINE AND THEN SHE ASKED ME IF I WANTED TO GO FOR A WALK, AND THAT'S HOW WE STARTED GOING OUT.

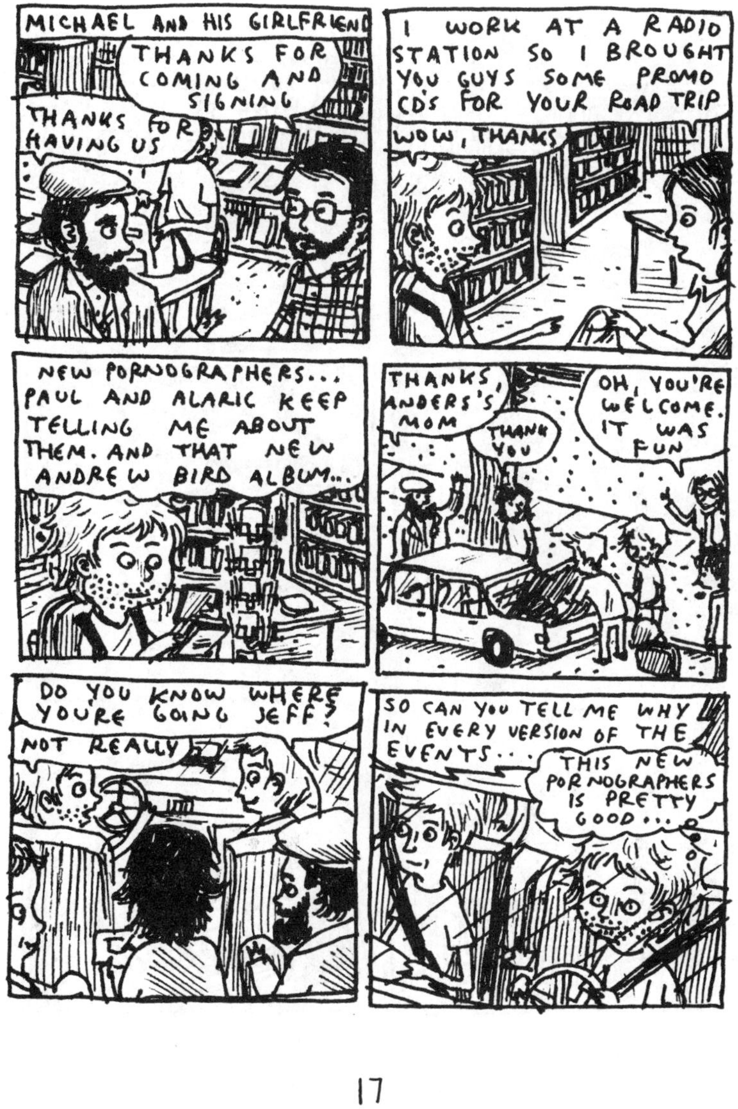
MICHAEL AND HIS GIRLFRIEND
THANKS FOR COMING AND SIGNING
THANKS FOR HAVING US
I WORK AT A RADIO STATION SO I BROUGHT YOU GUYS SOME PROMO CD'S FOR YOUR ROAD TRIP
WOW, THANKS
NEW PORNOGRAPHERS... PAUL AND ALARIC KEEP TELLING ME ABOUT THEM. AND THAT NEW ANDREW BIRD ALBUM...
THANKS, ANDERS'S MOM
THANK YOU
OH, YOU'RE WELCOME. IT WAS FUN
DO YOU KNOW WHERE YOU'RE GOING JEFF?
NOT REALLY
SO CAN YOU TELL ME WHY IN EVERY VERSION OF THE EVENTS...
THIS NEW PORNOGRAPHERS IS PRETTY GOOD...

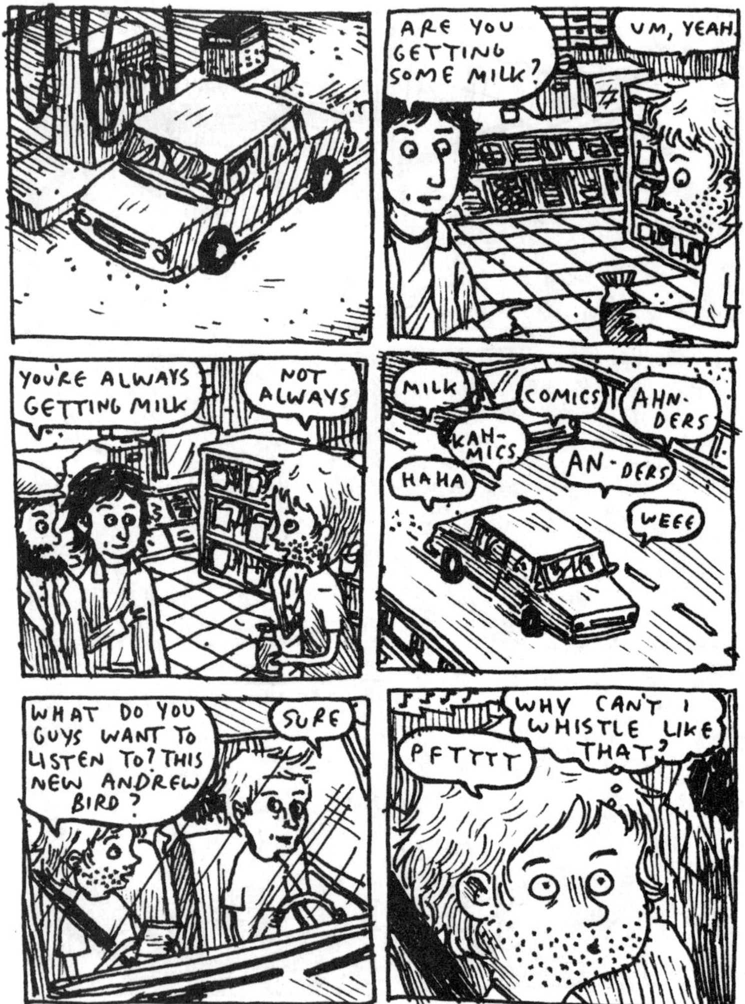
ARE YOU GETTING SOME MILK?
UM, YEAH.
YOU'RE ALWAYS GETTING MILK
NOT ALWAYS
MILK
COMICS
AHN-DERS
KAH-MICS
AN-DERS
HAHA
WEEE
WHAT DO YOU GUYS WANT TO LISTEN TO? THIS NEW ANDREW BIRD?
SURE
WHY CAN'T I WHISTLE LIKE THAT?
PFTTTTT

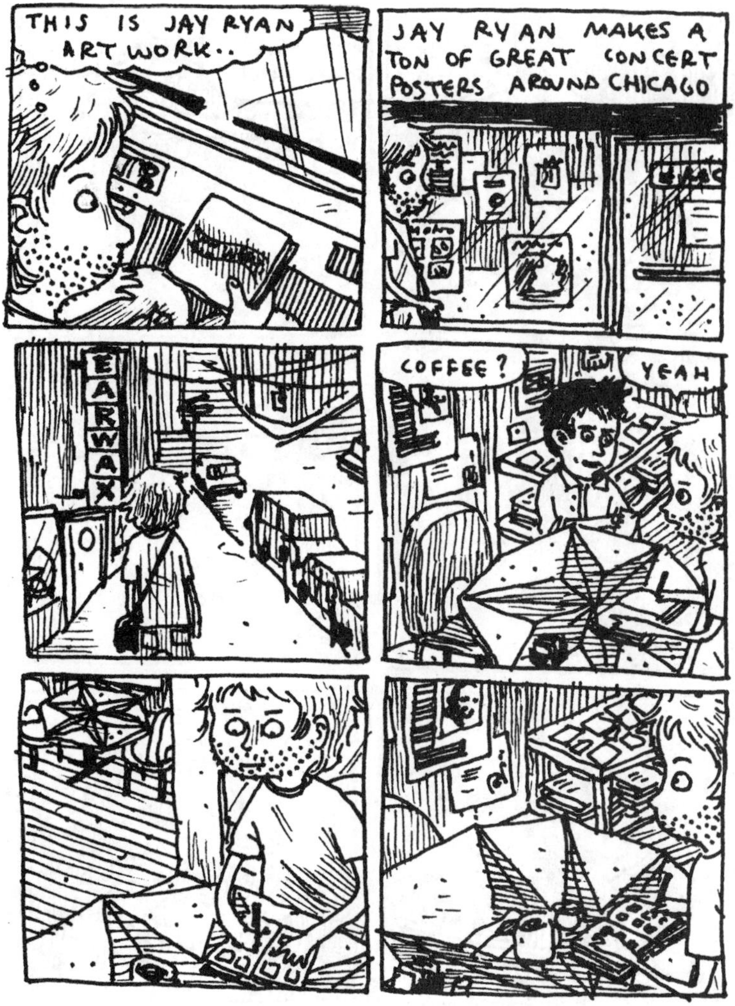
THIS IS JAY RYAN ARTWORK..
JAY RYAN MAKES A TON OF GREAT CONCERT POSTERS AROUND CHICAGO
EARWAX
COFFEE?
YEAH

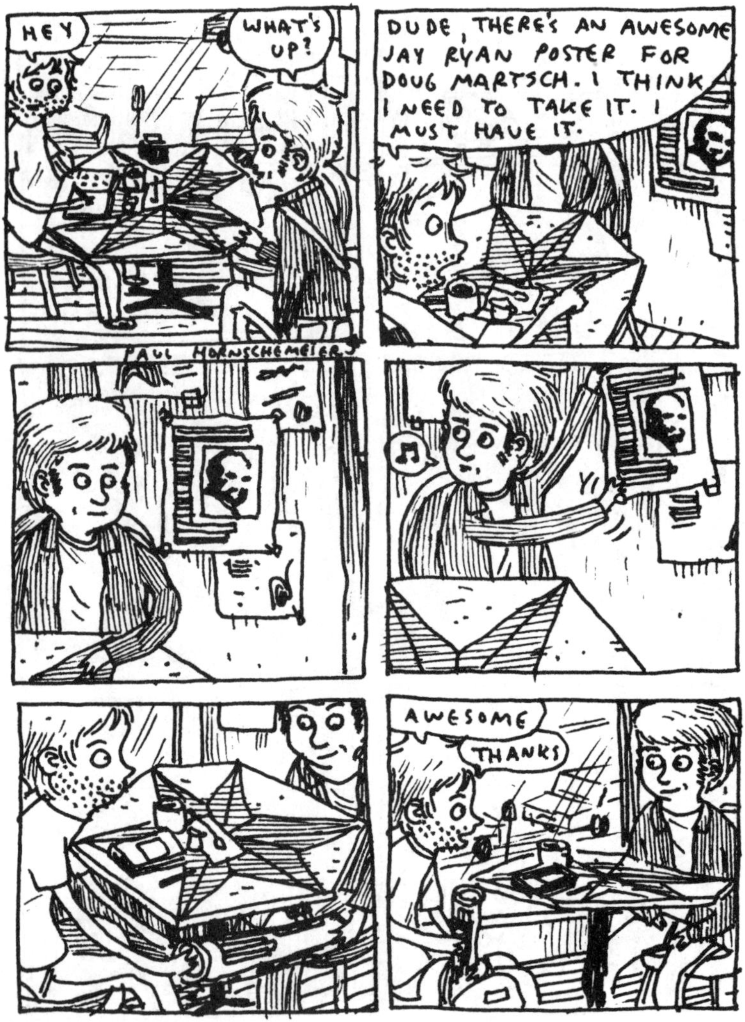
HEY
WHAT'S UP?
PAUL HORNSCHEMEIER
DUDE, THERE'S AN AWESOME JAY RYAN POSTER FOR DOUG MARTSCH. I THINK I NEED TO TAKE IT. I MUST HAVE IT.
AWESOME
THANKS

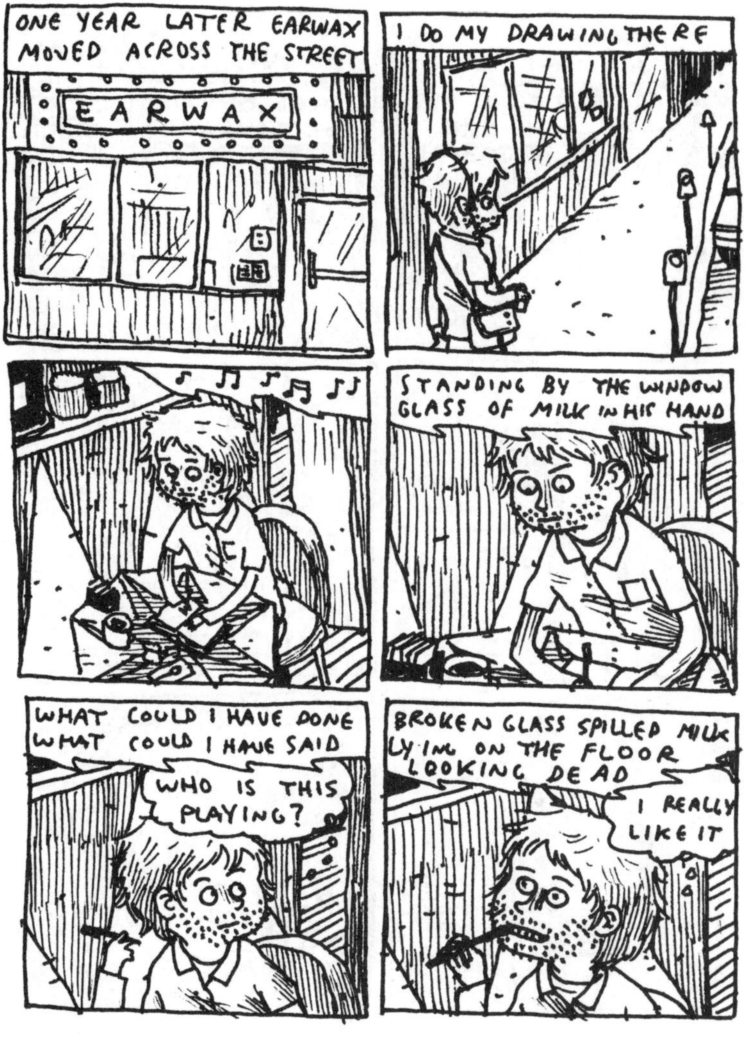
ONE YEAR LATER EARWAX MOVED ACROSS THE STREET
EARWAX
I DO MY DRAWING THERE
STANDING BY THE WINDOW GLASS OF MILK IN HIS HAND
WHAT COULD I HAVE DONE WHAT COULD I HAVE SAID
WHO IS THIS PLAYING?
BROKEN GLASS SPILLED MILK LYING ON THE FLOOR LOOKING DEAD
I REALLY LIKE IT

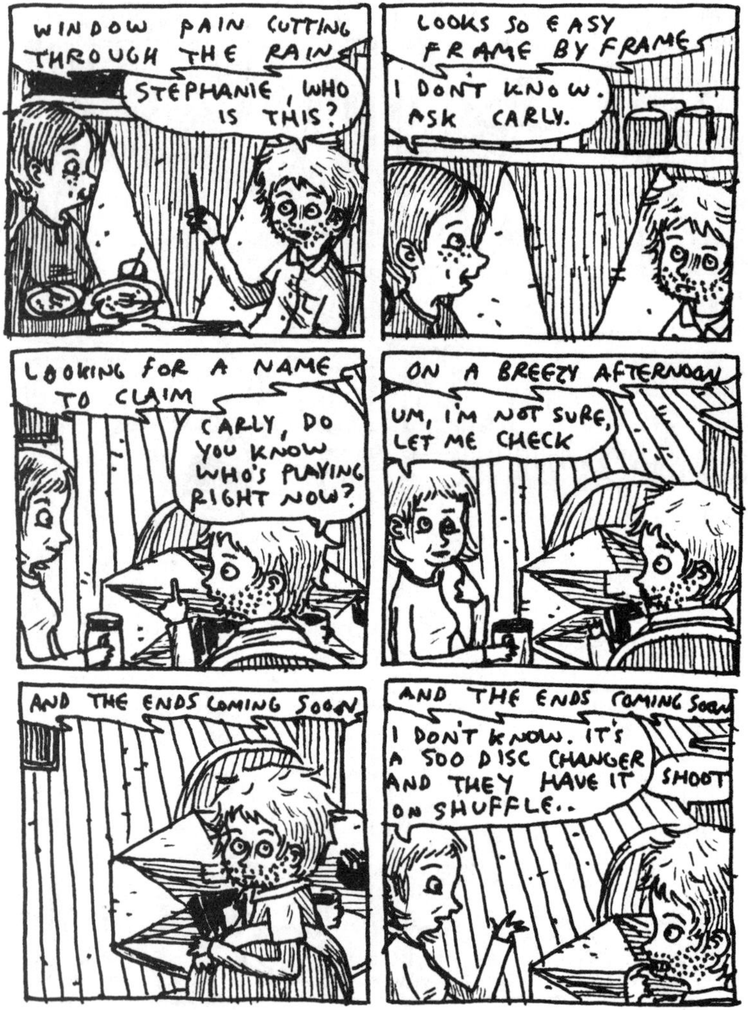
WINDOW PAIN CUTTING THROUGH THE RAIN
STEPHANIE, WHO IS THIS?
LOOKS SO EASY FRAME BY FRAME
I DON'T KNOW. ASK CARLY.
LOOKING FOR A NAME TO CLAIM
CARLY, DO YOU KNOW WHO'S PLAYING RIGHT NOW?
ON A BREEZY AFTERNOON
UM, I'M NOT SURE, LET ME CHECK
AND THE ENDS COMING SOON
AND THE ENDS COMING SOON
I DON'T KNOW. IT'S A 500 DISC CHANGER AND THEY HAVE IT ON SHUFFLE..
SHOOT

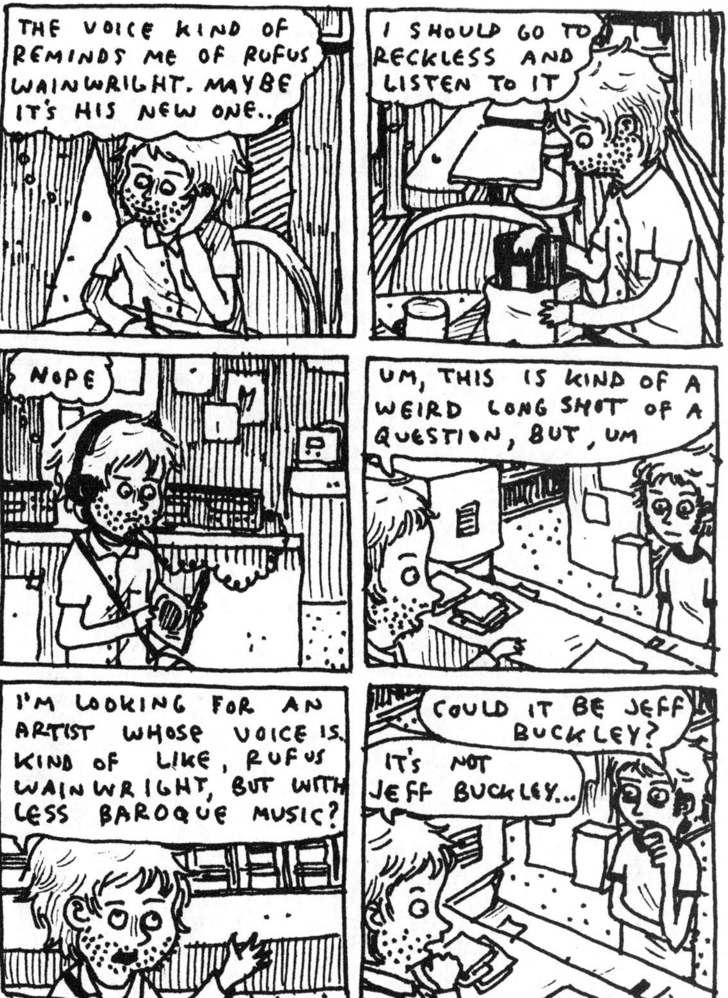
THE VOICE KIND OF REMINDS ME OF RUFUS WAINWRIGHT. MAYBE IT'S HIS NEW ONE..
I SHOULD GO TO RECKLESS AND LISTEN TO IT
NOPE
UM, THIS IS KIND OF A WEIRD LONG SHOT OF A QUESTION, BUT, UM
I'M LOOKING FOR AN ARTIST WHOSE VOICE IS KIND OF LIKE, RUFUS WAINWRIGHT, BUT WITH LESS BAROQUE MUSIC?
COULD IT BE JEFF BUCKLEY?
IT'S NOT JEFF BUCKLEY...

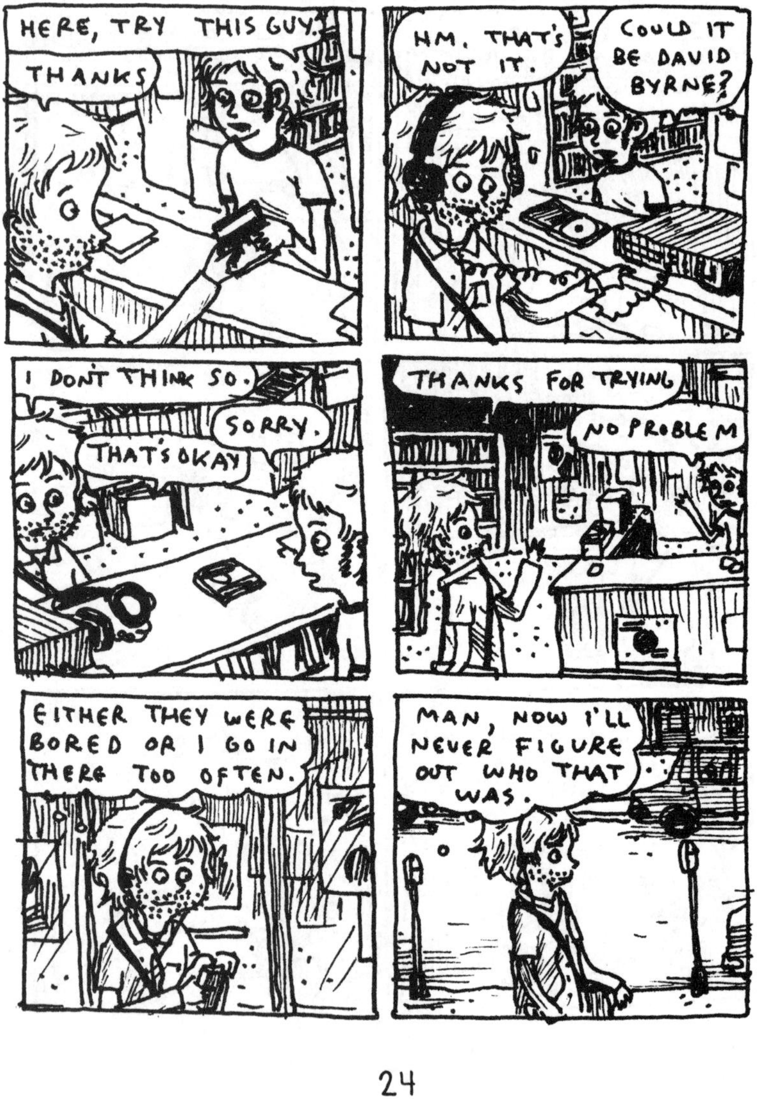
HERE, TRY THIS GUY.
THANKS
HM. THAT'S NOT IT.
COULD IT BE DAVID BYRNE?
I DONT THINK SO.
SORRY.
THAT'S OKAY
THANKS FOR TRYING
NO PROBLEM
EITHER THEY WERE BORED OR I GO IN THERE TOO OFTEN.
MAN, NOW I'LL NEVER FIGURE OUT WHO THAT WAS.

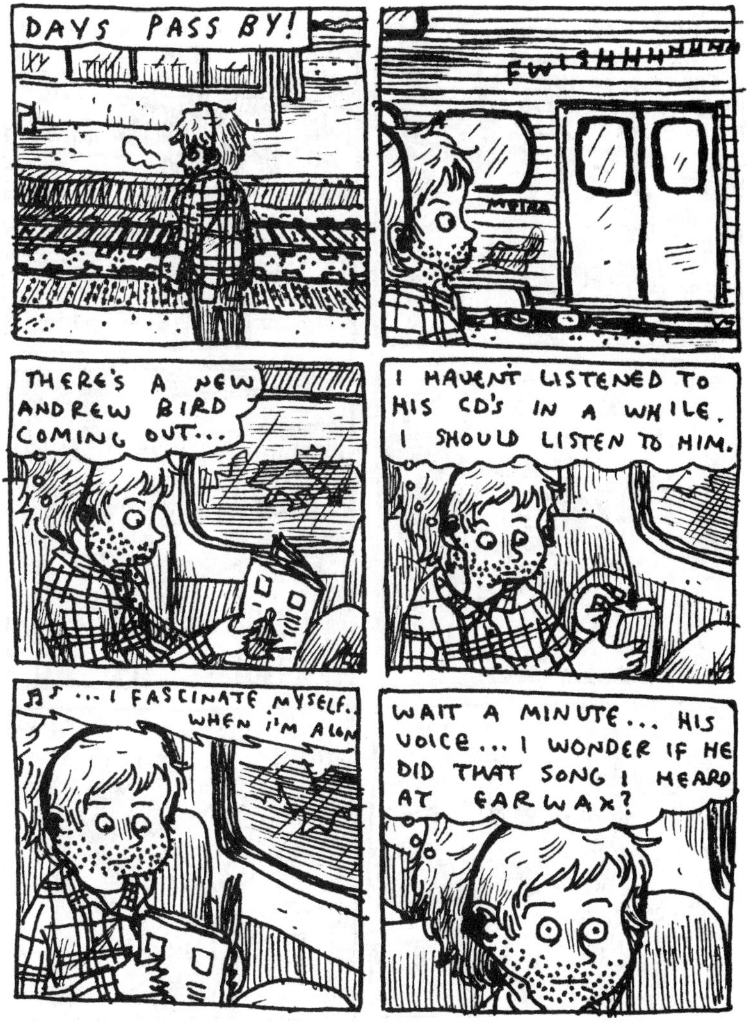
DAYS PASS BY!
FWISHHHHHHHH
THERE'S A NEW ANDREW BIRD COMING OUT...
I HAVEN'T LISTENED TO HIS CD'S IN A WHILE. I SHOULD LISTEN TO HIM.
♫ ...I FASCINATE MYSELF... WHEN I'M ALON
WAIT A MINUTE... HIS VOICE... I WONDER IF HE DID THAT SONG I HEARD AT EARWAX?

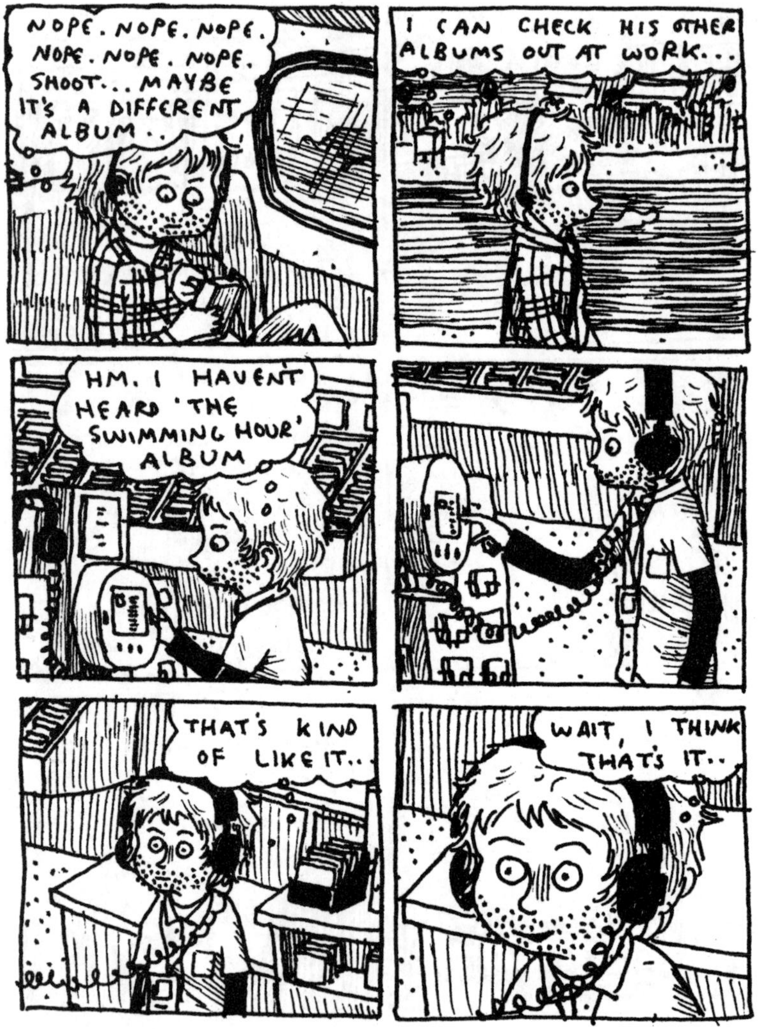
NOPE. NOPE. NOPE. NOPE. NOPE. NOPE. SHOOT... MAYBE IT'S A DIFFERENT ALBUM..
I CAN CHECK HIS OTHER ALBUMS OUT AT WORK...
HM. I HAVENT HEARD 'THE SWIMMING HOUR' ALBUM
THAT'S KIND OF LIKE IT..
WAIT, I THINK THAT'S IT..

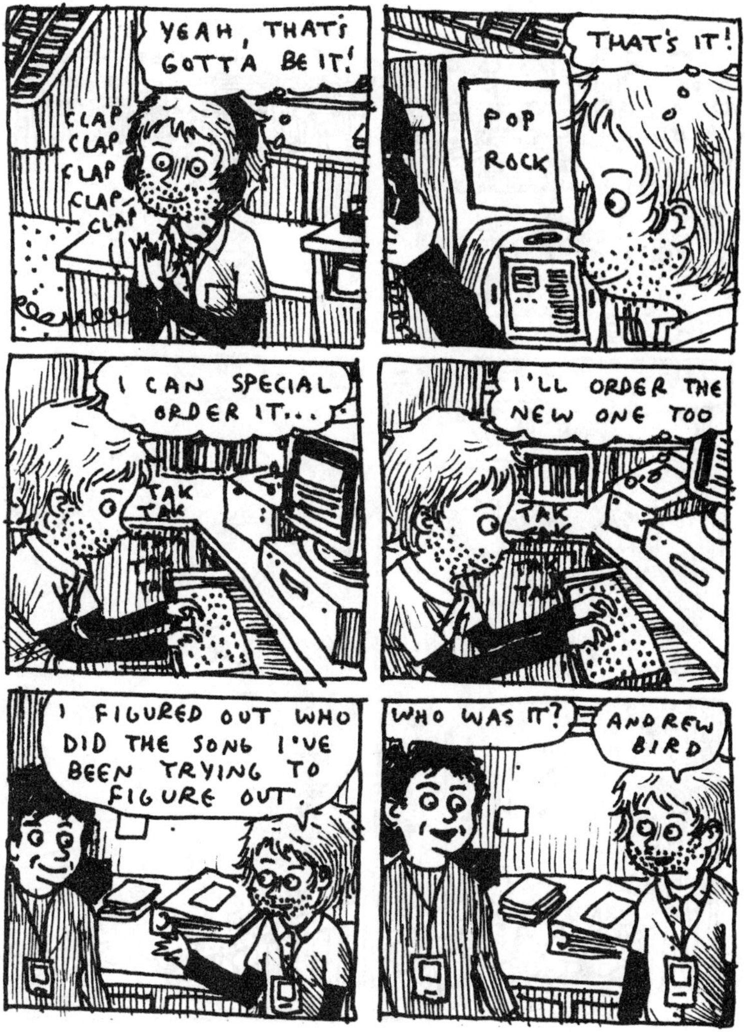
YEAH, THAT'S GOTTA BE IT!
CLAP CLAP FLAP CLAP CLAP
THAT'S IT!
POP ROCK
I CAN SPECIAL ORDER IT...
TAK TAK
I'LL ORDER THE NEW ONE TOO
TAK
I FIGURED OUT WHO DID THE SONG I'VE BEEN TRYING TO FIGURE OUT.
WHO WAS IT?
ANDREW BIRD

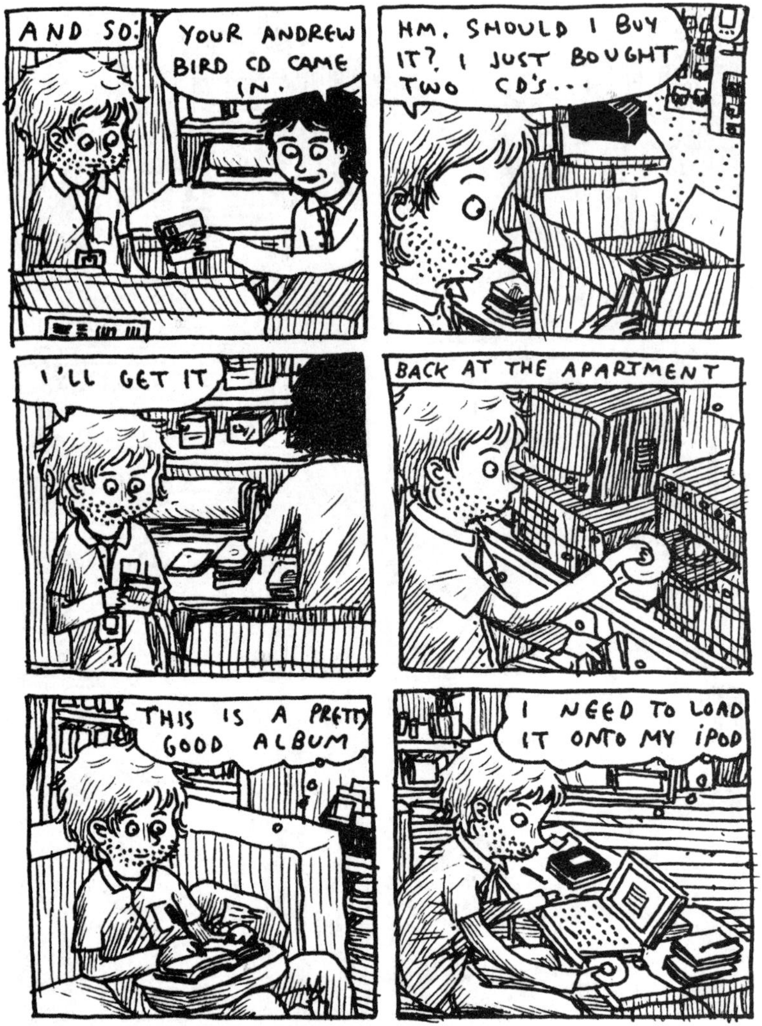
AND SO:
YOUR ANDREW BIRD CD CAME IN.
HM. SHOULD I BUY IT? I JUST BOUGHT TWO CD'S...
I'LL GET IT
BACK AT THE APARTMENT
THIS IS A PRETTY GOOD ALBUM
I NEED TO LOAD IT ONTO MY iPOD

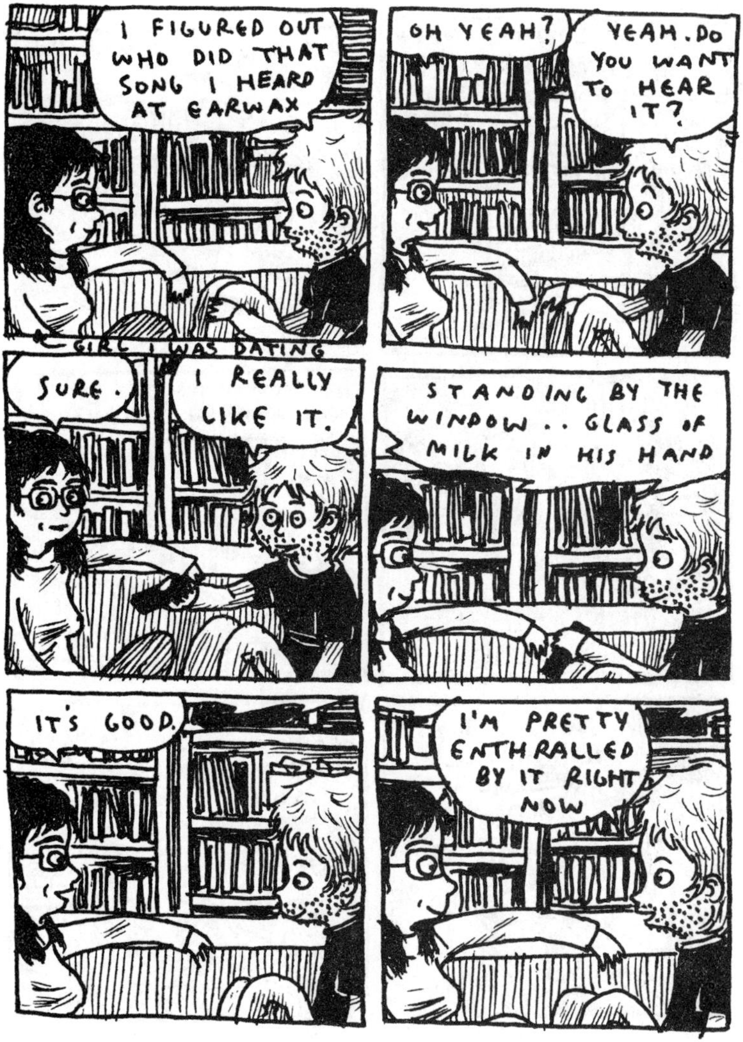
I FIGURED OUT WHO DID THAT SONG I HEARD AT EARWAX
OH YEAH?
YEAH. DO YOU WANT TO HEAR IT?
GIRL I WAS DATING
SURE.
I REALLY LIKE IT.
STANDING BY THE WINDOW.. GLASS OF MILK IN HIS HAND
IT'S GOOD.
I'M PRETTY ENTHRALLED BY IT RIGHT NOW

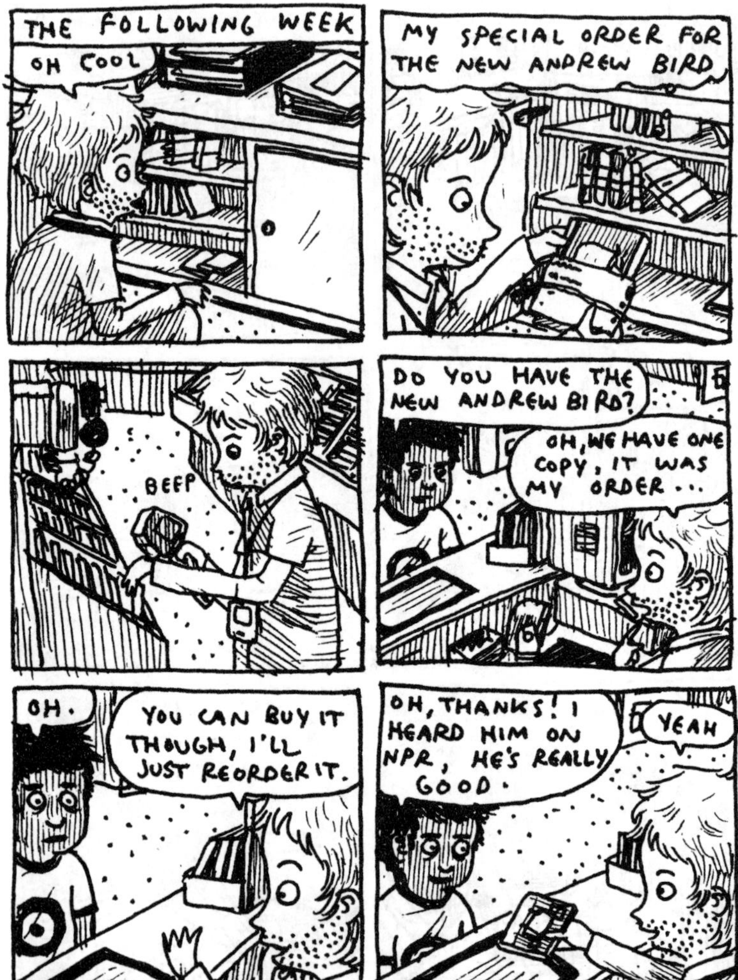
THE FOLLOWING WEEK
OH COOL
MY SPECIAL ORDER FOR THE NEW ANDREW BIRD
BEEP
DO YOU HAVE THE NEW ANDREW BIRD?
OH, WE HAVE ONE COPY, IT WAS MY ORDER...
OH.
YOU CAN BUY IT THOUGH, I'LL JUST REORDER IT.
OH, THANKS! I HEARD HIM ON NPR, HE'S REALLY GOOD.
YEAH

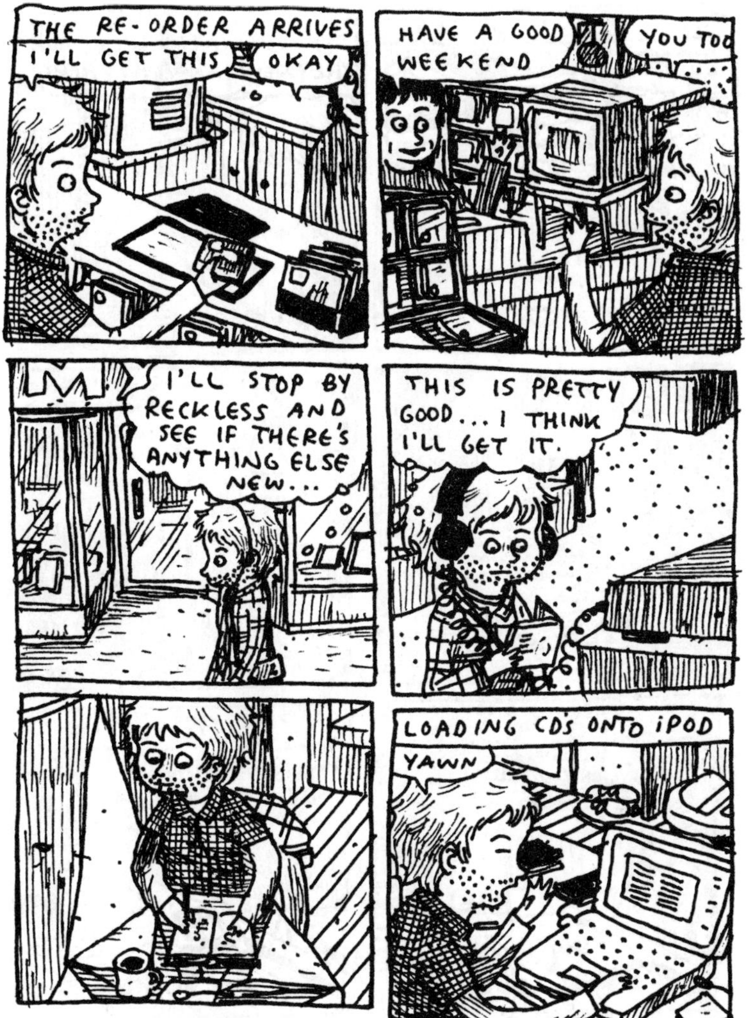
THE RE-ORDER ARRIVES
I'LL GET THIS
OKAY
HAVE A GOOD WEEKEND
YOU TOO
I'LL STOP BY RECKLESS AND SEE IF THERE'S ANYTHING ELSE NEW...
THIS IS PRETTY GOOD... I THINK I'LL GET IT.
LOADING CD'S ONTO iPOD
YAWN

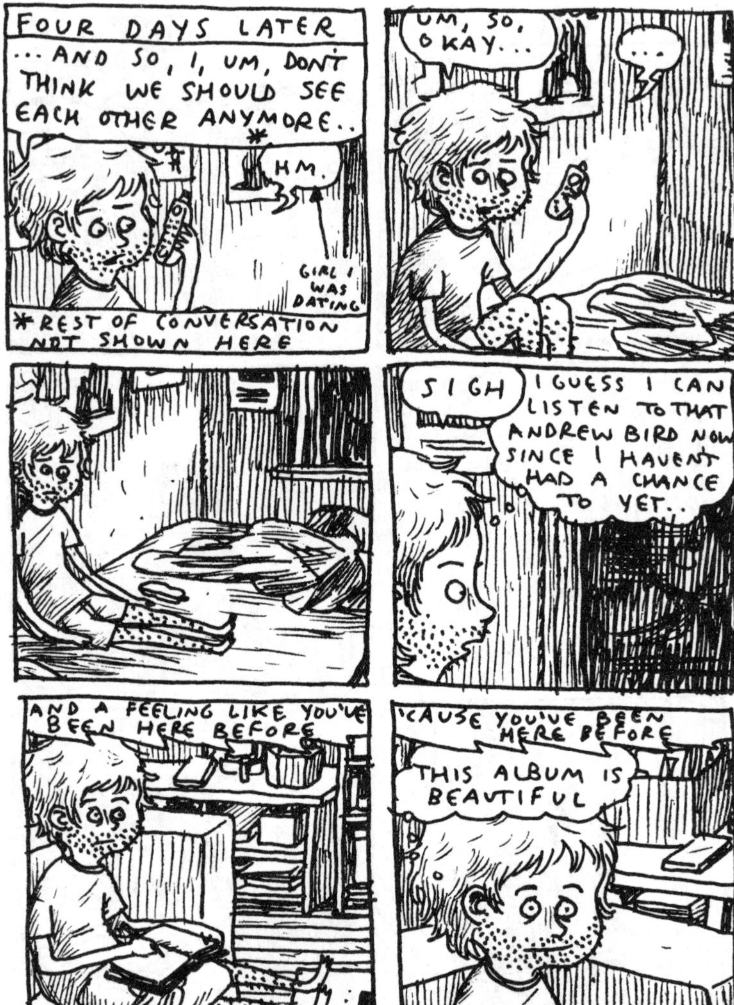
FOUR DAYS LATER
...AND SO, I, UM, DON'T THINK WE SHOULD SEE EACH OTHER ANYMORE..
HM.
GIRL I WAS DATING
* REST OF CONVERSATION NOT SHOWN HERE
UM, SO, OKAY...
...
SIGH
I GUESS I CAN LISTEN TO THAT ANDREW BIRD NOW SINCE I HAVEN'T HAD A CHANCE TO YET..
AND A FEELING LIKE YOU'VE BEEN HERE BEFORE
'CAUSE YOU'VE BEEN HERE BEFORE
THIS ALBUM IS BEAUTIFUL

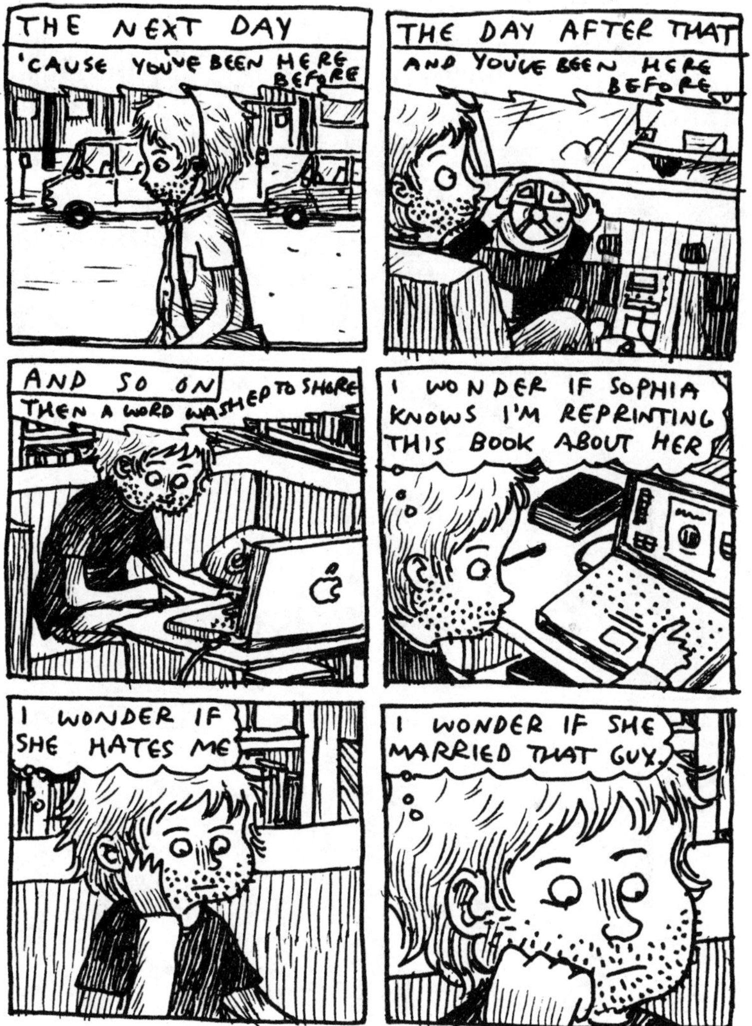
THE NEXT DAY
'CAUSE YOU'VE BEEN HERE BEFORE
THE DAY AFTER THAT
AND YOU'VE BEEN HERE BEFORE
AND SO ON
THEN A WORD WASHED TO SHORE
I WONDER IF SOPHIA KNOWS I'M REPRINTING THIS BOOK ABOUT HER
I WONDER IF SHE HATES ME
I WONDER IF SHE MARRIED THAT GUY

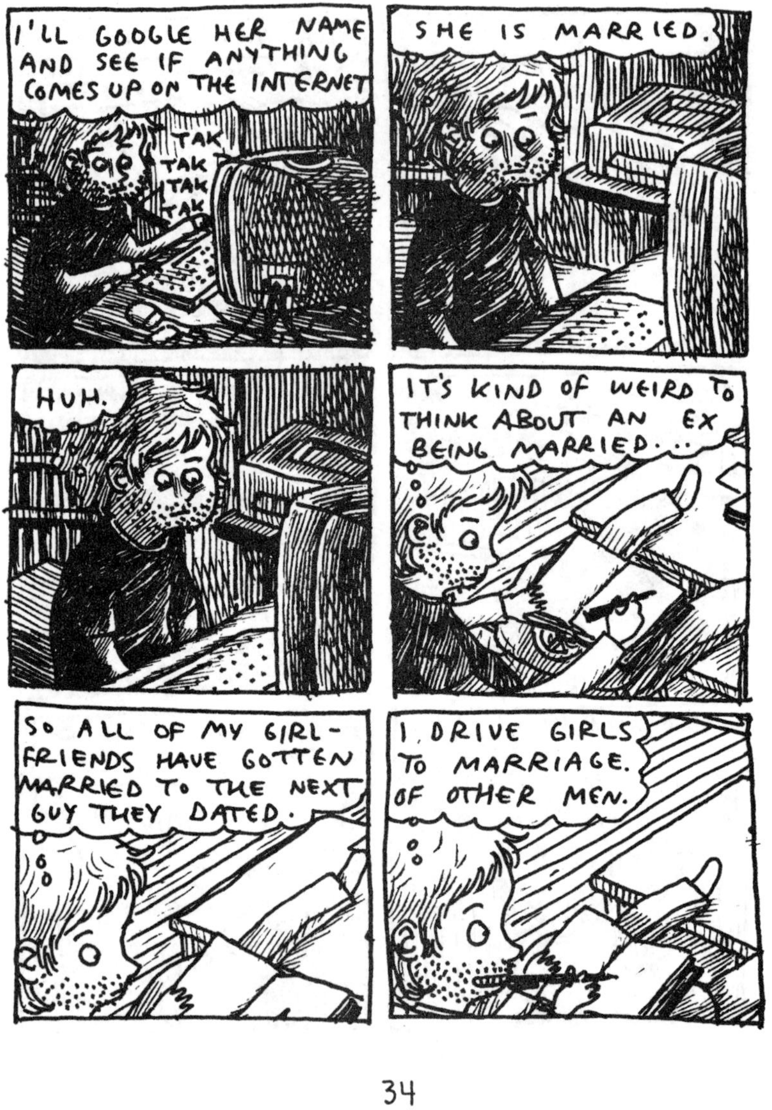
I'LL GOOGLE HER NAME AND SEE IF ANYTHING COMES UP ON THE INTERNET
TAK TAK TAK TAK
SHE IS MARRIED.
HUH.
IT'S KIND OF WEIRD TO THINK ABOUT AN EX BEING MARRIED...
SO ALL OF MY GIRL-FRIENDS HAVE GOTTEN MARRIED TO THE NEXT GUY THEY DATED.
I DRIVE GIRLS TO MARRIAGE. OF OTHER MEN.

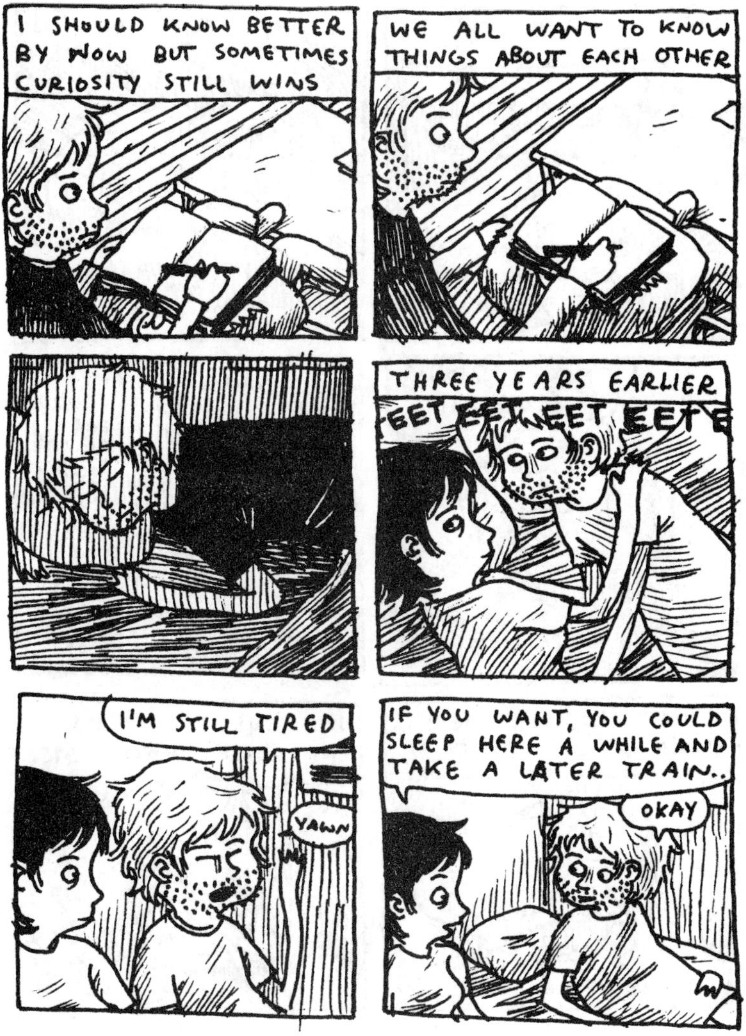
I SHOULD KNOW BETTER BY NOW BUT SOMETIMES CURIOSITY STILL WINS
WE ALL WANT TO KNOW THINGS ABOUT EACH OTHER
THREE YEARS EARLIER
EET EET EET EETE
I'M STILL TIRED
YAWN
IF YOU WANT, YOU COULD SLEEP HERE A WHILE AND TAKE A LATER TRAIN..
OKAY

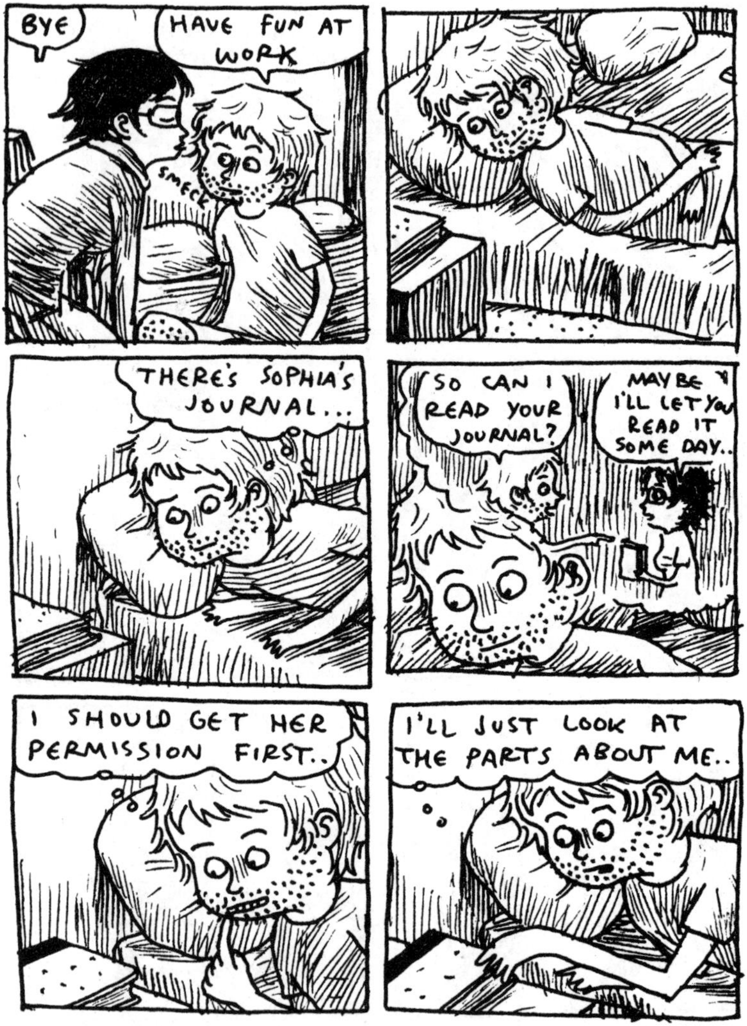
BYE
HAVE FUN AT WORK
SMECK
THERE'S SOPHIA'S JOURNAL...
SO CAN I READ YOUR JOURNAL?
MAYBE I'LL LET YOU READ IT SOME DAY..
I SHOULD GET HER PERMISSION FIRST..
I'LL JUST LOOK AT THE PARTS ABOUT ME..

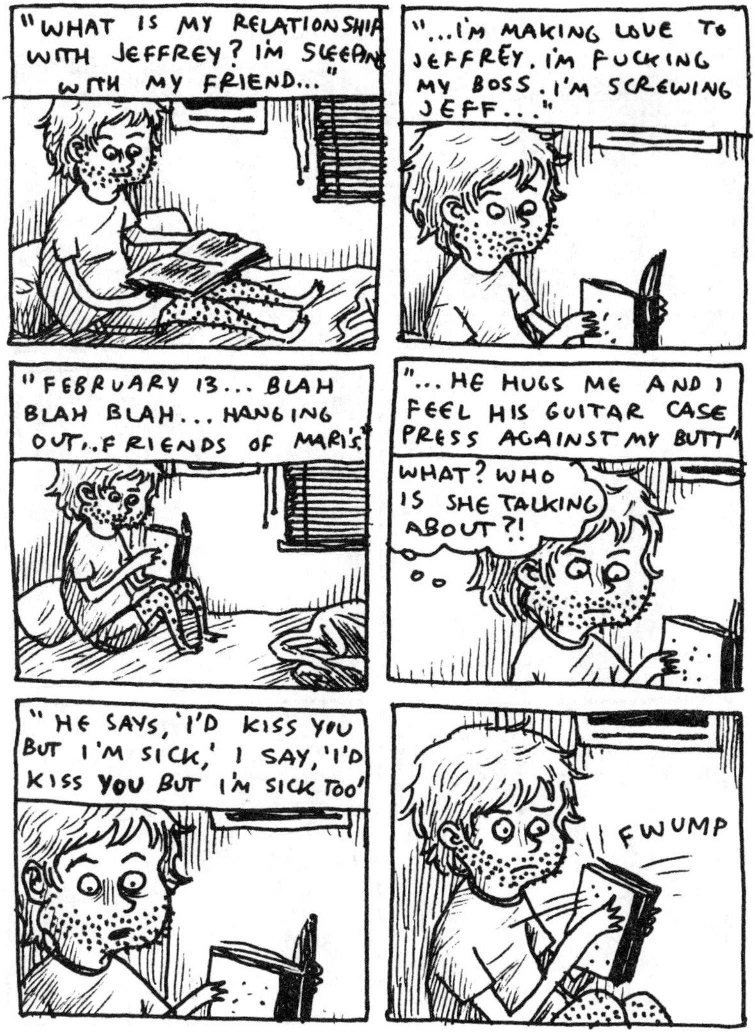
"WHAT IS MY RELATIONSHIP WITH JEFFREY? I'M SLEEPING WITH MY FRIEND..."
"...I'M MAKING LOVE TO JEFFREY. I'M FUCKING MY BOSS. I'M SCREWING JEFF..."
"FEBRUARY 13... BLAH BLAH BLAH... HANGING OUT... FRIENDS OF MARI'S."
"...HE HUGS ME AND I FEEL HIS GUITAR CASE PRESS AGAINST MY BUTT"
WHAT? WHO IS SHE TALKING ABOUT?!
"HE SAYS, 'I'D KISS YOU BUT I'M SICK,' I SAY, 'I'D KISS YOU BUT I'M SICK TOO'
FWUMP

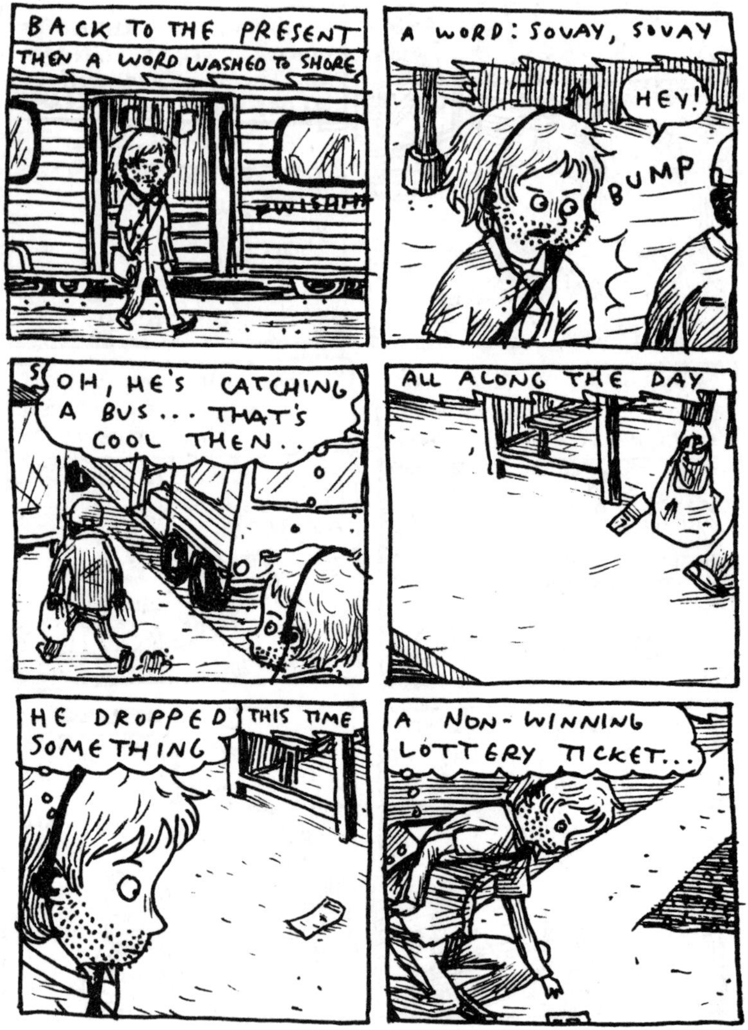
BACK TO THE PRESENT
THEN A WORD WASHED TO SHORE
A WORD: SOVAY, SOVAY
HEY!
BUMP
OH, HE'S CATCHING A BUS... THAT'S COOL THEN...
ALL ALONG THE DAY
HE DROPPED SOMETHING
THIS TIME
A NON-WINNING LOTTERY TICKET...

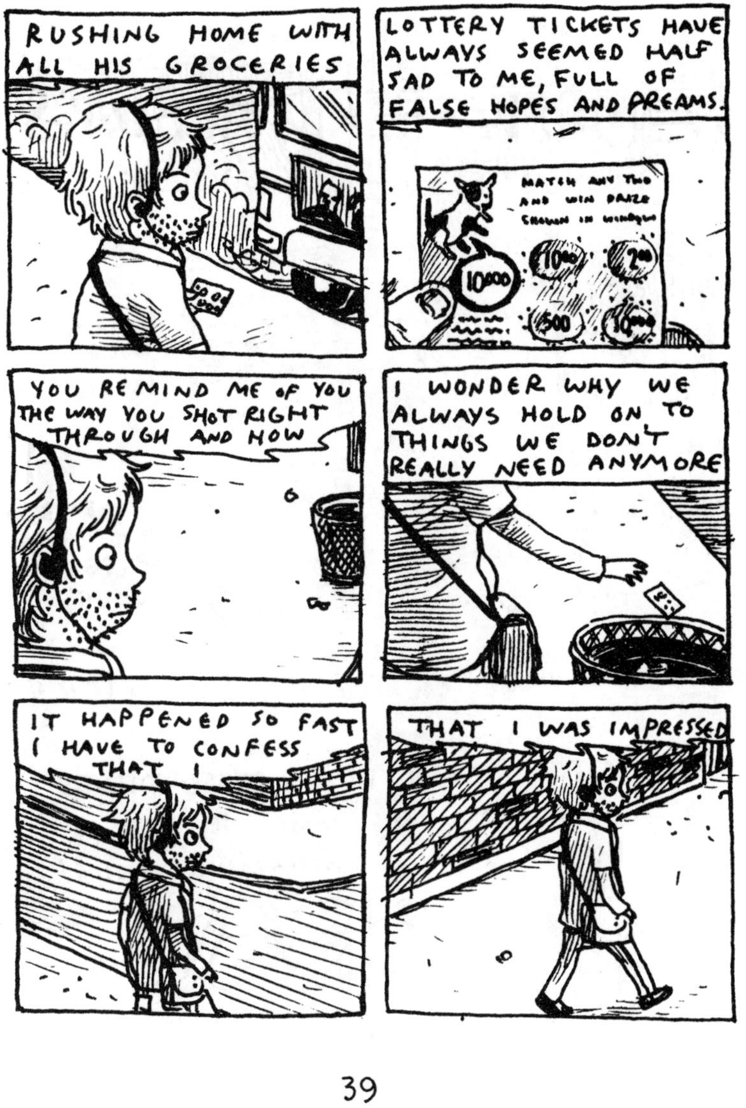
RUSHING HOME WITH ALL HIS GROCERIES
LOTTERY TICKETS HAVE ALWAYS SEEMED HALF SAD TO ME, FULL OF FALSE HOPES AND DREAMS.
MATCH ANY TWO AND WIN PRIZE SHOWN IN WINDOW
YOU REMIND ME OF YOU THE WAY YOU SHOT RIGHT THROUGH AND HOW
I WONDER WHY WE ALWAYS HOLD ON TO THINGS WE DON'T REALLY NEED ANYMORE
IT HAPPENED SO FAST I HAVE TO CONFESS THAT I
THAT I WAS IMPRESSED

ANDREW BIRD ALBUMS

FEATURED IN THIS STORY

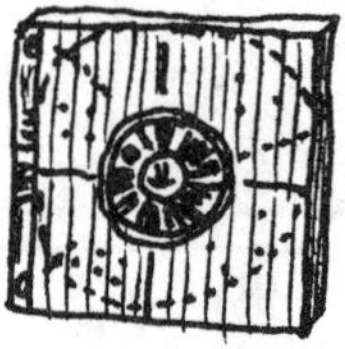

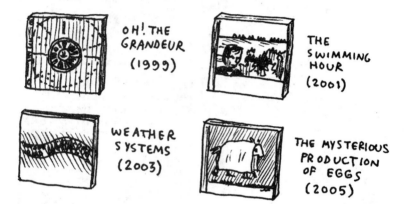

OH! THE GRANDEUR (1999)

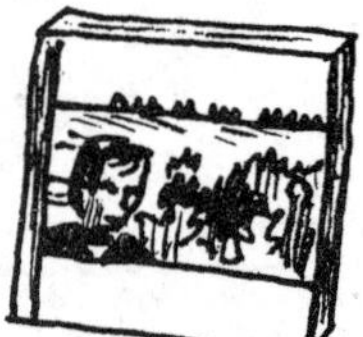

THE SWIMMING HOUR (2001)

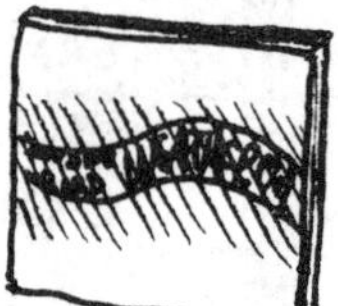

WEATHER SYSTEMS (2003)

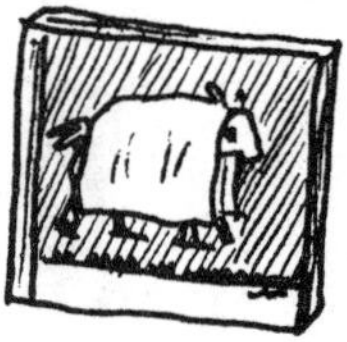

THE MYSTERIOUS PRODUCTION OF EGGS (2005)

SEE www.andrewbird.net FOR MORE

THE TITLE 'THESE THINGS THESE THINGS' IS TAKEN FROM THE SONG 'HEADSOAK' OFF THE ALBUM 'THE SWIMMING HOUR'

FOUND IN HIS HOME

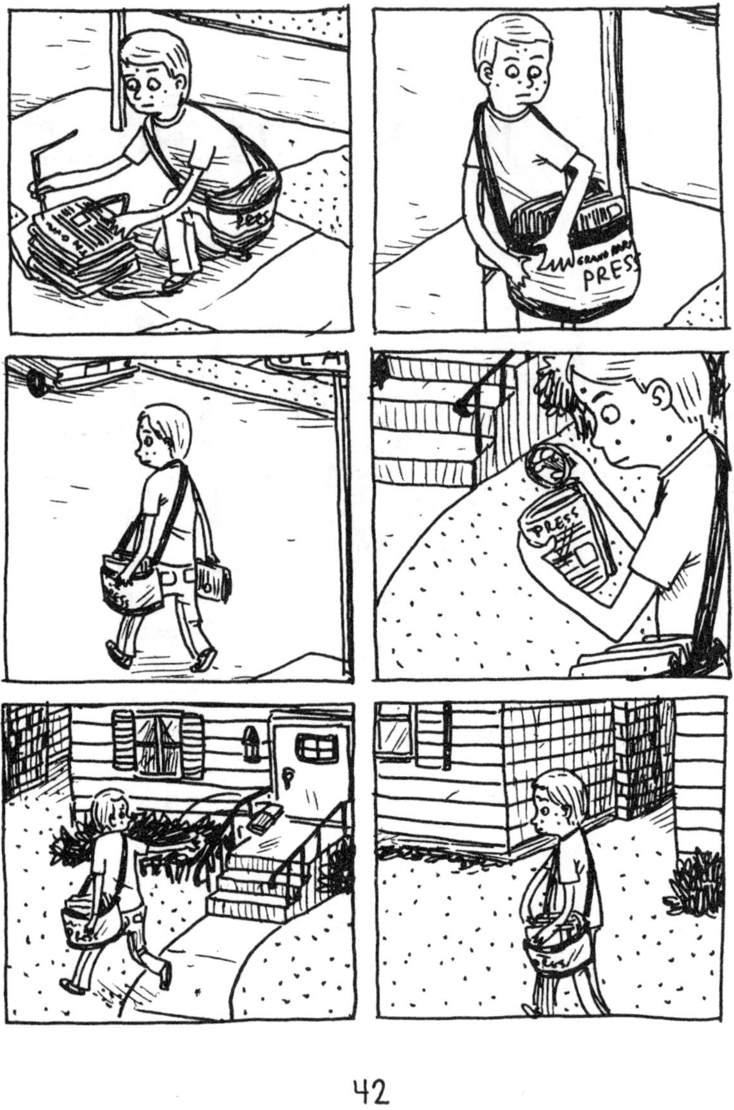
PRESS
PRESS

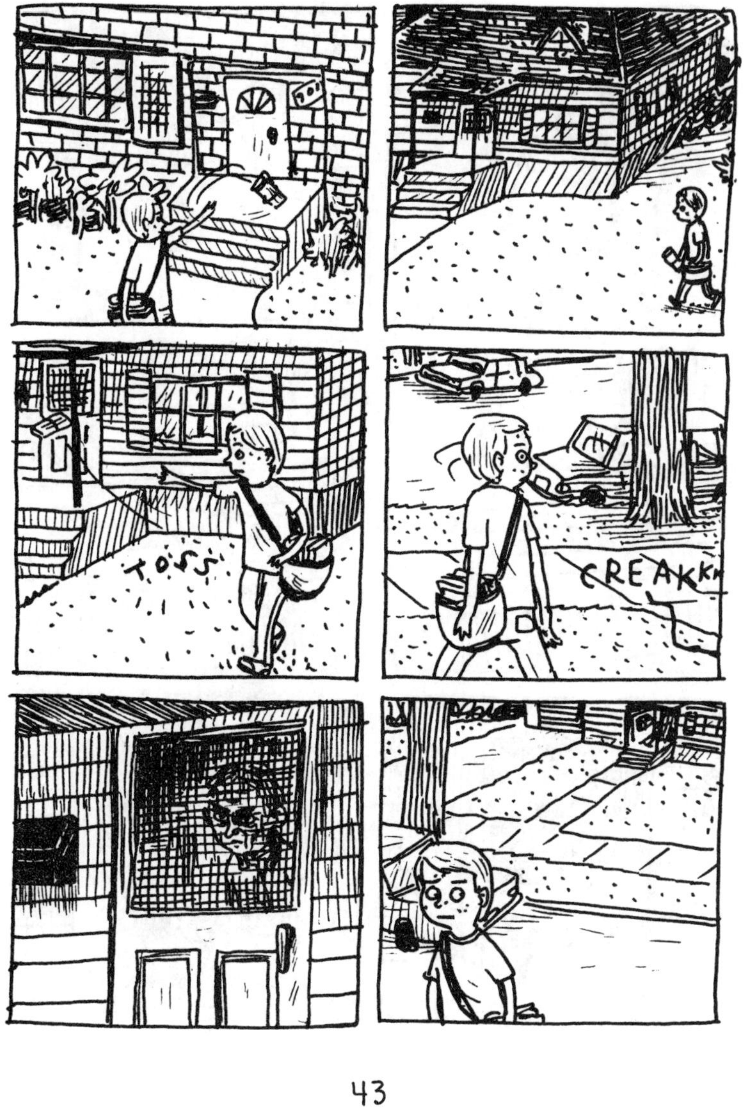
TOSS
CREAKK

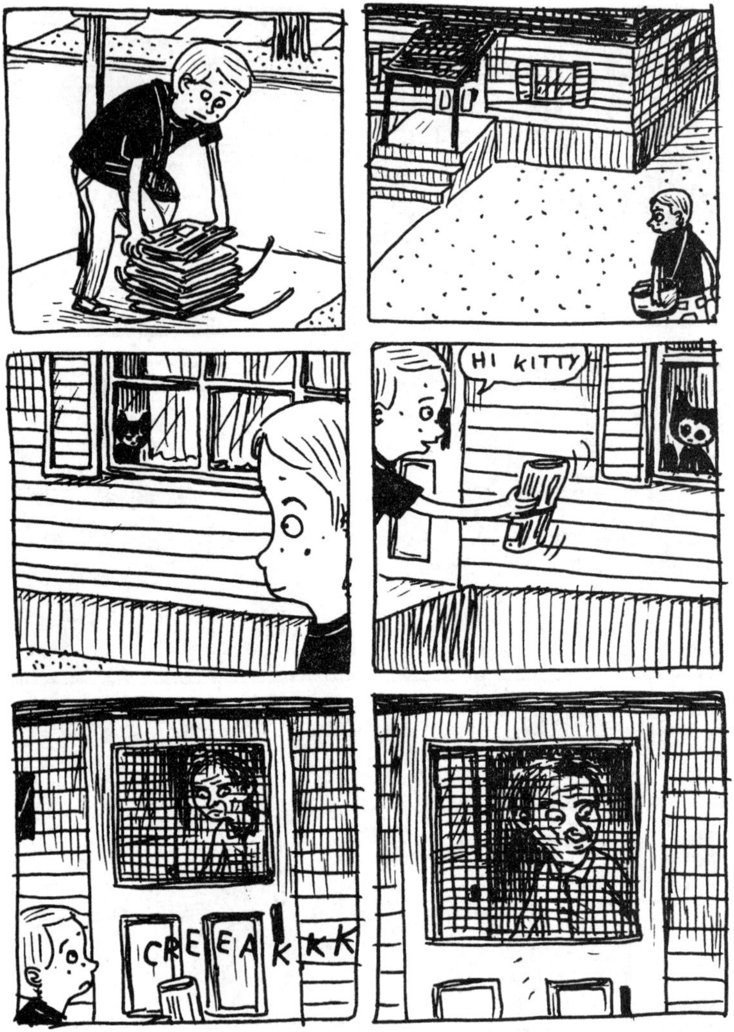
HI KITTY
CREEAKKK

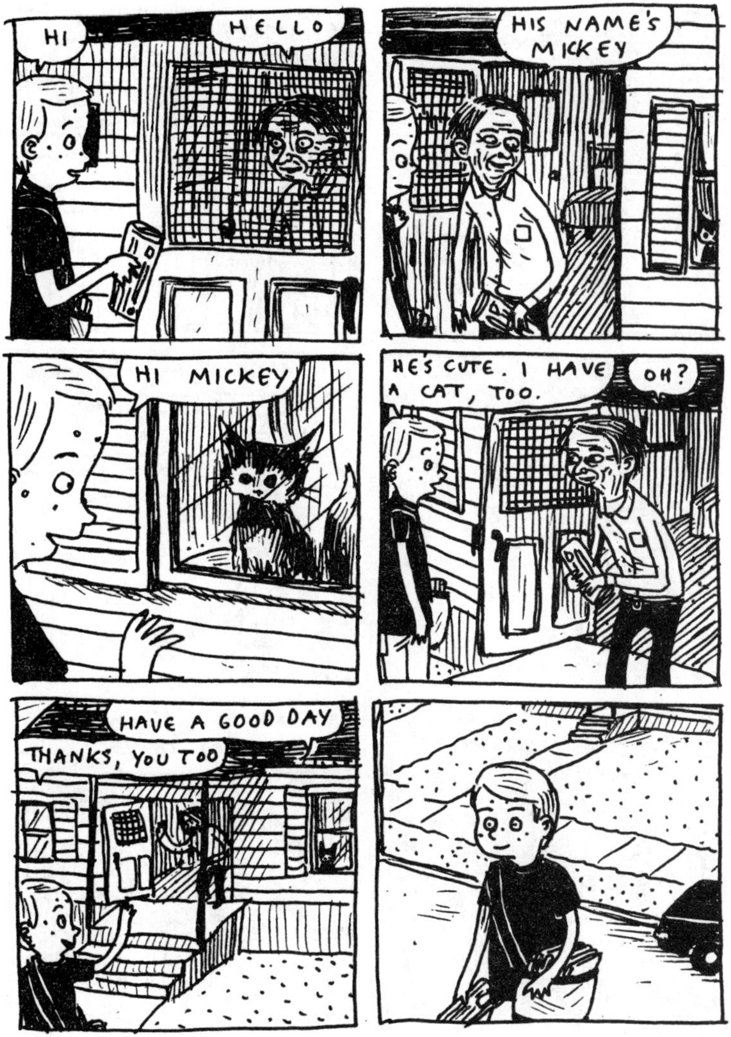
HI
HELLO
HIS NAME'S MICKEY
HI MICKEY
HE'S CUTE. I HAVE A CAT, TOO.
OH?
HAVE A GOOD DAY
THANKS, YOU TOO

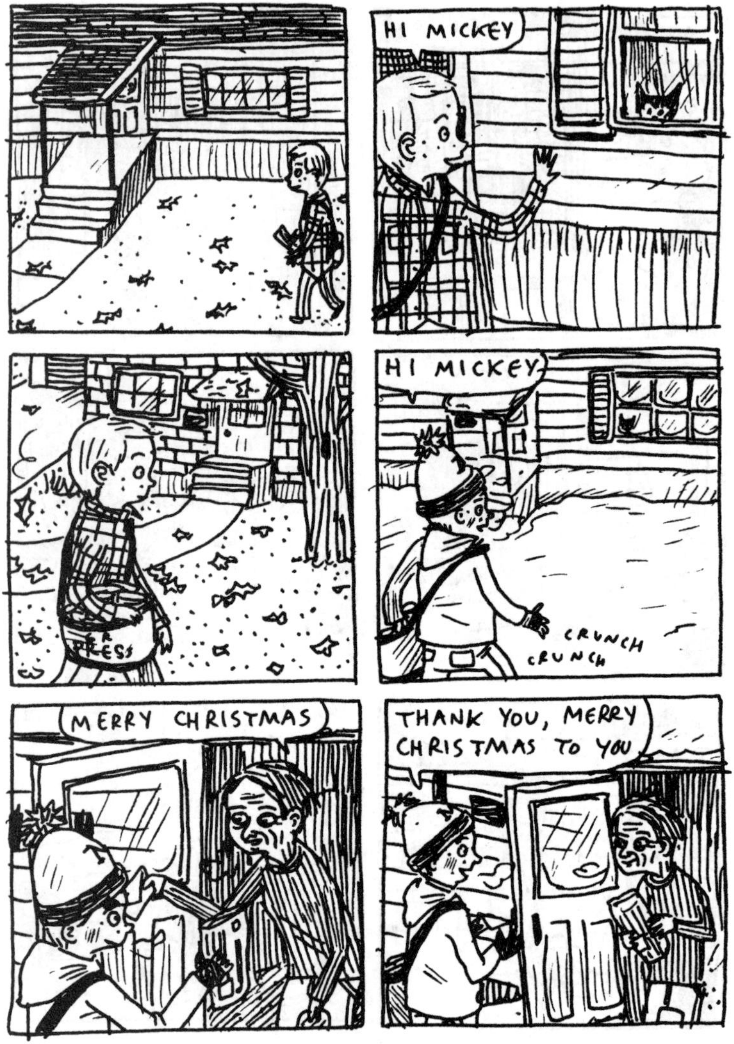
HI MICKEY
HI MICKEY
CRUNCH
CRUNCH
MERRY CHRISTMAS
THANK YOU, MERRY CHRISTMAS TO YOU

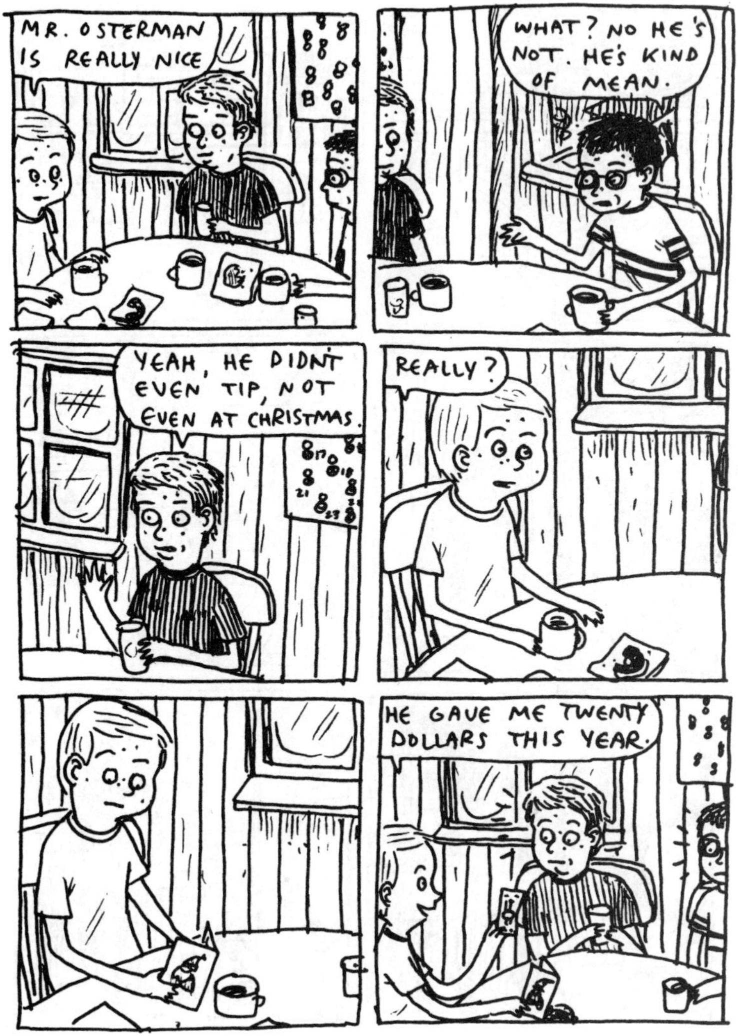
MR. OSTERMAN IS REALLY NICE
WHAT? NO HE'S NOT. HE'S KIND OF MEAN.
YEAH, HE DIDN'T EVEN TIP, NOT EVEN AT CHRISTMAS.
REALLY?
HE GAVE ME TWENTY DOLLARS THIS YEAR.

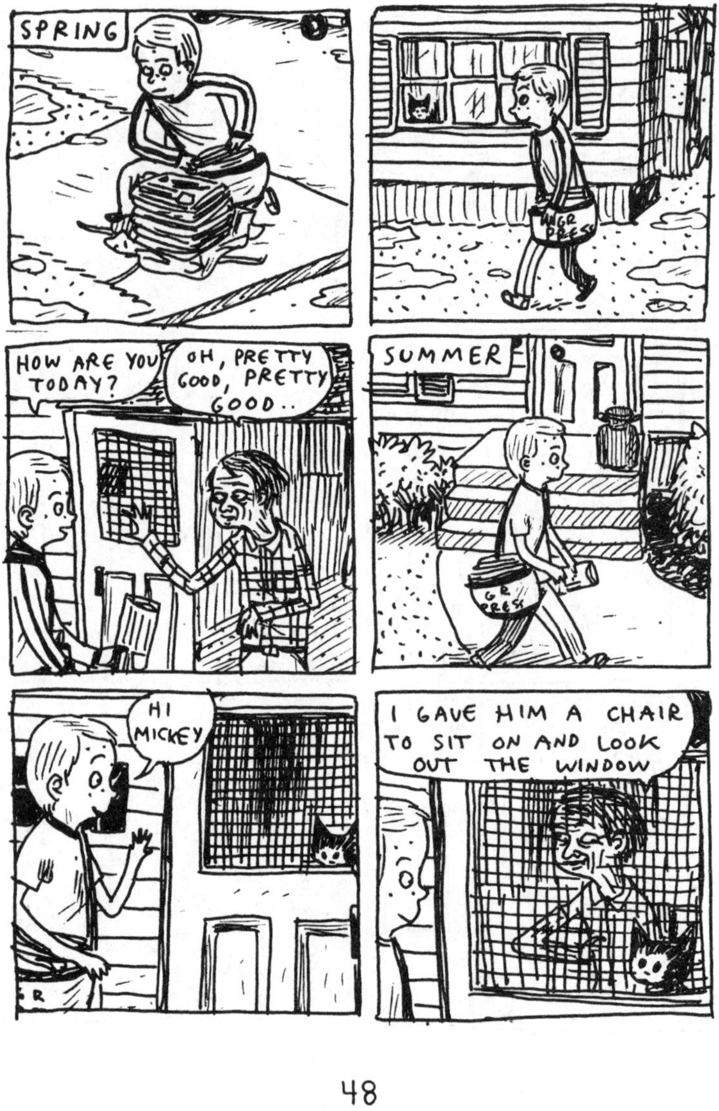
SPRING
HOW ARE YOU TODAY?
OH, PRETTY GOOD, PRETTY GOOD..
SUMMER
GR PRESS
HI MICKEY
I GAVE HIM A CHAIR TO SIT ON AND LOOK OUT THE WINDOW

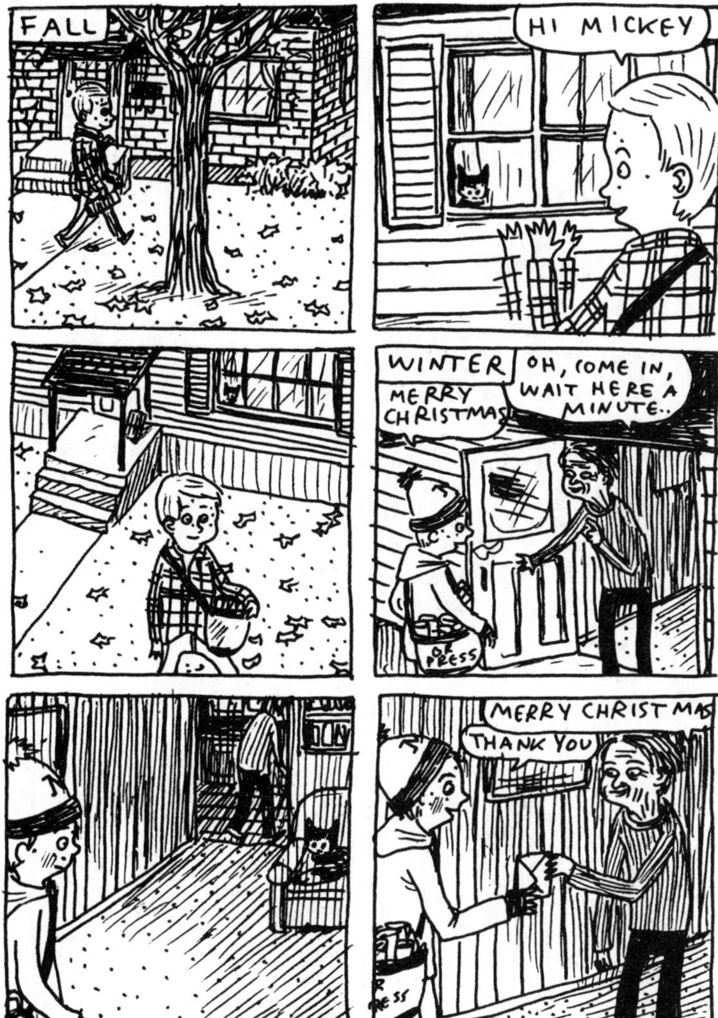
FALL
HI MICKEY
WINTER
MERRY CHRISTMAS
OH, COME IN, WAIT HERE A MINUTE.
MERRY CHRISTMAS
THANK YOU

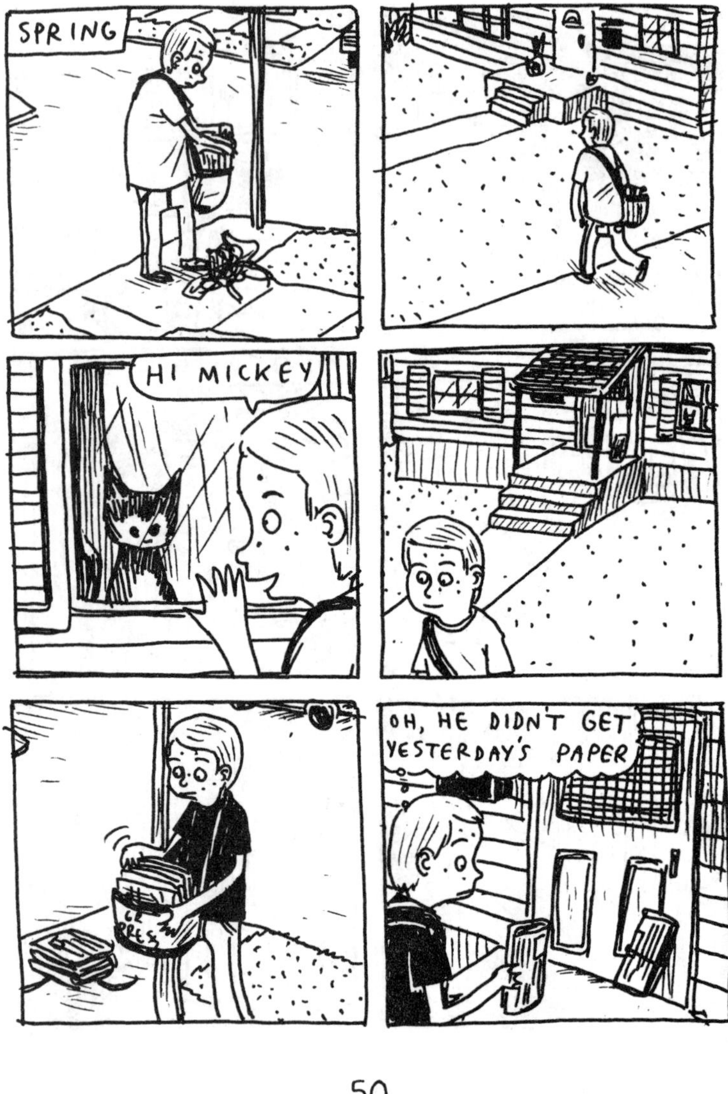
SPRING
HI MICKEY
OH, HE DIDN'T GET YESTERDAY'S PAPER

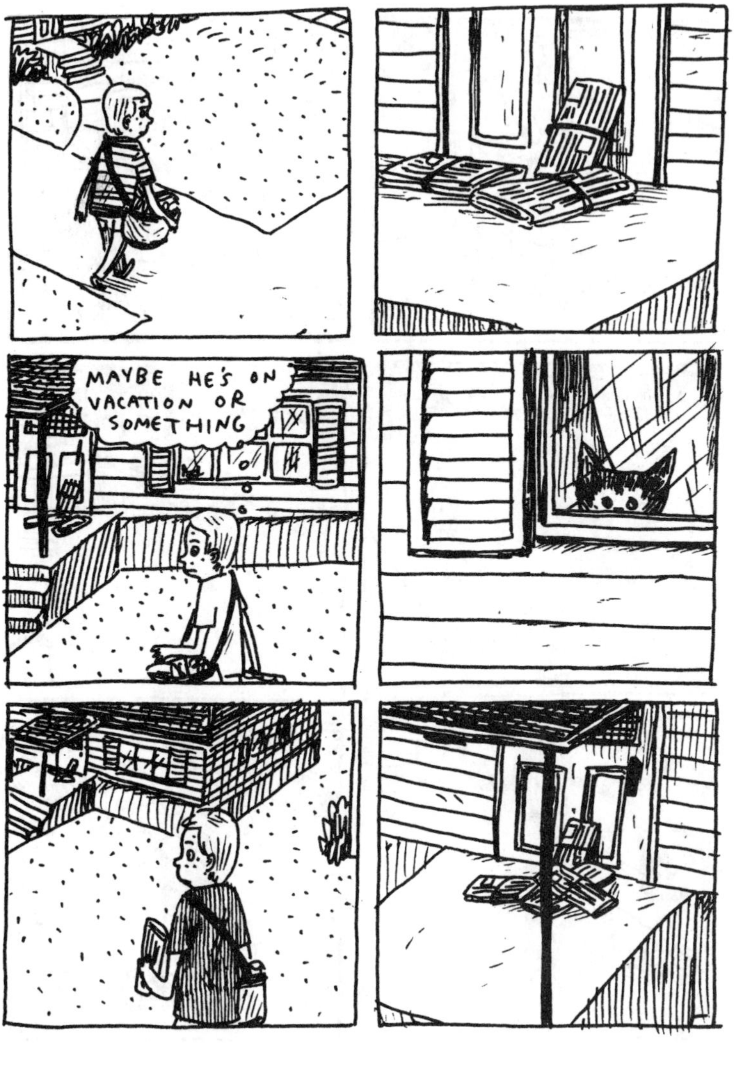
MAYBE HE'S ON VACATION OR SOMETHING

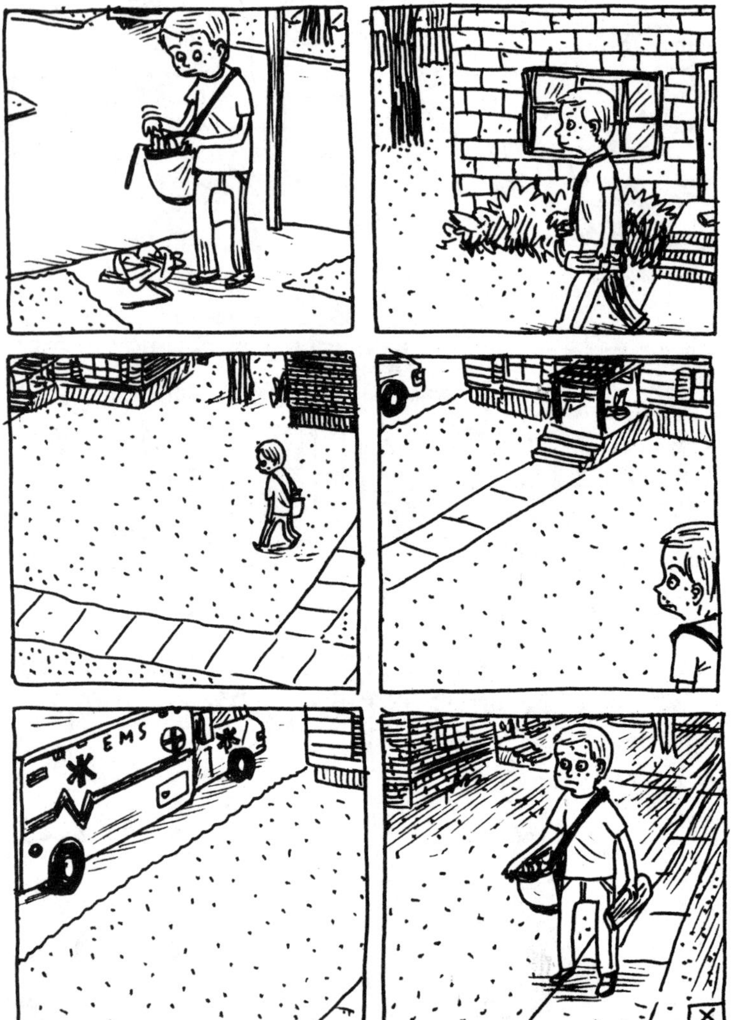
EMS

THAT'S WHAT I WAS AFRAID OF

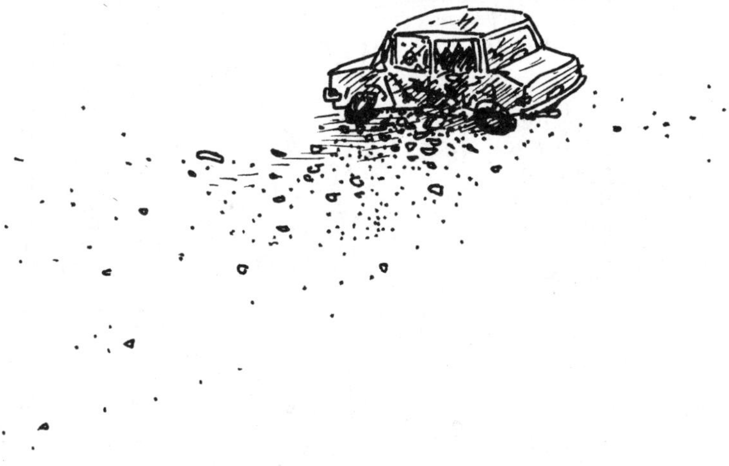

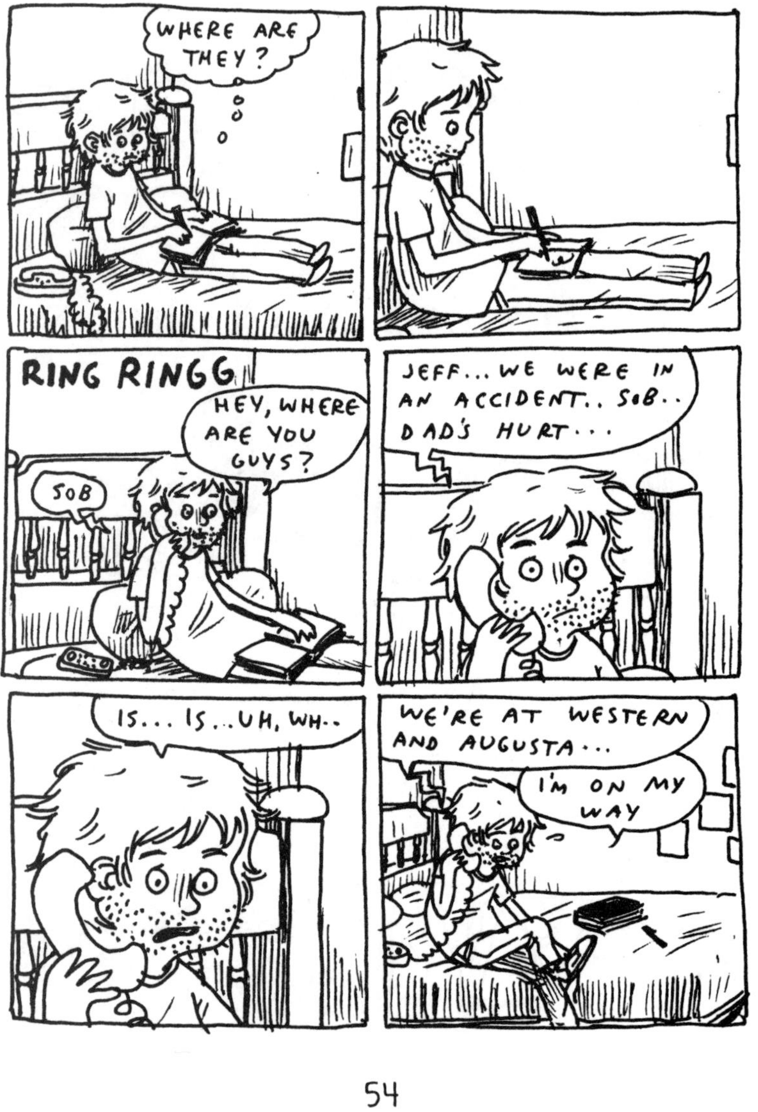
WHERE ARE THEY?
RING RINGG
HEY, WHERE ARE YOU GUYS?
SOB
JEFF... WE WERE IN AN ACCIDENT.. SOB.. DAD'S HURT...
IS... IS...UH, WH..
WE'RE AT WESTERN AND AUGUSTA...
I'M ON MY WAY

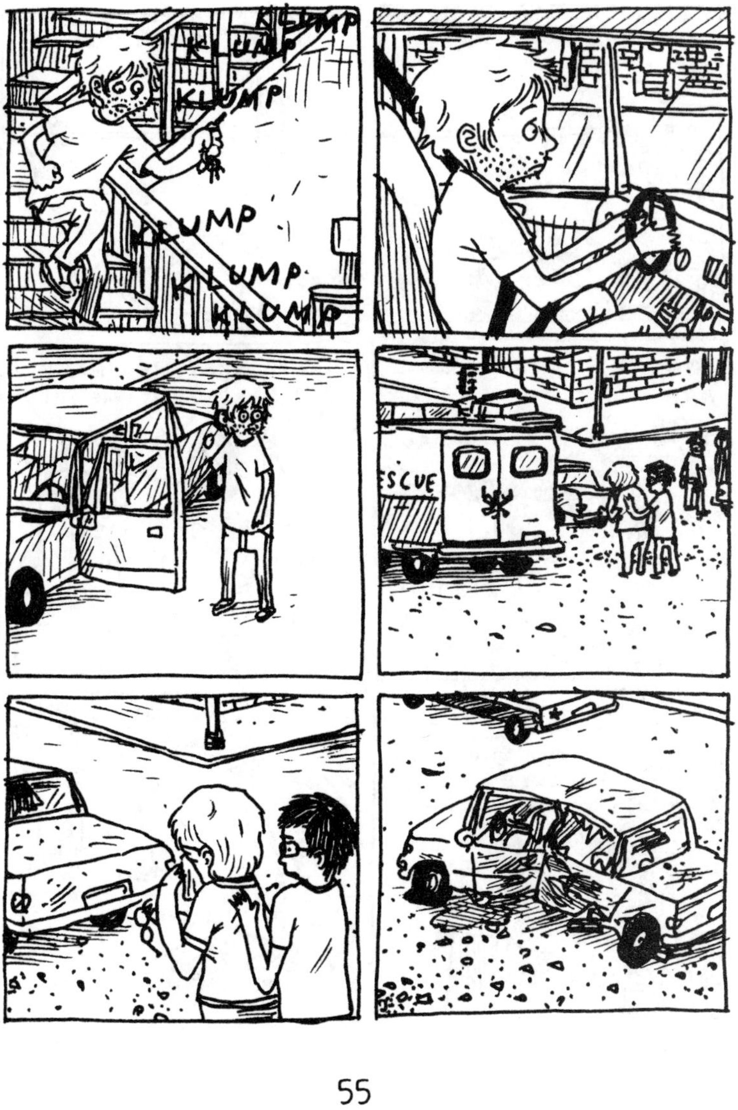
KLUMP
KLUMP
KLUMP
KLUMP
KLUMP
KLUMP
ESCUE

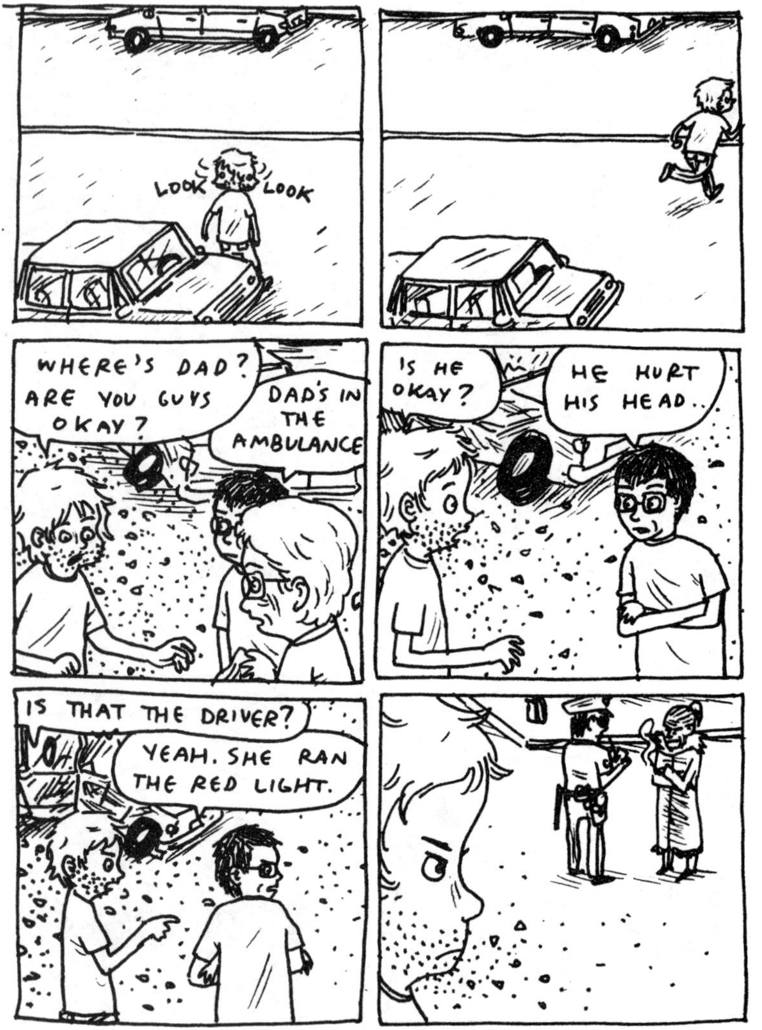
LOOK LOOK
WHERE'S DAD? ARE YOU GUYS OKAY?
DAD'S IN THE AMBULANCE
IS HE OKAY?
HE HURT HIS HEAD..
IS THAT THE DRIVER?
YEAH. SHE RAN THE RED LIGHT.

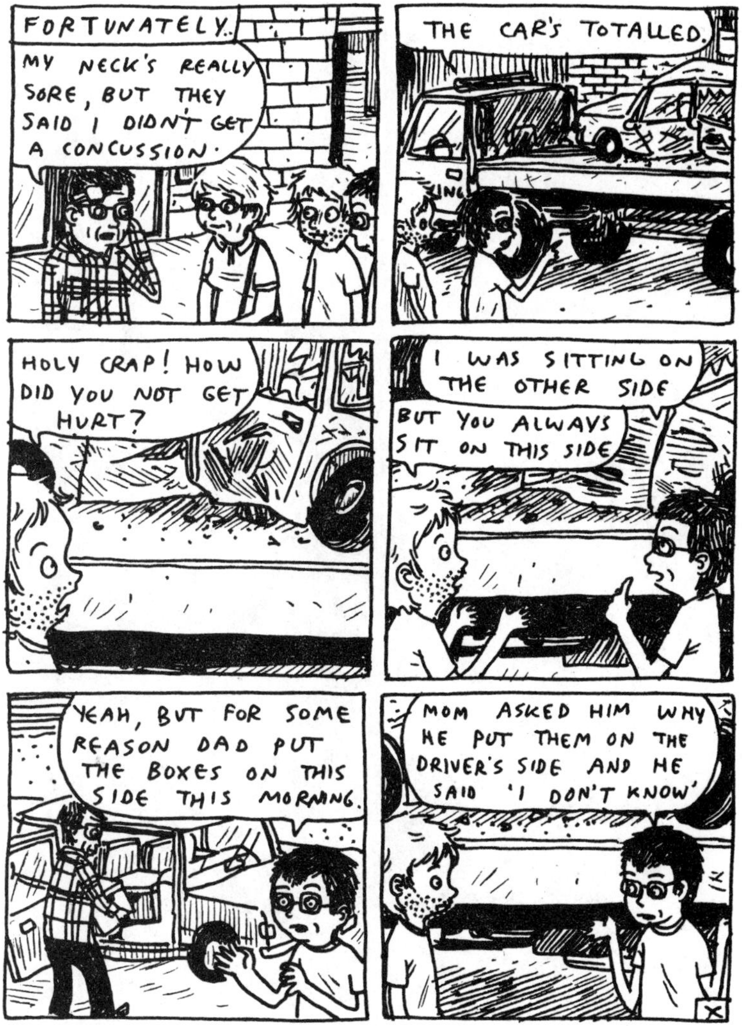
FORTUNATELY..
MY NECK'S REALLY SORE, BUT THEY SAID I DIDN'T GET A CONCUSSION.
THE CAR'S TOTALLED.
HOLY CRAP! HOW DID YOU NOT GET HURT?
I WAS SITTING ON THE OTHER SIDE
BUT YOU ALWAYS SIT ON THIS SIDE
YEAH, BUT FOR SOME REASON DAD PUT THE BOXES ON THIS SIDE THIS MORNING.
MOM ASKED HIM WHY HE PUT THEM ON THE DRIVER'S SIDE AND HE SAID 'I DON'T KNOW'

MISSING
THE
MOUNTAINS

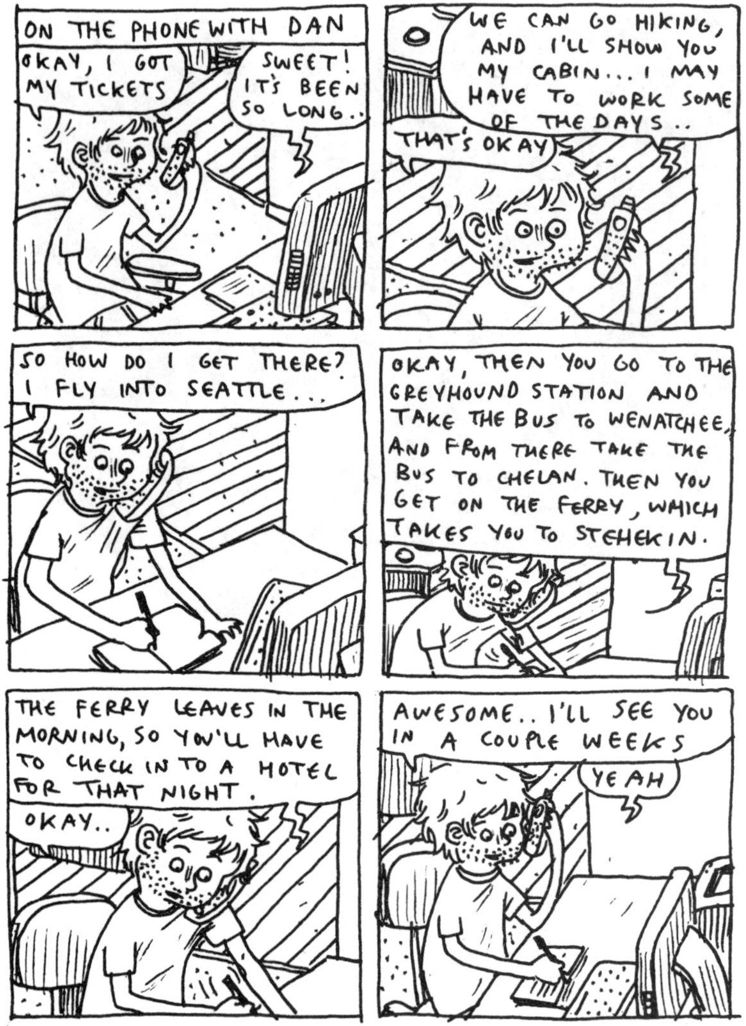
ON THE PHONE WITH DAN
OKAY, I GOT MY TICKETS
SWEET! IT'S BEEN SO LONG..
WE CAN GO HIKING, AND I'LL SHOW YOU MY CABIN... I MAY HAVE TO WORK SOME OF THE DAYS..
THAT'S OKAY
SO HOW DO I GET THERE? I FLY INTO SEATTLE...
OKAY, THEN YOU GO TO THE GREYHOUND STATION AND TAKE THE BUS TO WENATCHEE, AND FROM THERE TAKE THE BUS TO CHELAN. THEN YOU GET ON THE FERRY, WHICH TAKES YOU TO STEHEKIN.
THE FERRY LEAVES IN THE MORNING, SO YOU'LL HAVE TO CHECK IN TO A HOTEL FOR THAT NIGHT.
OKAY..
AWESOME.. I'LL SEE YOU IN A COUPLE WEEKS
YEAH

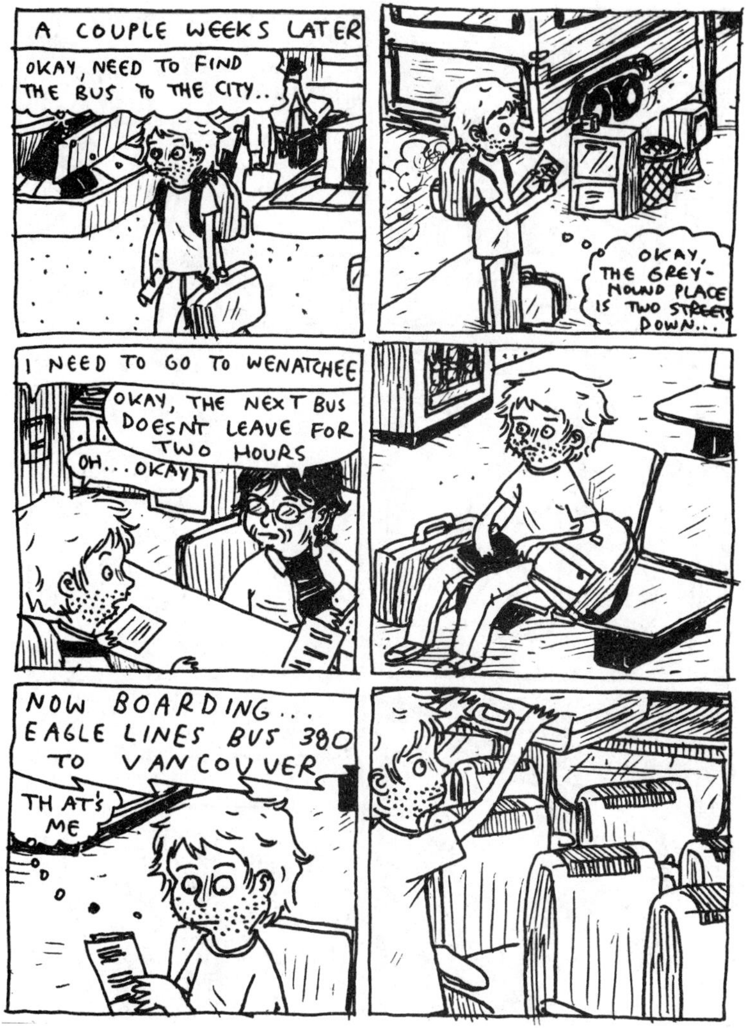
A COUPLE WEEKS LATER
OKAY, NEED TO FIND THE BUS TO THE CITY..
OKAY, THE GREY-HOUND PLACE IS TWO STREETS DOWN..
I NEED TO GO TO WENATCHEE
OKAY, THE NEXT BUS DOESN'T LEAVE FOR TWO HOURS
OH... OKAY
NOW BOARDING... EAGLE LINES BUS 380 TO VANCOUVER
THAT'S ME

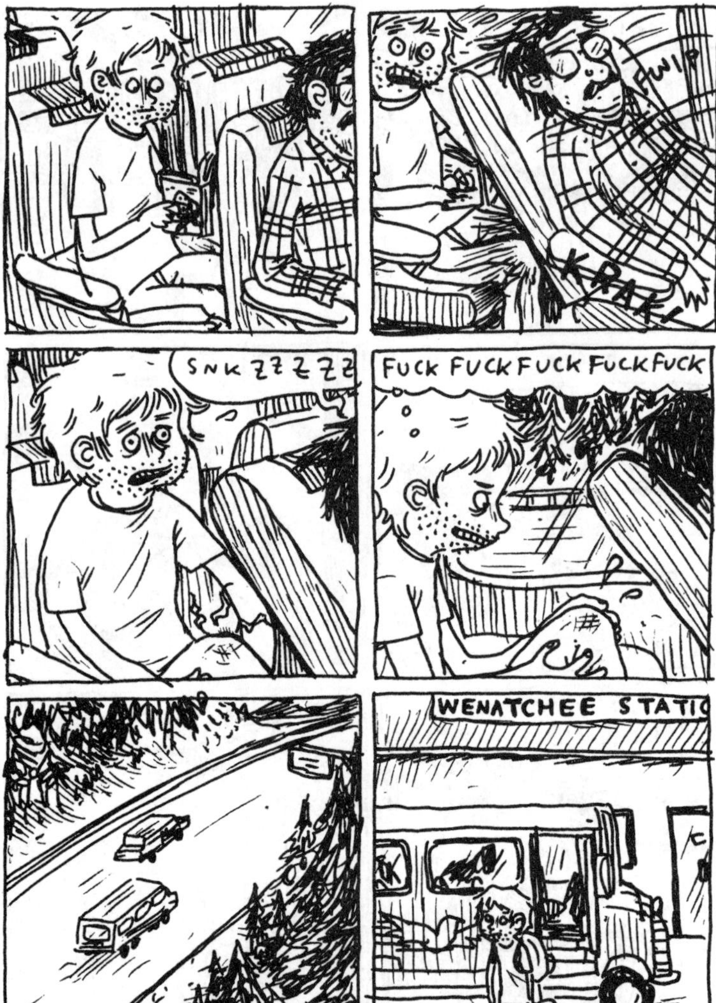
AWIP
KRAK!
SNK ZZZZZ
FUCK FUCK FUCK FUCK FUCK
WENATCHEE STATIO

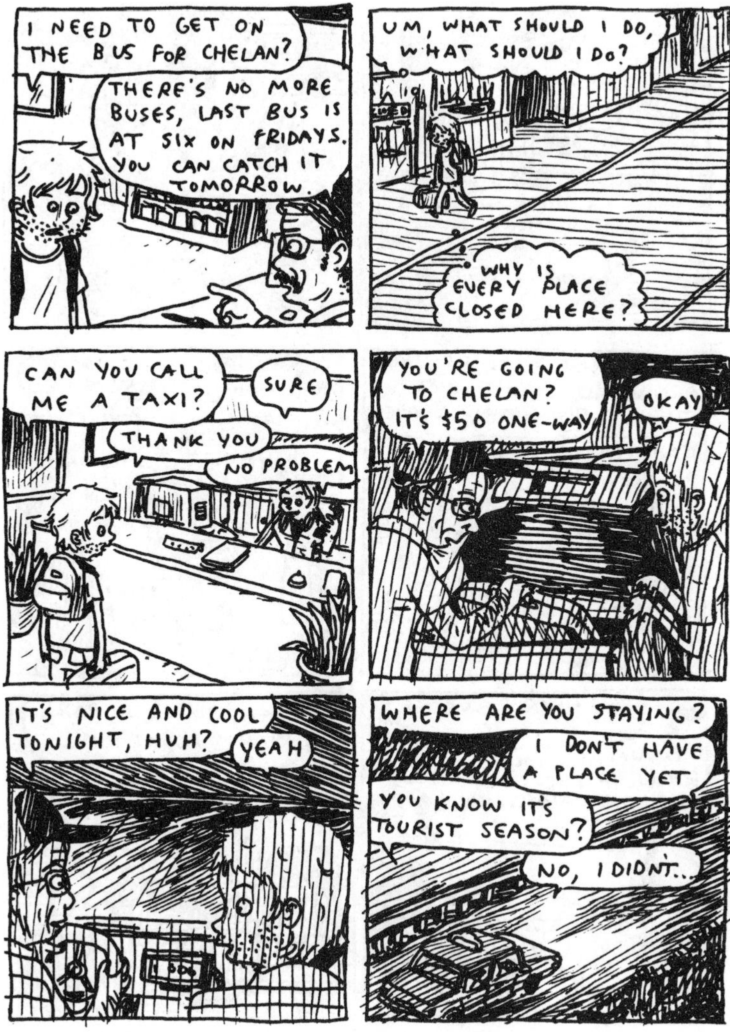
I NEED TO GET ON THE BUS FOR CHELAN?
THERE'S NO MORE BUSES, LAST BUS IS AT SIX ON FRIDAYS. YOU CAN CATCH IT TOMORROW.
UM, WHAT SHOULD I DO, WHAT SHOULD I DO?
WHY IS EVERY PLACE CLOSED HERE?
CAN YOU CALL ME A TAXI?
SURE
THANK YOU
NO PROBLEM
YOU'RE GOING TO CHELAN? IT'S $50 ONE-WAY
OKAY
IT'S NICE AND COOL TONIGHT, HUH?
YEAH
WHERE ARE YOU STAYING?
I DON'T HAVE A PLACE YET
YOU KNOW IT'S TOURIST SEASON?
NO, I DIDN'T...

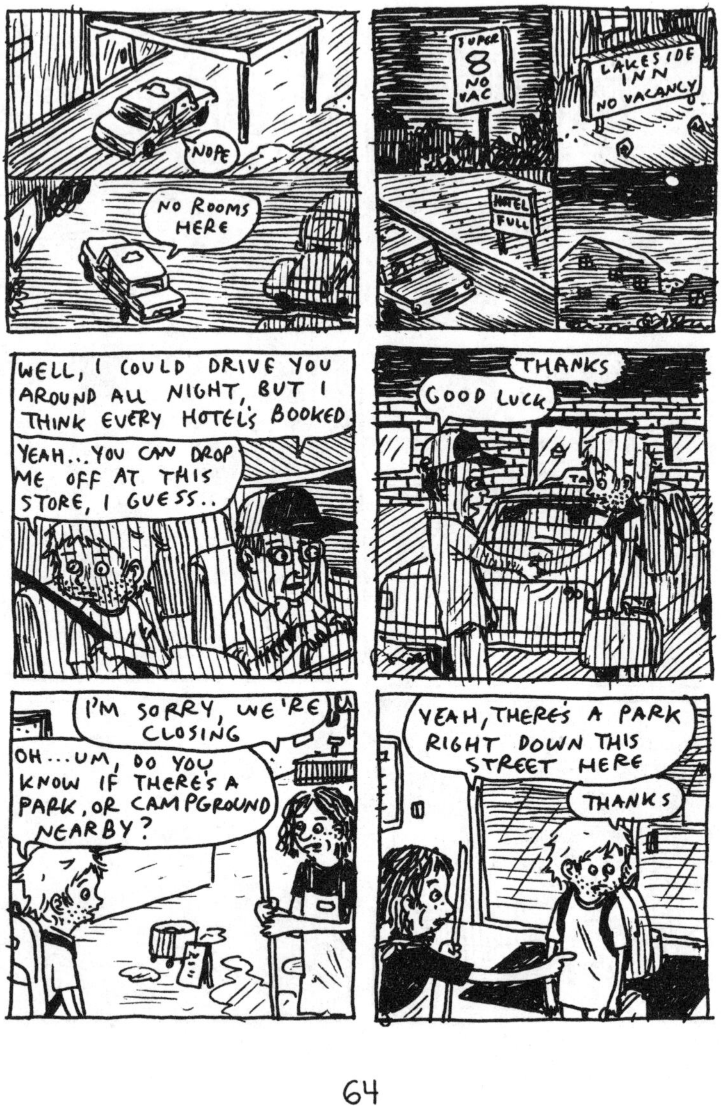
SUPER 8 NO VAC
LAKESIDE INN NO VACANCY
NOPE
NO ROOMS HERE
HOTEL FULL
WELL, I COULD DRIVE YOU AROUND ALL NIGHT, BUT I THINK EVERY HOTEL'S BOOKED
YEAH... YOU CAN DROP ME OFF AT THIS STORE, I GUESS..
THANKS
GOOD LUCK
I'M SORRY, WE'RE CLOSING
OH... UM, DO YOU KNOW IF THERE'S A PARK, OR CAMPGROUND NEARBY?
YEAH, THERE'S A PARK RIGHT DOWN THIS STREET HERE
THANKS

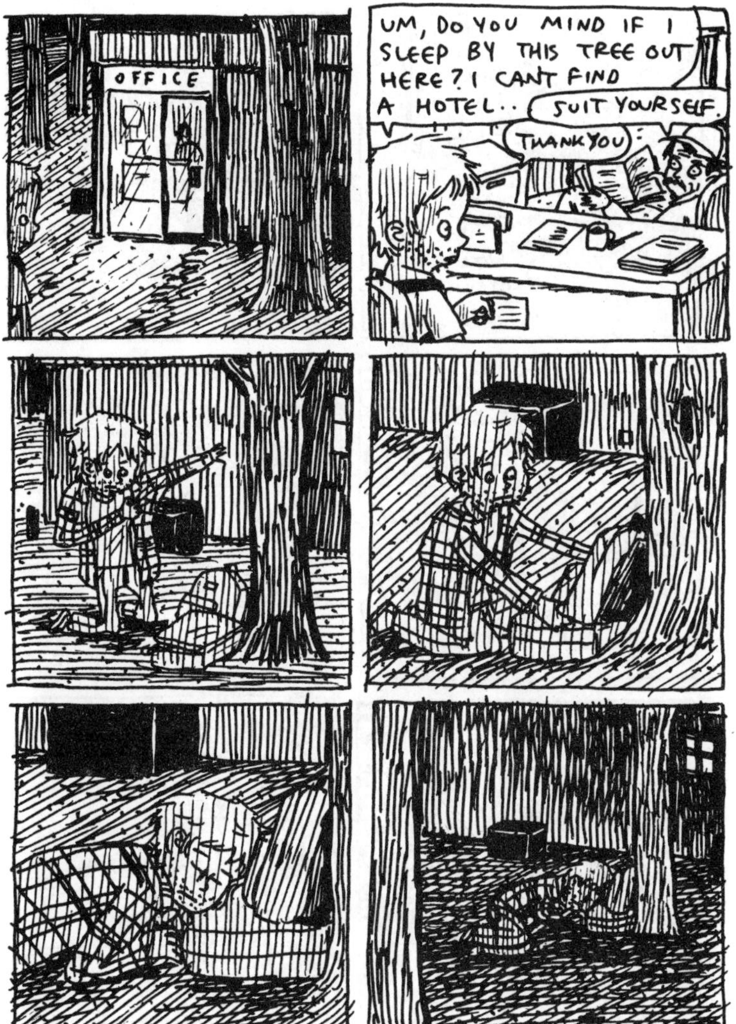
OFFICE
UM, DO YOU MIND IF I SLEEP BY THIS TREE OUT HERE? I CAN'T FIND A HOTEL..
SUIT YOURSELF.
THANK YOU

BLINK
BLINK
LAKE CHEL
I NEED THE FERRY TO STEHEKIN?
IT'S $50... THAT'LL LEAVE AT ELEVEN, SO YOU'VE GOT A COUPLE HOURS
THANKS

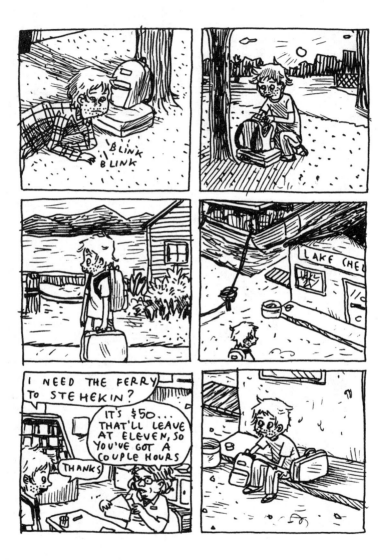

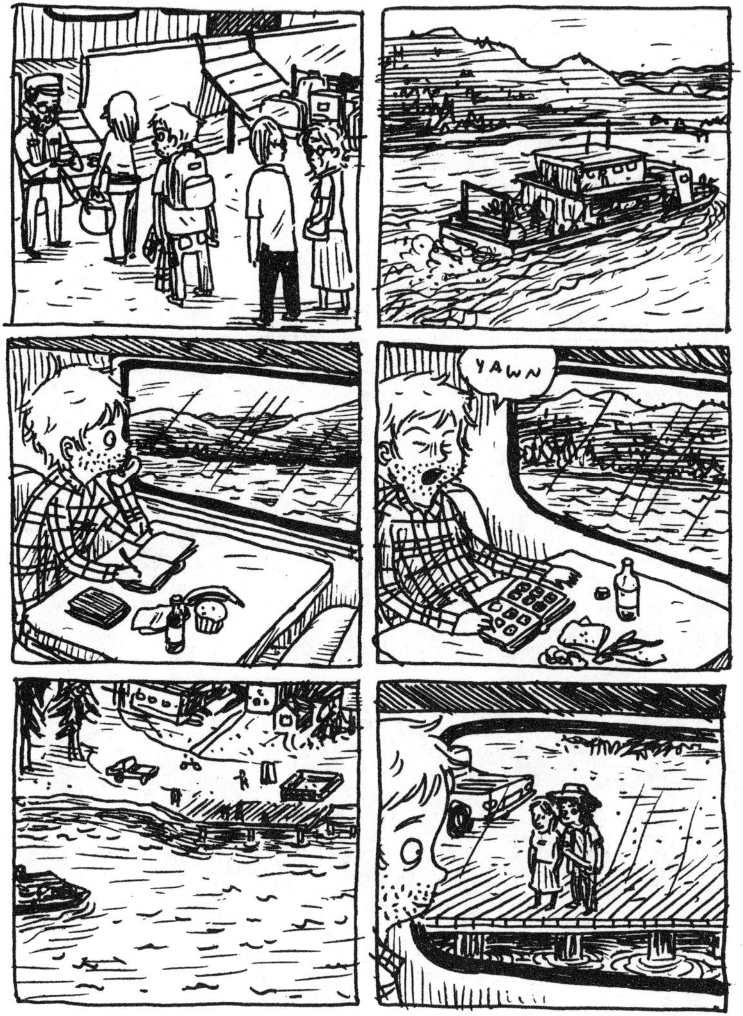
YAWN

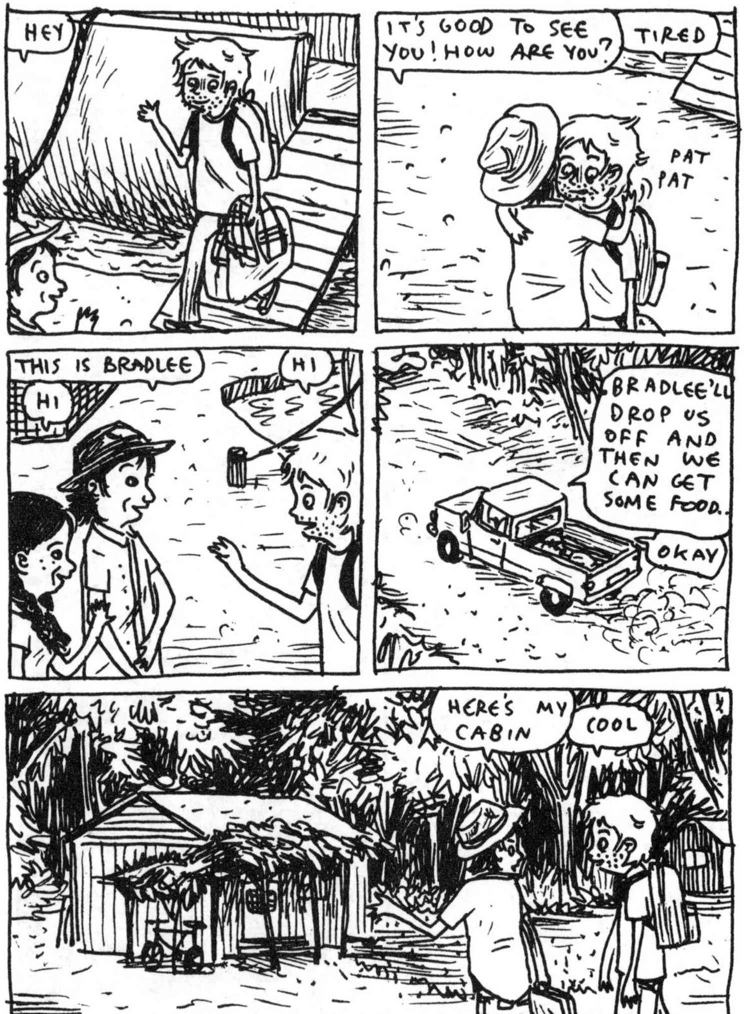
HEY
IT'S GOOD TO SEE YOU! HOW ARE YOU?
TIRED
PAT PAT
THIS IS BRADLEE
HI
HI
BRADLEE'LL DROP US OFF AND THEN WE CAN GET SOME FOOD...
OKAY
HERE'S MY CABIN
COOL

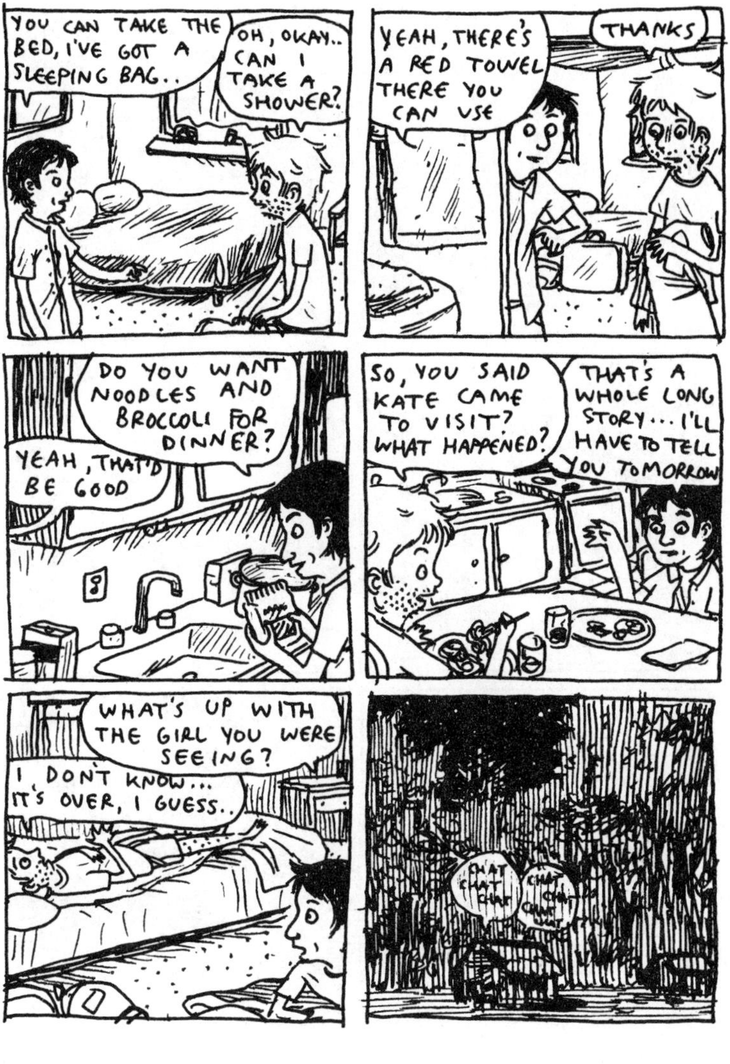
YOU CAN TAKE THE BED, I'VE GOT A SLEEPING BAG..
OH, OKAY.. CAN I TAKE A SHOWER?
YEAH, THERE'S A RED TOWEL THERE YOU CAN USE
THANKS
DO YOU WANT NOODLES AND BROCCOLI FOR DINNER?
YEAH, THAT'D BE GOOD
SO, YOU SAID KATE CAME TO VISIT? WHAT HAPPENED?
THAT'S A WHOLE LONG STORY... I'LL HAVE TO TELL YOU TOMORROW
WHAT'S UP WITH THE GIRL YOU WERE SEEING?
I DON'T KNOW... IT'S OVER, I GUESS..
CHAT CHAT CHAT

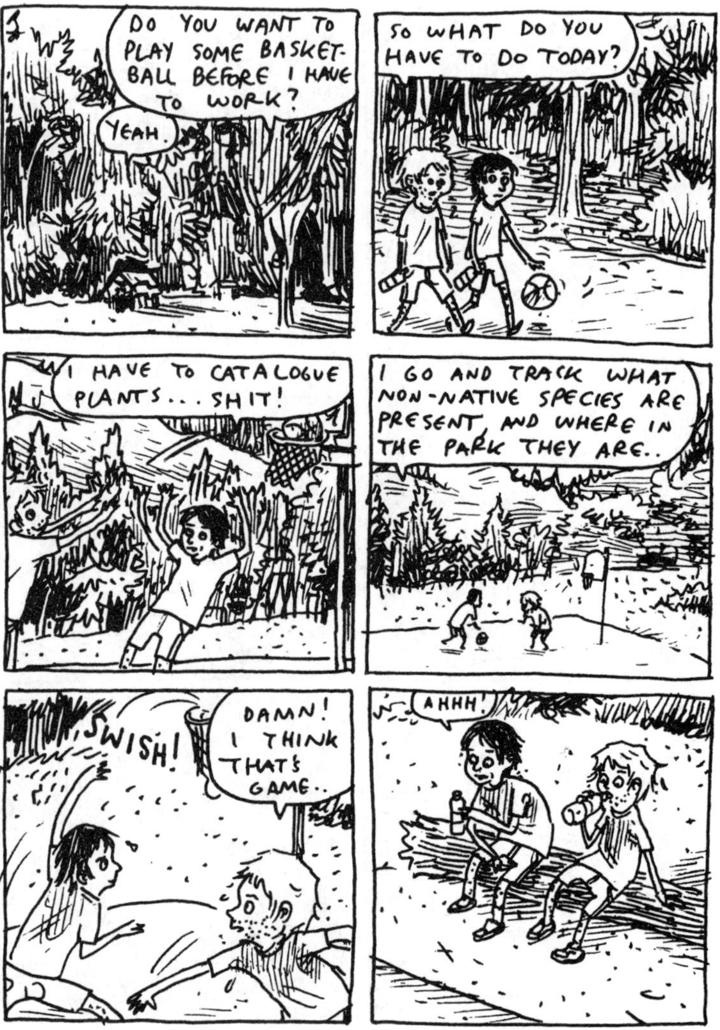
DO YOU WANT TO PLAY SOME BASKET-BALL BEFORE I HAVE TO WORK?
YEAH.
SO WHAT DO YOU HAVE TO DO TODAY?
I HAVE TO CATALOGUE PLANTS... SHIT!
I GO AND TRACK WHAT NON-NATIVE SPECIES ARE PRESENT, AND WHERE IN THE PARK THEY ARE..
SWISH!
DAMN! I THINK THAT'S GAME..
AHHH!

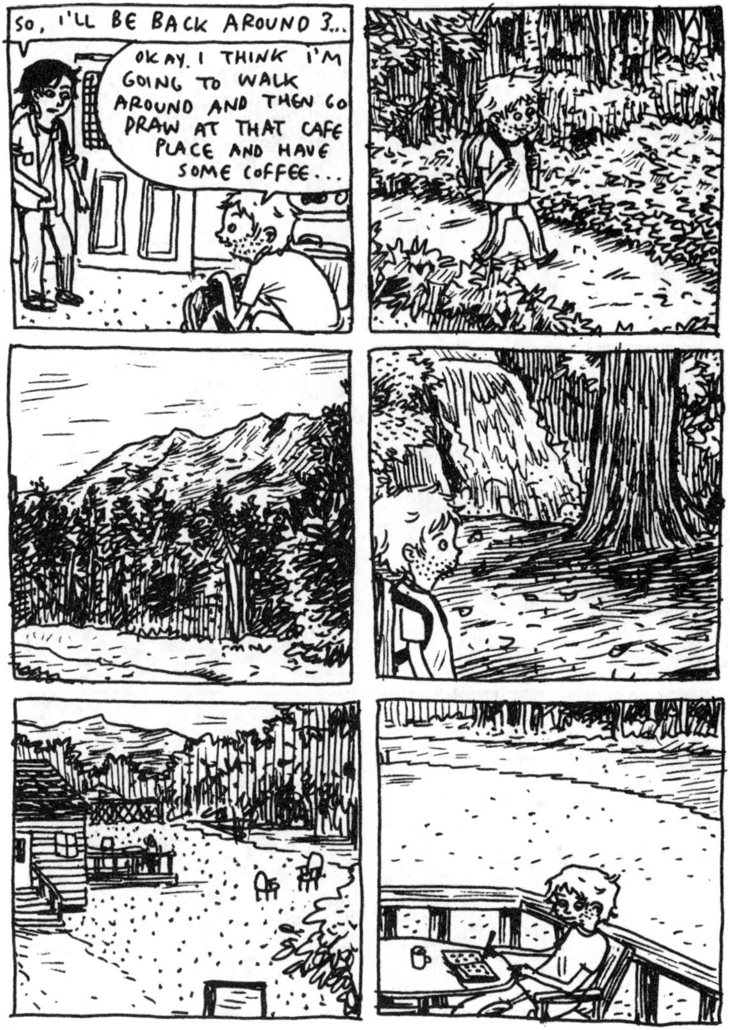
SO, I'LL BE BACK AROUND 3...
OKAY. I THINK I'M GOING TO WALK AROUND AND THEN GO DRAW AT THAT CAFE PLACE AND HAVE SOME COFFEE...

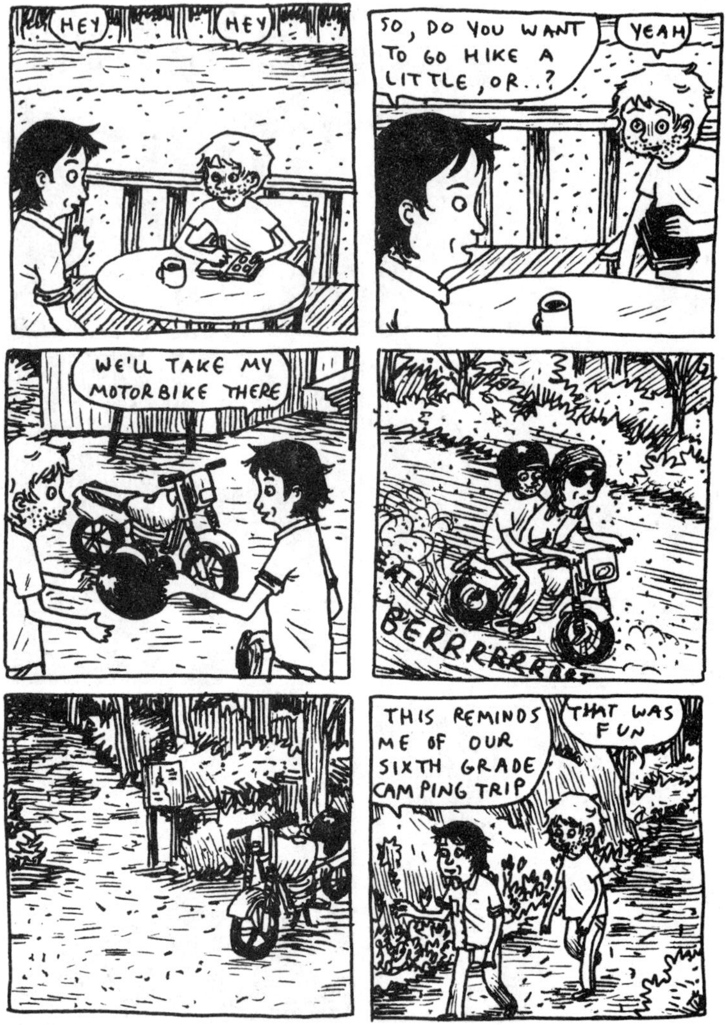
HEY
HEY
SO, DO YOU WANT TO GO HIKE A LITTLE, OR..?
YEAH
WE'LL TAKE MY MOTORBIKE THERE
BERRRRRRRRRT
THIS REMINDS ME OF OUR SIXTH GRADE CAMPING TRIP
THAT WAS FUN

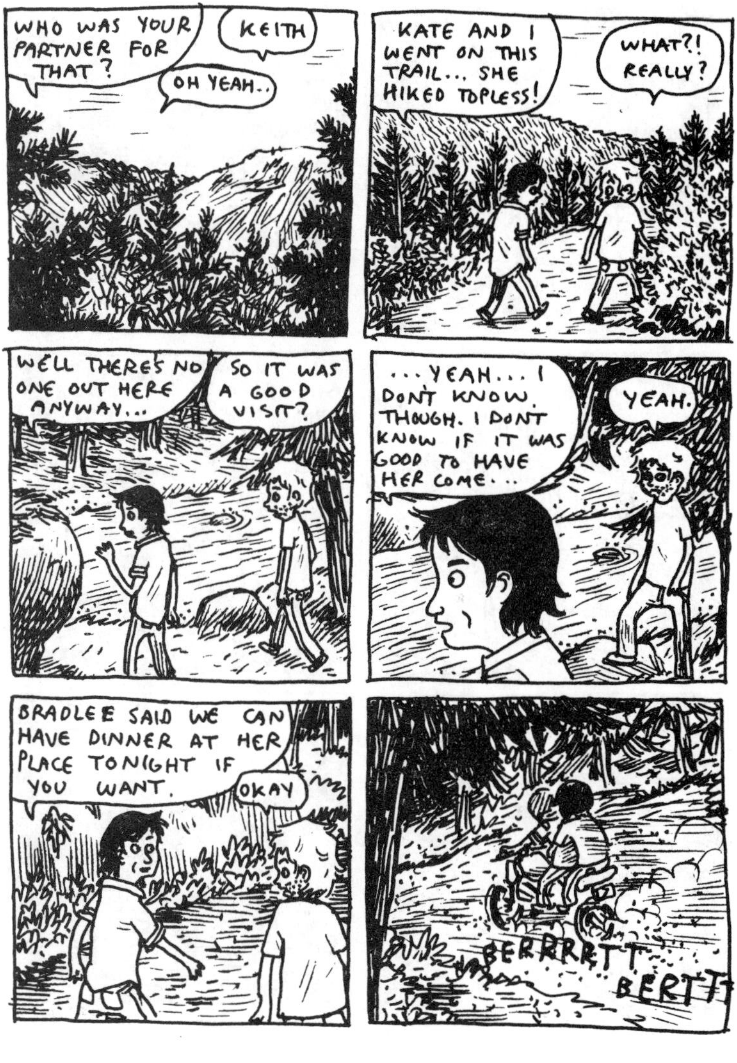
WHO WAS YOUR PARTNER FOR THAT?
KEITH
OH YEAH..
KATE AND I WENT ON THIS TRAIL... SHE HIKED TOPLESS!
WHAT?! REALLY?
WELL THERE'S NO ONE OUT HERE ANYWAY...
SO IT WAS A GOOD VISIT?
...YEAH... I DON'T KNOW. THOUGH. I DON'T KNOW IF IT WAS GOOD TO HAVE HER COME...
YEAH.
BRADLEE SAID WE CAN HAVE DINNER AT HER PLACE TONIGHT IF YOU WANT.
OKAY
BERRRRTT
BERTT

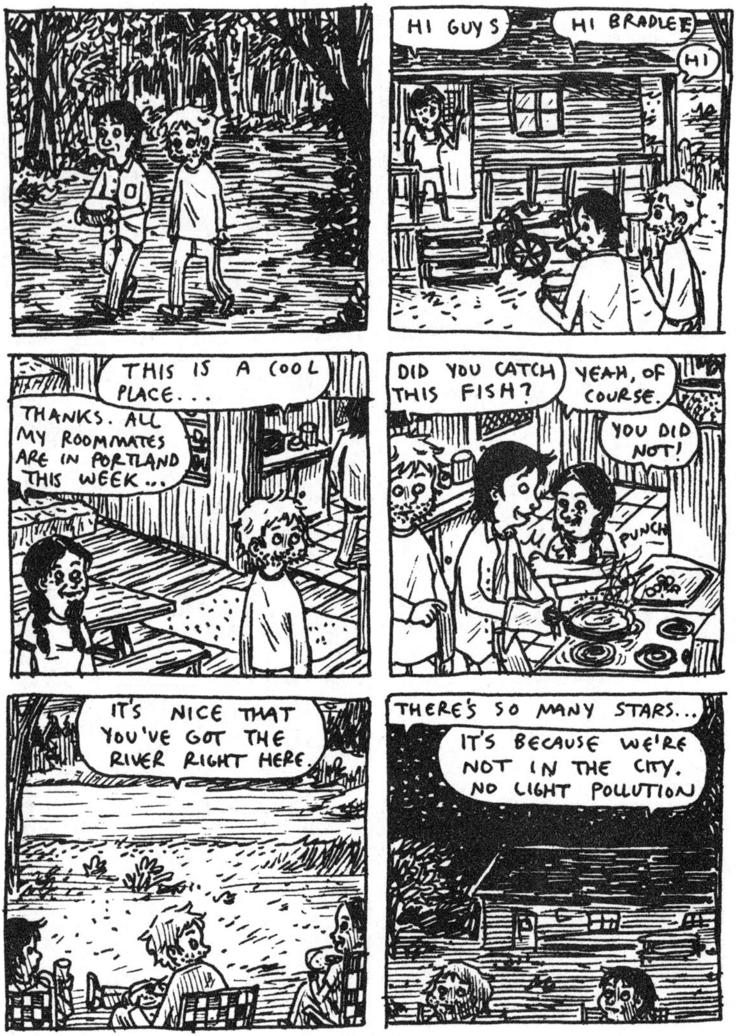
HI GUYS
HI BRADLEE
HI
THIS IS A COOL PLACE...
THANKS. ALL MY ROOMMATES ARE IN PORTLAND THIS WEEK...
DID YOU CATCH THIS FISH?
YEAH, OF COURSE.
YOU DID NOT!
PUNCH
IT'S NICE THAT YOU'VE GOT THE RIVER RIGHT HERE.
THERE'S SO MANY STARS...
IT'S BECAUSE WE'RE NOT IN THE CITY. NO LIGHT POLLUTION

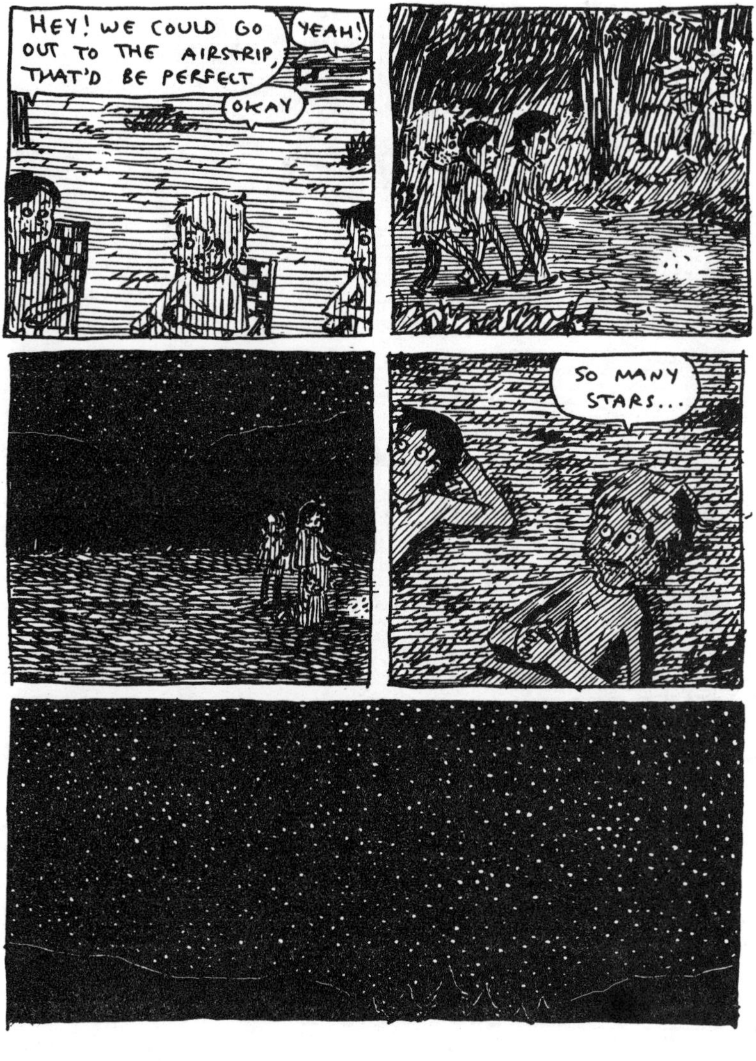
HEY! WE COULD GO OUT TO THE AIRSTRIP, THAT'D BE PERFECT
YEAH!
OKAY
SO MANY STARS...

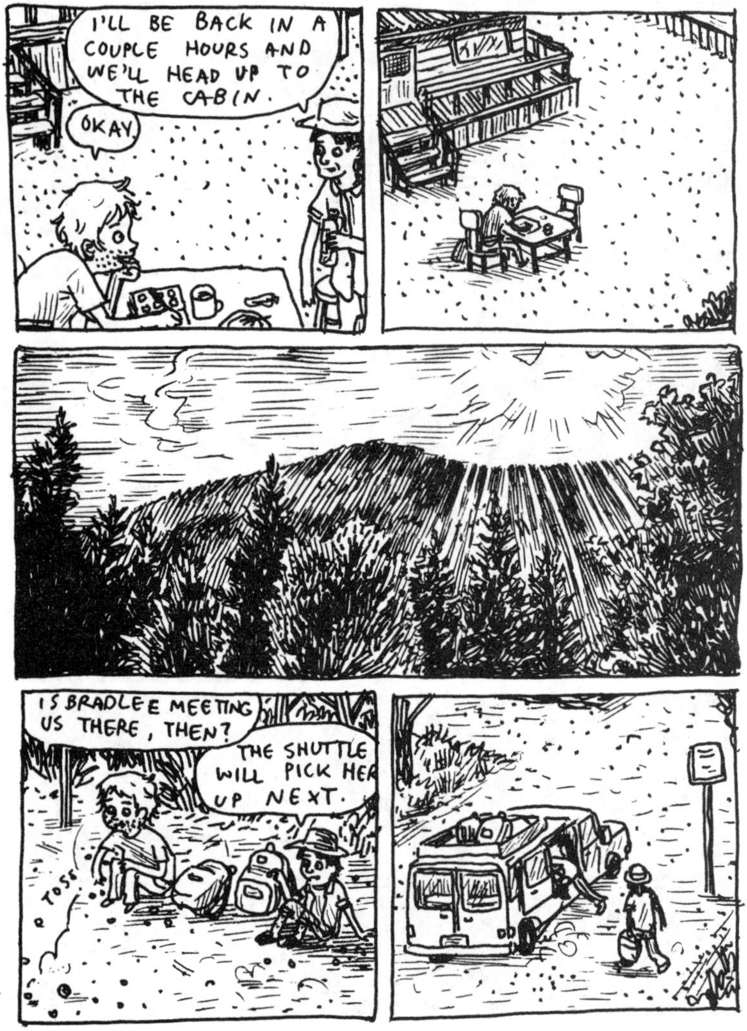
I'LL BE BACK IN A COUPLE HOURS AND WE'LL HEAD UP TO THE CABIN.
OKAY.
IS BRADLEE MEETING US THERE, THEN?
THE SHUTTLE WILL PICK HER UP NEXT.
TOSS

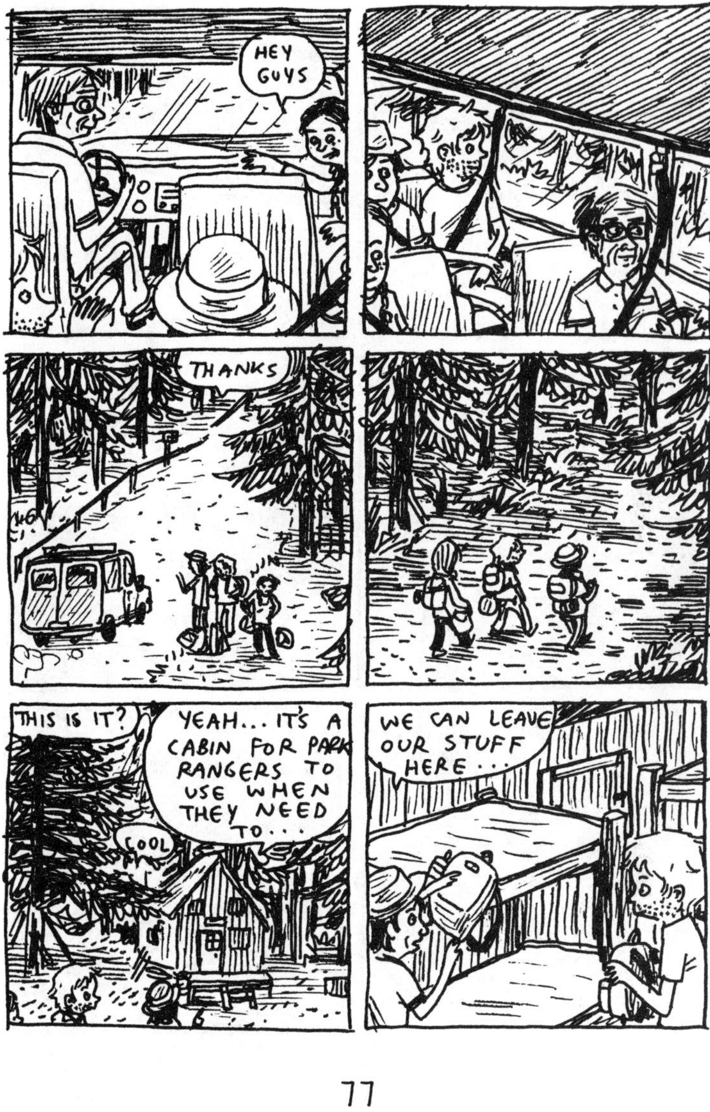
HEY GUYS
THANKS
THIS IS IT?
YEAH... IT'S A CABIN FOR PARK RANGERS TO USE WHEN THEY NEED TO...
COOL
WE CAN LEAVE OUR STUFF HERE...

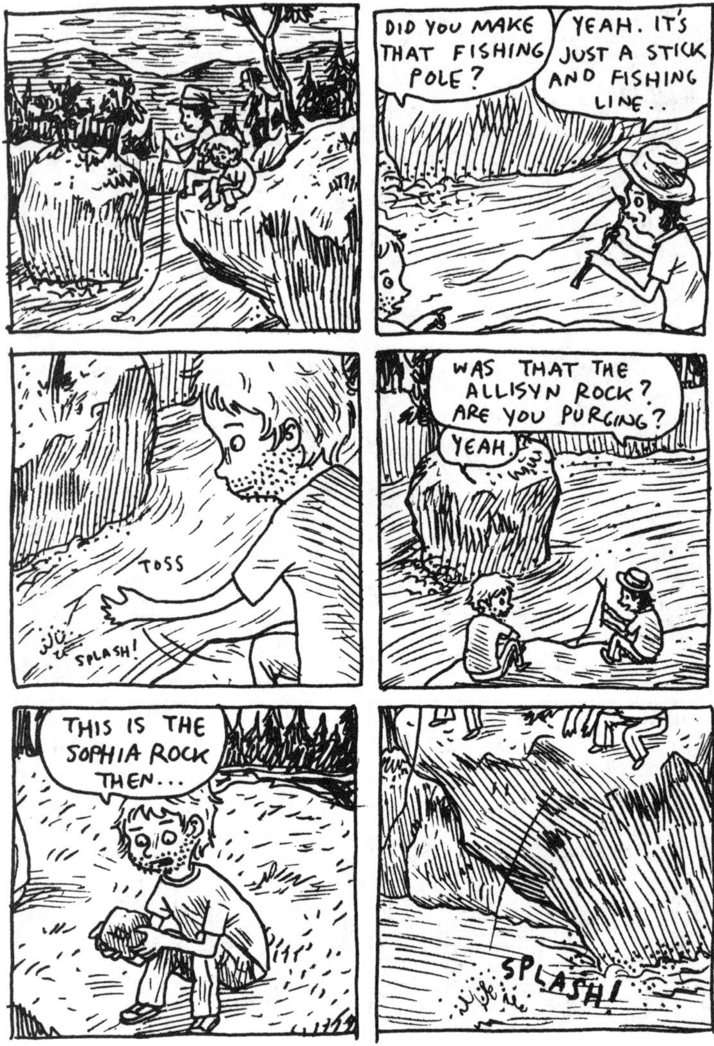
DID YOU MAKE THAT FISHING POLE?
YEAH. IT'S JUST A STICK AND FISHING LINE..
TOSS
SPLASH!
WAS THAT THE ALLISYN ROCK? ARE YOU PURGING?
YEAH.
THIS IS THE SOPHIA ROCK THEN...
SPLASH!

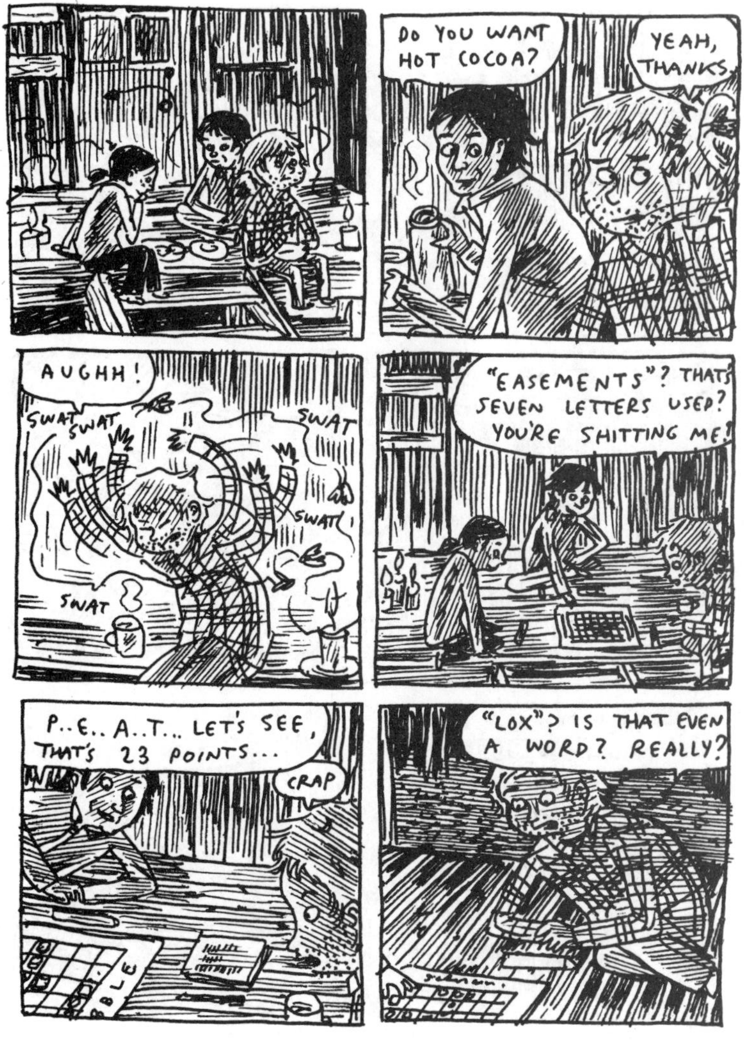
DO YOU WANT HOT COCOA?
YEAH, THANKS.
AUGHH!
SWAT SWAT
SWAT
SWAT
SWAT
"EASEMENTS"? THAT'S SEVEN LETTERS USED? YOU'RE SHITTING ME?
P.. E.. A.. T... LET'S SEE, THAT'S 23 POINTS...
CRAP
"LOX"? IS THAT EVEN A WORD? REALLY?

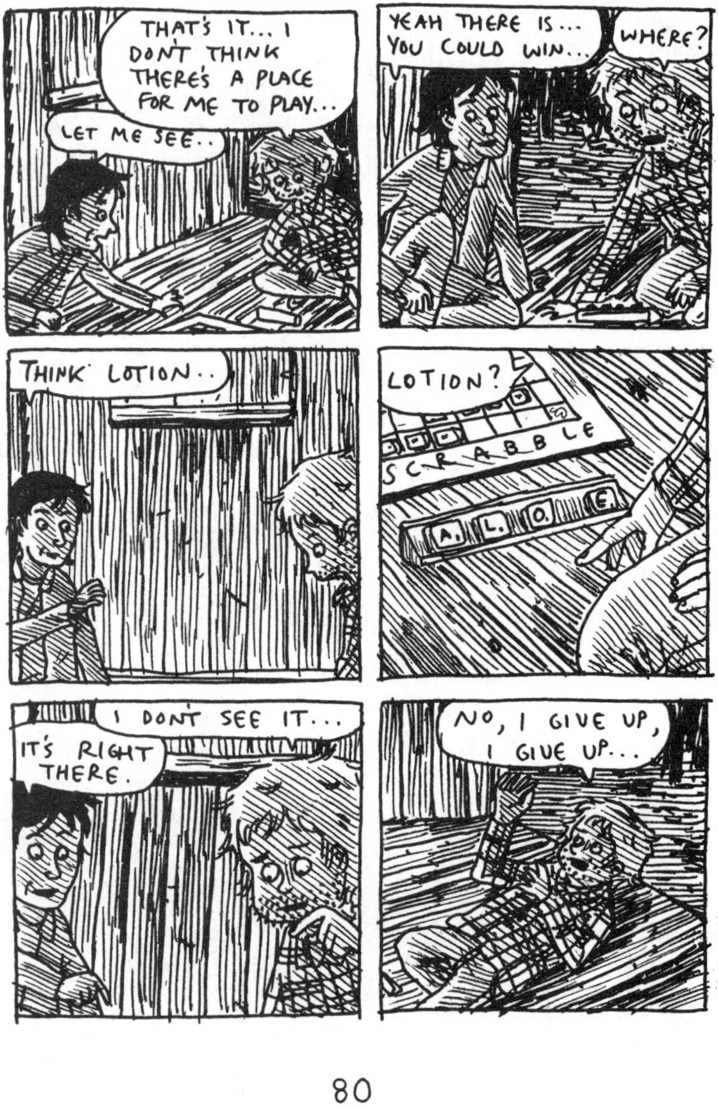
THAT'S IT... I DON'T THINK THERE'S A PLACE FOR ME TO PLAY...
LET ME SEE..
YEAH THERE IS... YOU COULD WIN...
WHERE?
THINK LOTION..
LOTION?
SCRABBLE
A L O E
I DONT SEE IT...
IT'S RIGHT THERE.
NO, I GIVE UP, I GIVE UP...

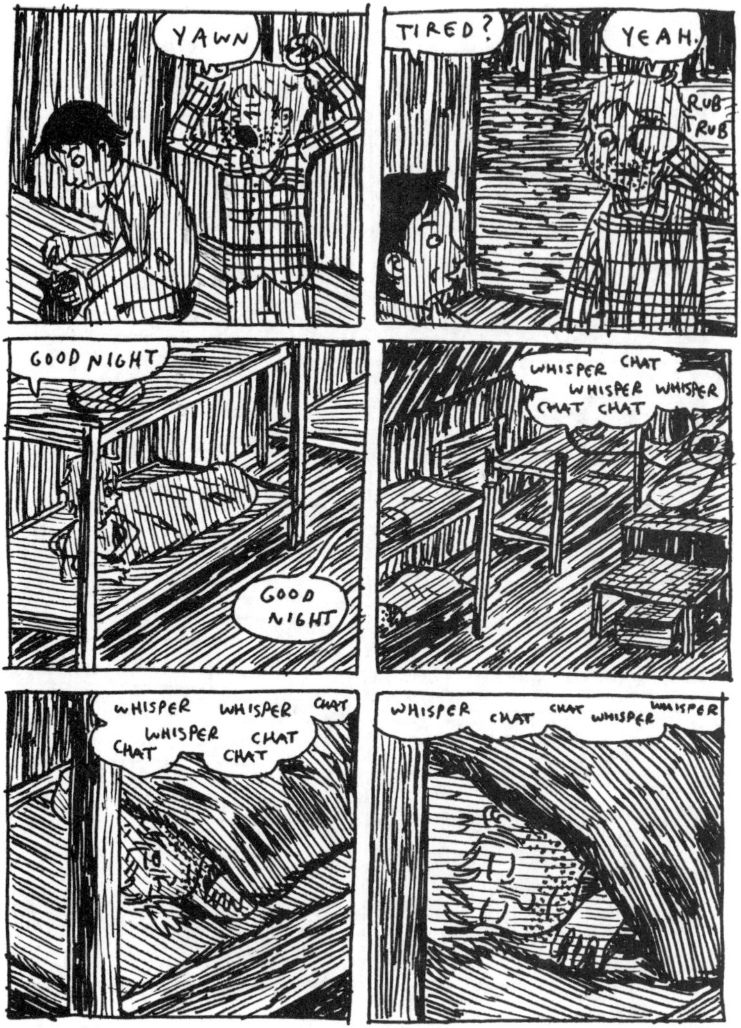
YAWN
TIRED?
YEAH.
RUB RUB
GOOD NIGHT
GOOD NIGHT
WHISPER CHAT WHISPER WHISPER CHAT CHAT
WHISPER WHISPER CHAT WHISPER CHAT CHAT CHAT
WHISPER CHAT CHAT WHISPER WHISPER

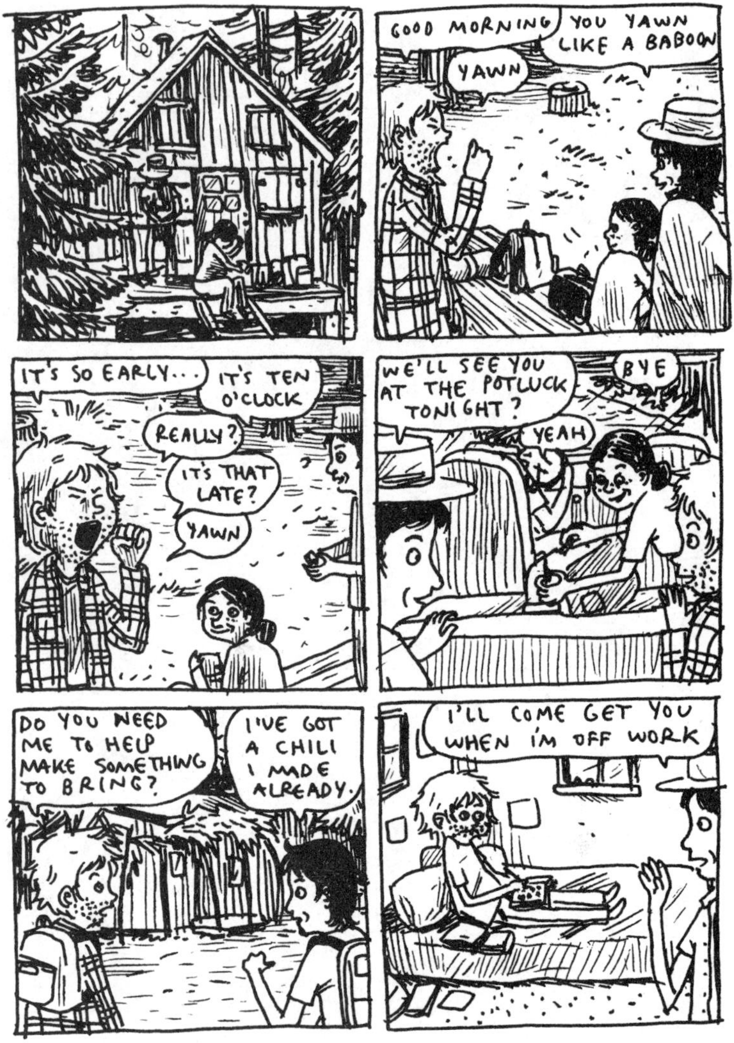

GOOD MORNING
YAWN
YOU YAWN LIKE A BABOON
IT'S SO EARLY...
IT'S TEN O'CLOCK
REALLY?
IT'S THAT LATE?
YAWN
WE'LL SEE YOU AT THE POTLUCK TONIGHT?
YEAH
BYE
DO YOU NEED ME TO HELP MAKE SOMETHING TO BRING?
I'VE GOT A CHILI I MADE ALREADY.
I'LL COME GET YOU WHEN I'M OFF WORK

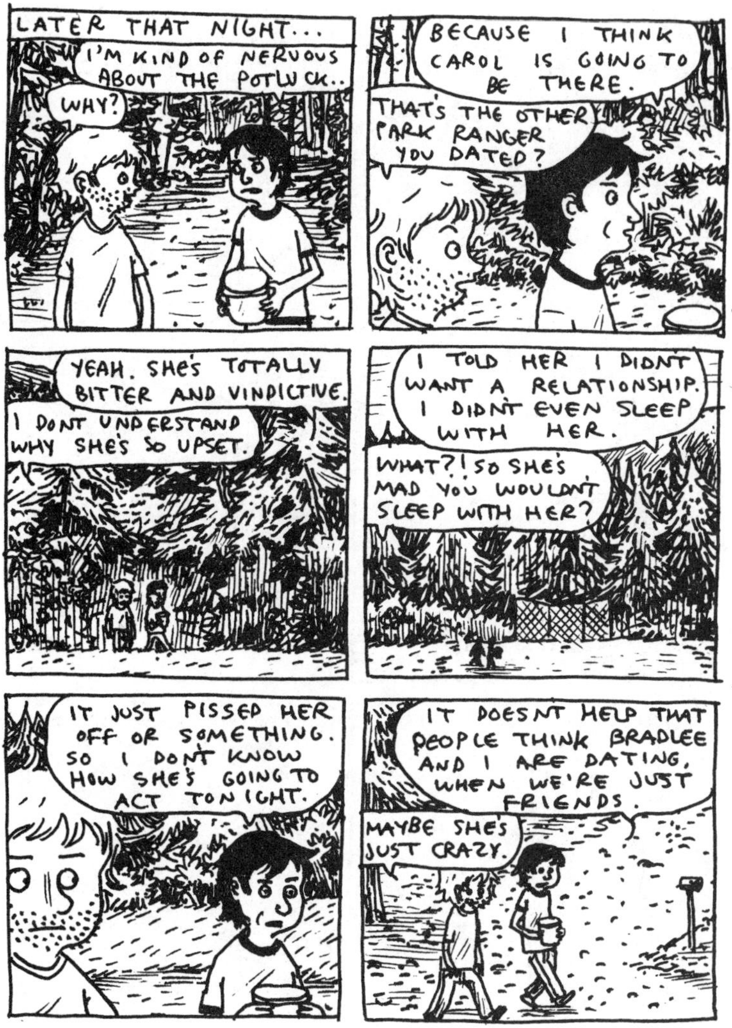
LATER THAT NIGHT...
I'M KIND OF NERVOUS ABOUT THE POTLUCK..
WHY?
BECAUSE I THINK CAROL IS GOING TO BE THERE.
THAT'S THE OTHER PARK RANGER YOU DATED?
YEAH. SHE'S TOTALLY BITTER AND VINDICTIVE.
I DONT UNDERSTAND WHY SHE'S SO UPSET.
I TOLD HER I DIDNT WANT A RELATIONSHIP. I DIDNT EVEN SLEEP WITH HER.
WHAT?! SO SHE'S MAD YOU WOULDNT SLEEP WITH HER?
IT JUST PISSED HER OFF OR SOMETHING. SO I DONT KNOW HOW SHE'S GOING TO ACT TONIGHT.
IT DOESNT HELP THAT PEOPLE THINK BRADLEE AND I ARE DATING, WHEN WE'RE JUST FRIENDS.
MAYBE SHE'S JUST CRAZY.

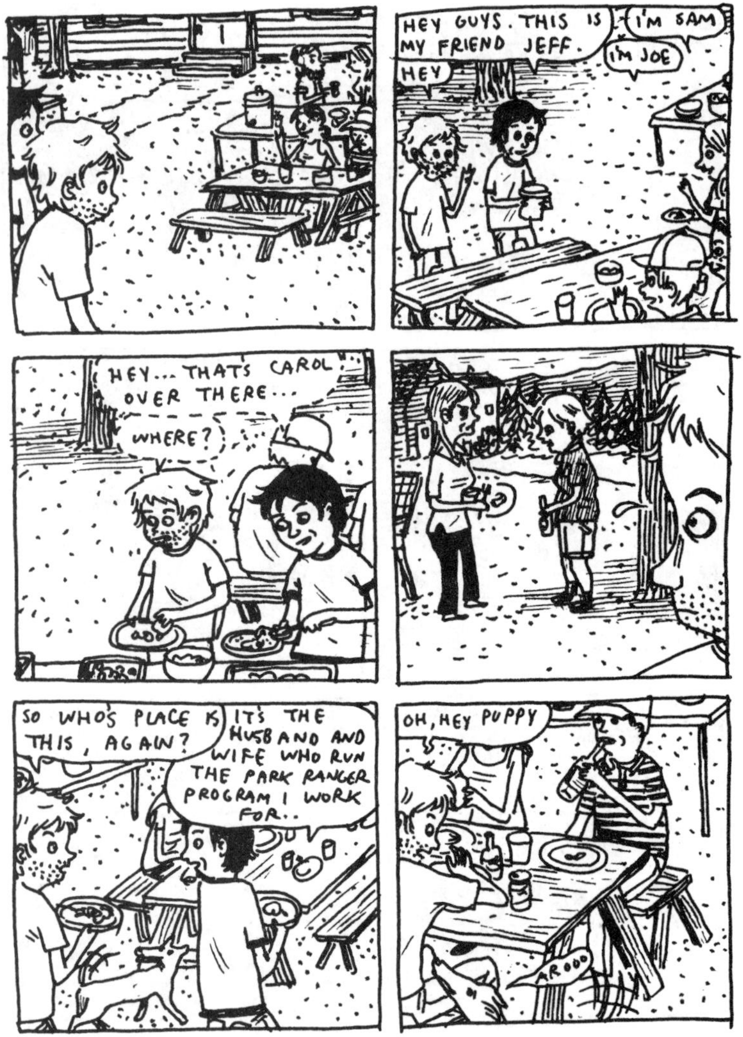
HEY GUYS. THIS IS MY FRIEND JEFF.
I'M SAM
I'M JOE
HEY
HEY... THAT'S CAROL OVER THERE...
WHERE?
SO WHO'S PLACE IS THIS, AGAIN?
IT'S THE HUSBAND AND WIFE WHO RUN THE PARK RANGER PROGRAM I WORK FOR..
OH, HEY PUPPY
AROOO

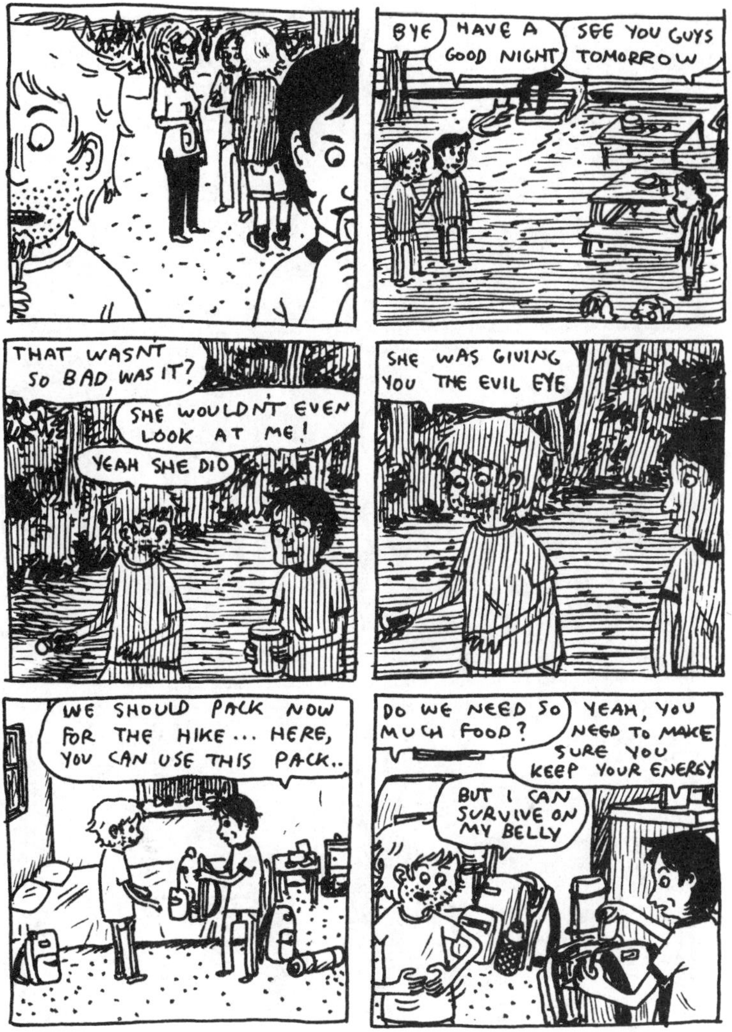
BYE
HAVE A GOOD NIGHT
SEE YOU GUYS TOMORROW
THAT WASNT SO BAD, WAS IT?
SHE WOULDN'T EVEN LOOK AT ME!
YEAH SHE DID
SHE WAS GIVING YOU THE EVIL EYE
WE SHOULD PACK NOW FOR THE HIKE... HERE, YOU CAN USE THIS PACK..
DO WE NEED SO MUCH FOOD?
YEAH, YOU NEED TO MAKE SURE YOU KEEP YOUR ENERGY
BUT I CAN SURVIVE ON MY BELLY

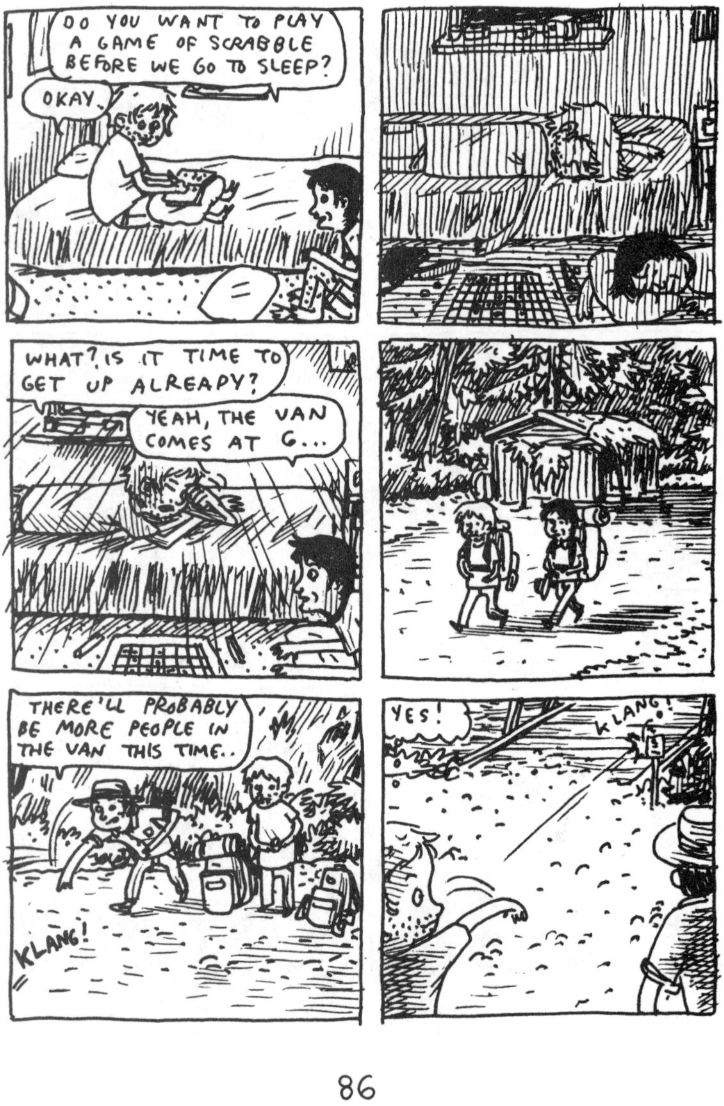
DO YOU WANT TO PLAY A GAME OF SCRABBLE BEFORE WE GO TO SLEEP?
OKAY.
WHAT? IS IT TIME TO GET UP ALREADY?
YEAH, THE VAN COMES AT 6...
THERE'LL PROBABLY BE MORE PEOPLE IN THE VAN THIS TIME..
KLANG!
YES!
KLANG!

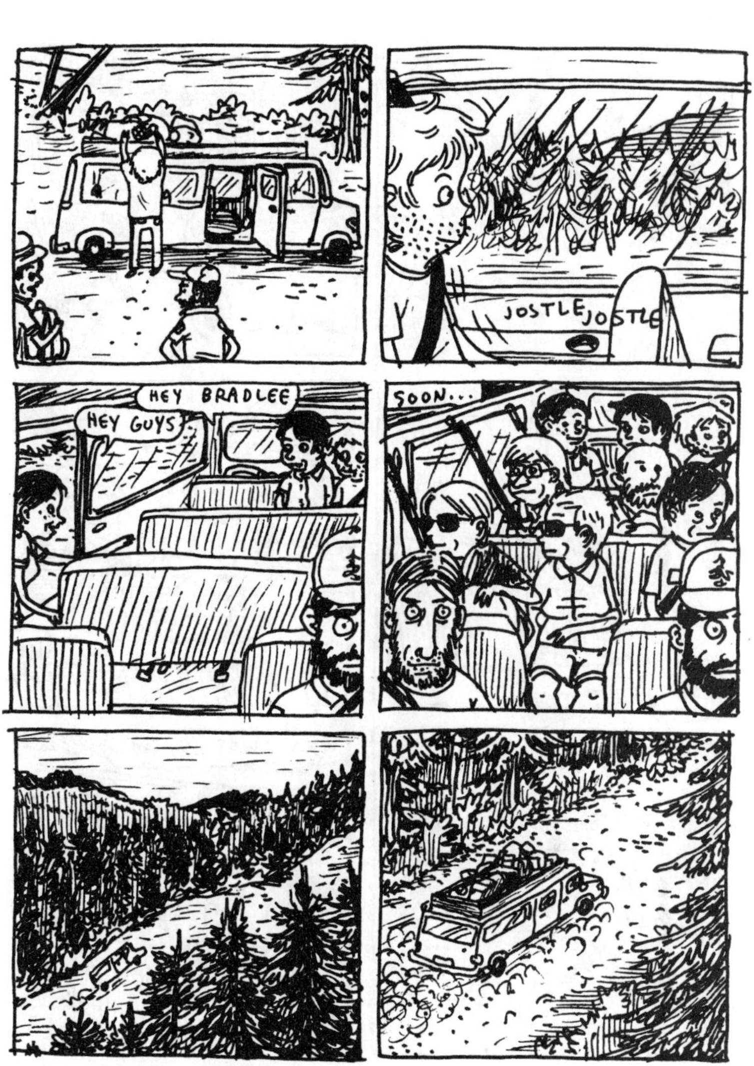
JOSTLE JOSTLE
HEY BRADLEE
HEY GUYS
SOON...

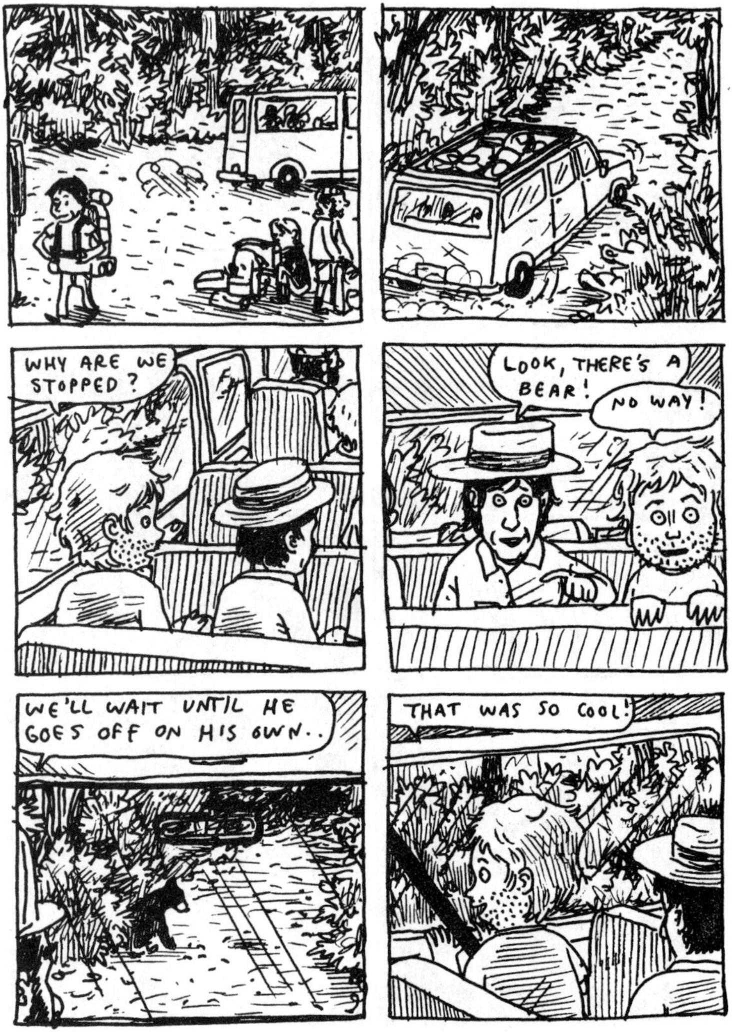
WHY ARE WE STOPPED?
LOOK, THERE'S A BEAR!
NO WAY!
WE'LL WAIT UNTIL HE GOES OFF ON HIS OWN..
THAT WAS SO COOL!

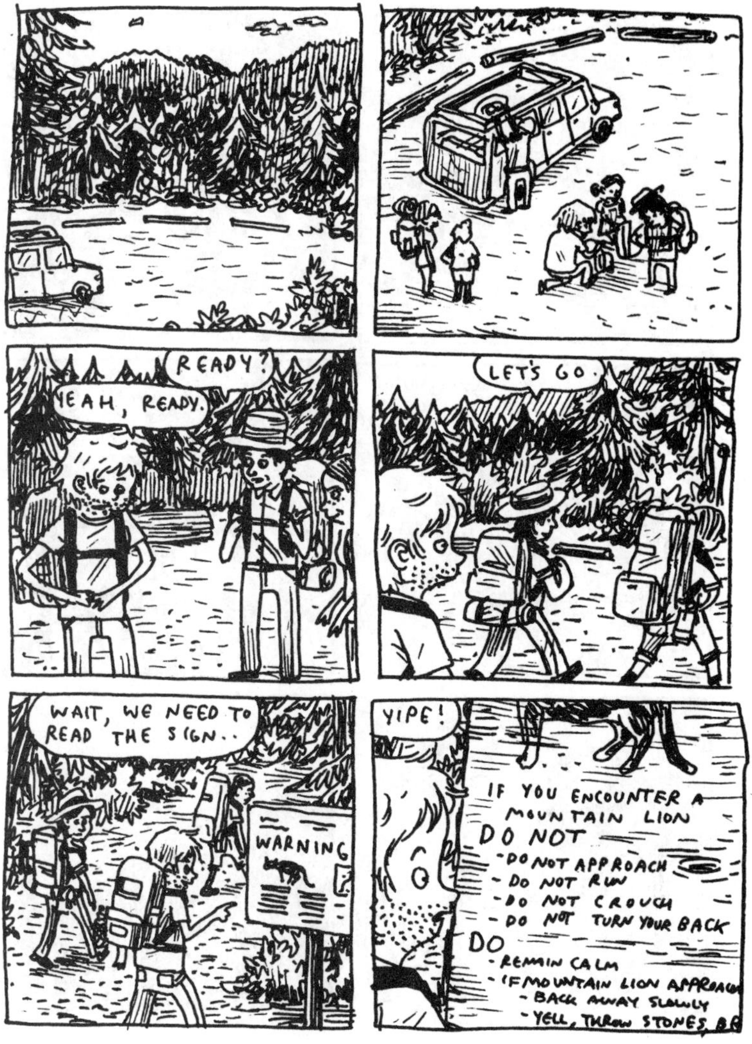
READY?
YEAH, READY.
LET'S GO.
WAIT, WE NEED TO READ THE SIGN..
WARNING
YIPE!
IF YOU ENCOUNTER A MOUNTAIN LION
DO NOT
-DO NOT APPROACH
-DO NOT RUN
-DO NOT CROUCH
-DO NOT TURN YOUR BACK
DO
-REMAIN CALM
-IF MOUNTAIN LION APPROAC
-BACK AWAY SLOWLY
-YELL, THROW STONES,

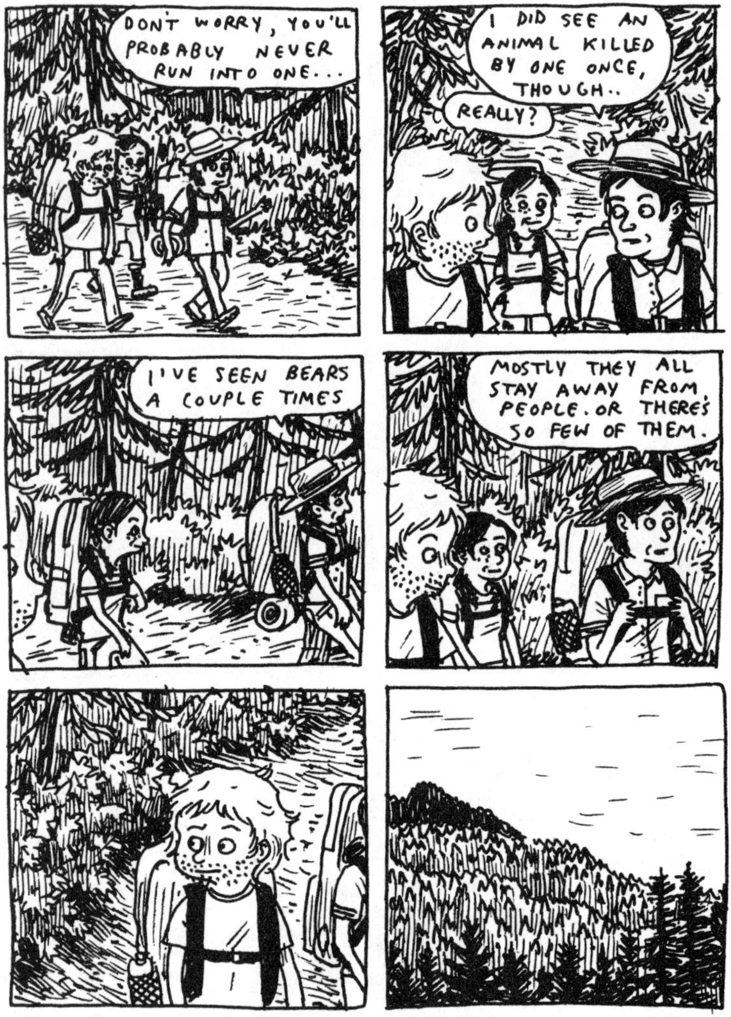
DON'T WORRY, YOU'LL PROBABLY NEVER RUN INTO ONE...
I DID SEE AN ANIMAL KILLED BY ONE ONCE, THOUGH..
REALLY?
I'VE SEEN BEARS A COUPLE TIMES
MOSTLY THEY ALL STAY AWAY FROM PEOPLE. OR THERE'S SO FEW OF THEM.

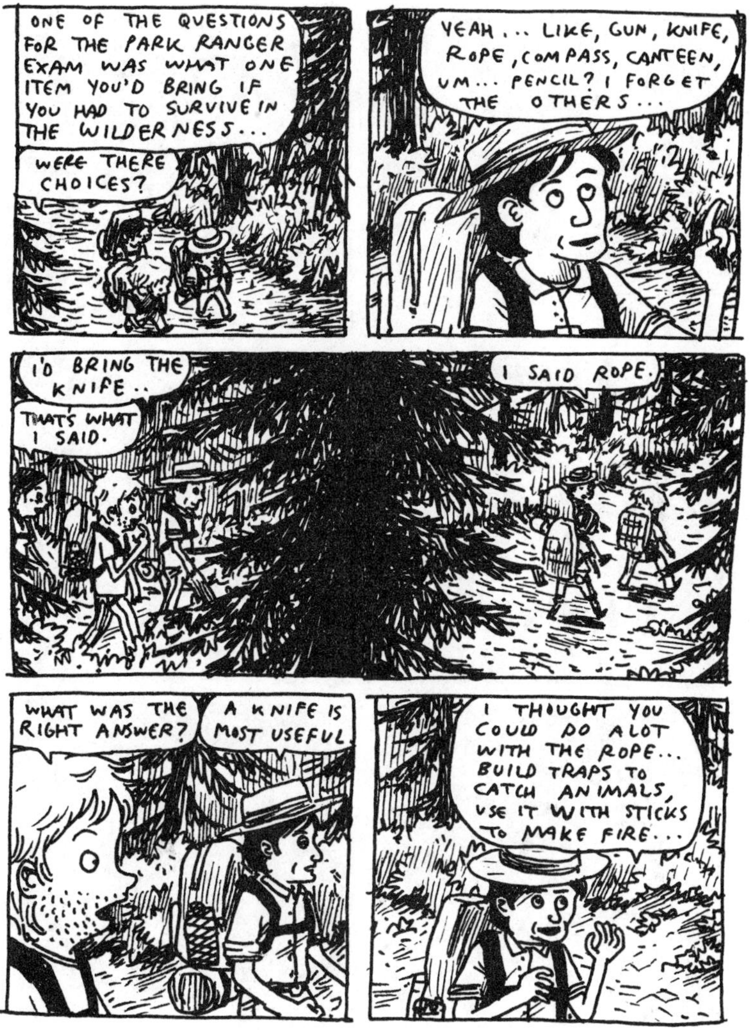
ONE OF THE QUESTIONS FOR THE PARK RANGER EXAM WAS WHAT ONE ITEM YOU'D BRING IF YOU HAD TO SURVIVE IN THE WILDERNESS...
WERE THERE CHOICES?
YEAH... LIKE, GUN, KNIFE, ROPE, COMPASS, CANTEEN, UM... PENCIL? I FORGET THE OTHERS...
I'D BRING THE KNIFE..
THAT'S WHAT I SAID.
I SAID ROPE.
WHAT WAS THE RIGHT ANSWER?
A KNIFE IS MOST USEFUL.
I THOUGHT YOU COULD DO ALOT WITH THE ROPE... BUILD TRAPS TO CATCH ANIMALS, USE IT WITH STICKS TO MAKE FIRE...

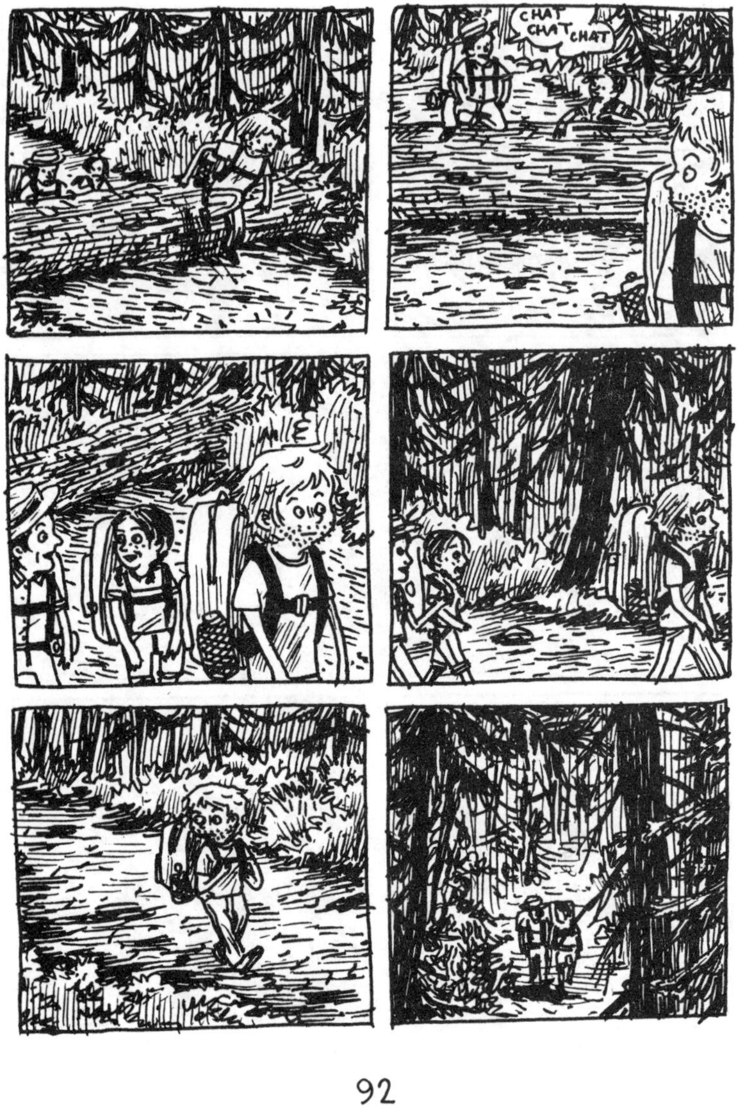
CHAT CHAT CHAT

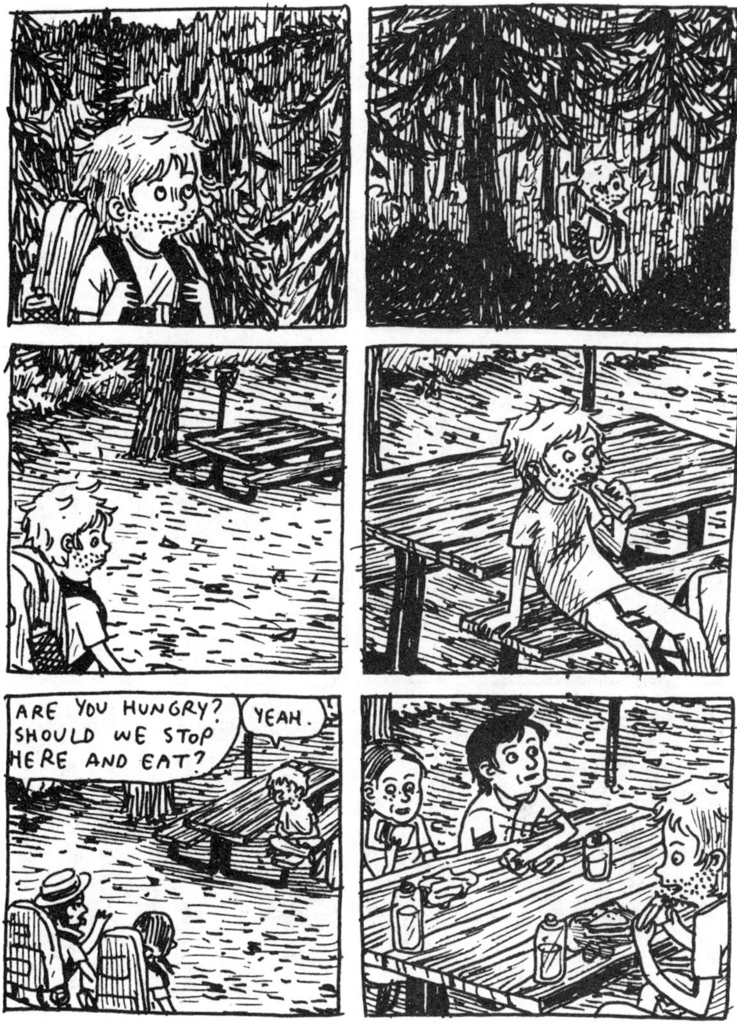
ARE YOU HUNGRY? SHOULD WE STOP HERE AND EAT?
YEAH.

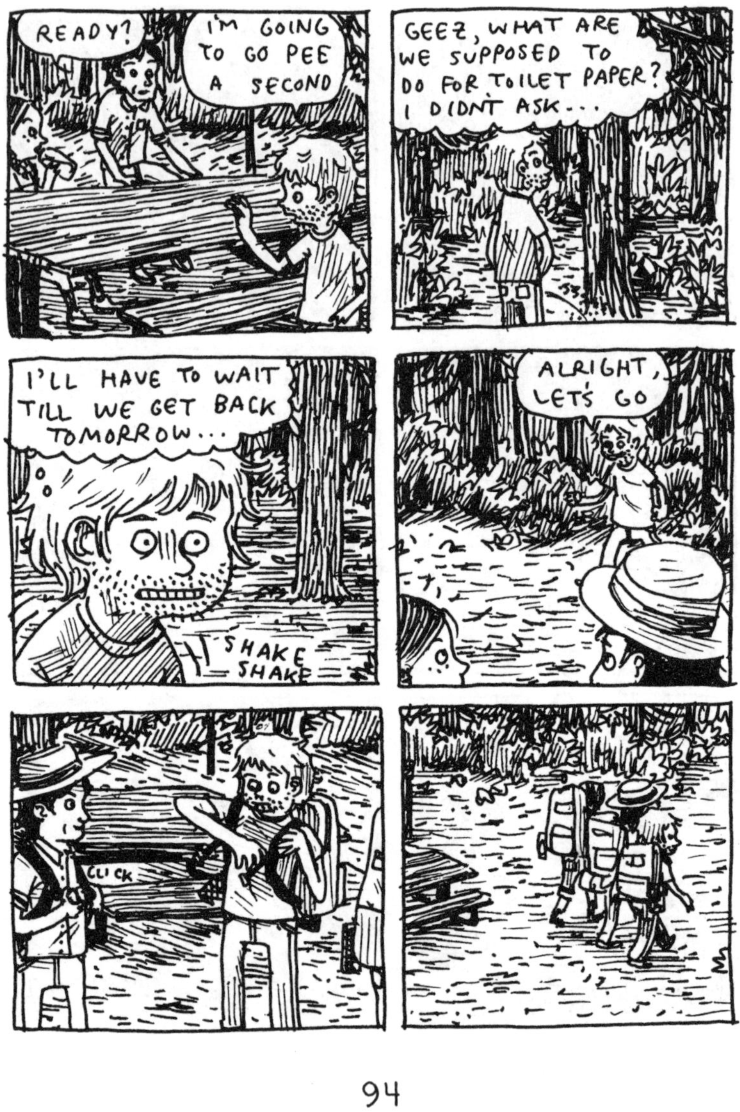
READY?
I'M GOING TO GO PEE A SECOND
GEEZ, WHAT ARE WE SUPPOSED TO DO FOR TOILET PAPER? I DIDN'T ASK...
I'LL HAVE TO WAIT TILL WE GET BACK TOMORROW...
SHAKE SHAKE
ALRIGHT, LET'S GO
CLICK

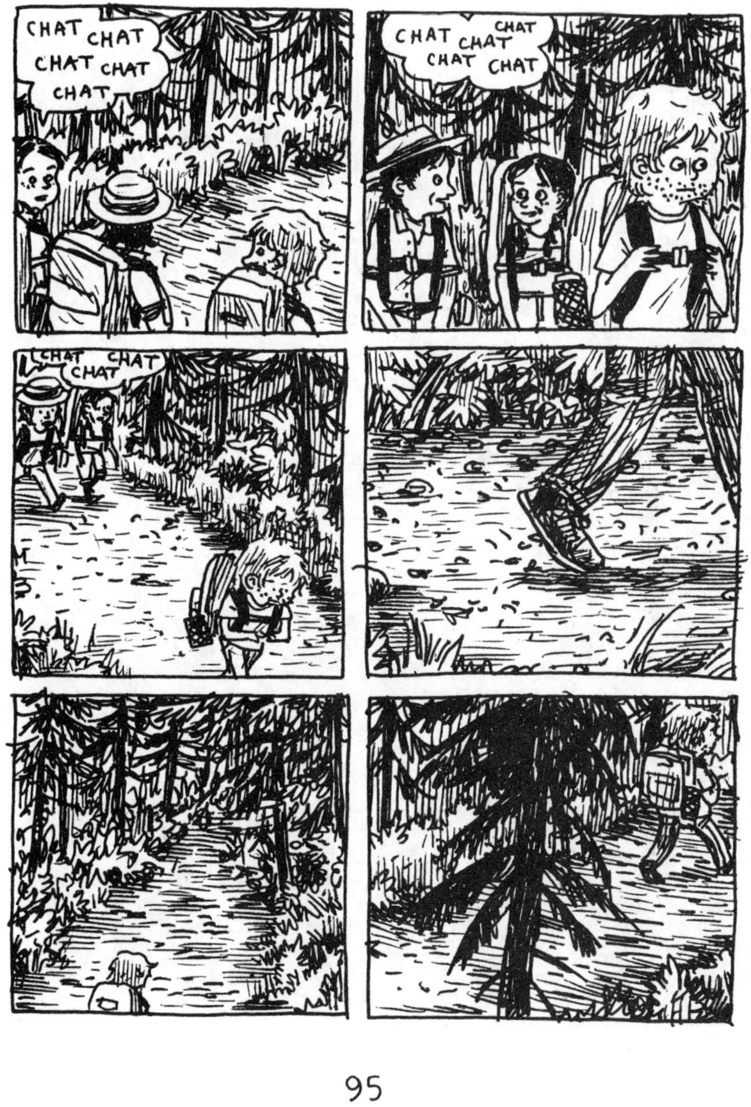
CHAT CHAT CHAT CHAT CHAT
CHAT CHAT CHAT CHAT CHAT
CHAT CHAT CHAT

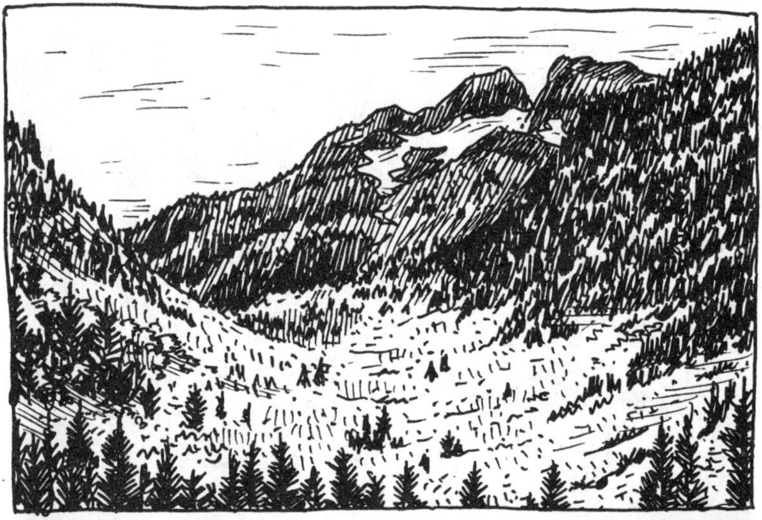

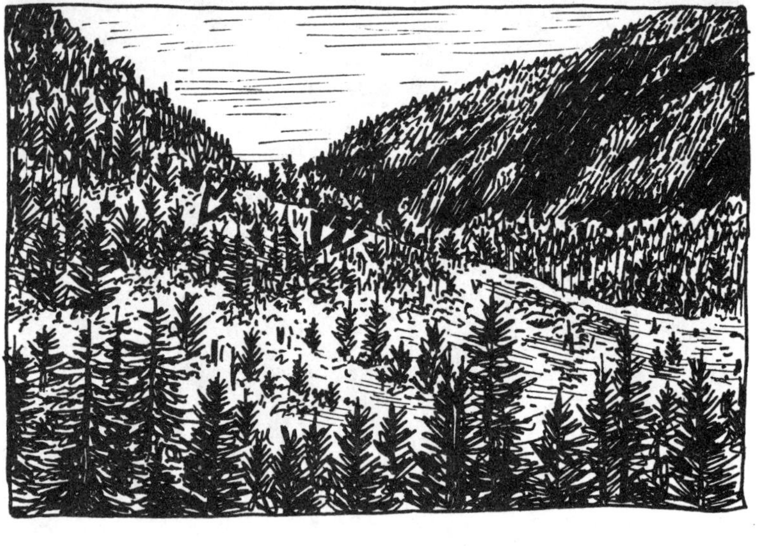

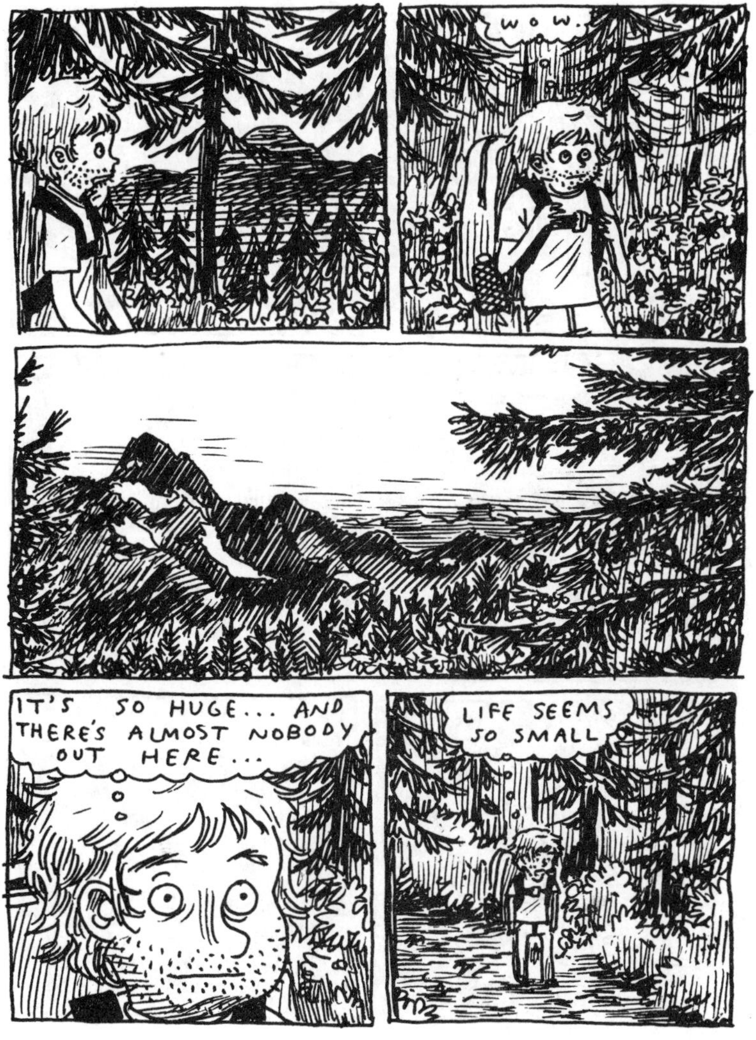
WOW.
IT'S SO HUGE... AND THERE'S ALMOST NOBODY OUT HERE...
LIFE SEEMS SO SMALL

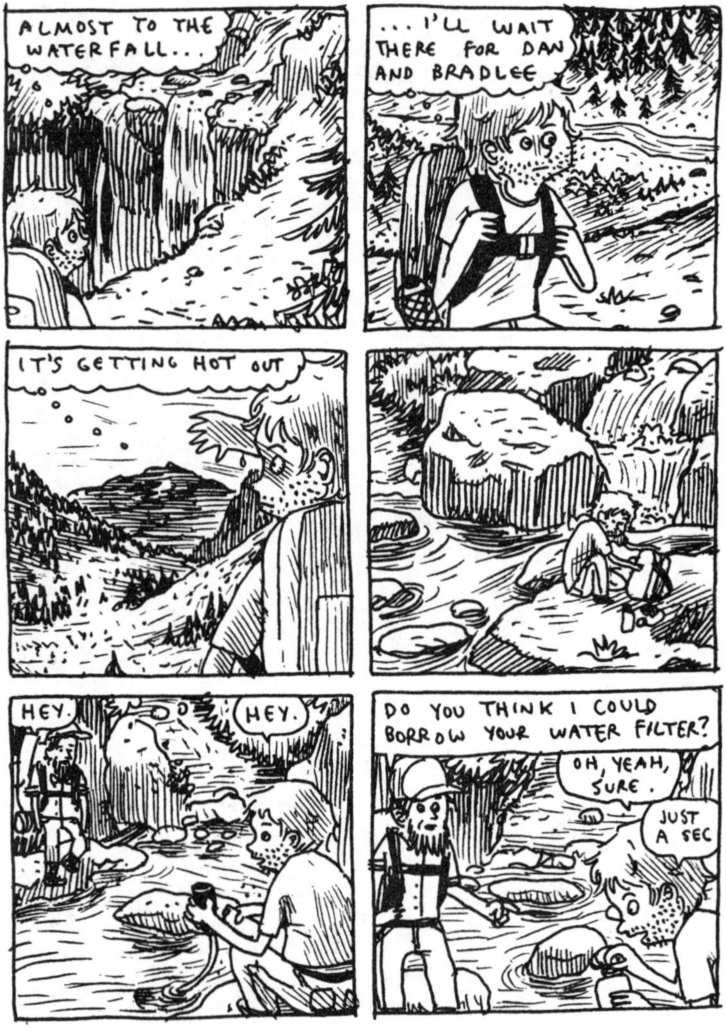
ALMOST TO THE WATERFALL...
...I'LL WAIT THERE FOR DAN AND BRADLEE
IT'S GETTING HOT OUT
HEY.
HEY.
DO YOU THINK I COULD BORROW YOUR WATER FILTER?
OH, YEAH, SURE.
JUST A SEC

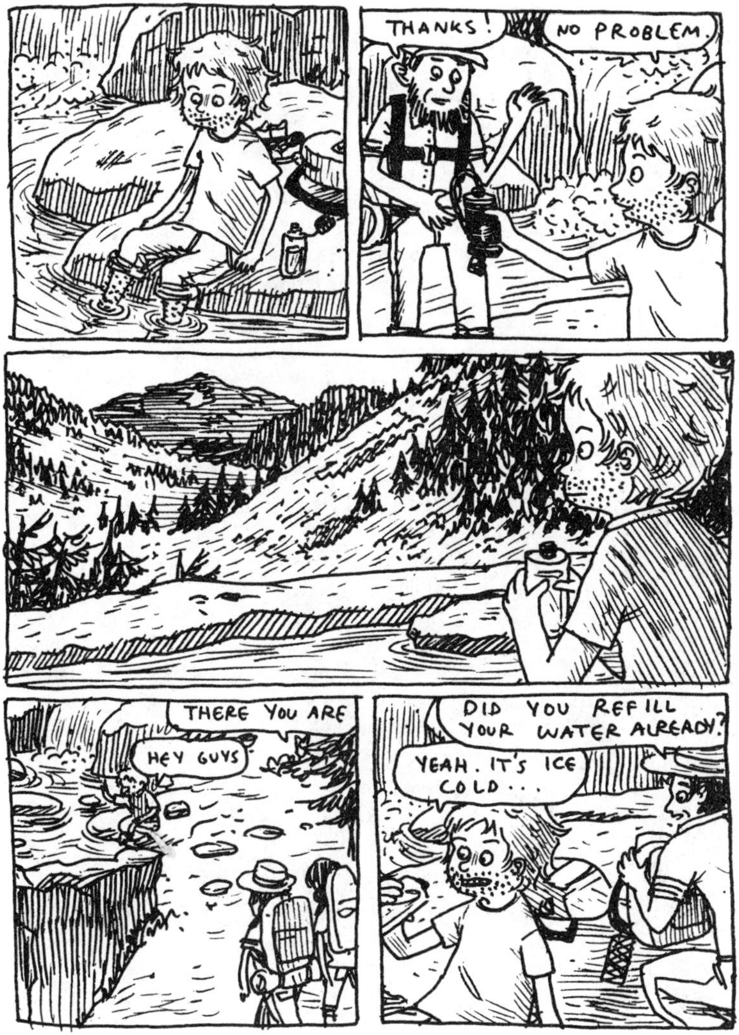
THANKS!
NO PROBLEM.
THERE YOU ARE
HEY GUYS
DID YOU REFILL YOUR WATER ALREADY?
YEAH. IT'S ICE COLD...

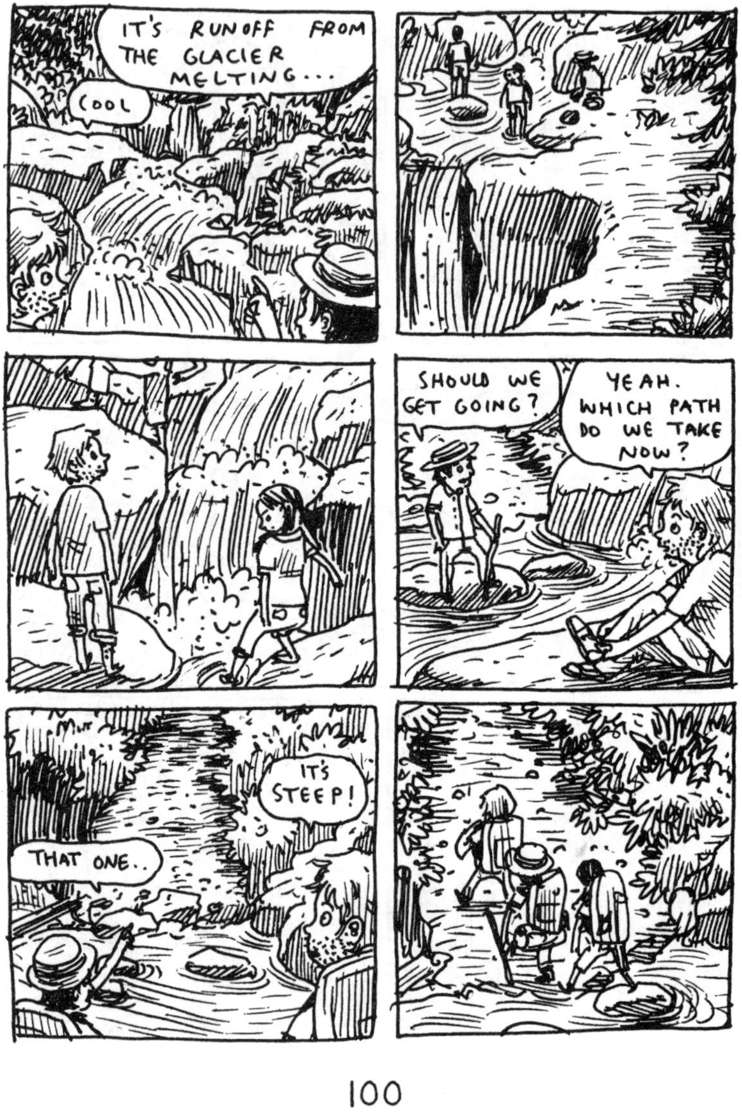
IT'S RUNOFF FROM THE GLACIER MELTING...
COOL
SHOULD WE GET GOING?
YEAH. WHICH PATH DO WE TAKE NOW?
THAT ONE..
IT'S STEEP!

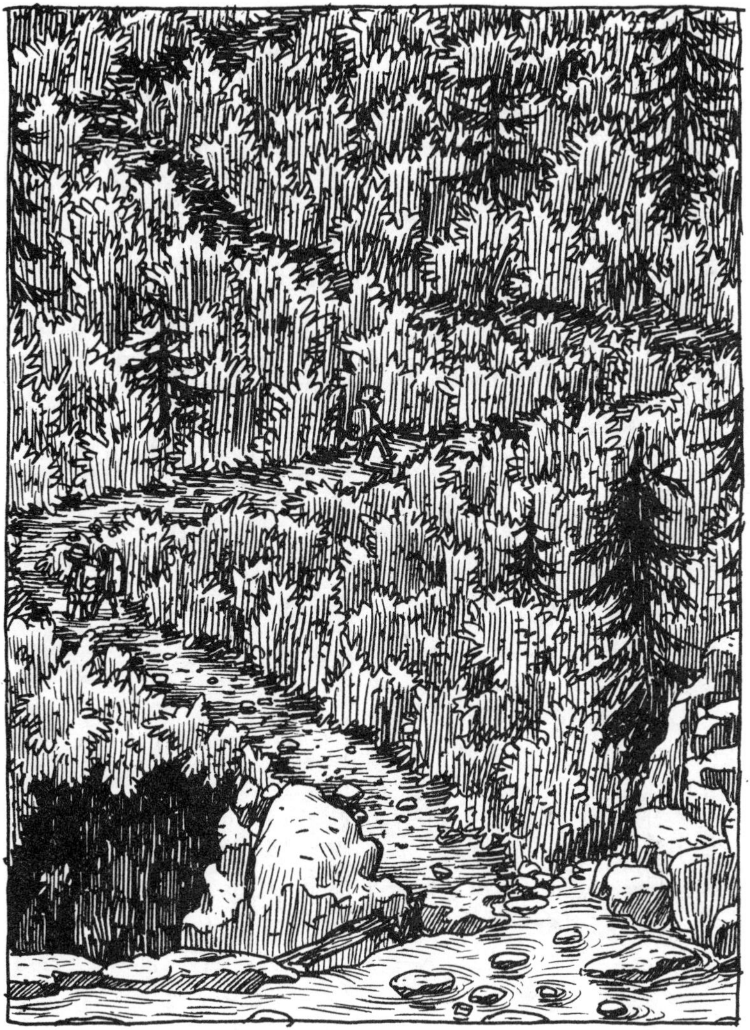

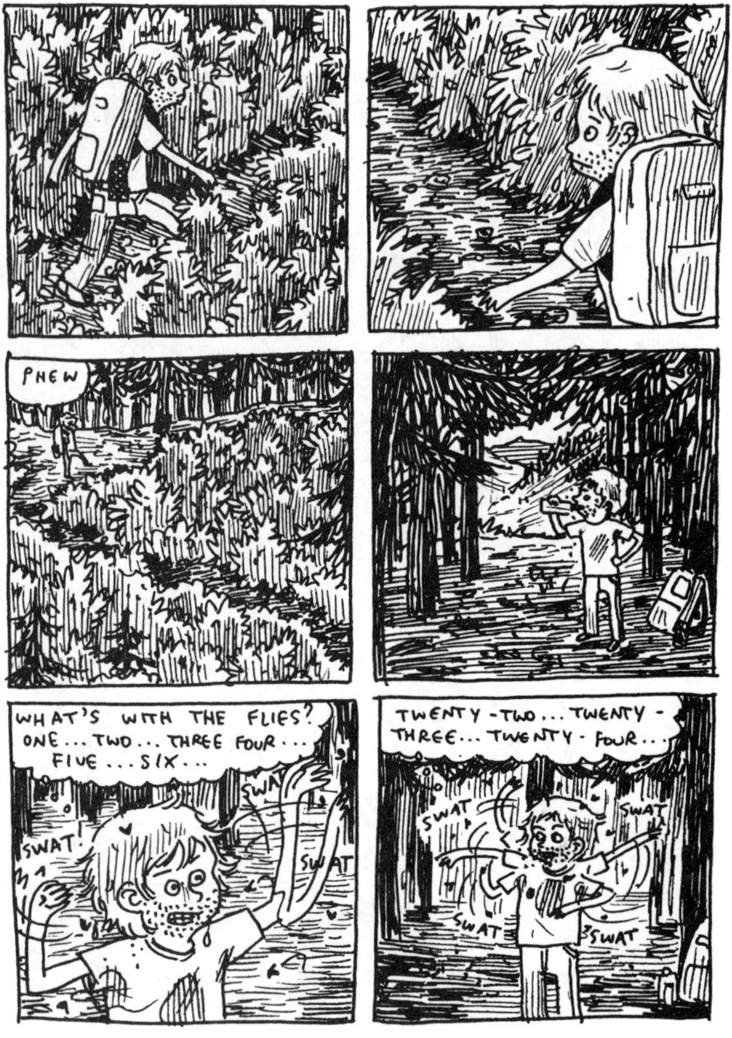
PHEW
WHAT'S WITH THE FLIES? ONE... TWO... THREE FOUR... FIVE... SIX...
SWAT!
SWAT
TWENTY-TWO... TWENTY-THREE... TWENTY-FOUR...
SWAT
SWAT
SWAT
SWAT

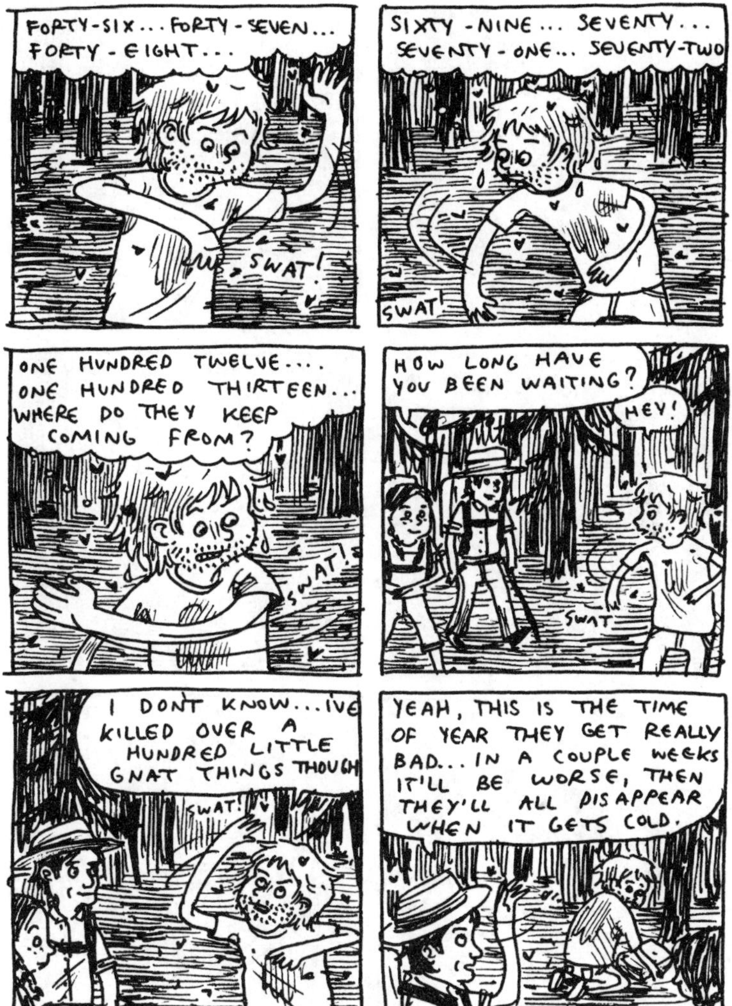

FORTY-SIX... FORTY-SEVEN... FORTY-EIGHT...
SWAT!
SIXTY-NINE... SEVENTY... SEVENTY-ONE... SEVENTY-TWO
SWAT!
ONE HUNDRED TWELVE.... ONE HUNDRED THIRTEEN... WHERE DO THEY KEEP COMING FROM?
SWAT!
HOW LONG HAVE YOU BEEN WAITING?
HEY!
SWAT
I DONT KNOW... IVE KILLED OVER A HUNDRED LITTLE GNAT THINGS THOUGH
SWAT!
YEAH, THIS IS THE TIME OF YEAR THEY GET REALLY BAD... IN A COUPLE WEEKS IT'LL BE WORSE, THEN THEY'LL ALL DISAPPEAR WHEN IT GETS COLD.

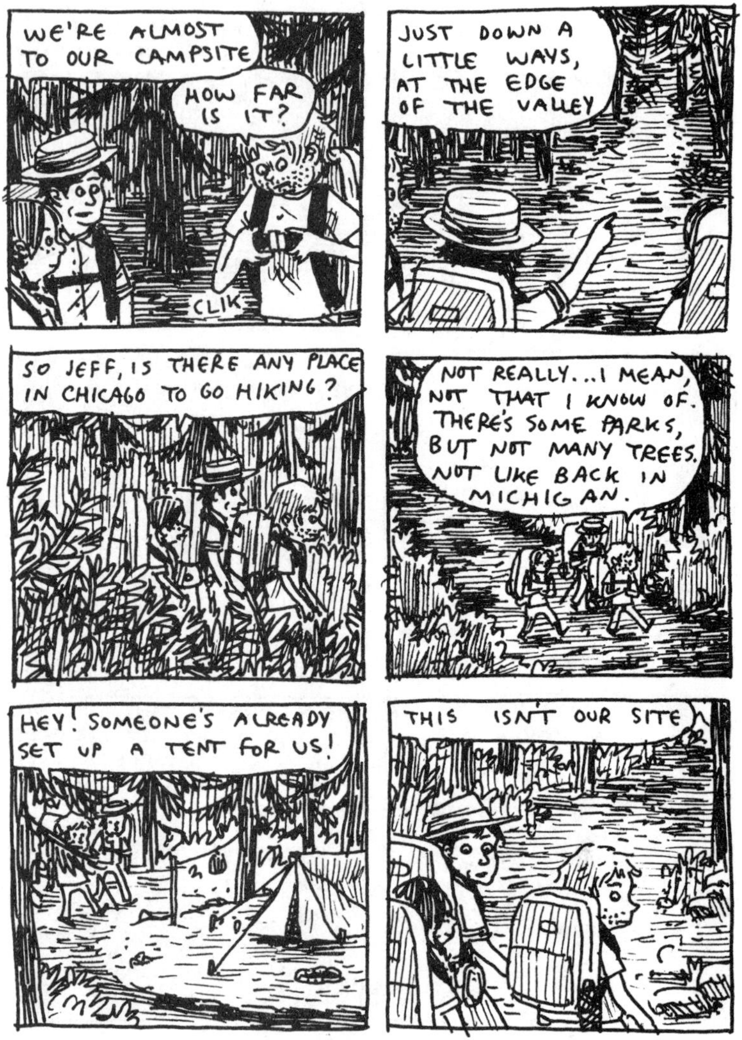
WE'RE ALMOST TO OUR CAMPSITE
HOW FAR IS IT?
CLIK
JUST DOWN A LITTLE WAYS, AT THE EDGE OF THE VALLEY
SO JEFF, IS THERE ANY PLACE IN CHICAGO TO GO HIKING?
NOT REALLY...I MEAN, NOT THAT I KNOW OF. THERE'S SOME PARKS, BUT NOT MANY TREES. NOT LIKE BACK IN MICHIGAN.
HEY! SOMEONE'S ALREADY SET UP A TENT FOR US!
THIS ISN'T OUR SITE

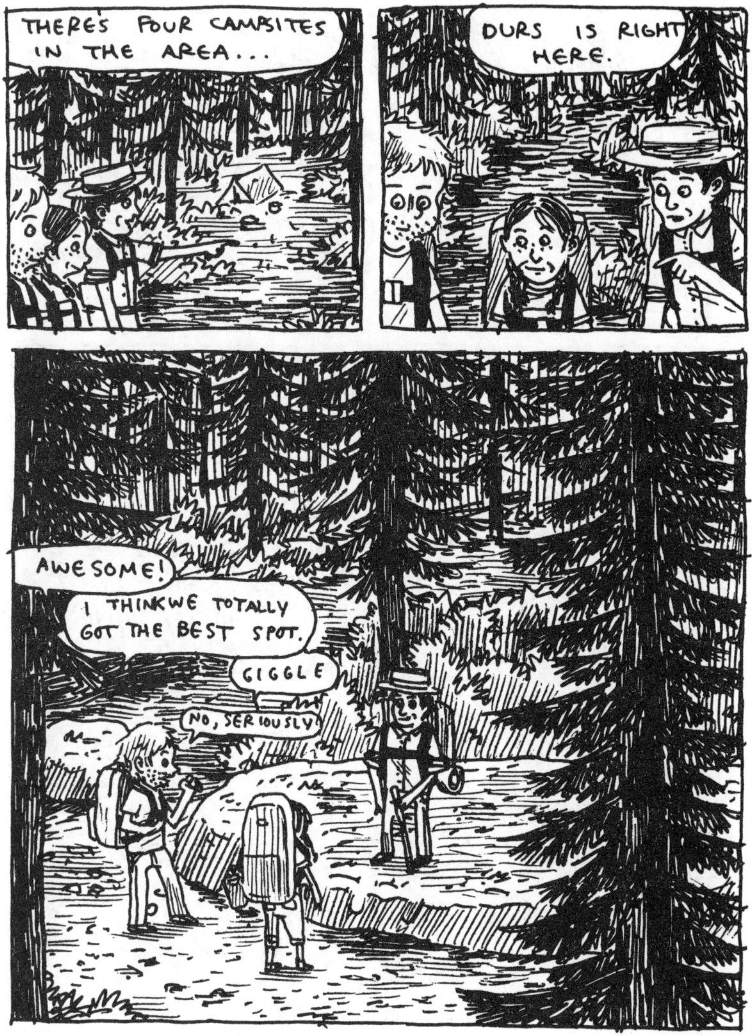
THERE'S FOUR CAMPSITES IN THE AREA...
OURS IS RIGHT HERE.
AWESOME!
I THINKWE TOTALLY GOT THE BEST SPOT.
GIGGLE
NO, SERIOUSLY!

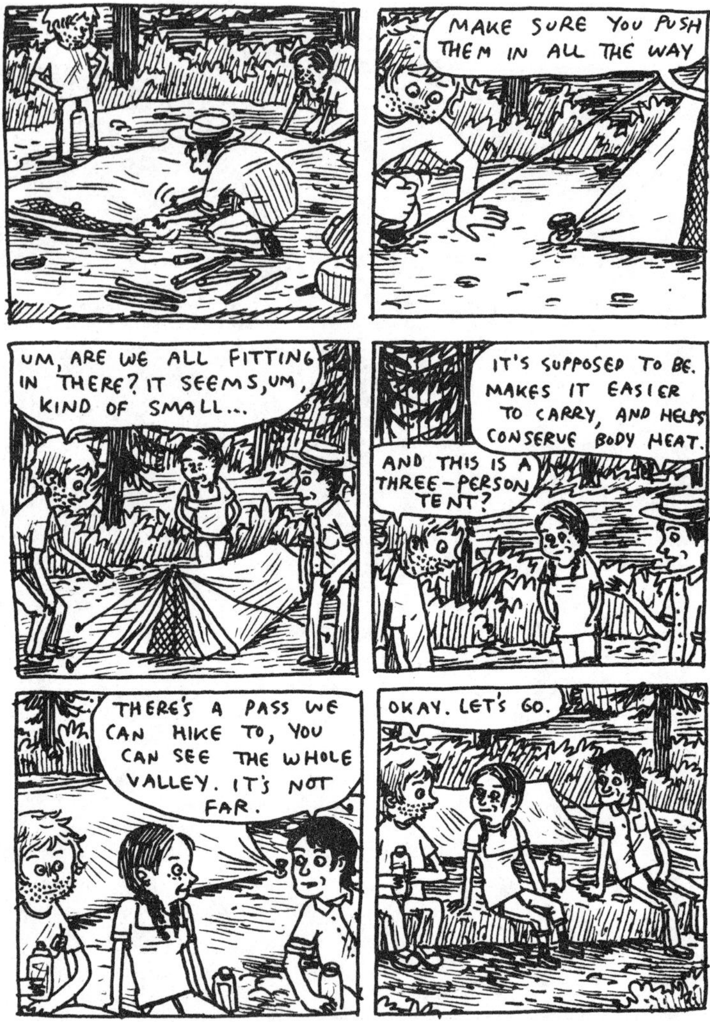
MAKE SURE YOU PUSH THEM IN ALL THE WAY
UM, ARE WE ALL FITTING IN THERE? IT SEEMS, UM, KIND OF SMALL...
IT'S SUPPOSED TO BE. MAKES IT EASIER TO CARRY, AND HELPS CONSERVE BODY HEAT.
AND THIS IS A THREE-PERSON TENT?
THERE'S A PASS WE CAN HIKE TO, YOU CAN SEE THE WHOLE VALLEY. IT'S NOT FAR.
OKAY. LET'S GO.

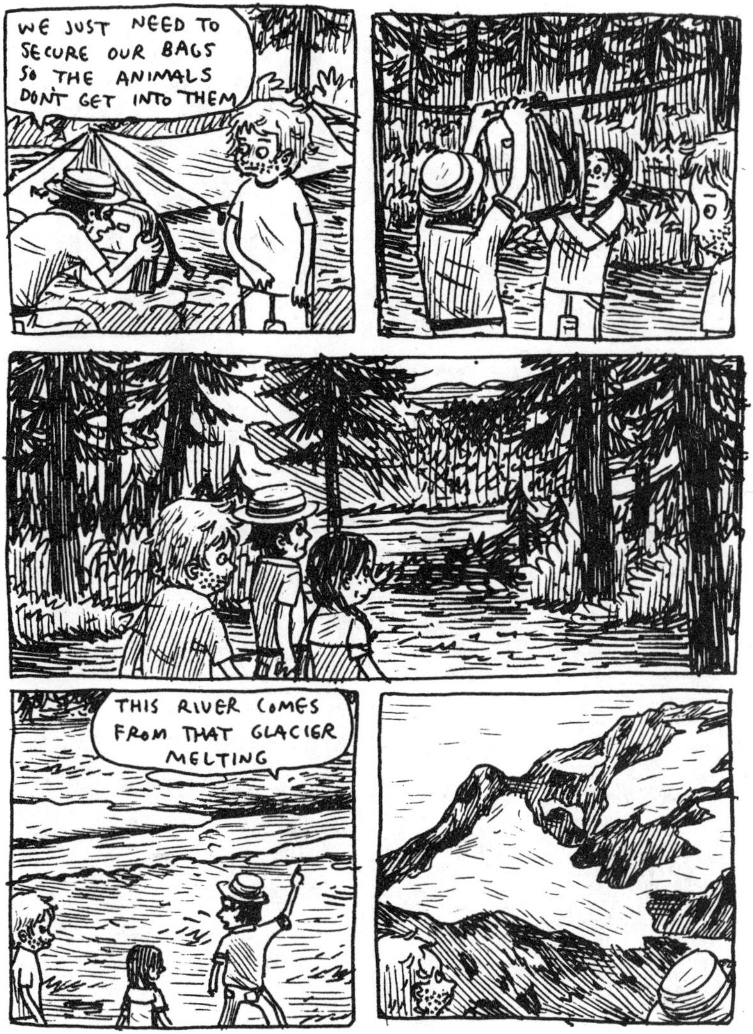
WE JUST NEED TO SECURE OUR BAGS SO THE ANIMALS DON'T GET INTO THEM
THIS RIVER COMES FROM THAT GLACIER MELTING

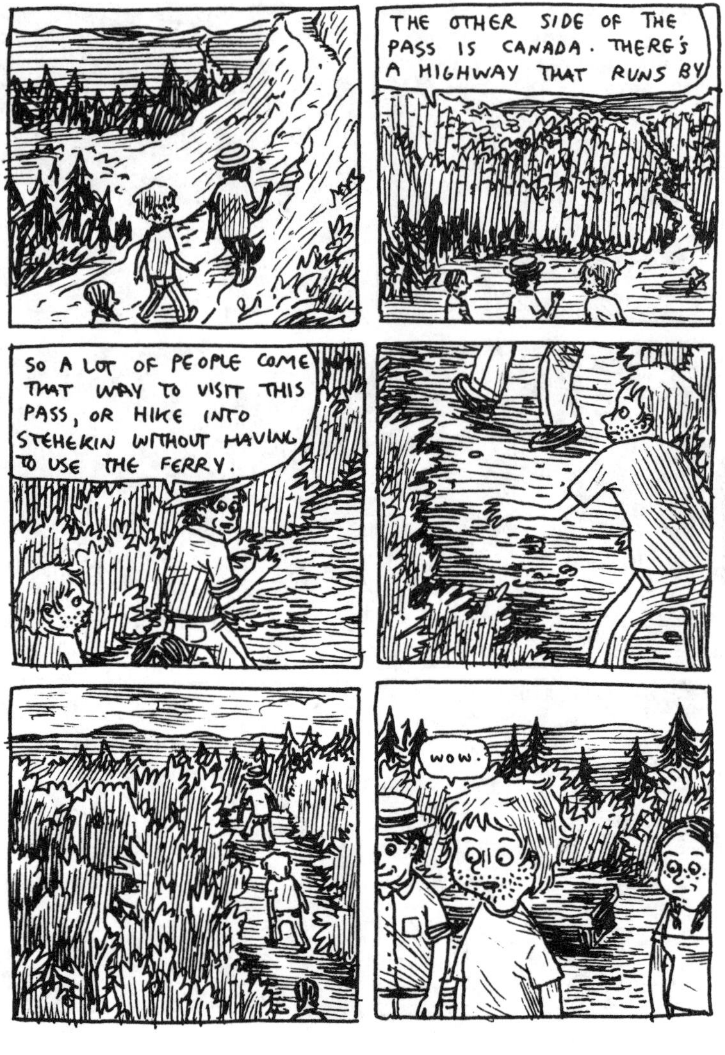
THE OTHER SIDE OF THE PASS IS CANADA. THERE'S A HIGHWAY THAT RUNS BY
SO A LOT OF PEOPLE COME THAT WAY TO VISIT THIS PASS, OR HIKE INTO STEHEKIN WITHOUT HAVING TO USE THE FERRY.
WOW.

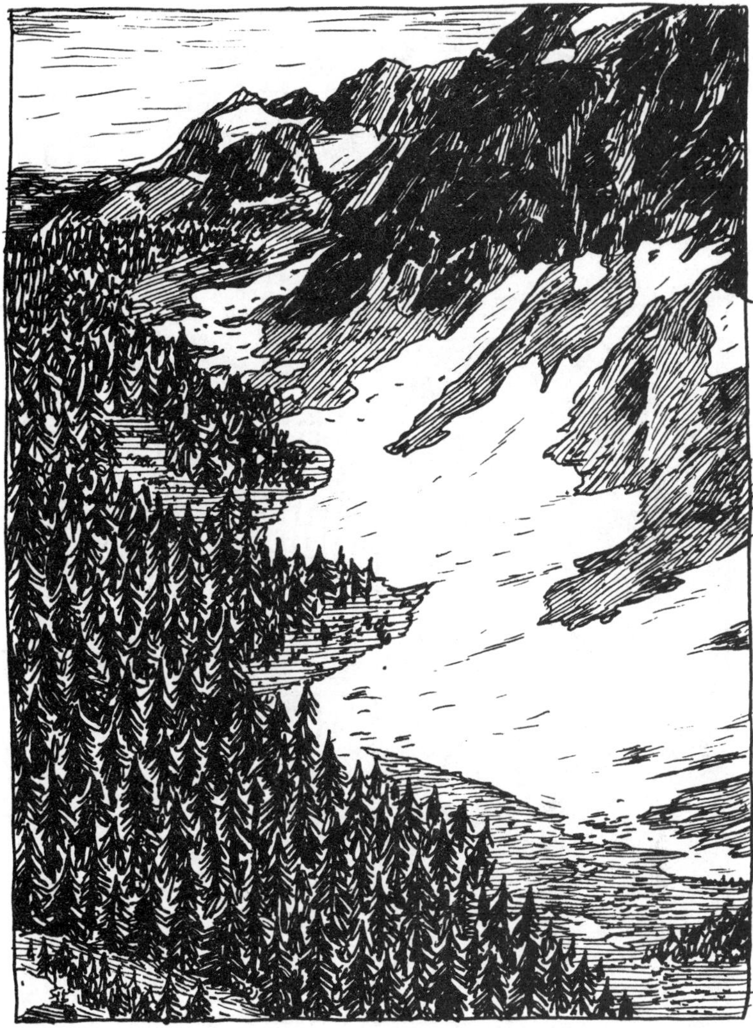

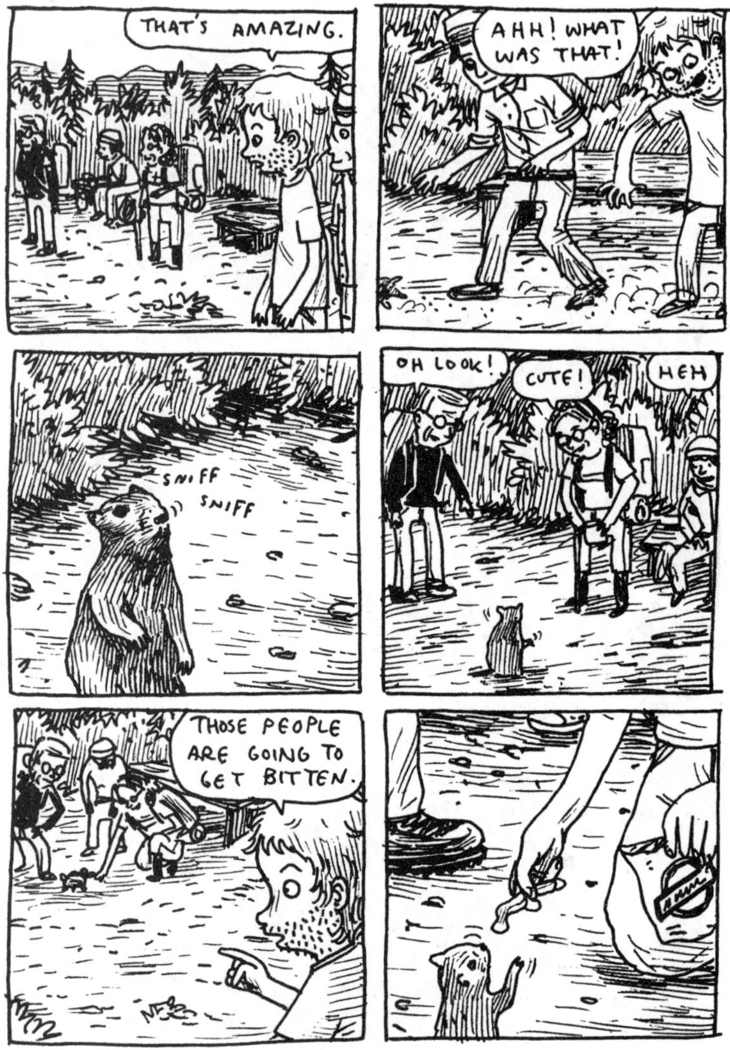
THAT'S AMAZING.
AHH! WHAT WAS THAT!
SNIFF
SNIFF
OH LOOK!
CUTE!
HEH
THOSE PEOPLE ARE GOING TO GET BITTEN.

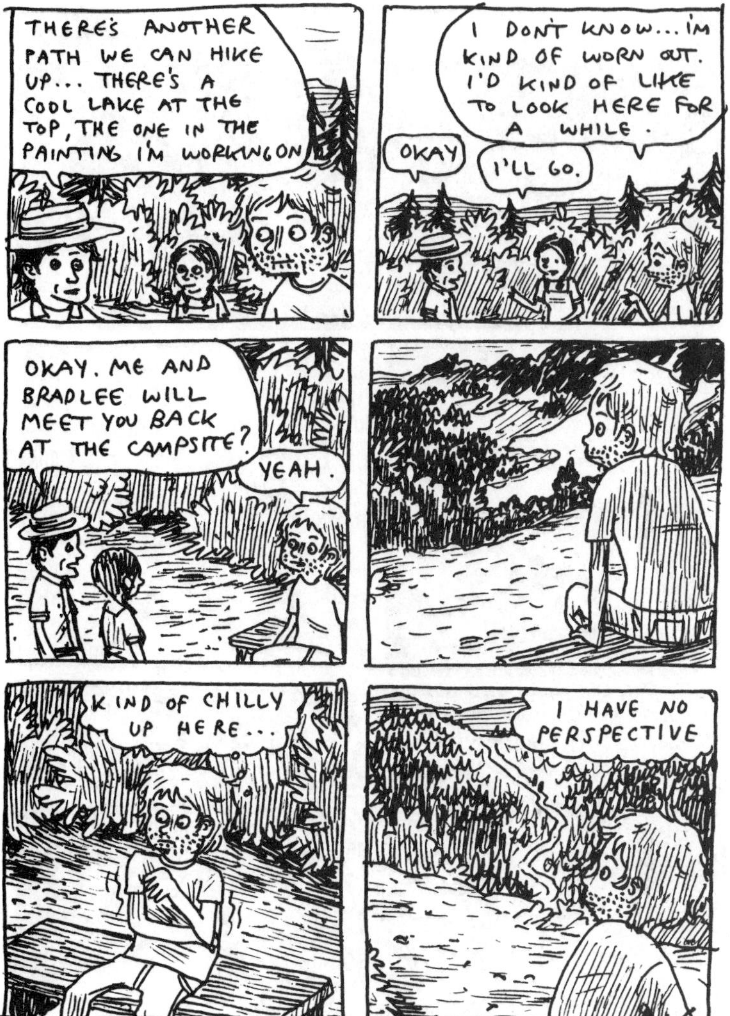
THERE'S ANOTHER PATH WE CAN HIKE UP... THERE'S A COOL LAKE AT THE TOP, THE ONE IN THE PAINTING I'M WORKING ON
I DON'T KNOW... I'M KIND OF WORN OUT. I'D KIND OF LIKE TO LOOK HERE FOR A WHILE.
OKAY
I'LL GO.
OKAY. ME AND BRADLEE WILL MEET YOU BACK AT THE CAMPSITE?
YEAH.
KIND OF CHILLY UP HERE...
I HAVE NO PERSPECTIVE

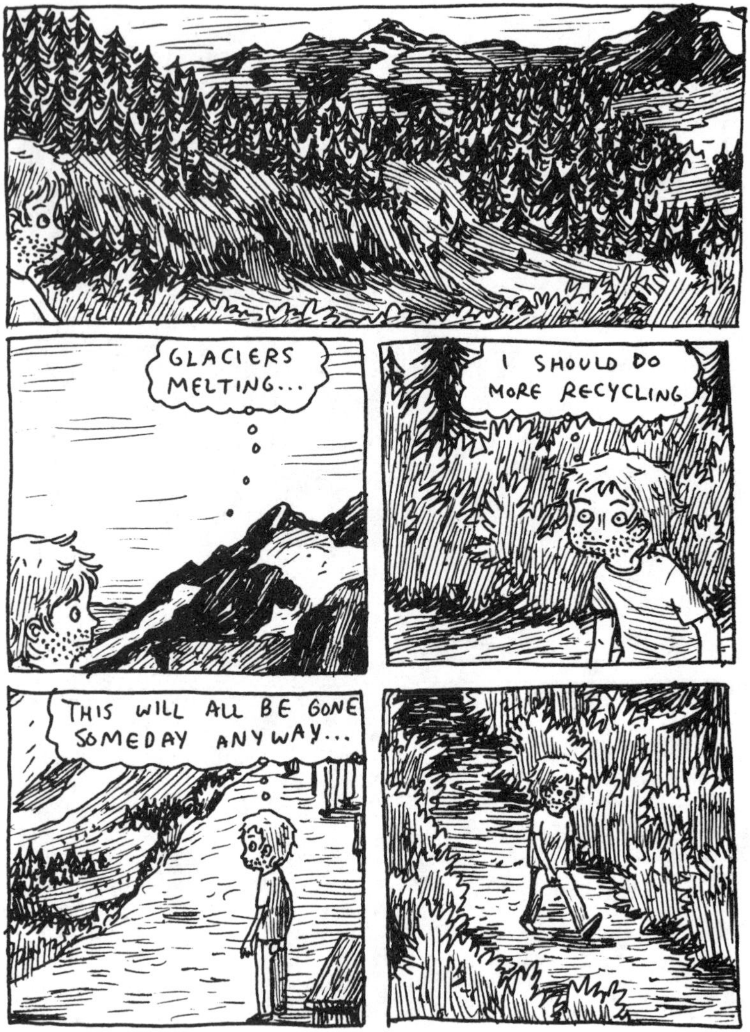
GLACIERS MELTING...
I SHOULD DO MORE RECYCLING
THIS WILL ALL BE GONE SOMEDAY ANYWAY...

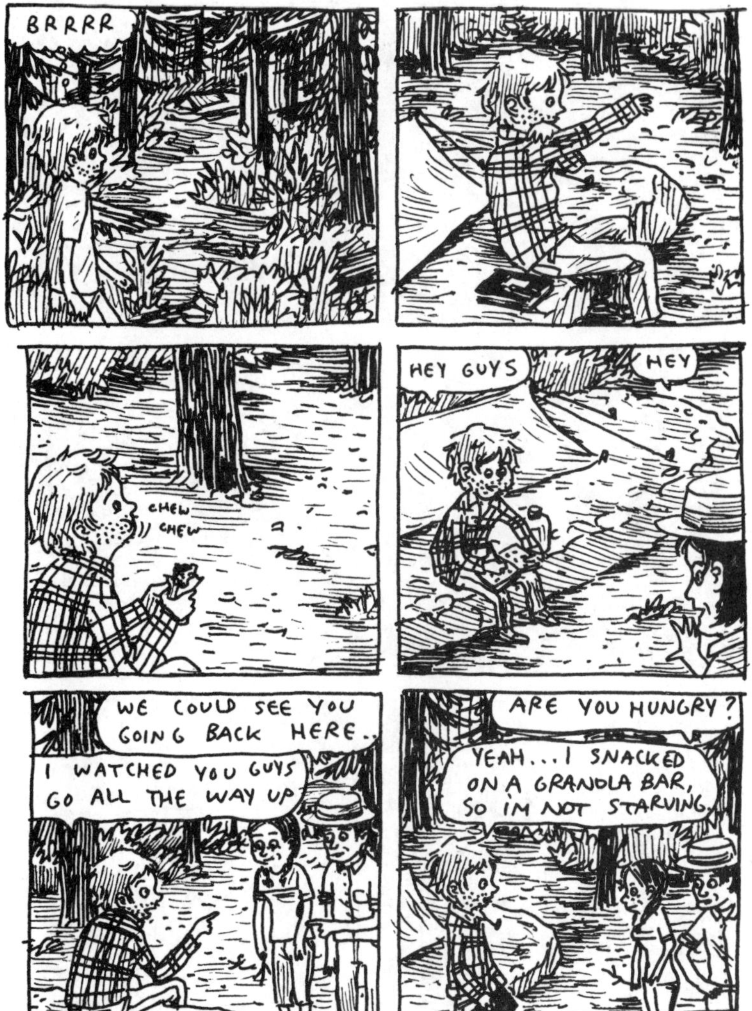
BRRRR
CHEW CHEW
HEY GUYS
HEY
WE COULD SEE YOU GOING BACK HERE..
I WATCHED YOU GUYS GO ALL THE WAY UP
ARE YOU HUNGRY?
YEAH...I SNACKED ON A GRANOLA BAR, SO IM NOT STARVING.

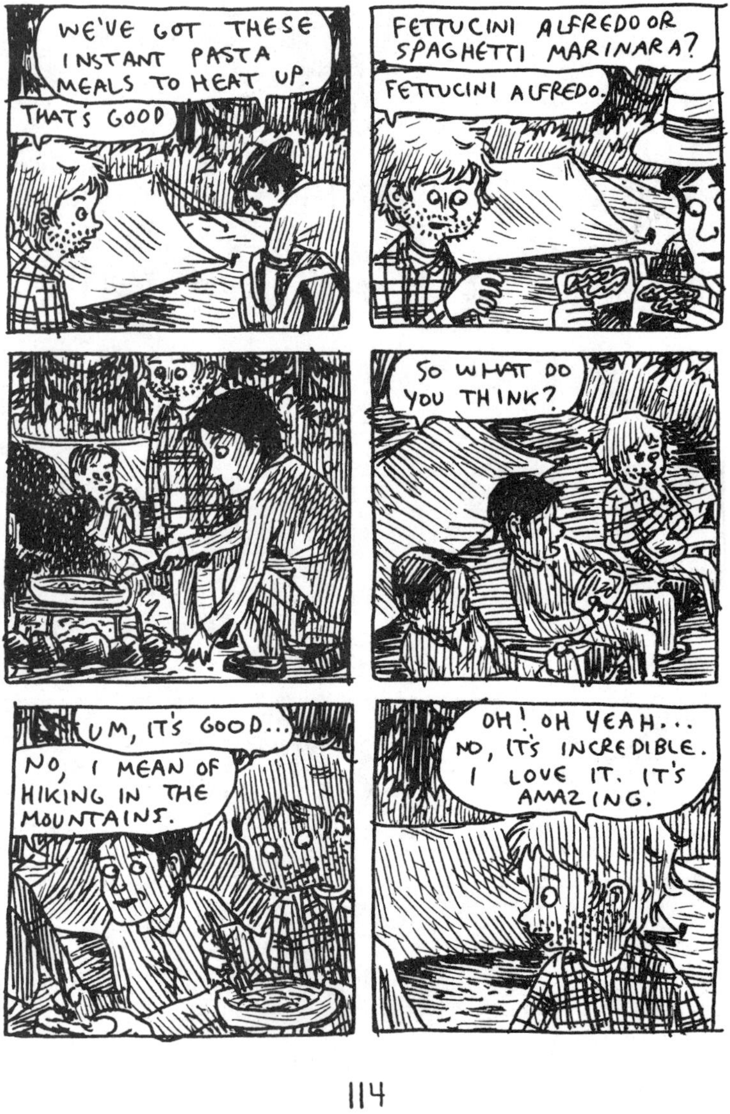
WE'VE GOT THESE INSTANT PASTA MEALS TO HEAT UP.
THAT'S GOOD
FETTUCINI ALFREDO OR SPAGHETTI MARINARA?
FETTUCINI ALFREDO.
SO WHAT DO YOU THINK?
UM, IT'S GOOD...
NO, I MEAN OF HIKING IN THE MOUNTAINS.
OH! OH YEAH... NO, IT'S INCREDIBLE. I LOVE IT. IT'S AMAZING.

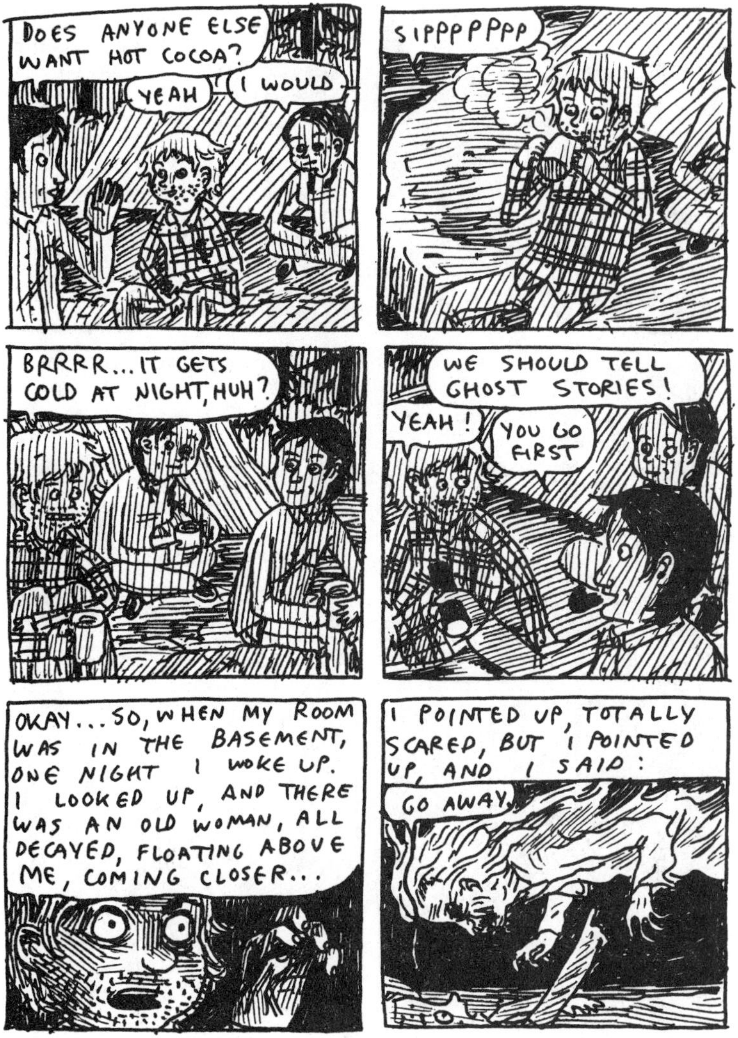
DOES ANYONE ELSE WANT HOT COCOA?
YEAH
I WOULD
SIPPPPPPP
BRRRR... IT GETS COLD AT NIGHT, HUH?
WE SHOULD TELL GHOST STORIES!
YEAH!
YOU GO FIRST
OKAY... SO, WHEN MY ROOM WAS IN THE BASEMENT, ONE NIGHT I WOKE UP. I LOOKED UP, AND THERE WAS AN OLD WOMAN, ALL DECAYED, FLOATING ABOVE ME, COMING CLOSER...
I POINTED UP, TOTALLY SCARED, BUT I POINTED UP, AND I SAID:
GO AWAY.

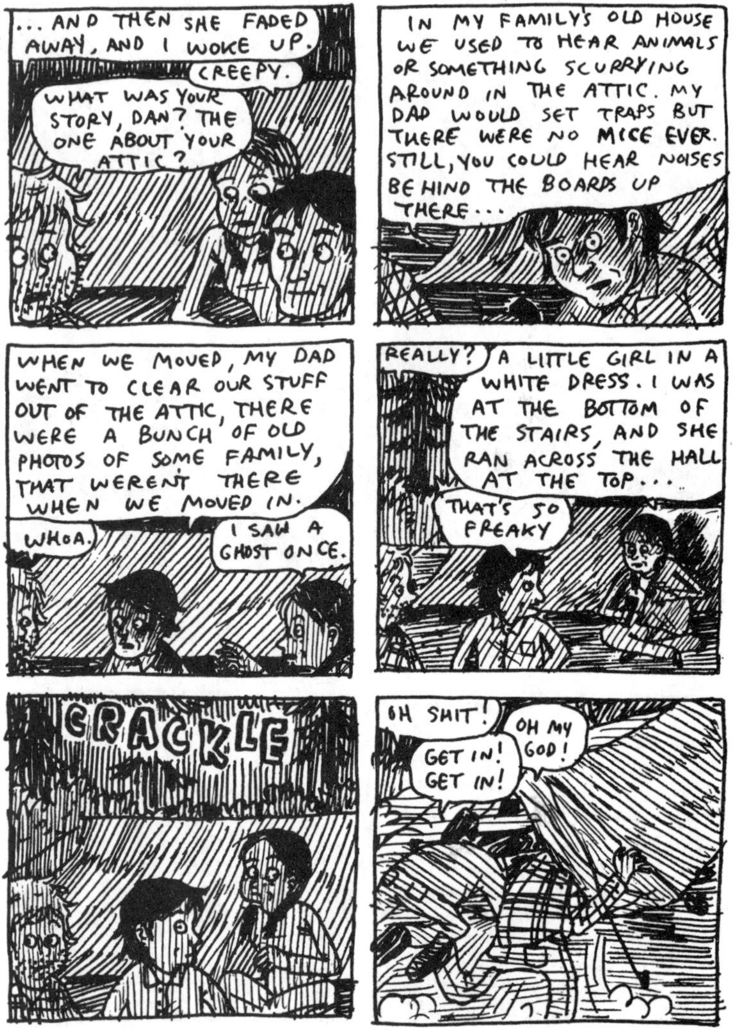

...AND THEN SHE FADED AWAY, AND I WOKE UP.
CREEPY.
WHAT WAS YOUR STORY, DAN? THE ONE ABOUT YOUR ATTIC?
IN MY FAMILY'S OLD HOUSE WE USED TO HEAR ANIMALS OR SOMETHING SCURRYING AROUND IN THE ATTIC. MY DAD WOULD SET TRAPS BUT THERE WERE NO MICE EVER. STILL, YOU COULD HEAR NOISES BEHIND THE BOARDS UP THERE...
WHEN WE MOVED, MY DAD WENT TO CLEAR OUR STUFF OUT OF THE ATTIC, THERE WERE A BUNCH OF OLD PHOTOS OF SOME FAMILY, THAT WERENT THERE WHEN WE MOVED IN.
WHOA.
I SAW A GHOST ONCE.
REALLY?
A LITTLE GIRL IN A WHITE DRESS. I WAS AT THE BOTTOM OF THE STAIRS, AND SHE RAN ACROSS THE HALL AT THE TOP...
THAT'S SO FREAKY
CRACKLE
OH SHIT!
OH MY GOD!
GET IN! GET IN!

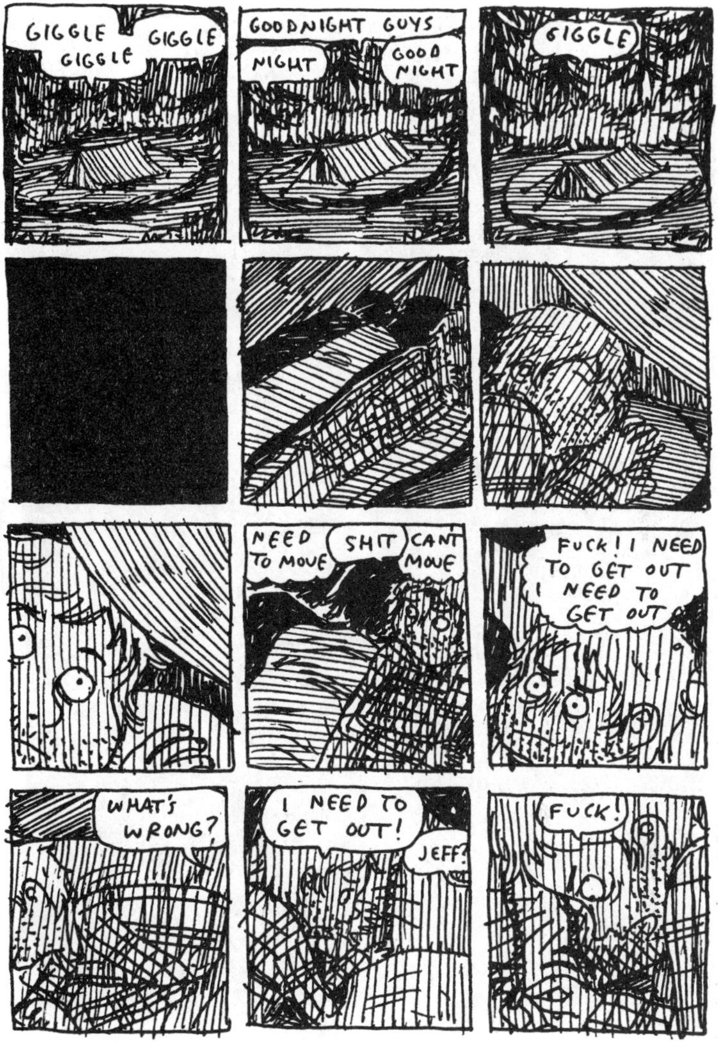
GIGGLE
GIGGLE
GIGGLE
GOODNIGHT GUYS
NIGHT
GOOD NIGHT
GIGGLE
NEED TO MOVE
SHIT
CANT MOVE
FUCK! I NEED TO GET OUT NEED TO GET OUT
WHAT'S WRONG?
I NEED TO GET OUT!
JEFF?
FUCK!

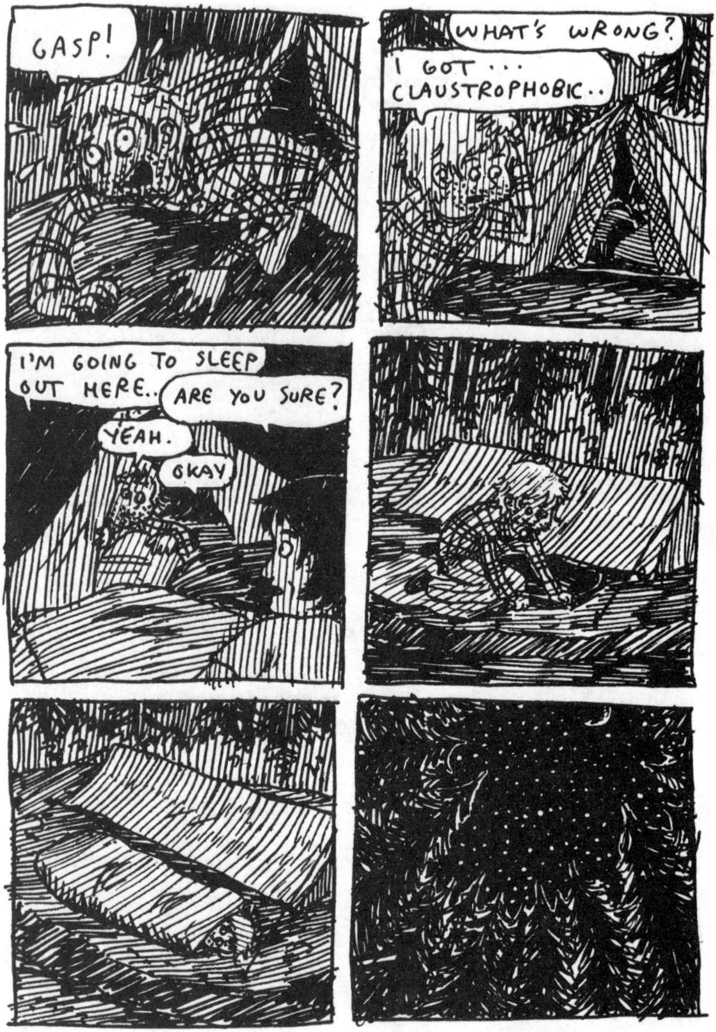
GASP!
WHAT'S WRONG?
I GOT ... CLAUSTROPHOBIC..
I'M GOING TO SLEEP OUT HERE..
ARE YOU SURE?
YEAH.
OKAY

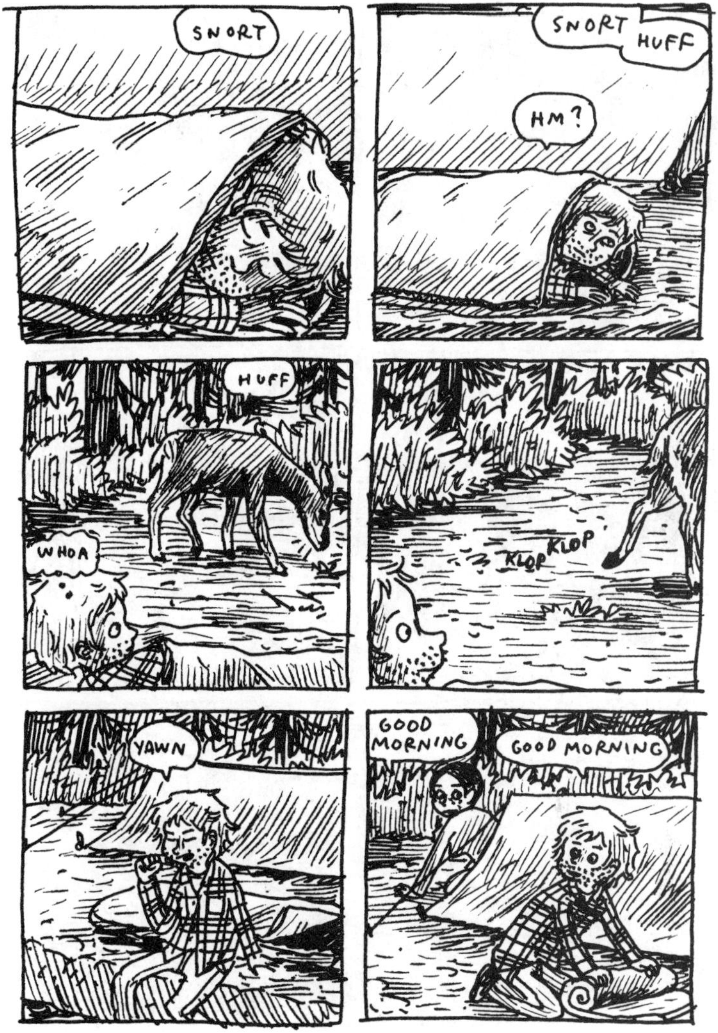
SNORT
SNORT
HUFF
HM?
HUFF
WHOA
KLOP
KLOP
YAWN
GOOD MORNING
GOOD MORNING

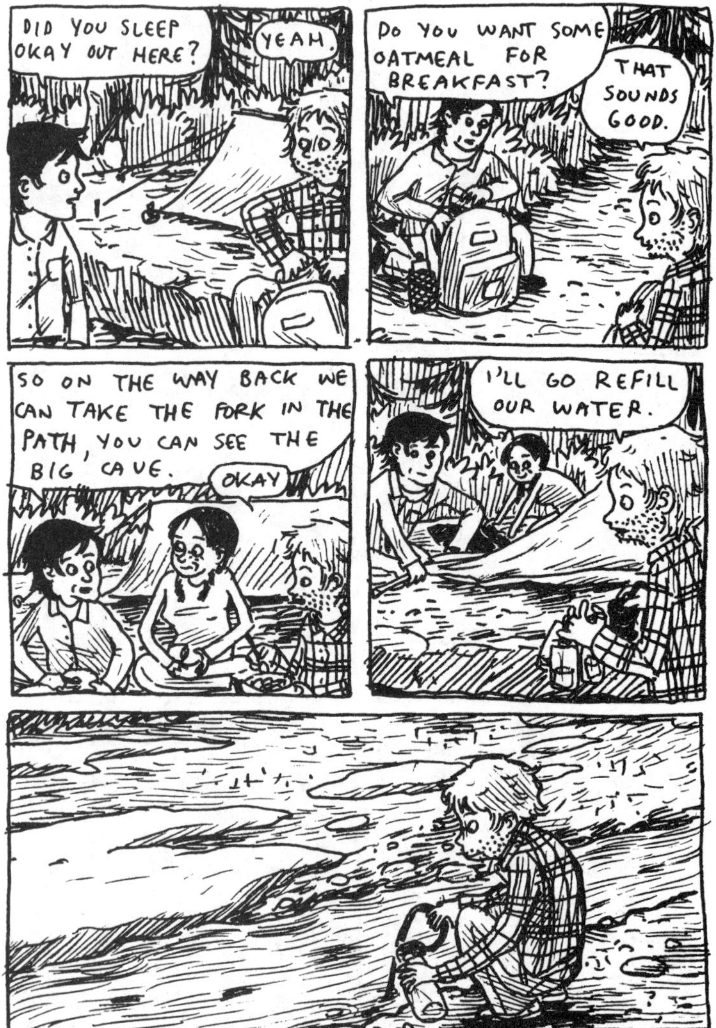
DID YOU SLEEP OKAY OUT HERE?
YEAH.
DO YOU WANT SOME OATMEAL FOR BREAKFAST?
THAT SOUNDS GOOD.
SO ON THE WAY BACK WE CAN TAKE THE FORK IN THE PATH, YOU CAN SEE THE BIG CAVE.
OKAY
I'LL GO REFILL OUR WATER.

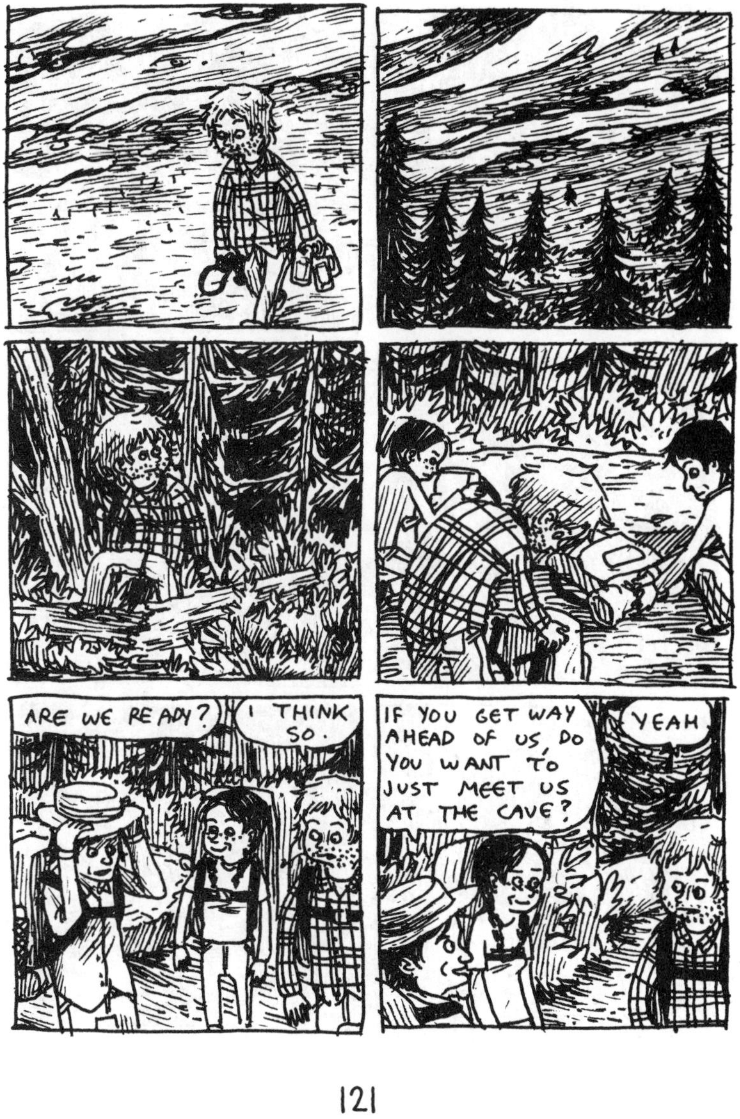
ARE WE READY?
I THINK SO.
IF YOU GET WAY AHEAD OF US, DO YOU WANT TO JUST MEET US AT THE CAVE?
YEAH

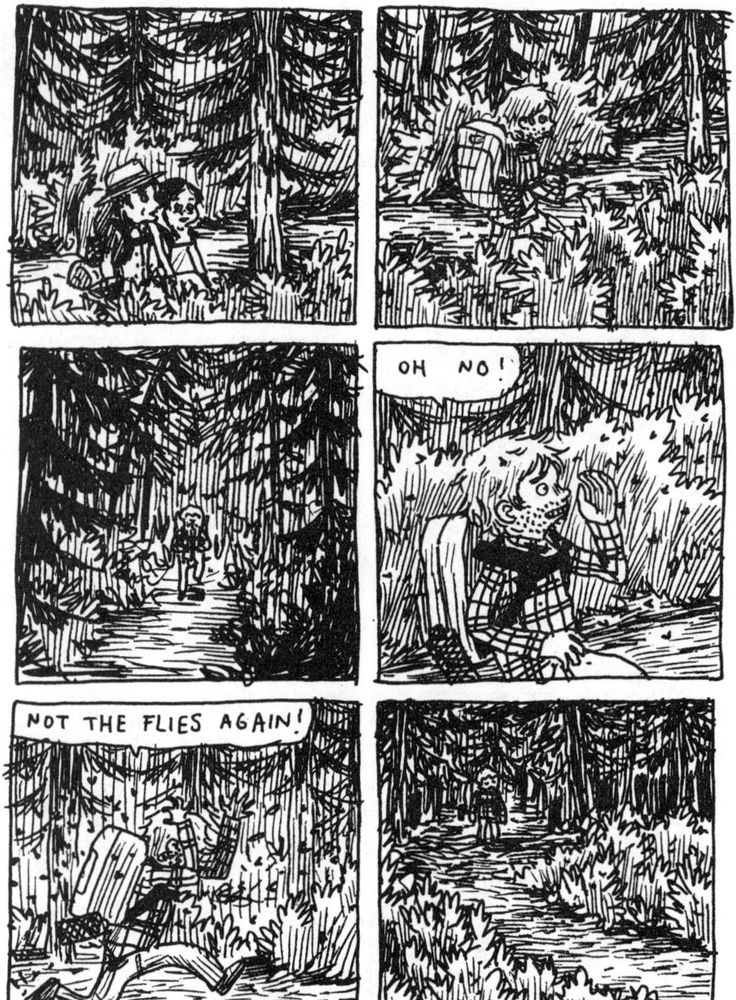
OH NO!
NOT THE FLIES AGAIN!

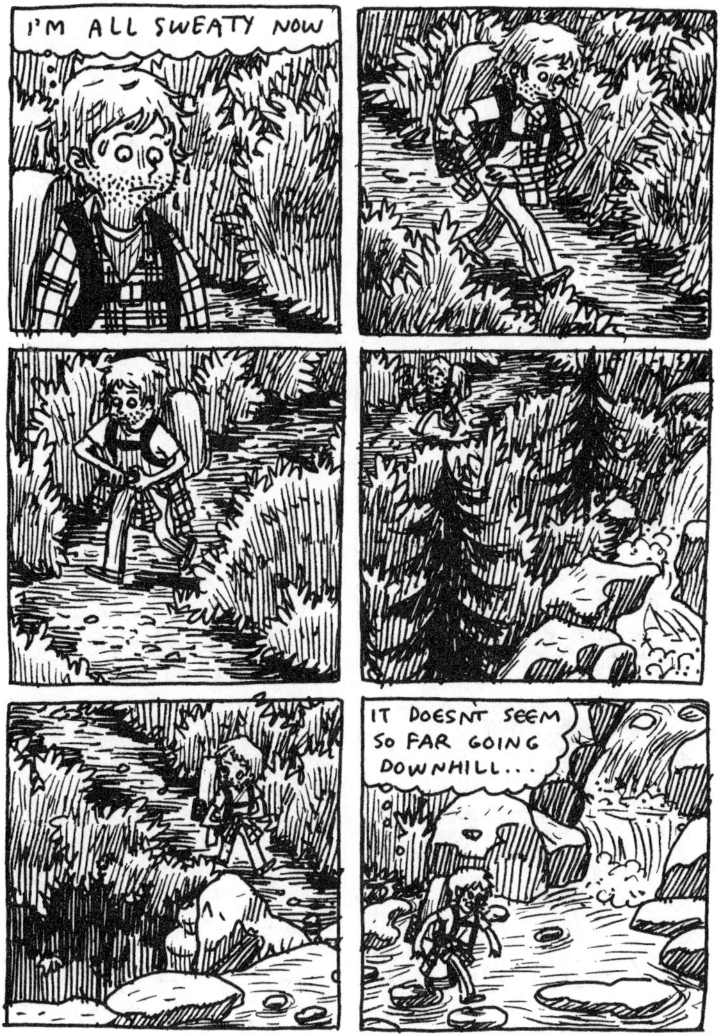
I'M ALL SWEATY NOW
IT DOESNT SEEM SO FAR GOING DOWNHILL...

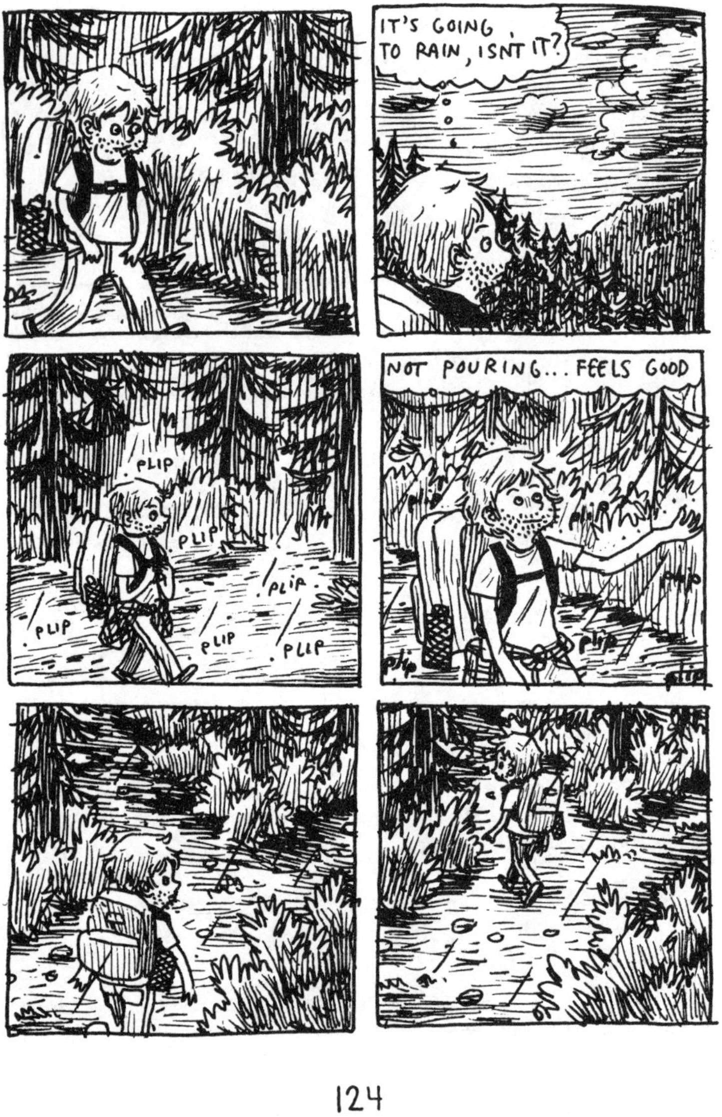
IT'S GOING TO RAIN, ISN'T IT?
PLIP
PLIP
PLIP
PLIP
PLIP
PLIP
NOT POURING... FEELS GOOD

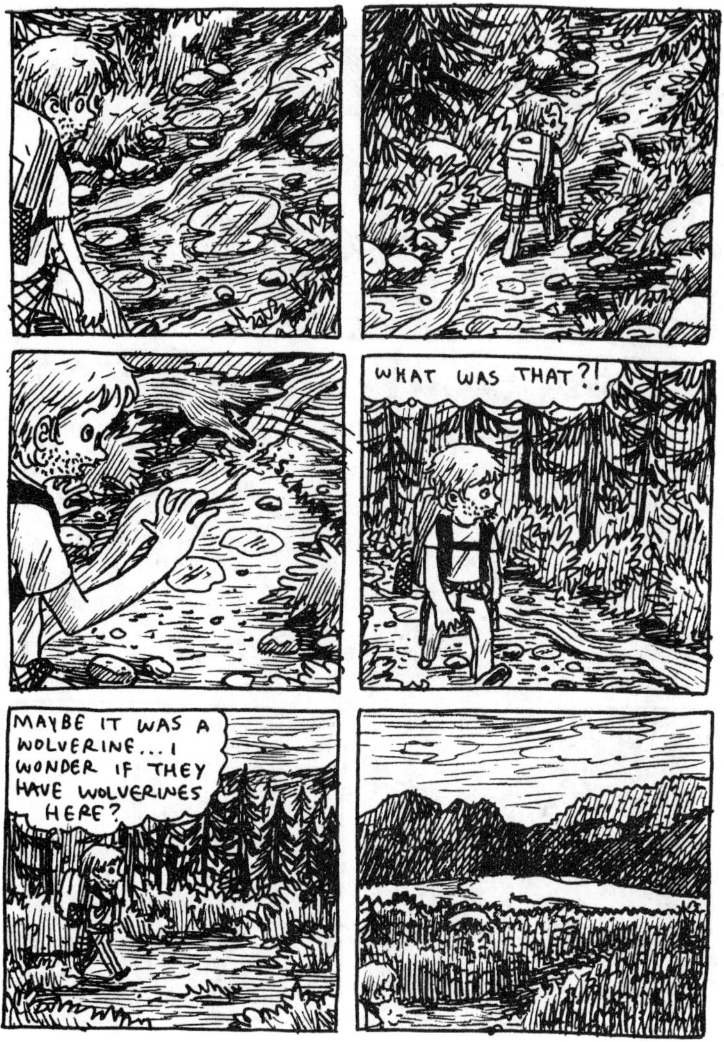
WHAT WAS THAT?!
MAYBE IT WAS A WOLVERINE... I WONDER IF THEY HAVE WOLVERINES HERE?

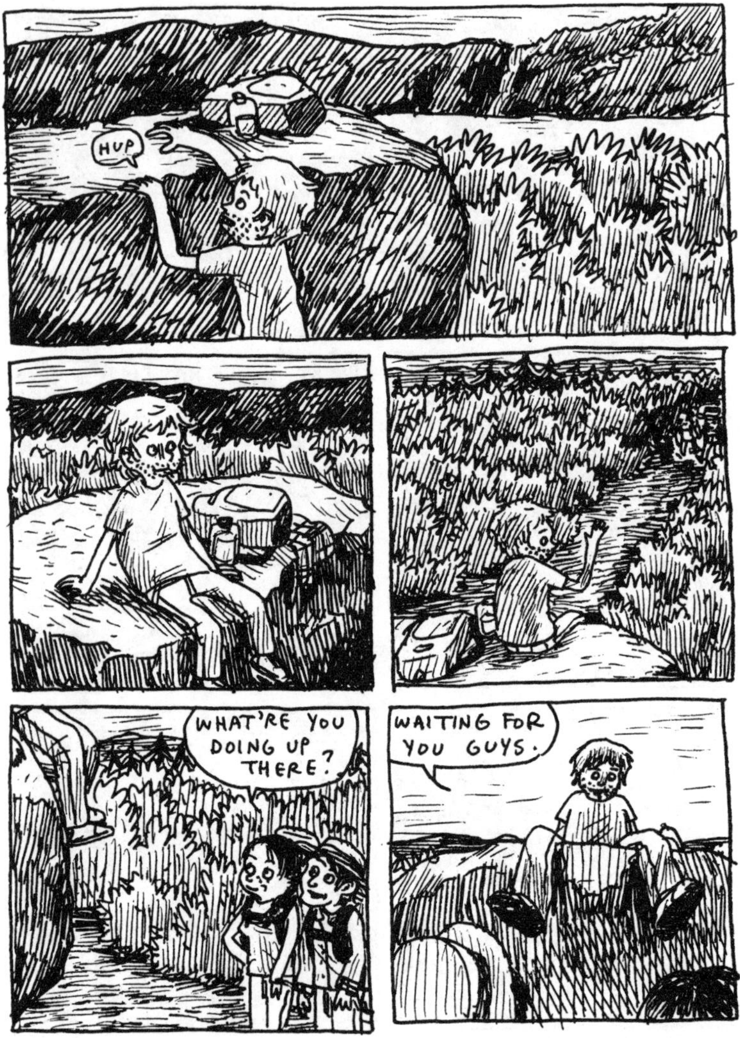
HUP
WHAT'RE YOU DOING UP THERE?
WAITING FOR YOU GUYS.

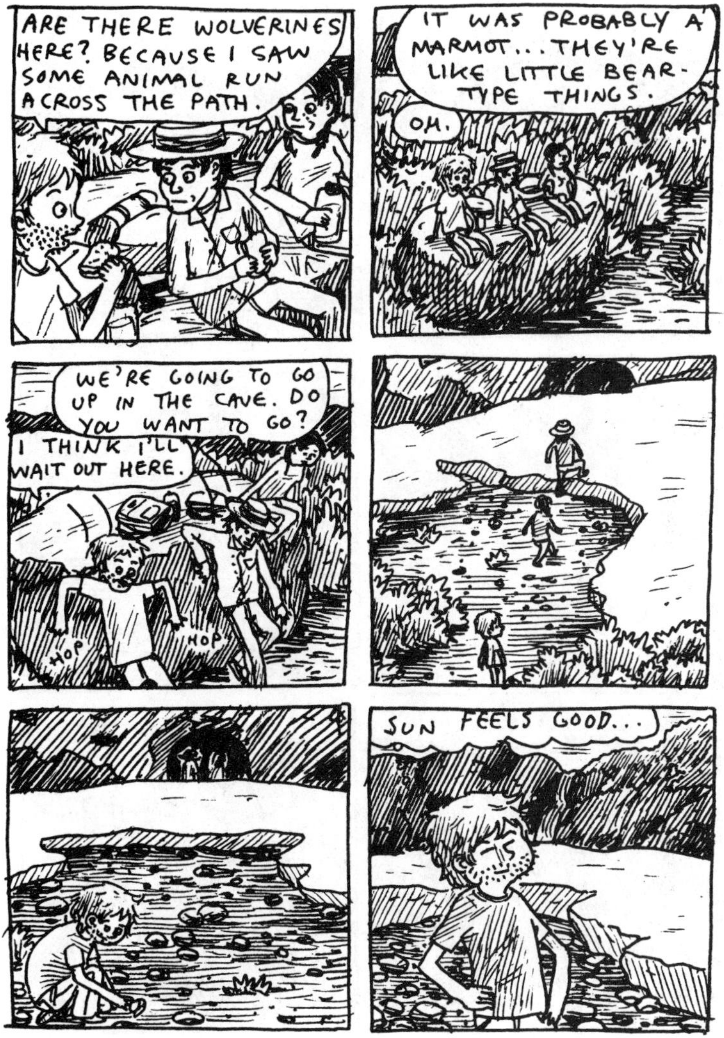
ARE THERE WOLVERINES HERE? BECAUSE I SAW SOME ANIMAL RUN ACROSS THE PATH.
IT WAS PROBABLY A MARMOT... THEY'RE LIKE LITTLE BEAR-TYPE THINGS.
OH.
WE'RE GOING TO GO UP IN THE CAVE. DO YOU WANT TO GO?
I THINK I'LL WAIT OUT HERE.
HOP
HOP
SUN FEELS GOOD...

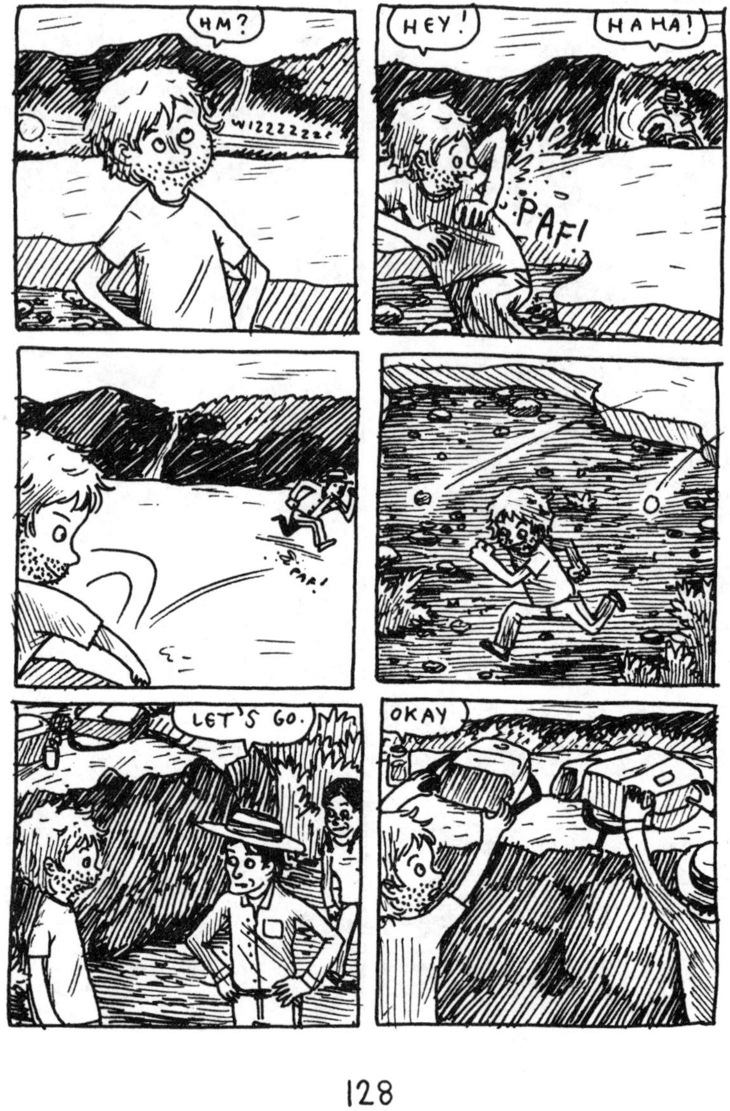
HM?
WIZZZZZZZ
HEY!
HAHA!
PAF!
PAF!
LET'S GO.
OKAY

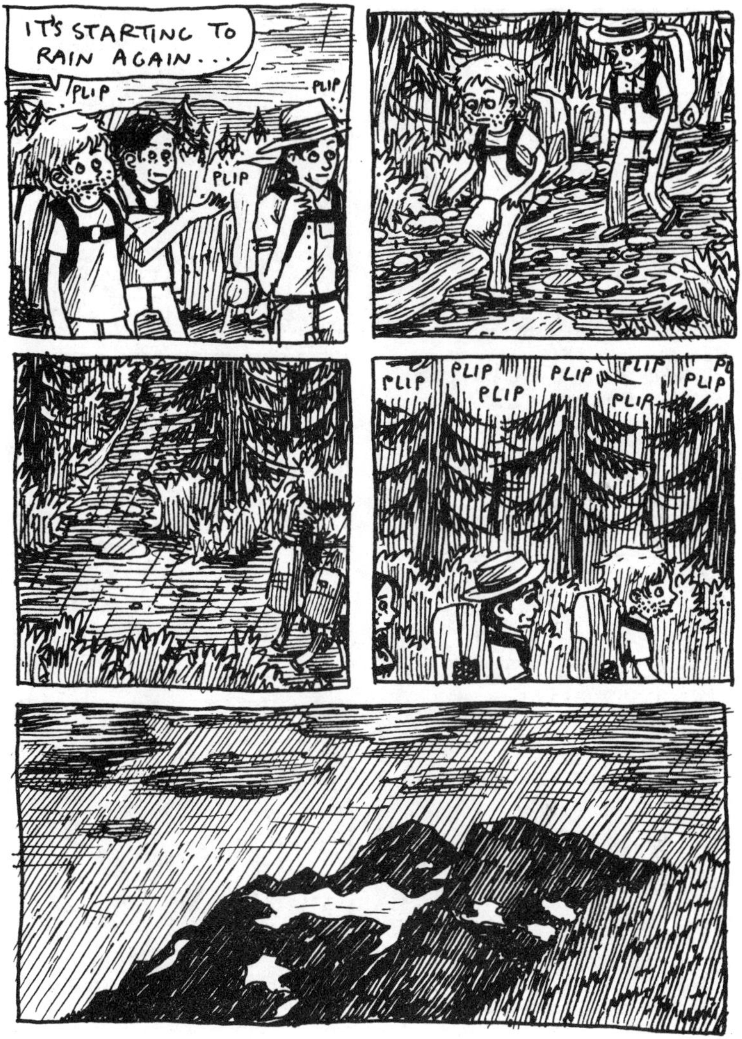
IT'S STARTING TO RAIN AGAIN...
PLIP
PLIP
PLIP
PLIP
PLIP
PLIP
PLIP
PLIP
PLIP
PLIP
PLIP

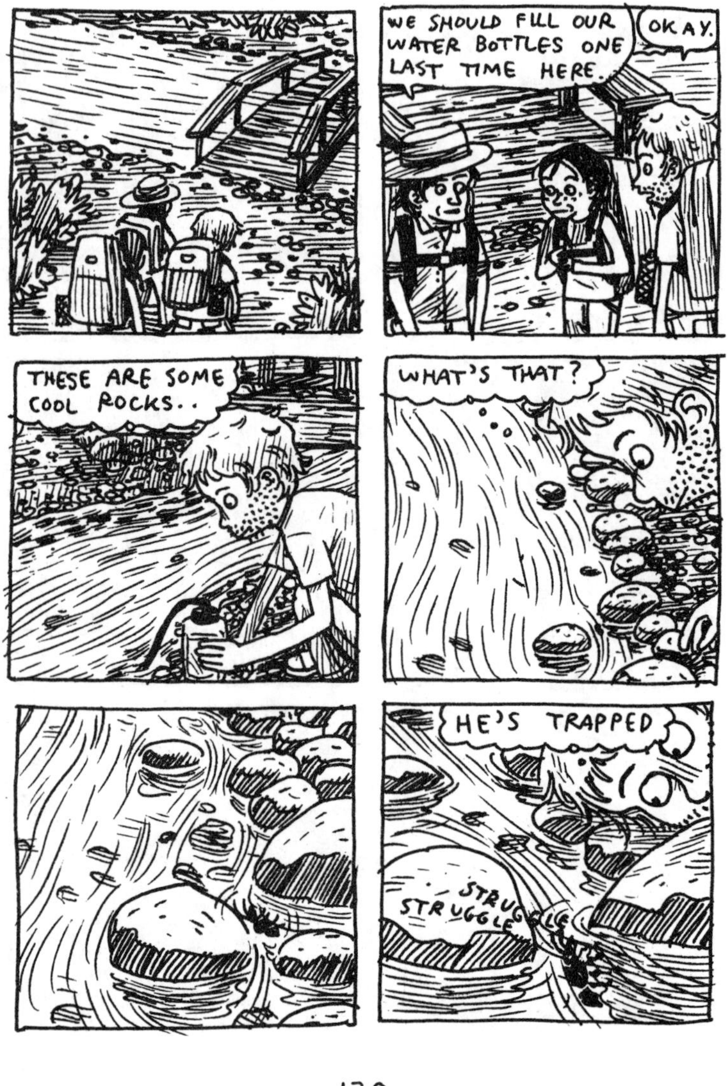
WE SHOULD FILL OUR WATER BOTTLES ONE LAST TIME HERE.
OKAY.
THESE ARE SOME COOL ROCKS..
WHAT'S THAT?
HE'S TRAPPED
STRUGGLE
STRUGGLE

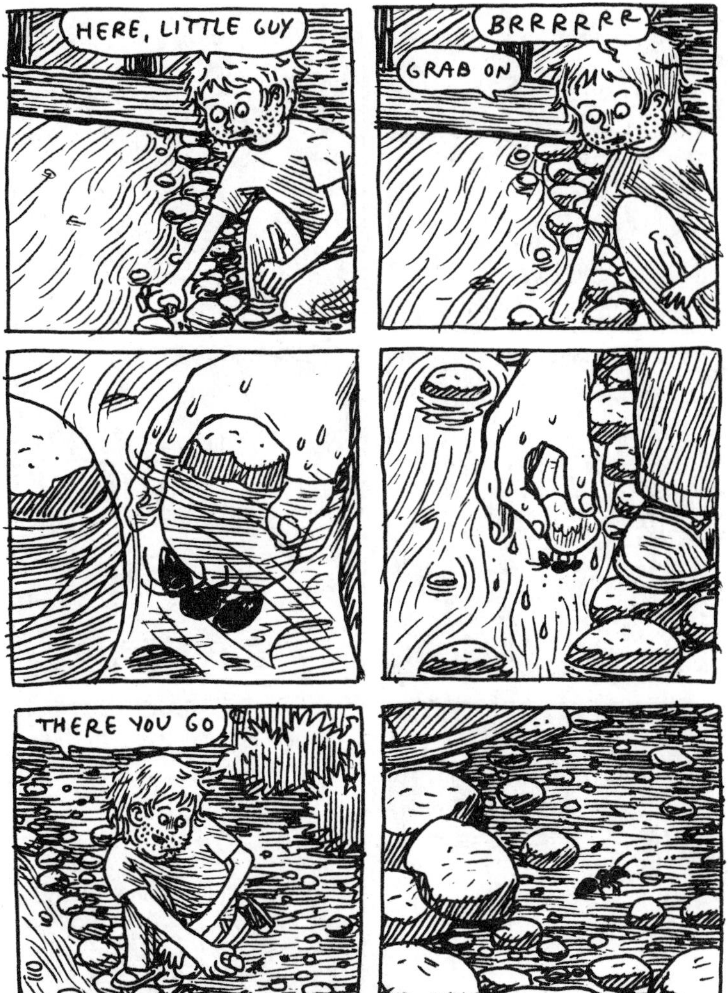
HERE, LITTLE GUY
BRRRRRR
GRAB ON
THERE YOU GO

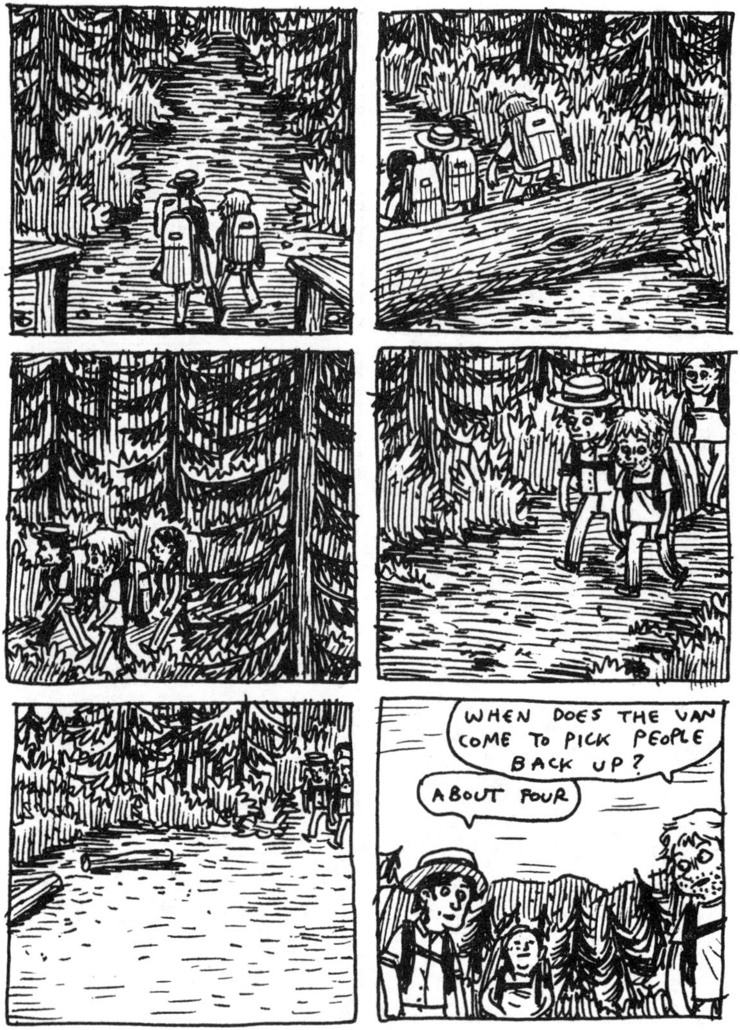
WHEN DOES THE VAN COME TO PICK PEOPLE BACK UP?
ABOUT FOUR

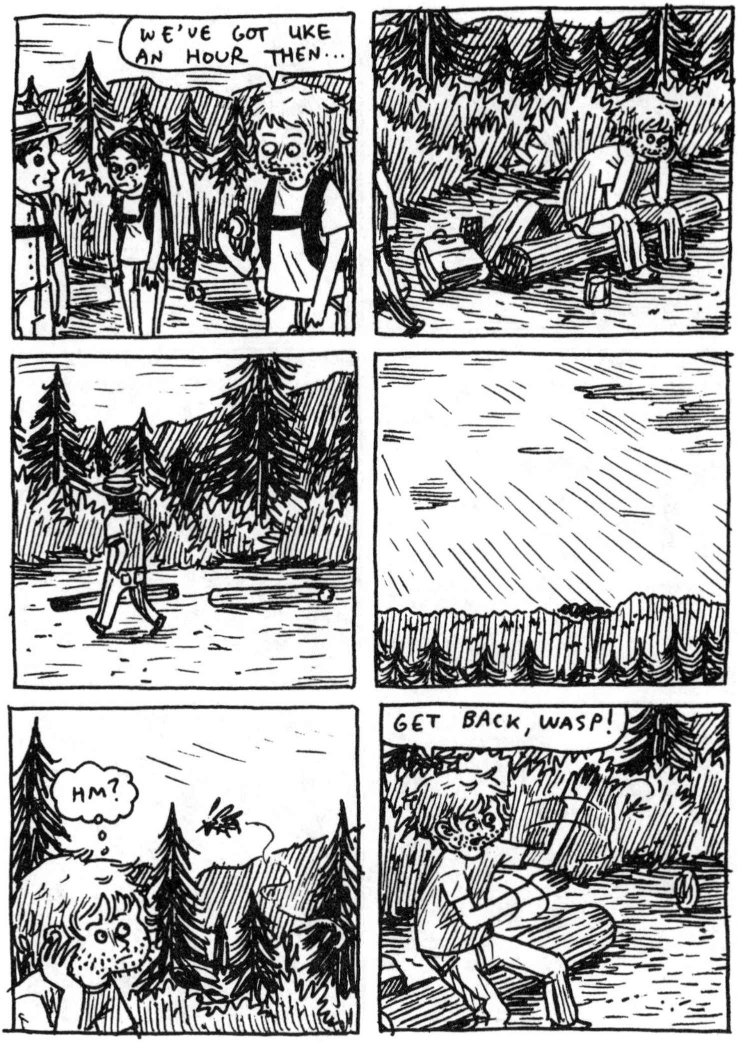
WE'VE GOT LIKE AN HOUR THEN...
HM?
GET BACK, WASP!

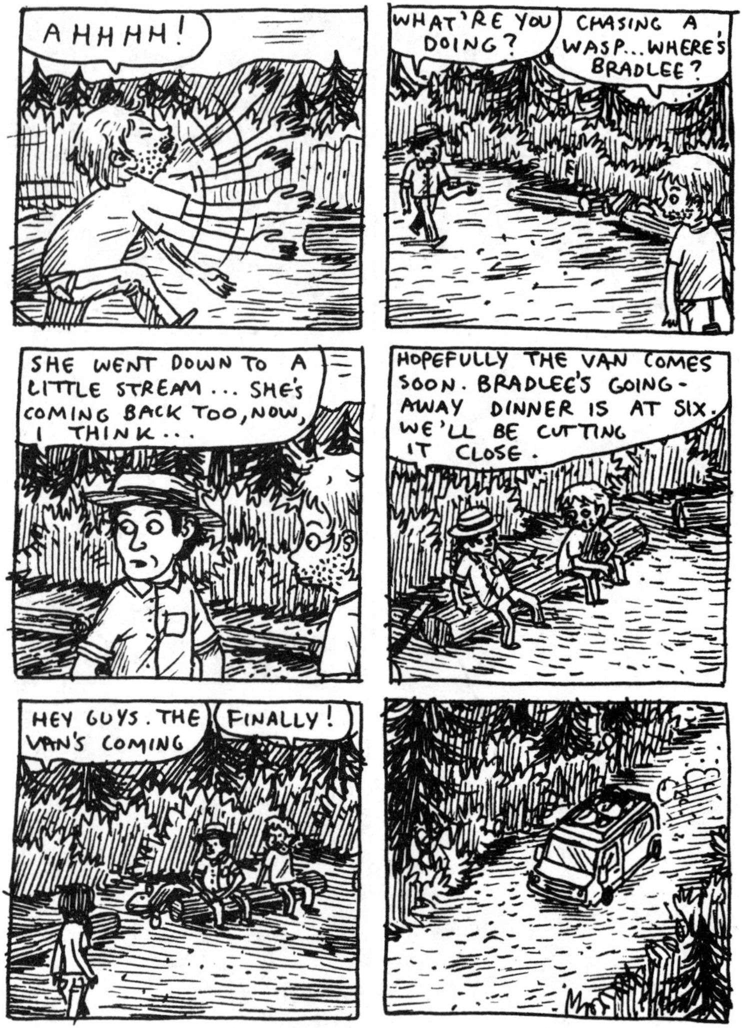
AHHHH!
WHAT'RE YOU DOING?
CHASING A WASP... WHERE'S BRADLEE?
SHE WENT DOWN TO A LITTLE STREAM... SHE'S COMING BACK TOO, NOW, I THINK...
HOPEFULLY THE VAN COMES SOON. BRADLEE'S GOING-AWAY DINNER IS AT SIX. WE'LL BE CUTTING IT CLOSE.
HEY GUYS. THE VAN'S COMING
FINALLY!

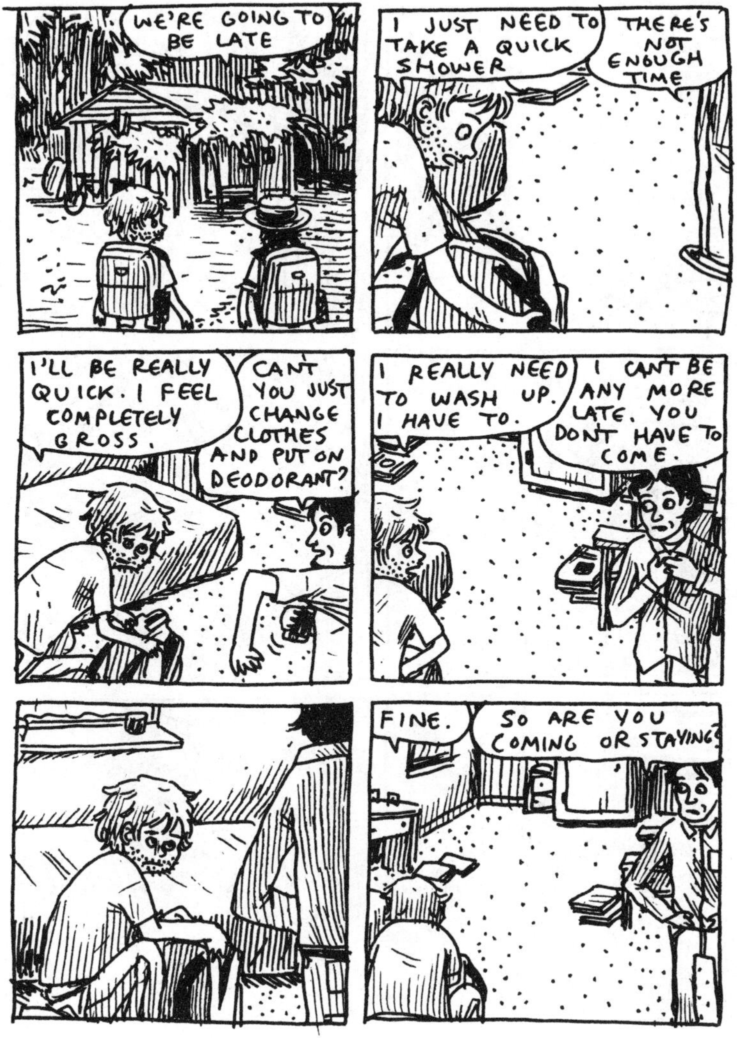
WE'RE GOING TO BE LATE
I JUST NEED TO TAKE A QUICK SHOWER
THERE'S NOT ENOUGH TIME
I'LL BE REALLY QUICK. I FEEL COMPLETELY GROSS.
CAN'T YOU JUST CHANGE CLOTHES AND PUT ON DEODORANT?
I REALLY NEED TO WASH UP. I HAVE TO.
I CAN'T BE ANY MORE LATE. YOU DON'T HAVE TO COME.
FINE.
SO ARE YOU COMING OR STAYING?

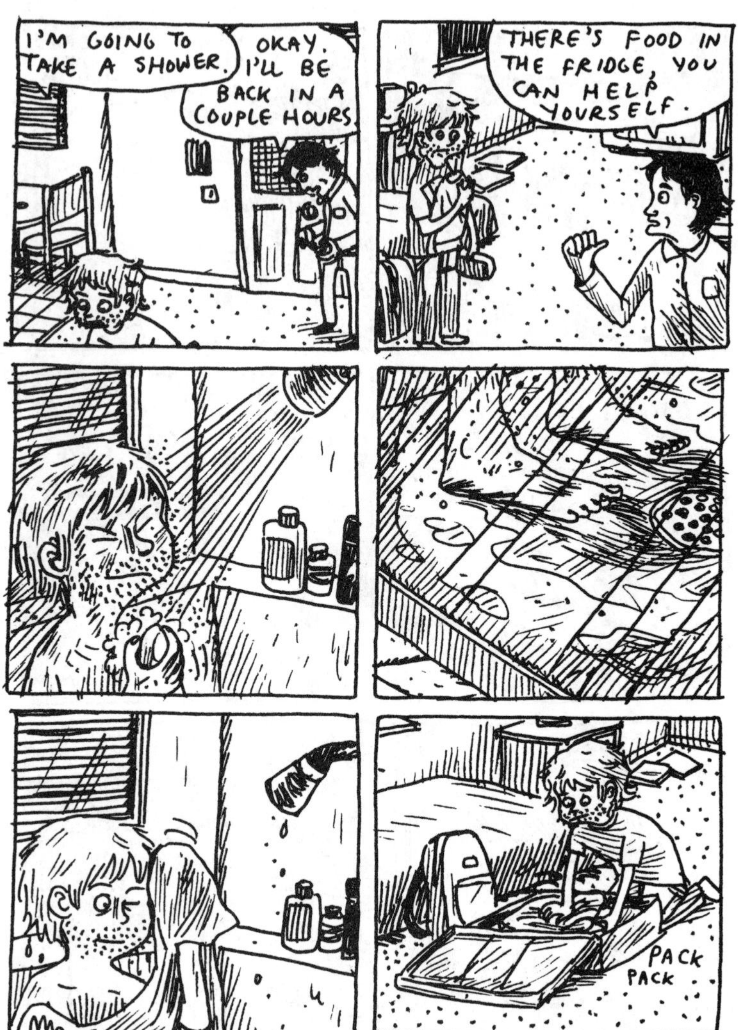
I'M GOING TO TAKE A SHOWER.
OKAY. I'LL BE BACK IN A COUPLE HOURS.
THERE'S FOOD IN THE FRIDGE, YOU CAN HELP YOURSELF.
PACK PACK

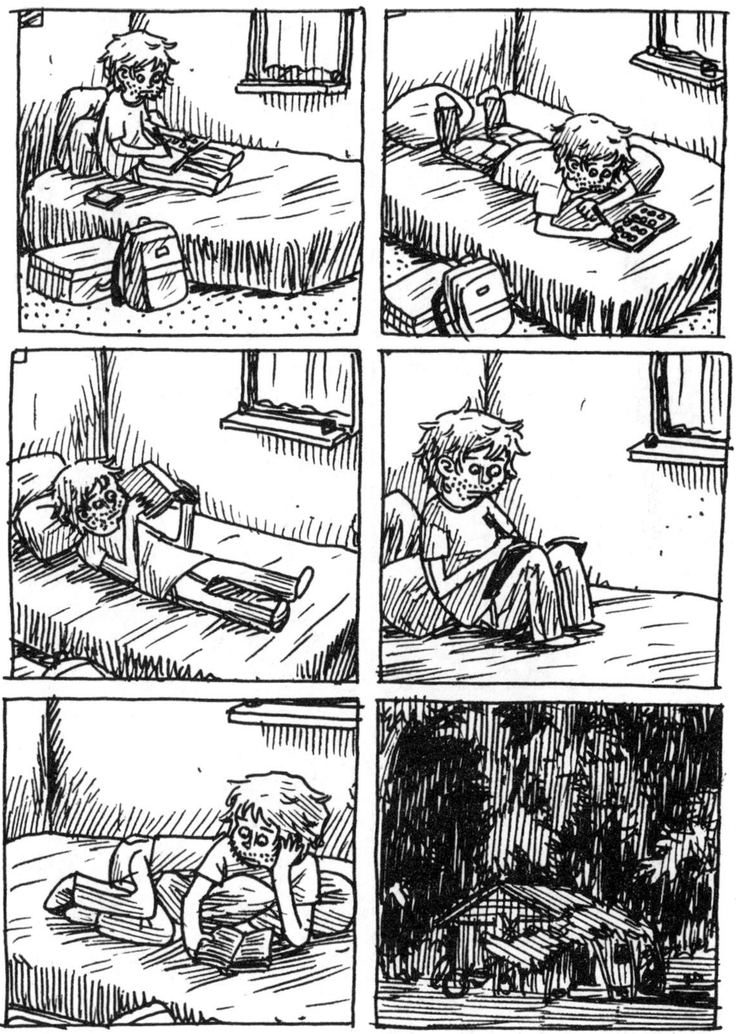

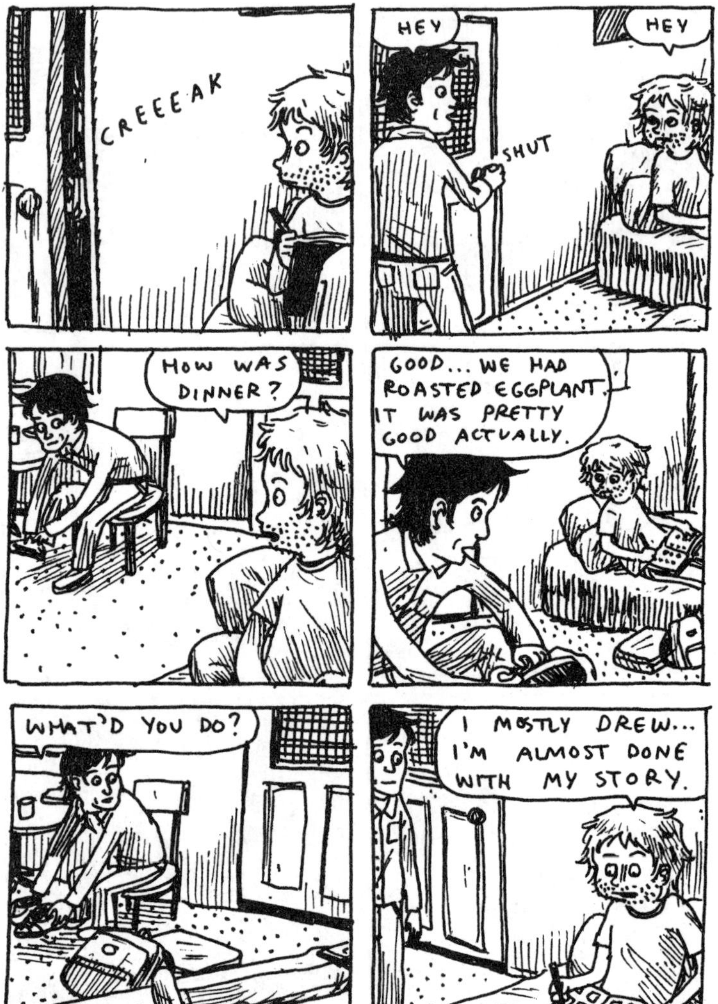
CREEEAK
HEY
SHUT
HEY
HOW WAS DINNER?
GOOD... WE HAD ROASTED EGGPLANT. IT WAS PRETTY GOOD ACTUALLY.
WHAT'D YOU DO?
I MOSTLY DREW... I'M ALMOST DONE WITH MY STORY.

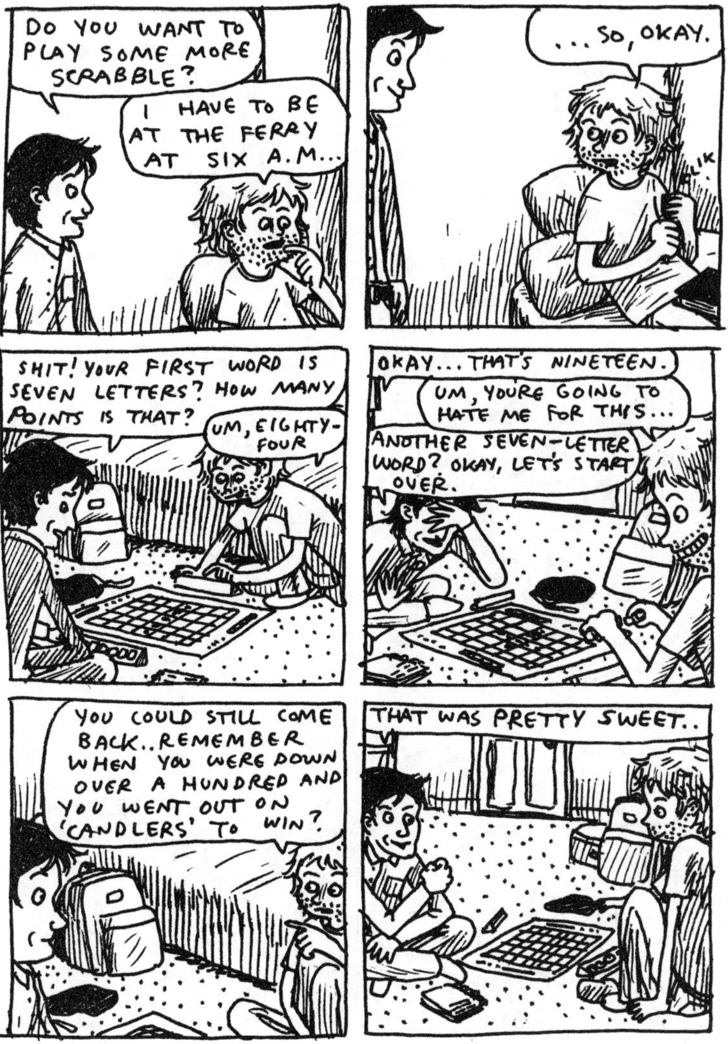
DO YOU WANT TO PLAY SOME MORE SCRABBLE?
I HAVE TO BE AT THE FERRY AT SIX A.M...
...SO, OKAY.
LIK
SHIT! YOUR FIRST WORD IS SEVEN LETTERS? HOW MANY POINTS IS THAT?
UM, EIGHTY-FOUR
OKAY... THAT'S NINETEEN.
UM, YOU'RE GOING TO HATE ME FOR THIS...
ANOTHER SEVEN-LETTER WORD? OKAY, LET'S START OVER.
YOU COULD STILL COME BACK..REMEMBER WHEN YOU WERE DOWN OVER A HUNDRED AND YOU WENT OUT ON 'CANDLERS' TO WIN?
THAT WAS PRETTY SWEET..

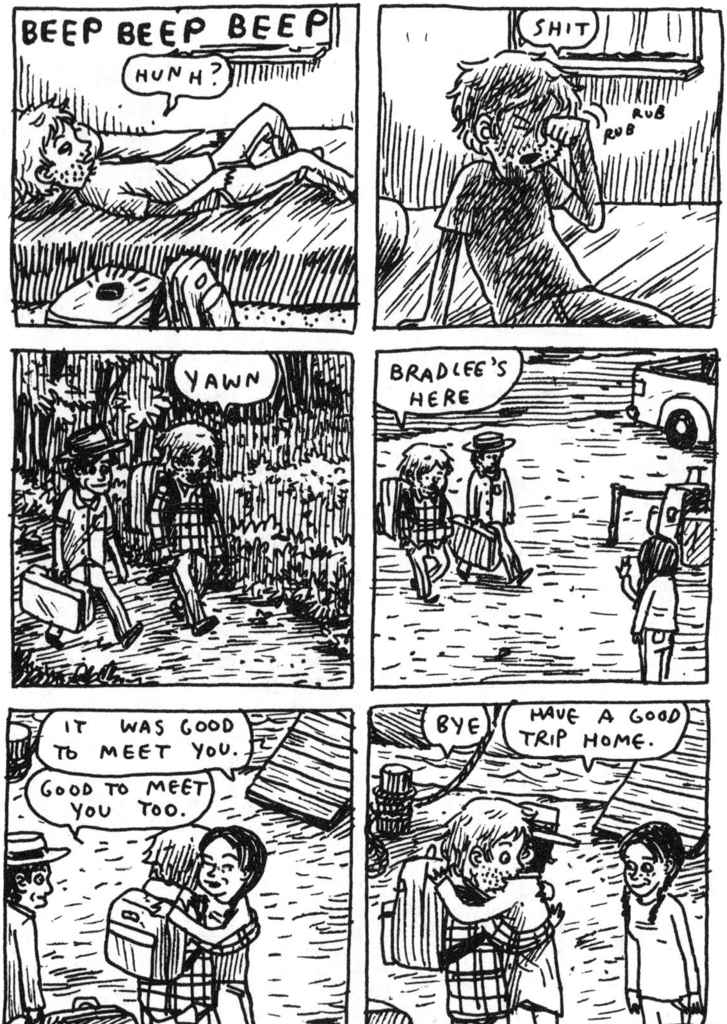

BEEP BEEP BEEP
HUNH?
SHIT
RUB RUB
YAWN
BRADLEE'S HERE
IT WAS GOOD TO MEET YOU.
GOOD TO MEET YOU TOO.
BYE
HAVE A GOOD TRIP HOME.

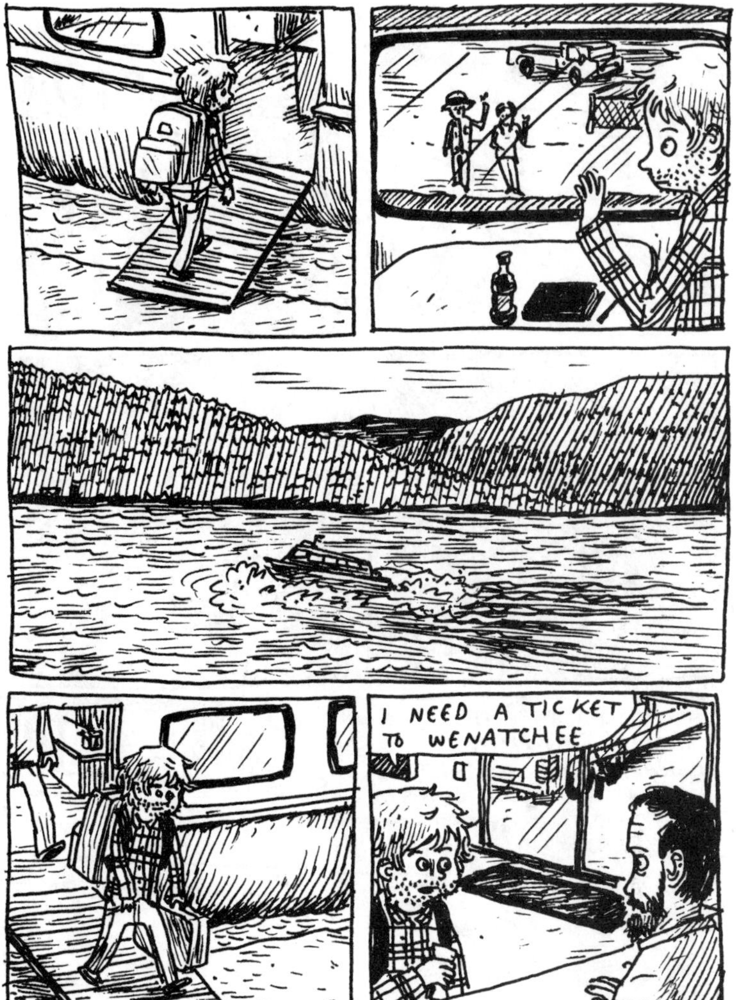
I NEED A TICKET TO WENATCHEE

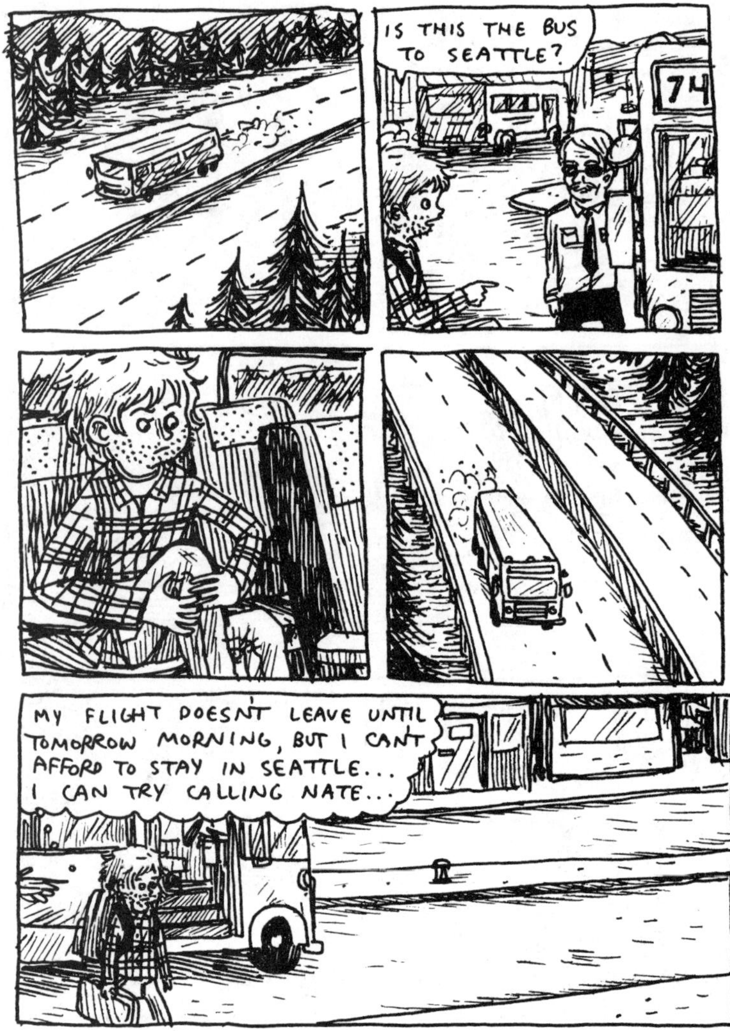
IS THIS THE BUS TO SEATTLE?
MY FLIGHT DOESN'T LEAVE UNTIL TOMORROW MORNING, BUT I CAN'T AFFORD TO STAY IN SEATTLE... I CAN TRY CALLING NATE...
74

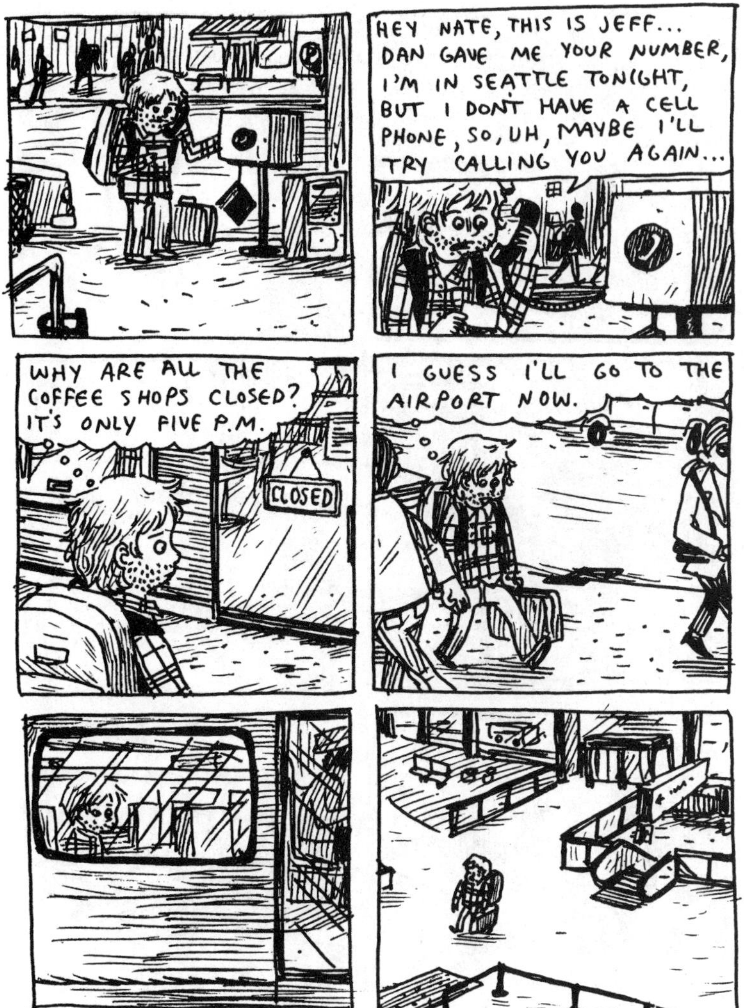
HEY NATE, THIS IS JEFF... DAN GAVE ME YOUR NUMBER, I'M IN SEATTLE TONIGHT, BUT I DON'T HAVE A CELL PHONE, SO, UH, MAYBE I'LL TRY CALLING YOU AGAIN...
WHY ARE ALL THE COFFEE SHOPS CLOSED? IT'S ONLY FIVE P.M.
CLOSED
I GUESS I'LL GO TO THE AIRPORT NOW.

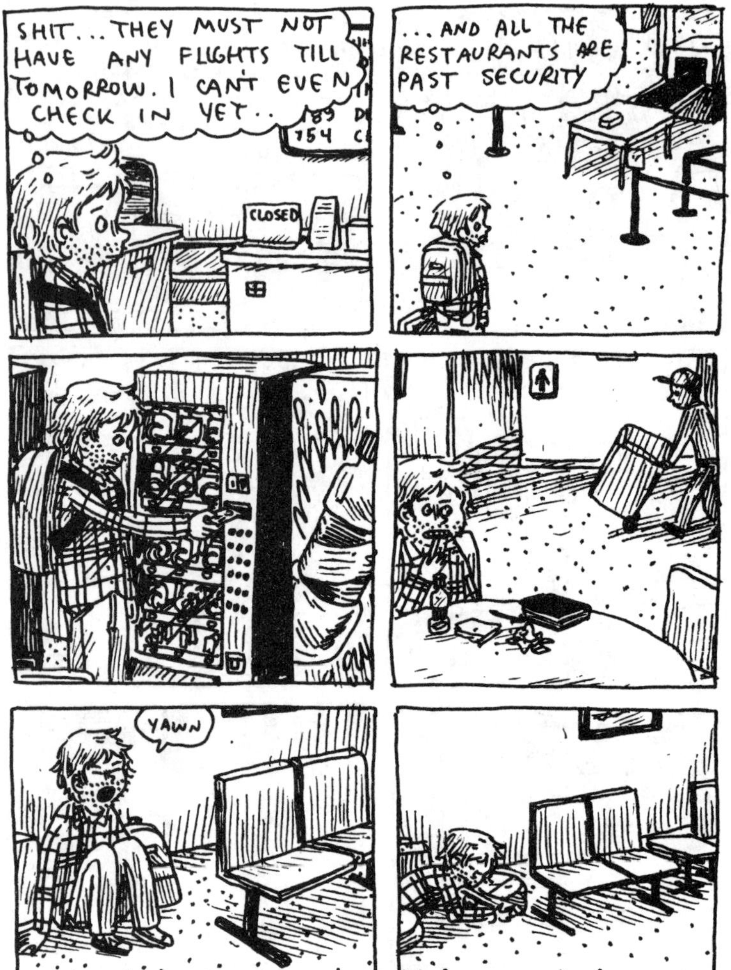
SHIT... THEY MUST NOT HAVE ANY FLIGHTS TILL TOMORROW. I CAN'T EVEN CHECK IN YET..
CLOSED
...AND ALL THE RESTAURANTS ARE PAST SECURITY
YAWN

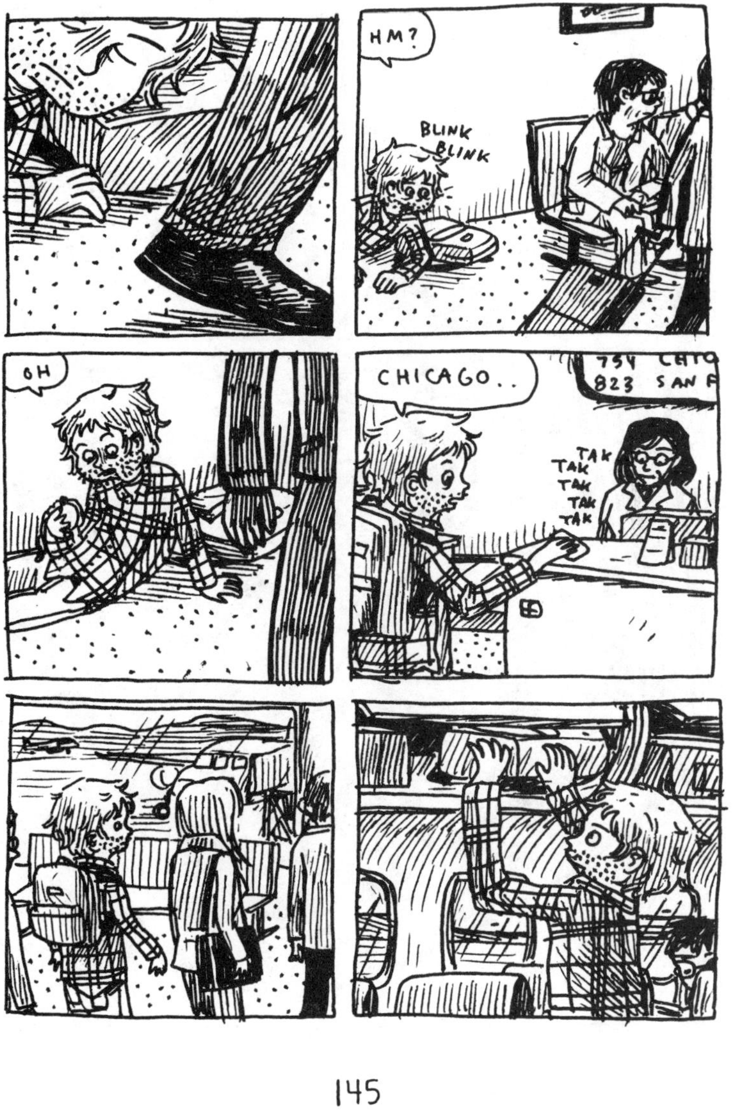
HM?
BLINK
BLINK
OH
CHICAGO..
754
823 SAN
TAK
TAK
TAK
TAK
TAK

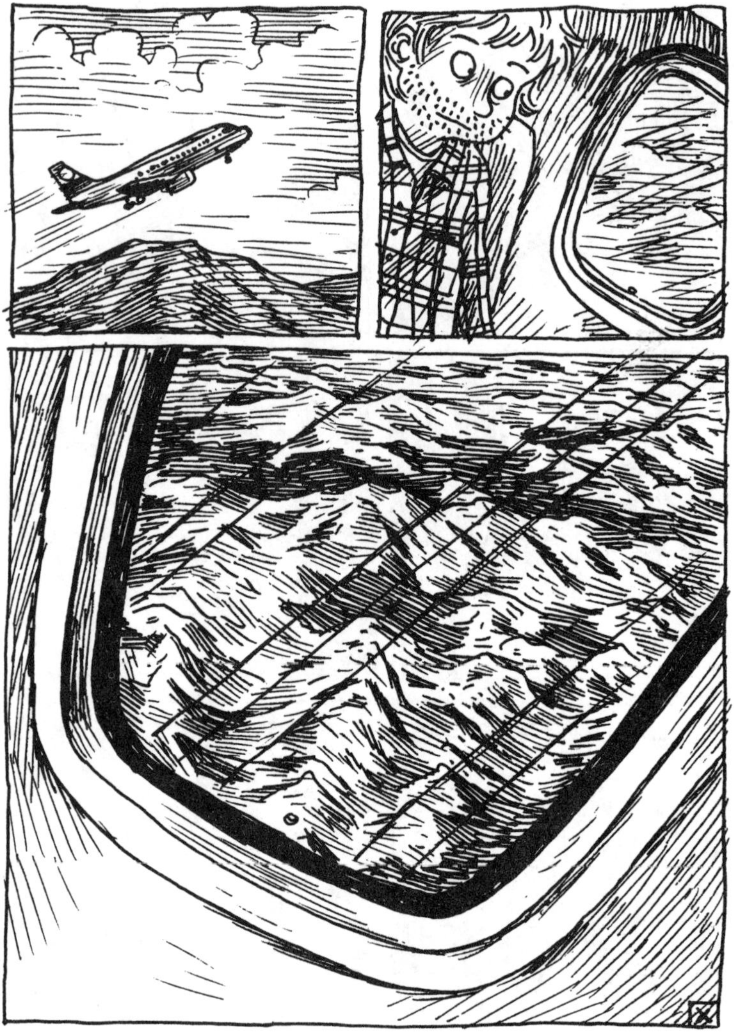

MARIE

VERSUS:

THE CAR

SOME DIALOGUE IS
< TRANSLATED FROM
THE FRENCH >

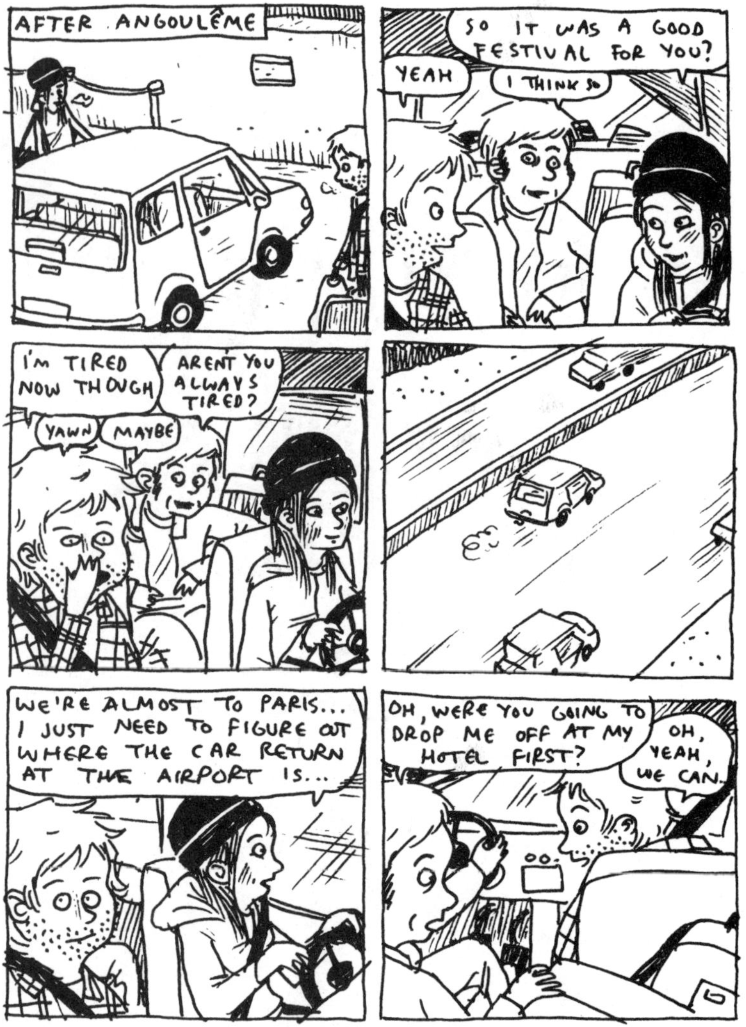

AFTER ANGOULÊME
SO IT WAS A GOOD FESTIVAL FOR YOU?
YEAH
I THINK SO
I'M TIRED NOW THOUGH
ARENT YOU ALWAYS TIRED?
YAWN
MAYBE
WE'RE ALMOST TO PARIS... I JUST NEED TO FIGURE OUT WHERE THE CAR RETURN AT THE AIRPORT IS...
OH, WERE YOU GOING TO DROP ME OFF AT MY HOTEL FIRST?
OH, YEAH, WE CAN.

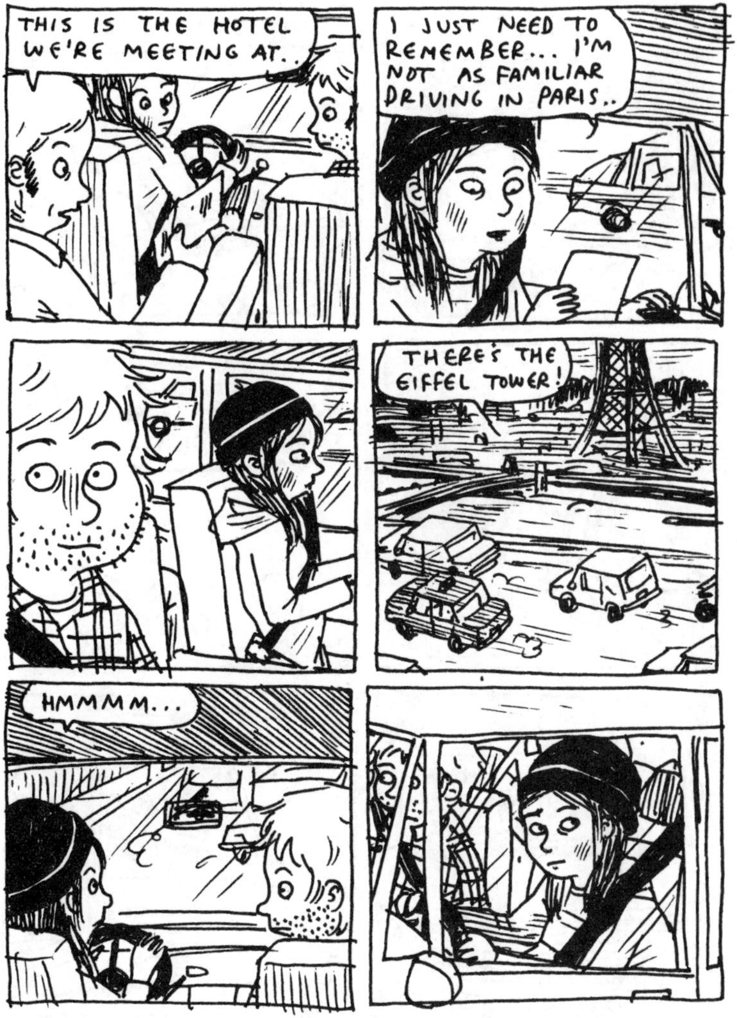
THIS IS THE HOTEL WE'RE MEETING AT..
I JUST NEED TO REMEMBER... I'M NOT AS FAMILIAR DRIVING IN PARIS..
THERE'S THE EIFFEL TOWER!
HMMMM...

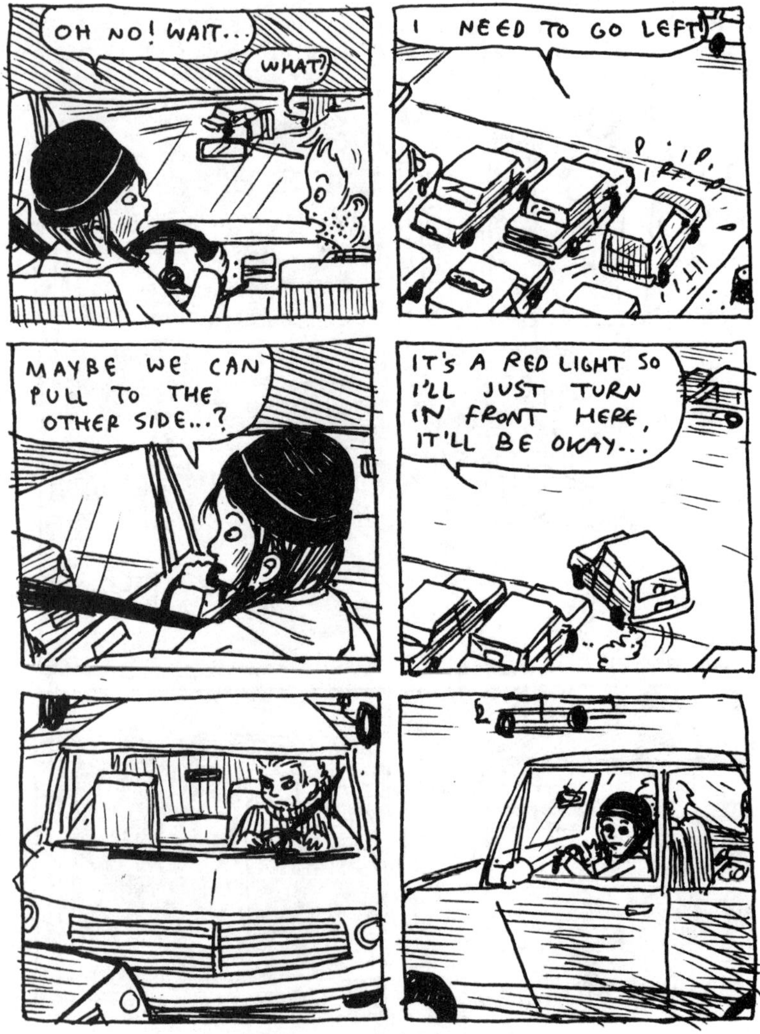
OH NO! WAIT...
WHAT?
I NEED TO GO LEFT!
MAYBE WE CAN PULL TO THE OTHER SIDE...?
IT'S A RED LIGHT SO I'LL JUST TURN IN FRONT HERE, IT'LL BE OKAY...

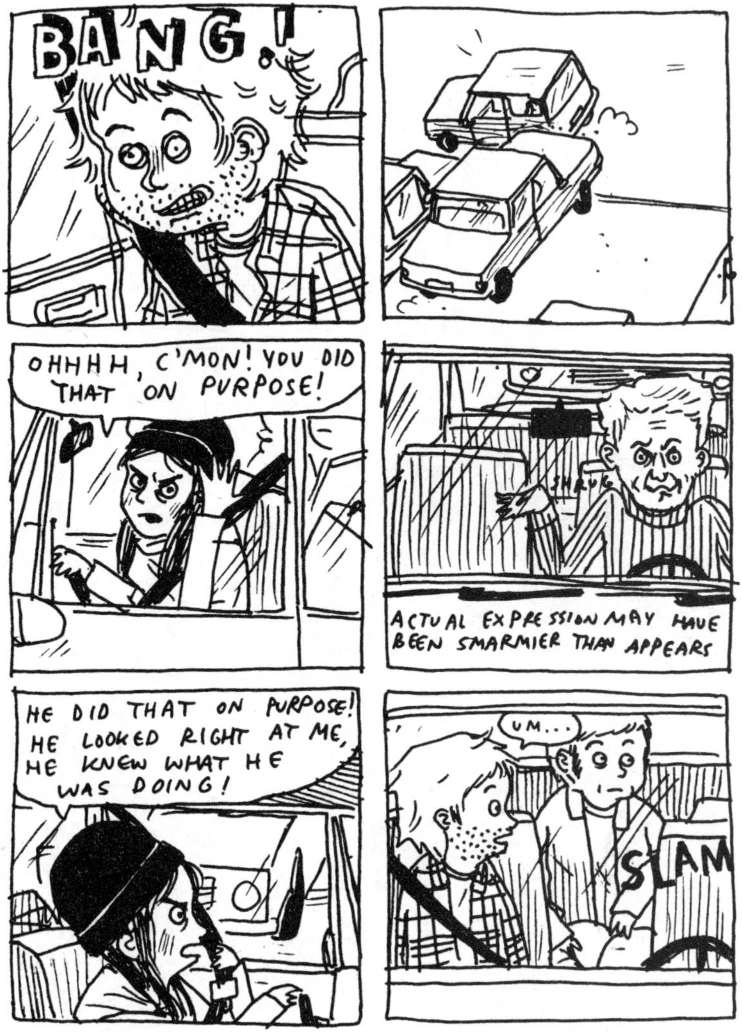
BANG!
OHHHH, C'MON! YOU DID THAT ON PURPOSE!
SHRUG
ACTUAL EXPRESSION MAY HAVE BEEN SMARMIER THAN APPEARS
HE DID THAT ON PURPOSE! HE LOOKED RIGHT AT ME, HE KNEW WHAT HE WAS DOING!
UM...
SLAM

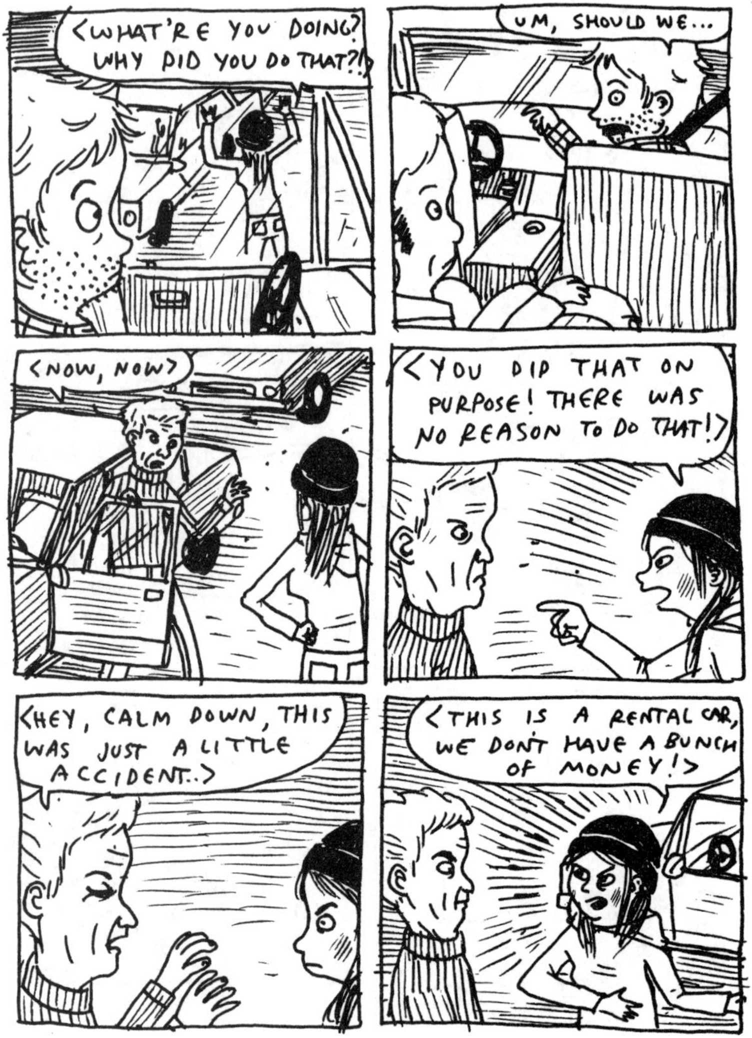
<WHAT'RE YOU DOING? WHY DID YOU DO THAT?!>
UM, SHOULD WE...
<NOW, NOW>
<YOU DID THAT ON PURPOSE! THERE WAS NO REASON TO DO THAT!>
<HEY, CALM DOWN, THIS WAS JUST A LITTLE ACCIDENT..>
<THIS IS A RENTAL CAR, WE DON'T HAVE A BUNCH OF MONEY!>

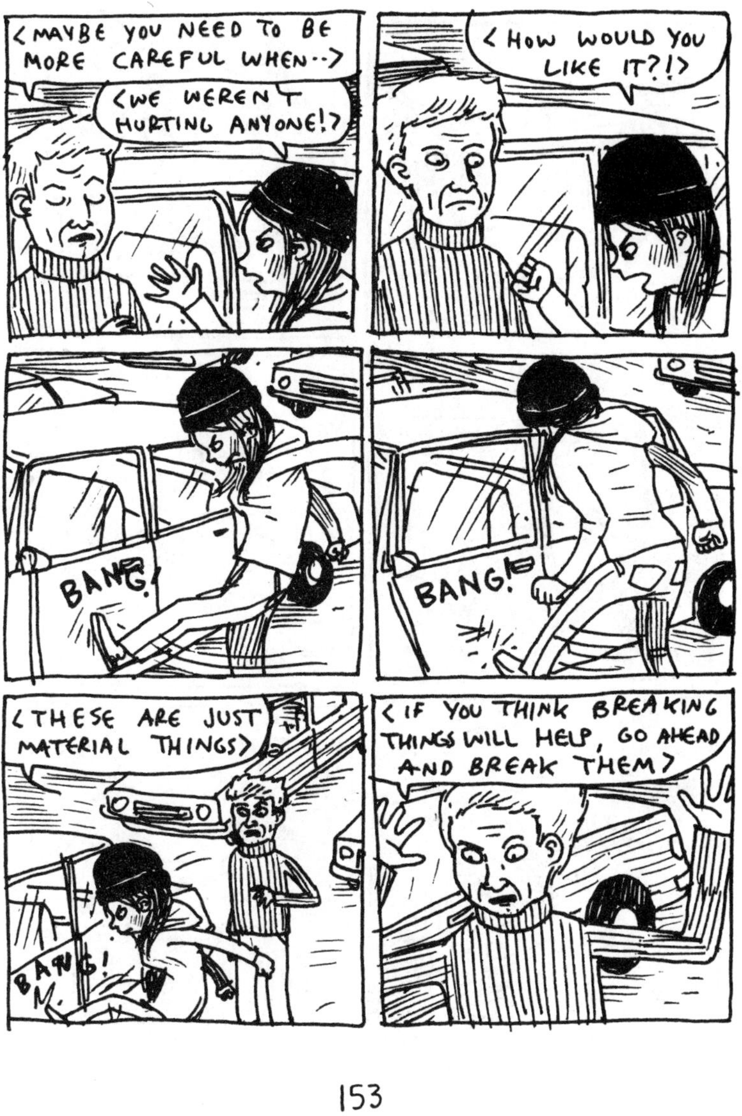
<MAYBE YOU NEED TO BE MORE CAREFUL WHEN-->
<WE WERENT HURTING ANYONE!>
<HOW WOULD YOU LIKE IT?!>
BANG!
BANG!
<THESE ARE JUST MATERIAL THINGS>
BANG!
<IF YOU THINK BREAKING THINGS WILL HELP, GO AHEAD AND BREAK THEM>

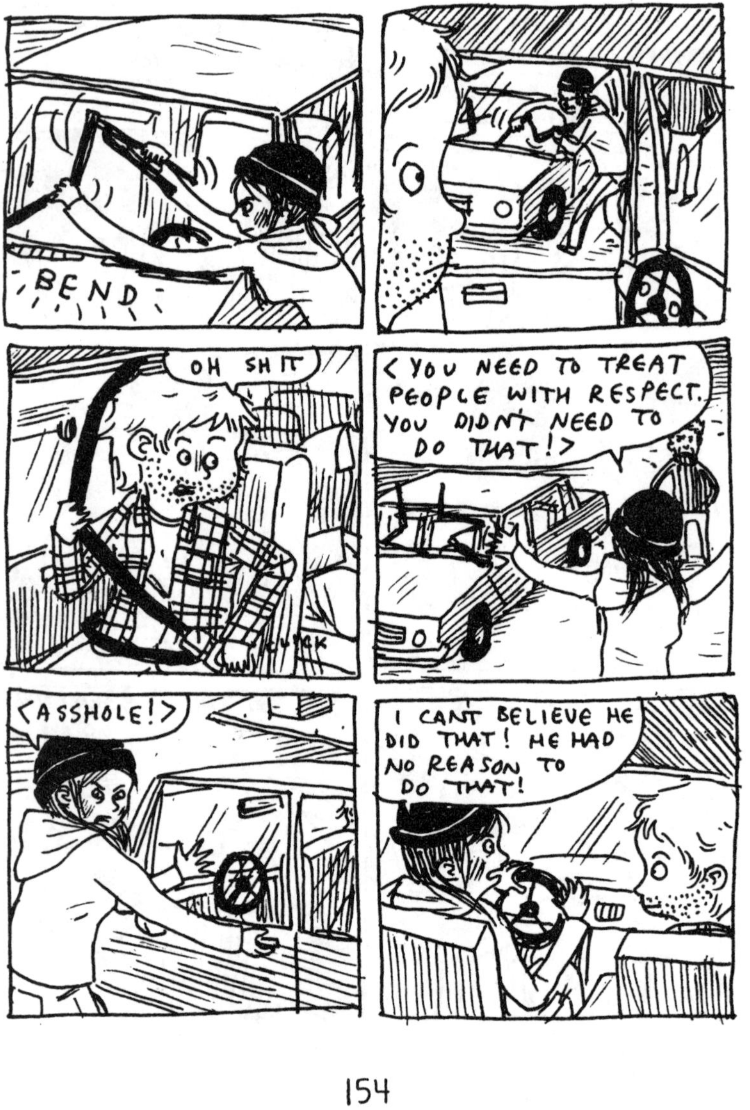
BEND
OH SHIT
<YOU NEED TO TREAT PEOPLE WITH RESPECT. YOU DIDN'T NEED TO DO THAT!>
<ASSHOLE!>
I CANT BELIEVE HE DID THAT! HE HAD NO REASON TO DO THAT!

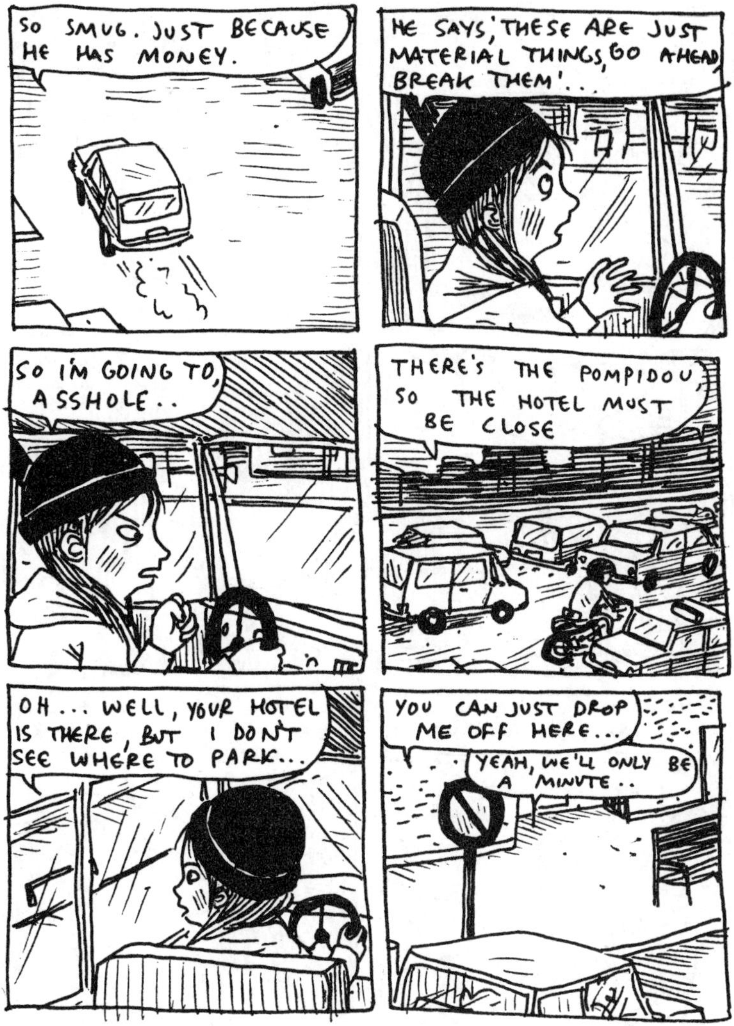
SO SMUG. JUST BECAUSE HE HAS MONEY.
HE SAYS, 'THESE ARE JUST MATERIAL THINGS, GO AHEAD, BREAK THEM'...
SO I'M GOING TO, ASSHOLE..
THERE'S THE POMPIDOU, SO THE HOTEL MUST BE CLOSE
OH... WELL, YOUR HOTEL IS THERE, BUT I DON'T SEE WHERE TO PARK...
YOU CAN JUST DROP ME OFF HERE...
YEAH, WE'LL ONLY BE A MINUTE..

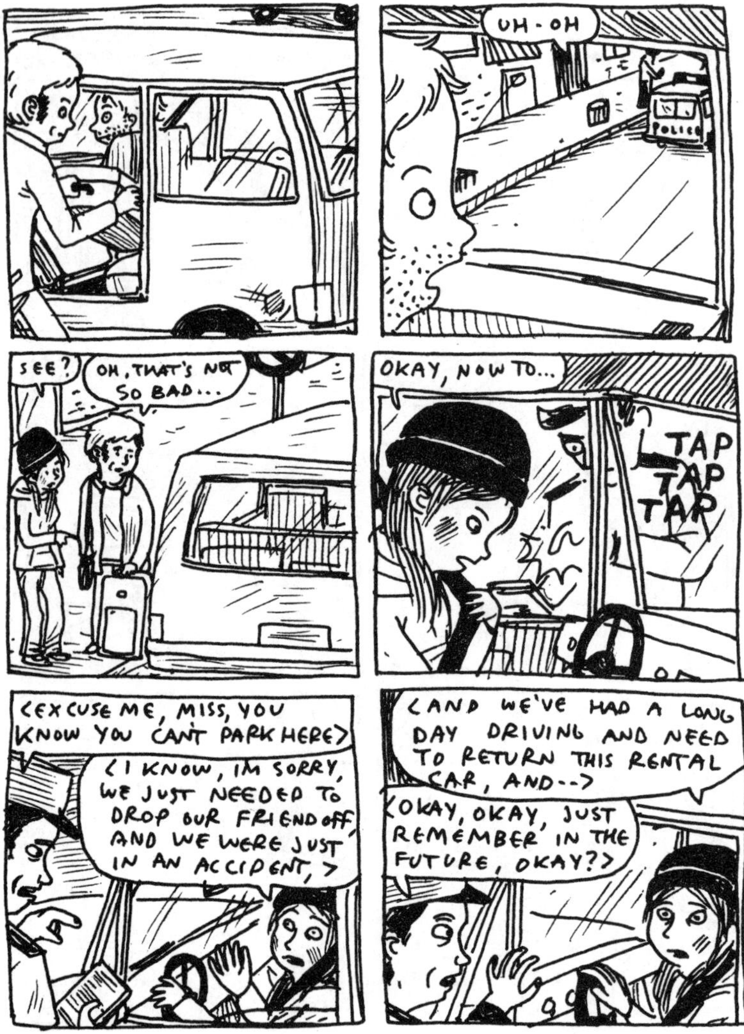
UH-OH
SEE?
OH, THAT'S NOT SO BAD...
OKAY, NOW TO...
TAP TAP TAP
<EXCUSE ME, MISS, YOU KNOW YOU CAN'T PARK HERE>
<I KNOW, I'M SORRY, WE JUST NEEDED TO DROP OUR FRIEND OFF AND WE WERE JUST IN AN ACCIDENT,>
<AND WE'VE HAD A LONG DAY DRIVING AND NEED TO RETURN THIS RENTAL CAR, AND-->
<OKAY, OKAY, JUST REMEMBER IN THE FUTURE, OKAY?>

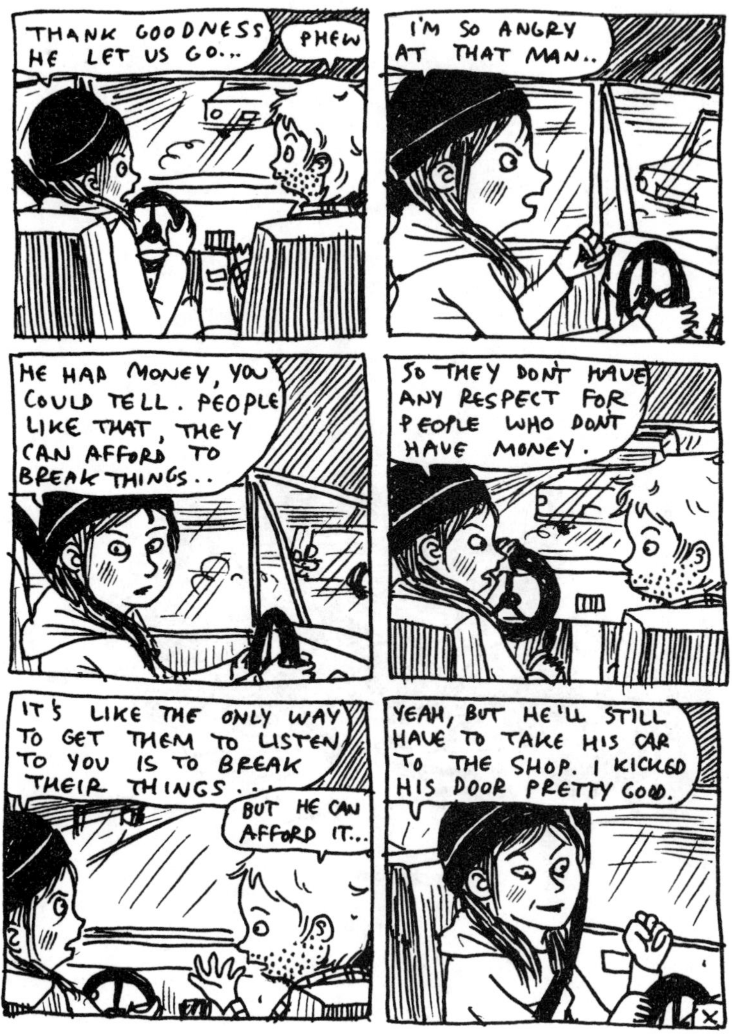
THANK GOODNESS HE LET US GO...
PHEW
I'M SO ANGRY AT THAT MAN..
HE HAD MONEY, YOU COULD TELL. PEOPLE LIKE THAT, THEY CAN AFFORD TO BREAK THINGS..
SO THEY DON'T HAVE ANY RESPECT FOR PEOPLE WHO DONT HAVE MONEY.
IT'S LIKE THE ONLY WAY TO GET THEM TO LISTEN TO YOU IS TO BREAK THEIR THINGS...
BUT HE CAN AFFORD IT...
YEAH, BUT HE'LL STILL HAVE TO TAKE HIS CAR TO THE SHOP. I KICKED HIS DOOR PRETTY GOOD.

EVERYTHING GETS FUCKED UP

BUT OCCASIONALLY GETS REPAIRED

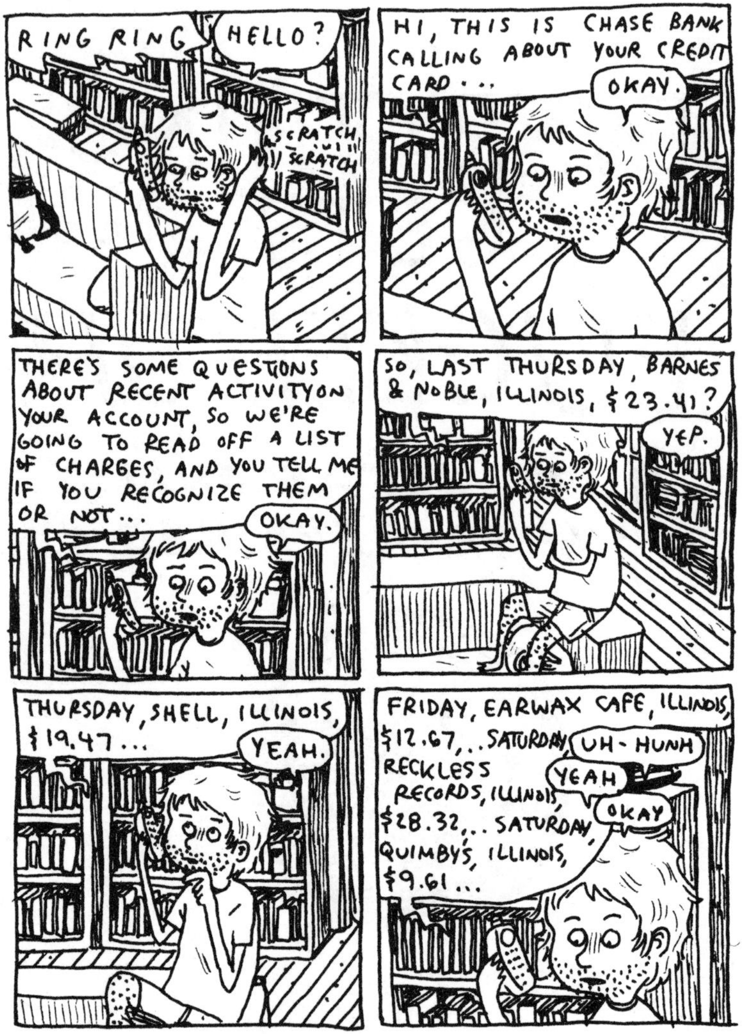
RING RING
HELLO?
SCRATCH SCRATCH
HI, THIS IS CHASE BANK CALLING ABOUT YOUR CREDIT CARD...
OKAY.
THERE'S SOME QUESTIONS ABOUT RECENT ACTIVITY ON YOUR ACCOUNT, SO WE'RE GOING TO READ OFF A LIST OF CHARGES, AND YOU TELL ME IF YOU RECOGNIZE THEM OR NOT...
OKAY.
SO, LAST THURSDAY, BARNES & NOBLE, ILLINOIS, $23.41?
YEP.
THURSDAY, SHELL, ILLINOIS, $19.47...
YEAH.
FRIDAY, EARWAX CAFE, ILLINOIS, $12.67,.. SATURDAY, RECKLESS RECORDS, ILLINOIS, $28.32,.. SATURDAY, QUIMBY'S, ILLINOIS, $9.61...
UH-HUNH
YEAH
OKAY

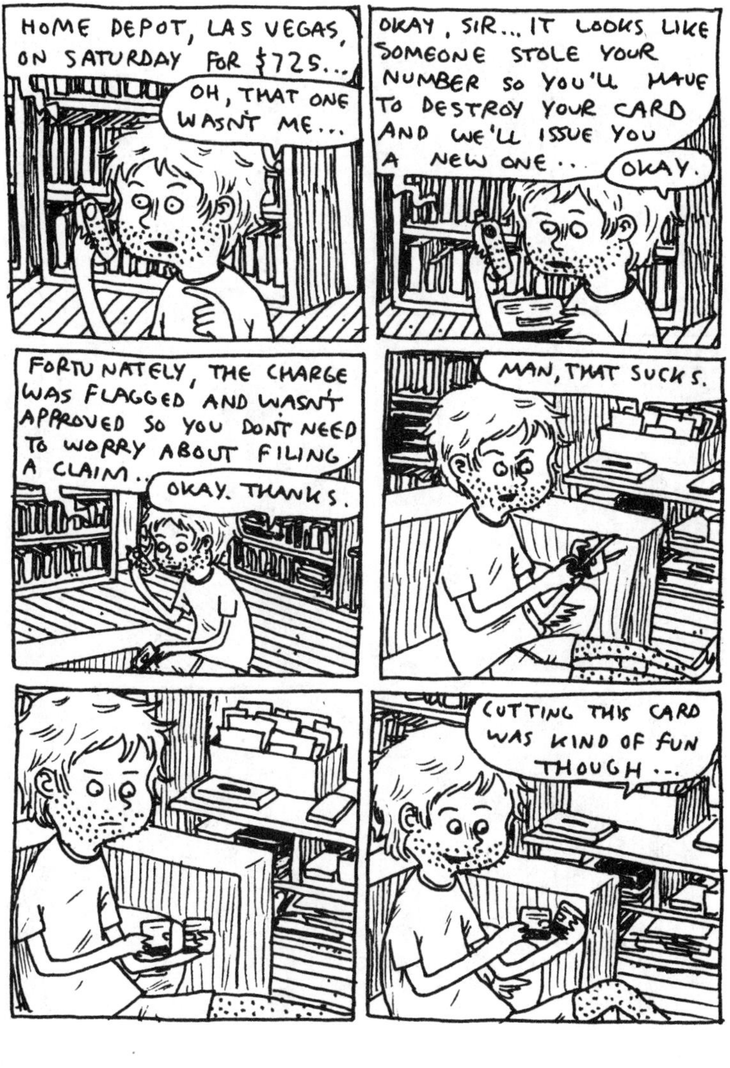
HOME DEPOT, LAS VEGAS, ON SATURDAY FOR $725...
OH, THAT ONE WASN'T ME...
OKAY, SIR... IT LOOKS LIKE SOMEONE STOLE YOUR NUMBER SO YOU'LL HAVE TO DESTROY YOUR CARD AND WE'LL ISSUE YOU A NEW ONE...
OKAY.
FORTUNATELY, THE CHARGE WAS FLAGGED AND WASN'T APPROVED SO YOU DON'T NEED TO WORRY ABOUT FILING A CLAIM...
OKAY. THANKS.
MAN, THAT SUCKS.
CUTTING THIS CARD WAS KIND OF FUN THOUGH...

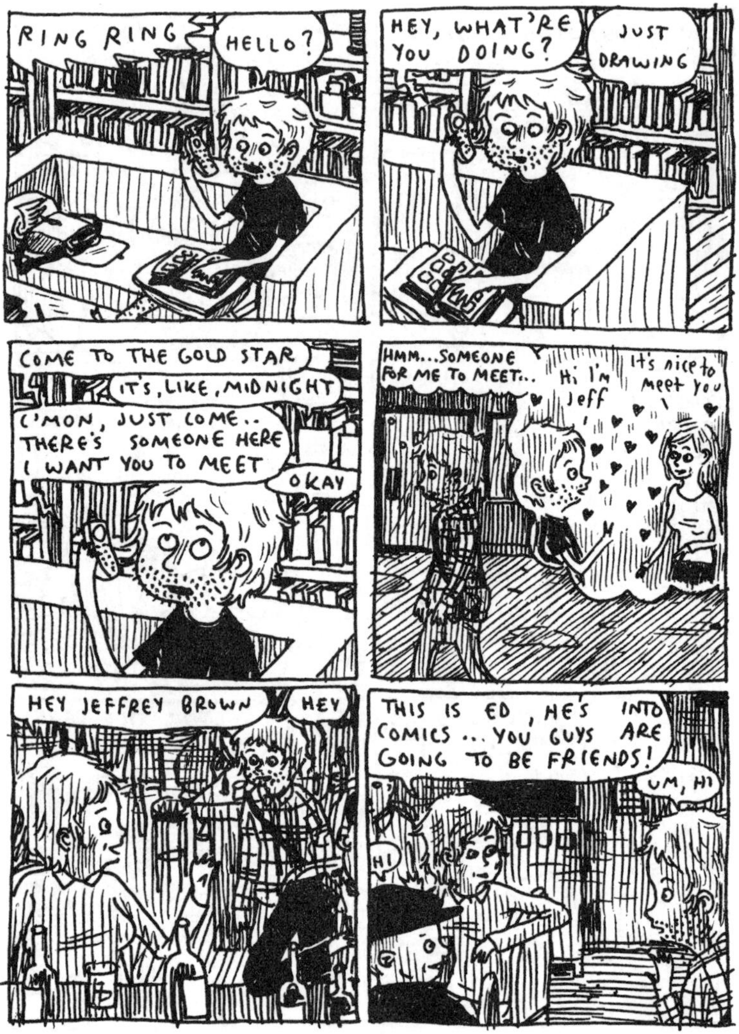
RING RING
HELLO?
HEY, WHAT'RE YOU DOING?
JUST DRAWING
COME TO THE GOLD STAR
IT'S, LIKE, MIDNIGHT
C'MON, JUST COME.. THERE'S SOMEONE HERE I WANT YOU TO MEET
OKAY
HMM...SOMEONE FOR ME TO MEET...
Hi I'm Jeff
It's nice to meet you
HEY JEFFREY BROWN
HEY
THIS IS ED, HE'S INTO COMICS ... YOU GUYS ARE GOING TO BE FRIENDS!
UM, HI
HI

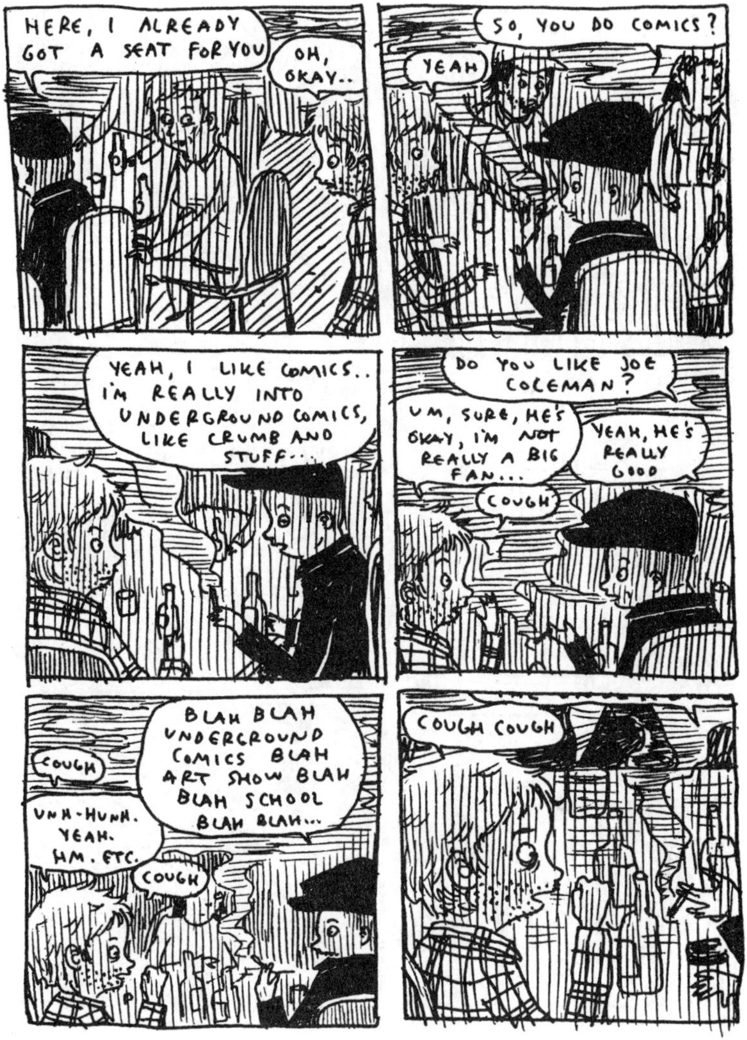
HERE, I ALREADY GOT A SEAT FOR YOU
OH, OKAY..
SO, YOU DO COMICS?
YEAH
YEAH, I LIKE COMICS.. I'M REALLY INTO UNDERGROUND COMICS, LIKE CRUMB AND STUFF...
DO YOU LIKE JOE COLEMAN?
UM, SURE, HE'S OKAY, I'M NOT REALLY A BIG FAN...
YEAH, HE'S REALLY GOOD
COUGH
COUGH
BLAH BLAH UNDERGROUND COMICS BLAH ART SHOW BLAH BLAH SCHOOL BLAH BLAH...
UNH-HUNH. YEAH. HM. ETC.
COUGH
COUGH COUGH

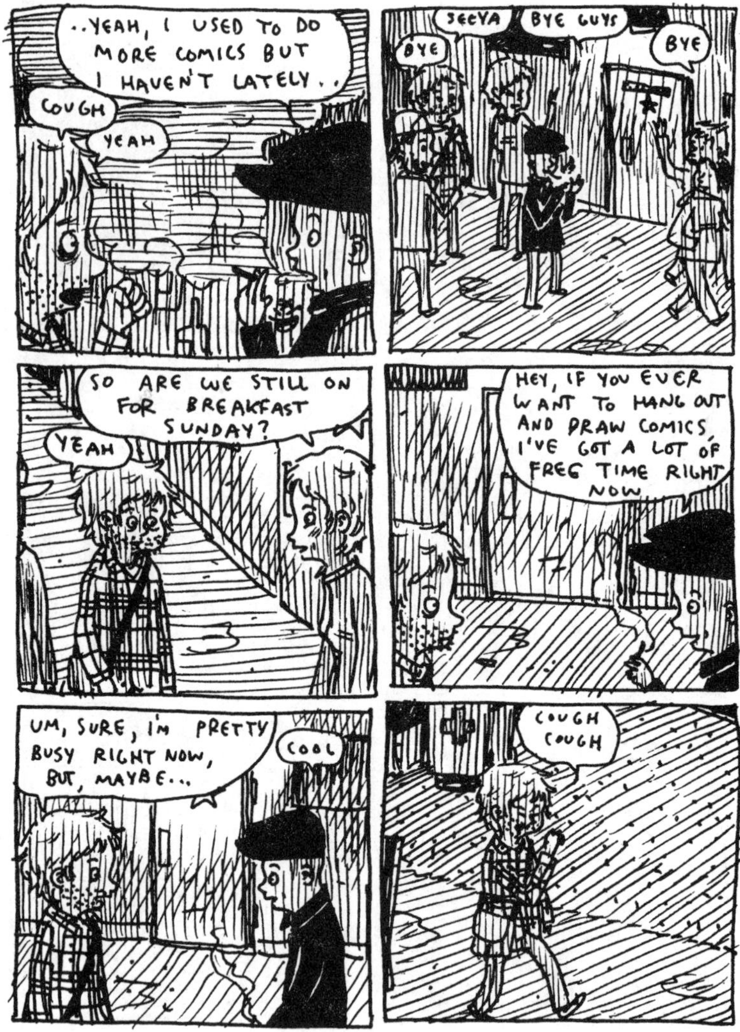
..YEAH, I USED TO DO MORE COMICS BUT I HAVEN'T LATELY..
COUGH
YEAH
SEEYA
BYE GUYS
BYE
BYE
SO ARE WE STILL ON FOR BREAKFAST SUNDAY?
YEAH
HEY, IF YOU EVER WANT TO HANG OUT AND DRAW COMICS, I'VE GOT A LOT OF FREE TIME RIGHT NOW
UM, SURE, I'M PRETTY BUSY RIGHT NOW, BUT, MAYBE...
COOL
COUGH COUGH

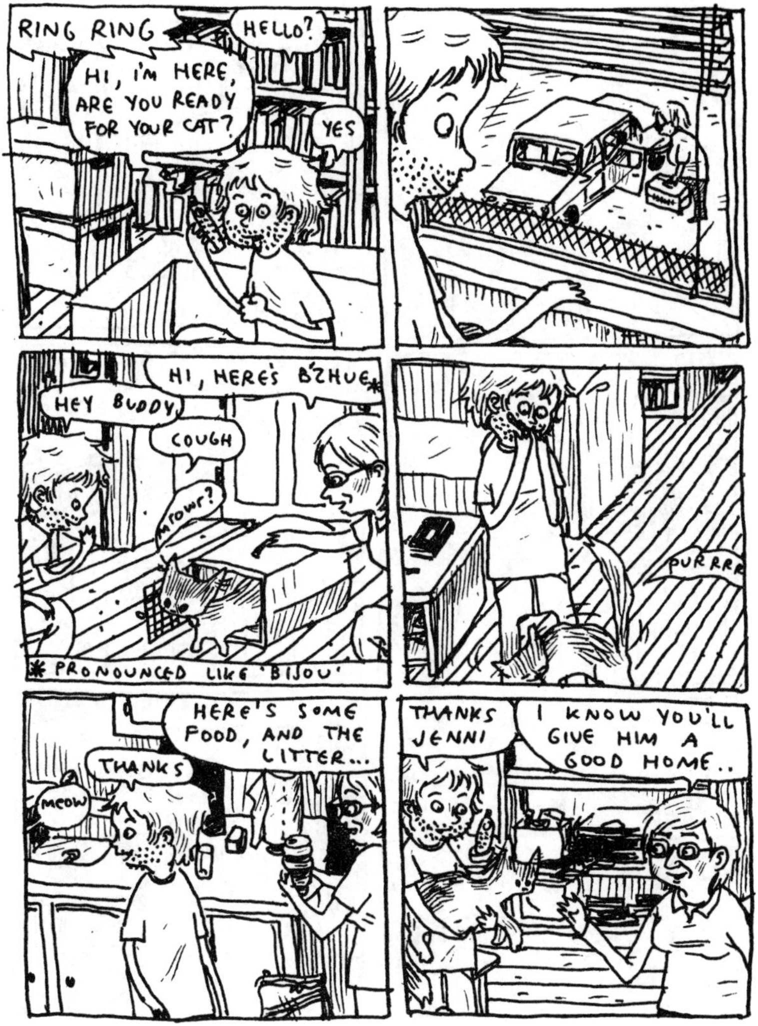
RING RING
HELLO?
HI, I'M HERE, ARE YOU READY FOR YOUR CAT?
YES
HI, HERE'S B'ZHUE*
HEY BUDDY
COUGH
MROWR?
* PRONOUNCED LIKE 'BIJOU'
PURRRR
HERE'S SOME FOOD, AND THE LITTER...
THANKS
MEOW
THANKS JENNI
I KNOW YOU'LL GIVE HIM A GOOD HOME..

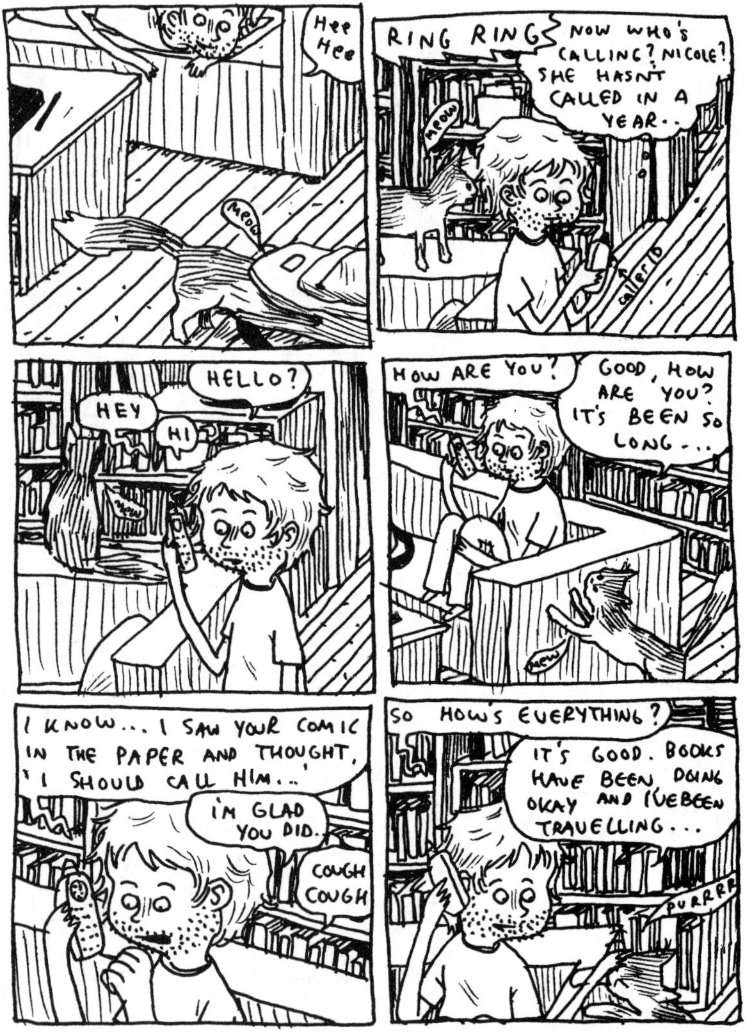
Hee Hee
MEOW
RING RING
NOW WHO'S CALLING? NICOLE? SHE HASN'T CALLED IN A YEAR..
MEOW
caller ID
HELLO?
HEY
HI
MEOW
HOW ARE YOU?
GOOD, HOW ARE YOU? IT'S BEEN SO LONG...
MEW
I KNOW... I SAW YOUR COMIC IN THE PAPER AND THOUGHT, 'I SHOULD CALL HIM..'
I'M GLAD YOU DID..
COUGH COUGH
SO HOW'S EVERYTHING?
IT'S GOOD. BOOKS HAVE BEEN DOING OKAY AND I'VE BEEN TRAVELLING...
PURRRR

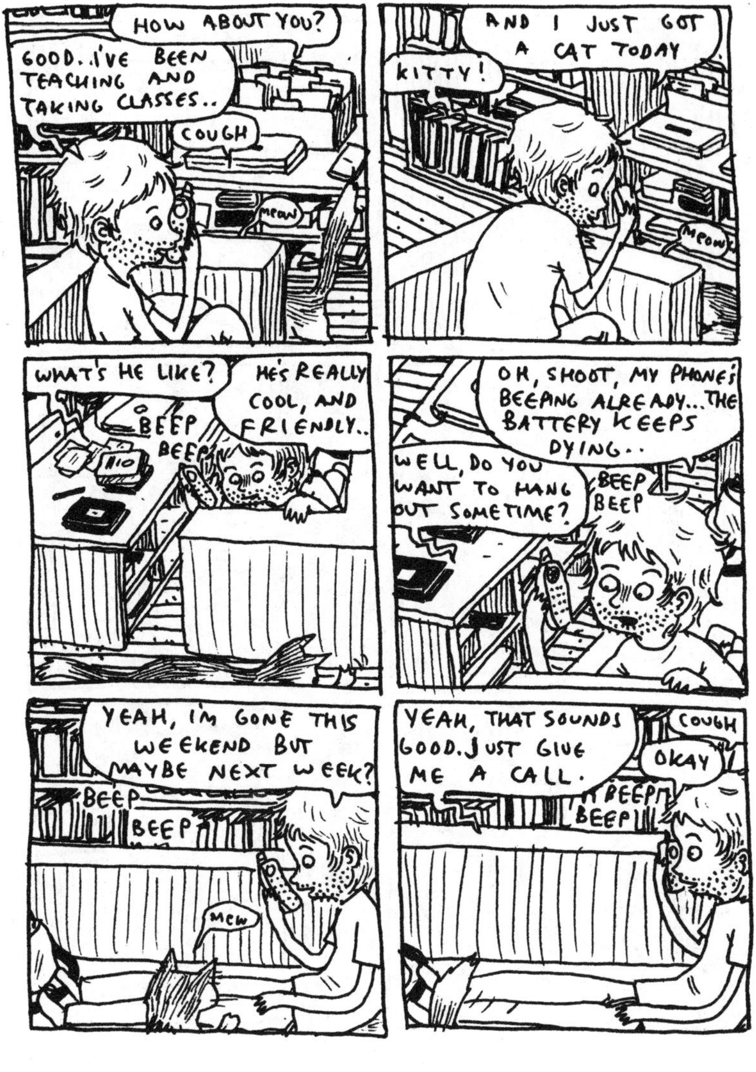
HOW ABOUT YOU?
GOOD. I'VE BEEN TEACHING AND TAKING CLASSES..
COUGH
MEOW
AND I JUST GOT A CAT TODAY
KITTY!
MEOW
WHAT'S HE LIKE?
HE'S REALLY COOL, AND FRIENDLY..
BEEP
BEEP
OH, SHOOT, MY PHONE'S BEEPING ALREADY... THE BATTERY KEEPS DYING..
WELL, DO YOU WANT TO HANG OUT SOMETIME?
BEEP
BEEP
YEAH, I'M GONE THIS WEEKEND BUT MAYBE NEXT WEEK?
BEEP
BEEP
MEW
YEAH, THAT SOUNDS GOOD. JUST GIVE ME A CALL.
COUGH
OKAY
BEEP
BEEP

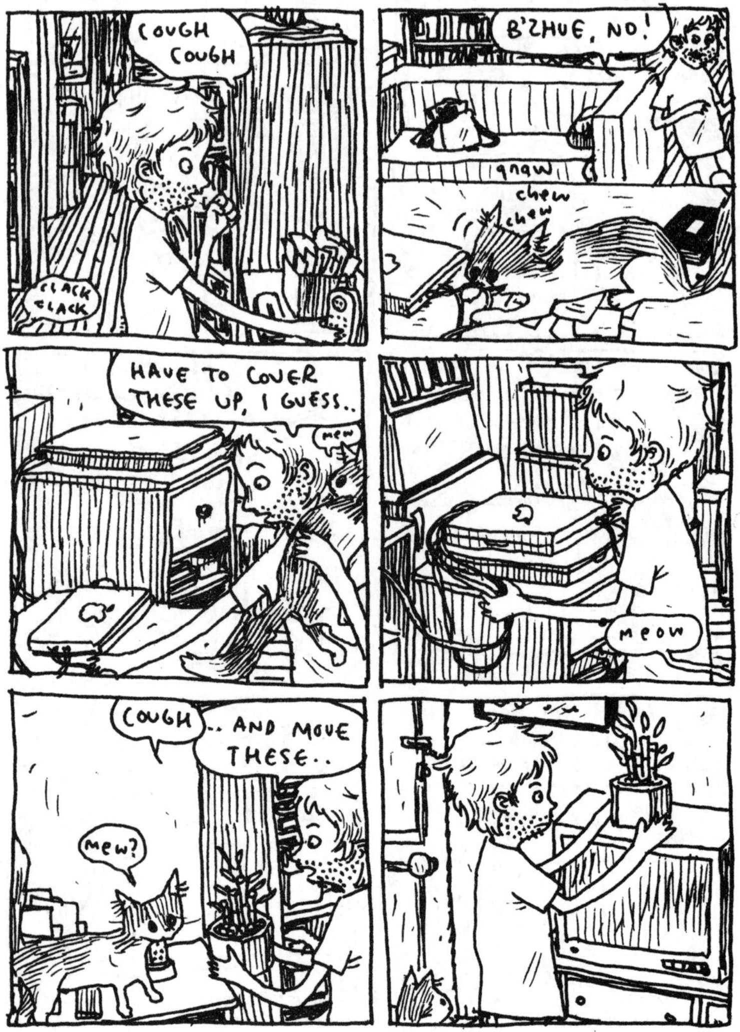
COUGH COUGH
CLACK CLACK
B'ZHUE, NO!
gnaw
chew chew
HAVE TO COVER THESE UP, I GUESS..
mew
MEOW
COUGH
.. AND MOVE THESE..
mew?

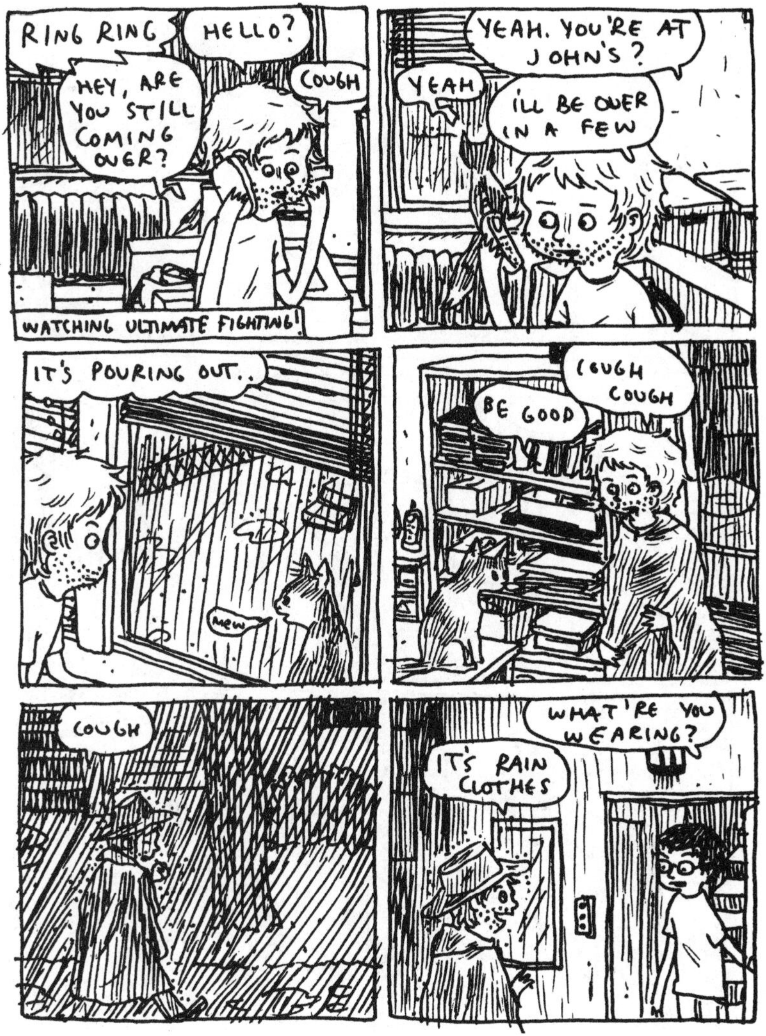
RING RING
HELLO?
HEY, ARE YOU STILL COMING OVER?
COUGH
WATCHING ULTIMATE FIGHTING!
YEAH. YOU'RE AT JOHN'S?
YEAH
I'LL BE OVER IN A FEW
IT'S POURING OUT..
MEW
COUGH COUGH
BE GOOD
COUGH
WHAT'RE YOU WEARING?
IT'S RAIN CLOTHES

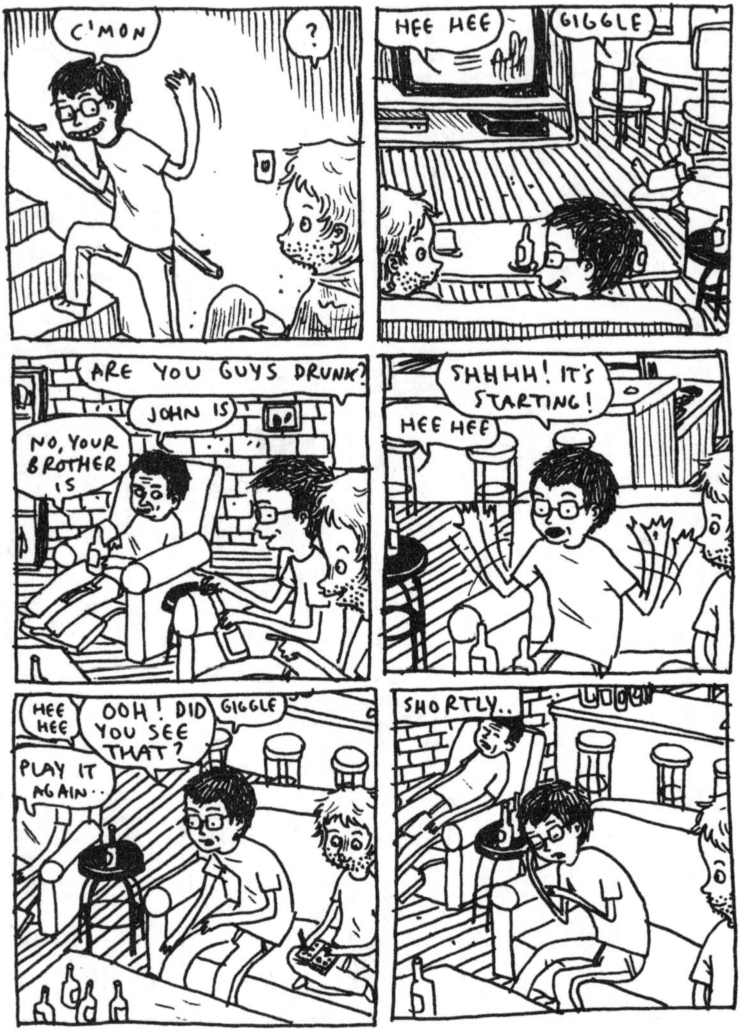
C'MON
?
HEE HEE
GIGGLE
ARE YOU GUYS DRUNK?
JOHN IS
NO, YOUR BROTHER IS
SHHHH! IT'S STARTING!
HEE HEE
HEE HEE
OOH! DID YOU SEE THAT?
GIGGLE
PLAY IT AGAIN..
SHORTLY..

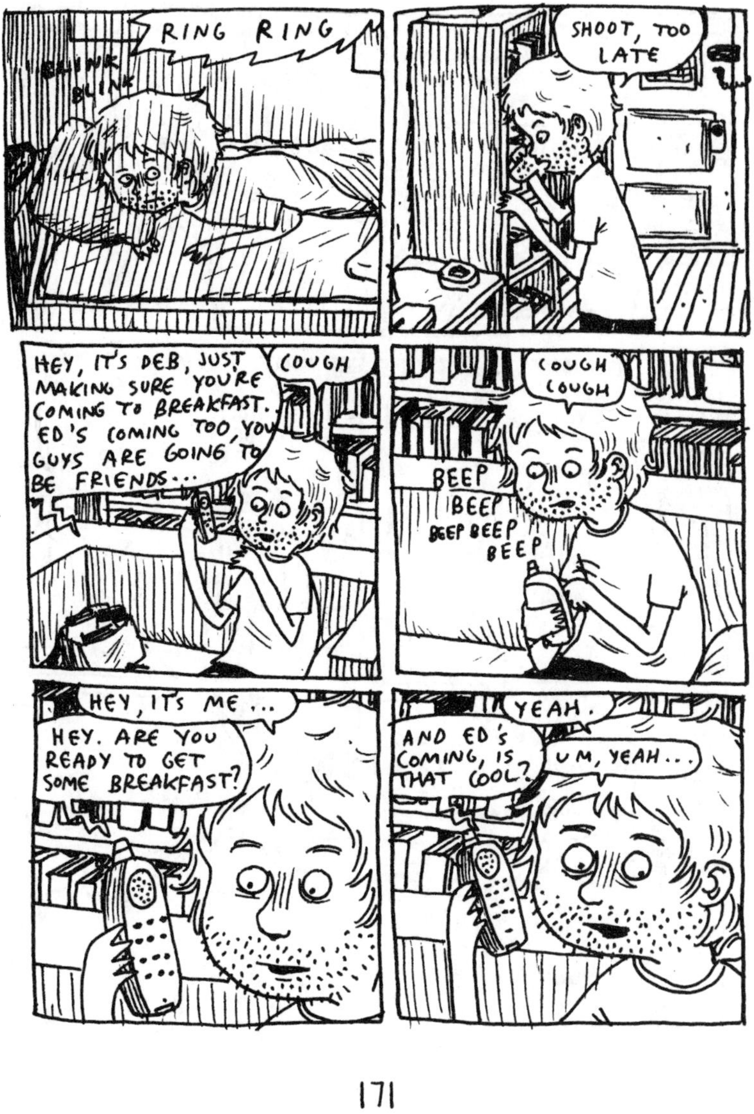
RING RING
BLINK BLINK
SHOOT, TOO LATE
HEY, IT'S DEB, JUST MAKING SURE YOU'RE COMING TO BREAKFAST... ED'S COMING TOO, YOU GUYS ARE GOING TO BE FRIENDS...
COUGH
COUGH COUGH
BEEP BEEP BEEP BEEP BEEP
HEY, IT'S ME...
HEY. ARE YOU READY TO GET SOME BREAKFAST?
YEAH.
AND ED'S COMING, IS THAT COOL?
UM, YEAH...

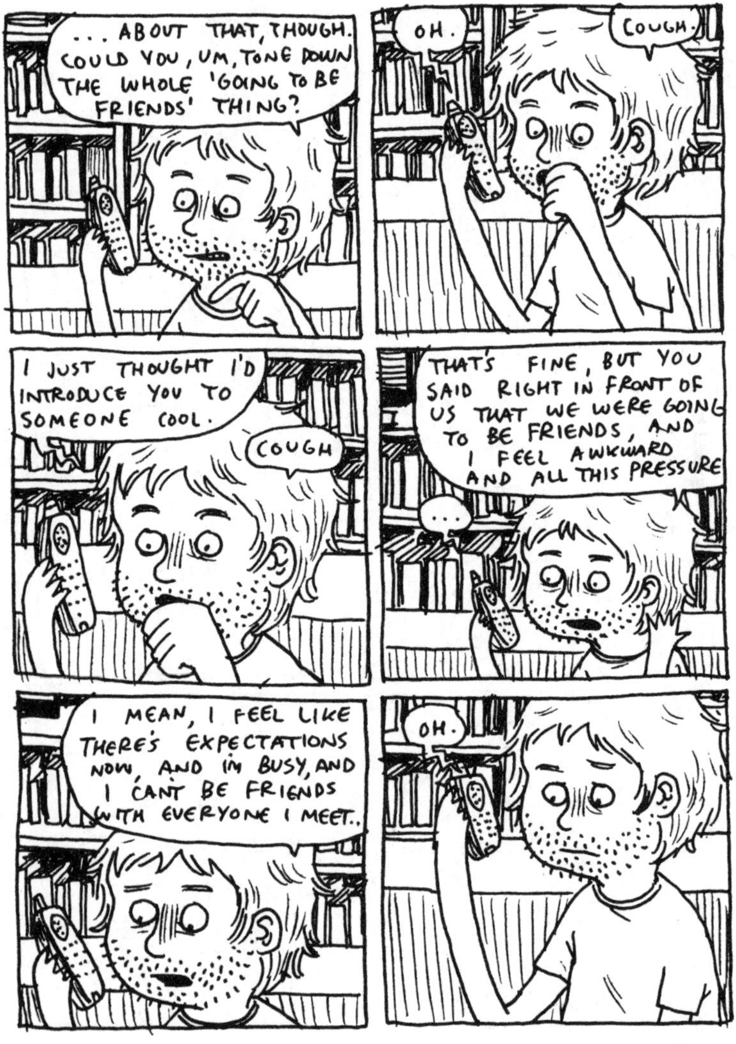
... ABOUT THAT, THOUGH. COULD YOU, UM, TONE DOWN THE WHOLE 'GOING TO BE FRIENDS' THING?
OH.
COUGH.
I JUST THOUGHT I'D INTRODUCE YOU TO SOMEONE COOL.
COUGH
THAT'S FINE, BUT YOU SAID RIGHT IN FRONT OF US THAT WE WERE GOING TO BE FRIENDS, AND I FEEL AWKWARD AND ALL THIS PRESSURE
...
I MEAN, I FEEL LIKE THERE'S EXPECTATIONS NOW, AND I'M BUSY, AND I CAN'T BE FRIENDS WITH EVERYONE I MEET.
OH.

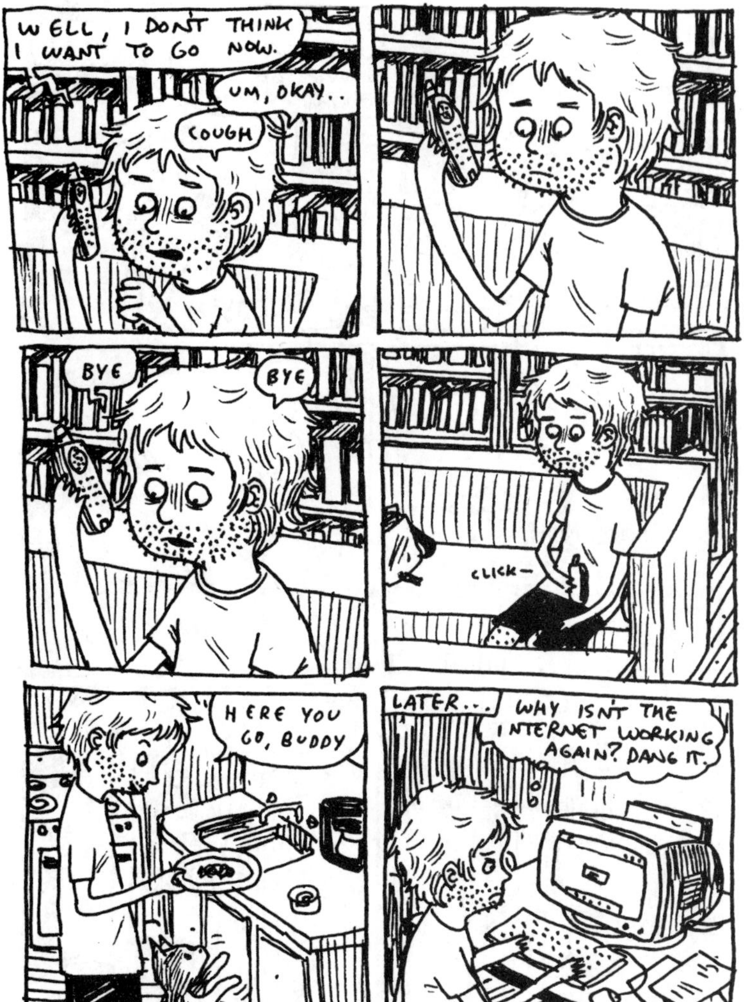
WELL, I DON'T THINK I WANT TO GO NOW.
UM, OKAY..
COUGH
BYE
BYE
CLICK—
HERE YOU GO, BUDDY
LATER...
WHY ISN'T THE INTERNET WORKING AGAIN? DANG IT.

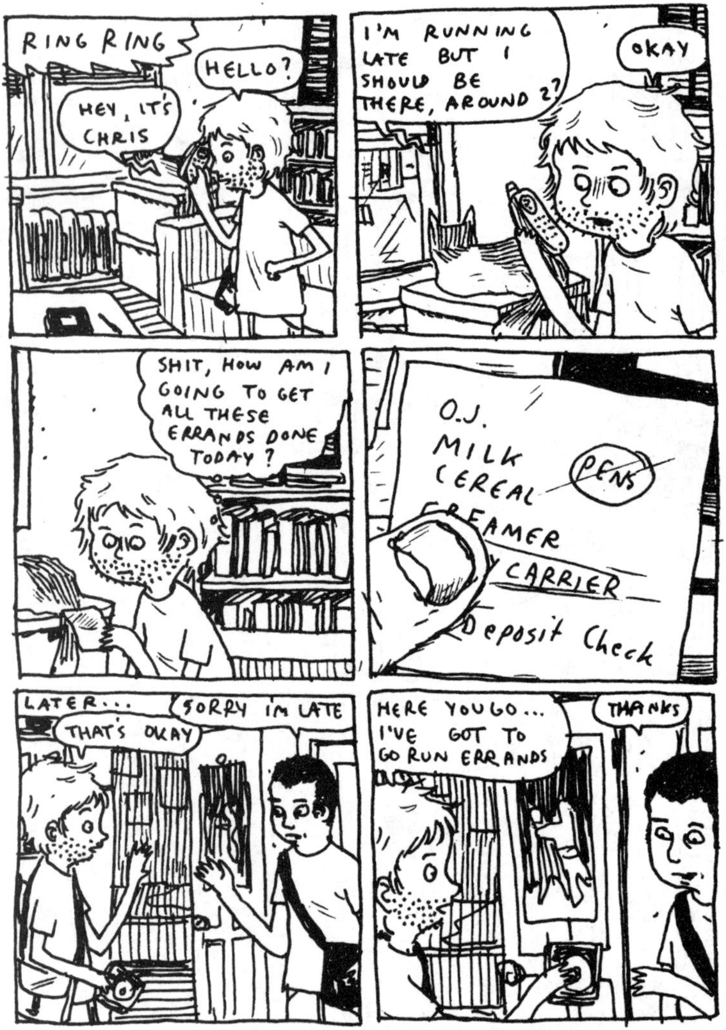
RING RING
HELLO?
HEY, IT'S CHRIS
I'M RUNNING LATE BUT I SHOULD BE THERE, AROUND 2?
OKAY
SHIT, HOW AM I GOING TO GET ALL THESE ERRANDS DONE TODAY?
O.J.
MILK
CEREAL
PENS
CREAMER
CARRIER
Deposit Check
LATER...
SORRY IM LATE
THAT'S OKAY
HERE YOU GO... I'VE GOT TO GO RUN ERRANDS
THANKS

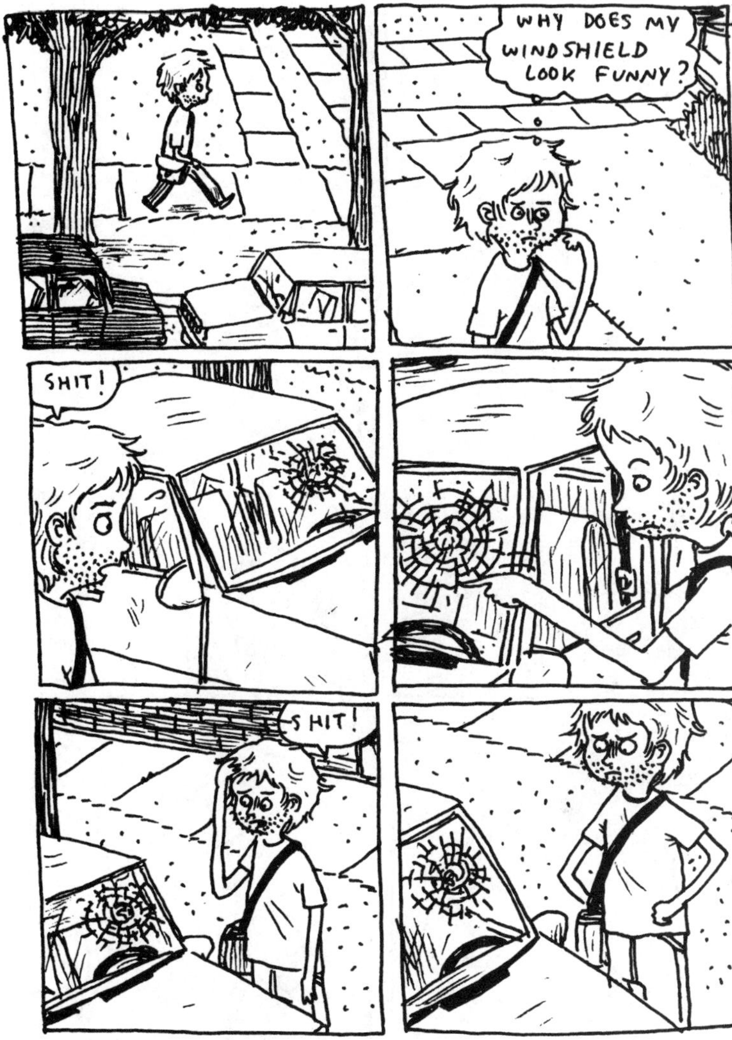
WHY DOES MY WINDSHIELD LOOK FUNNY?
SHIT!
SHIT!

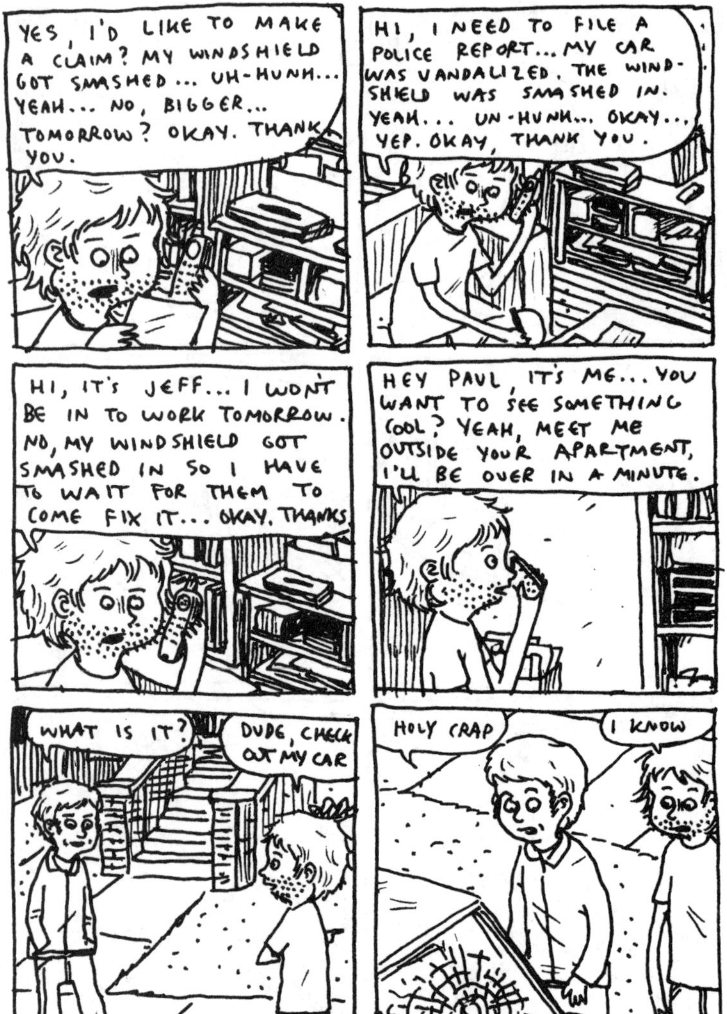
YES, I'D LIKE TO MAKE A CLAIM? MY WINDSHIELD GOT SMASHED... UH-HUNH... YEAH... NO, BIGGER... TOMORROW? OKAY. THANK YOU.
HI, I NEED TO FILE A POLICE REPORT... MY CAR WAS VANDALIZED. THE WINDSHIELD WAS SMASHED IN. YEAH... UN-HUNH... OKAY... YEP. OKAY, THANK YOU.
HI, IT'S JEFF... I WON'T BE IN TO WORK TOMORROW. NO, MY WINDSHIELD GOT SMASHED IN SO I HAVE TO WAIT FOR THEM TO COME FIX IT... OKAY. THANKS
HEY PAUL, IT'S ME... YOU WANT TO SEE SOMETHING COOL? YEAH, MEET ME OUTSIDE YOUR APARTMENT, I'LL BE OVER IN A MINUTE.
WHAT IS IT?
DUDE, CHECK OUT MY CAR
HOLY CRAP
I KNOW

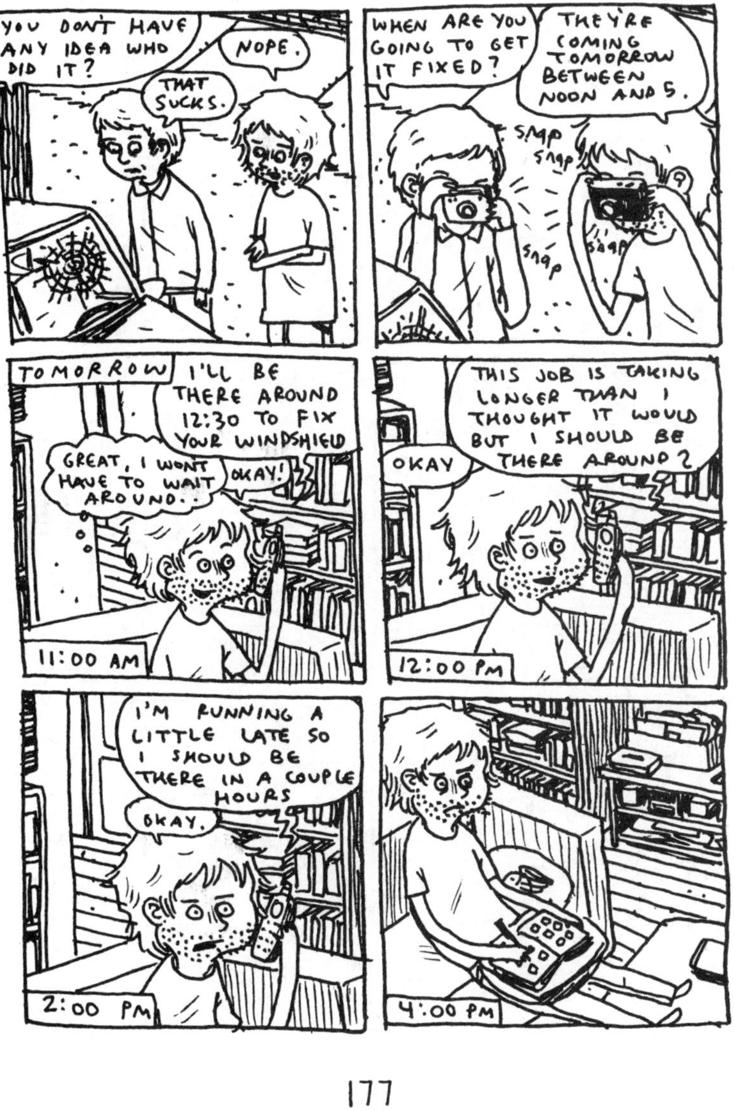
YOU DON'T HAVE ANY IDEA WHO DID IT?
NOPE.
THAT SUCKS.
WHEN ARE YOU GOING TO GET IT FIXED?
THEY'RE COMING TOMORROW BETWEEN NOON AND 5.
SNAP
SNAP
SNAP
SNAP
TOMORROW
I'LL BE THERE AROUND 12:30 TO FIX YOUR WINDSHIELD
GREAT, I WONT HAVE TO WAIT AROUND..
OKAY!
11:00 AM
THIS JOB IS TAKING LONGER THAN I THOUGHT IT WOULD BUT I SHOULD BE THERE AROUND 2
OKAY
12:00 PM
I'M RUNNING A LITTLE LATE SO I SHOULD BE THERE IN A COUPLE HOURS
OKAY.
2:00 PM
4:00 PM

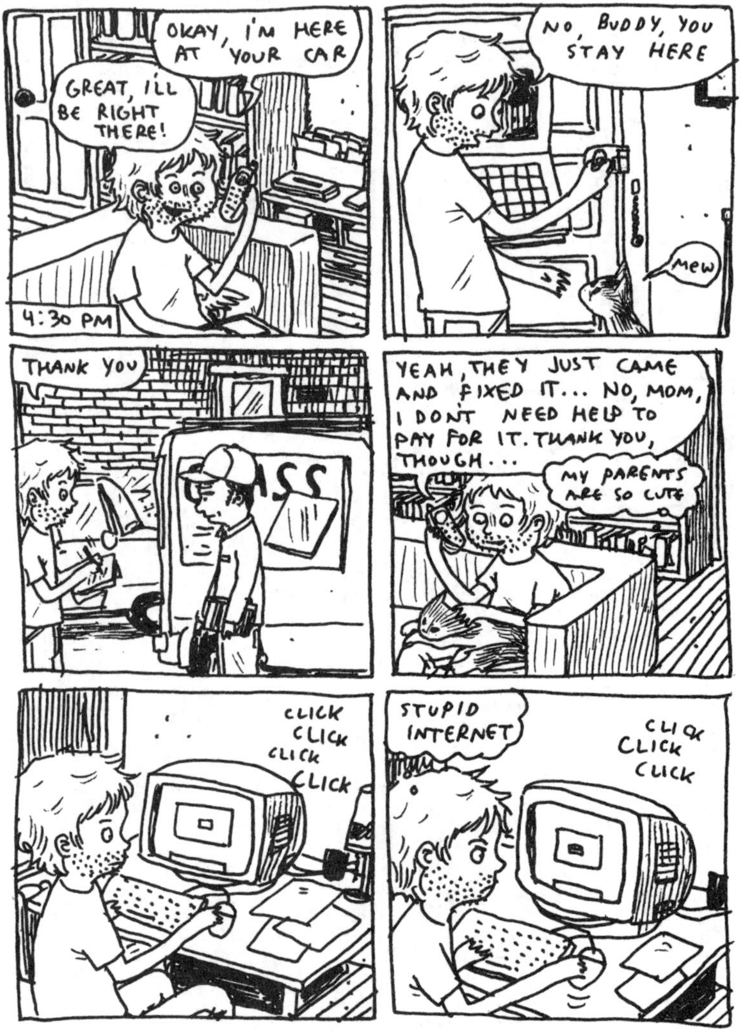
OKAY, I'M HERE AT YOUR CAR
GREAT, I'LL BE RIGHT THERE!
4:30 PM
NO, BUDDY, YOU STAY HERE
MEW
THANK YOU
YEAH, THEY JUST CAME AND FIXED IT... NO, MOM, I DONT NEED HELP TO PAY FOR IT. THANK YOU, THOUGH...
MY PARENTS ARE SO CUTE
CLICK CLICK CLICK CLICK
STUPID INTERNET
CLICK CLICK CLICK

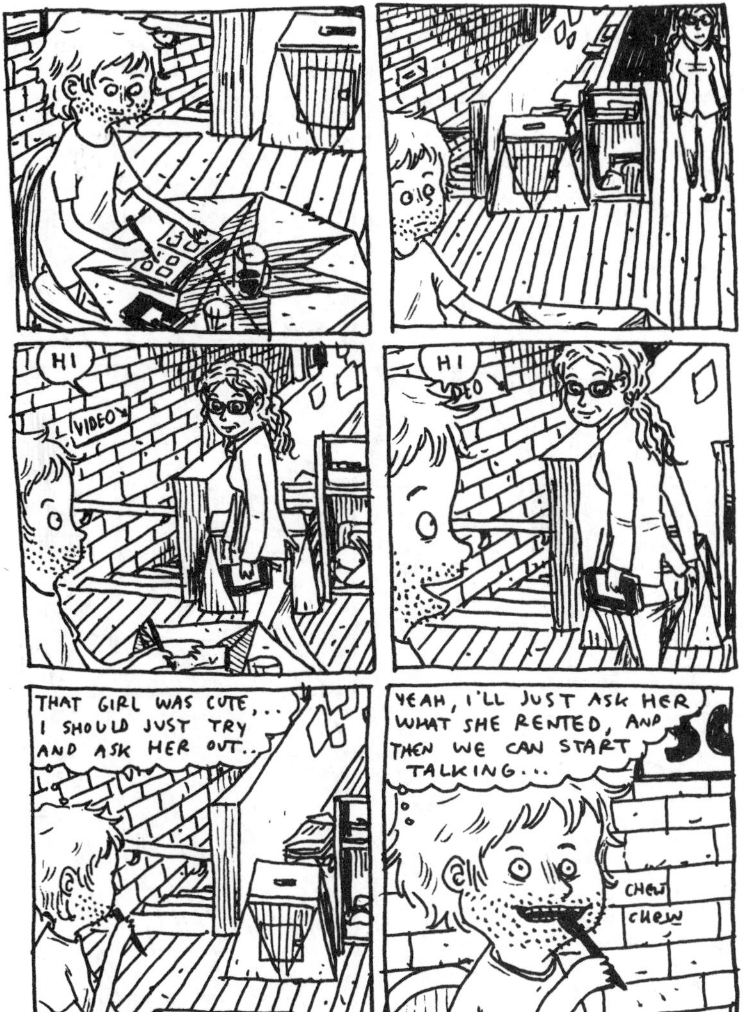
HI
VIDEO
HI
THAT GIRL WAS CUTE,... I SHOULD JUST TRY AND ASK HER OUT...
YEAH, I'LL JUST ASK HER WHAT SHE RENTED, AND THEN WE CAN START TALKING...
CHEW
CHEW

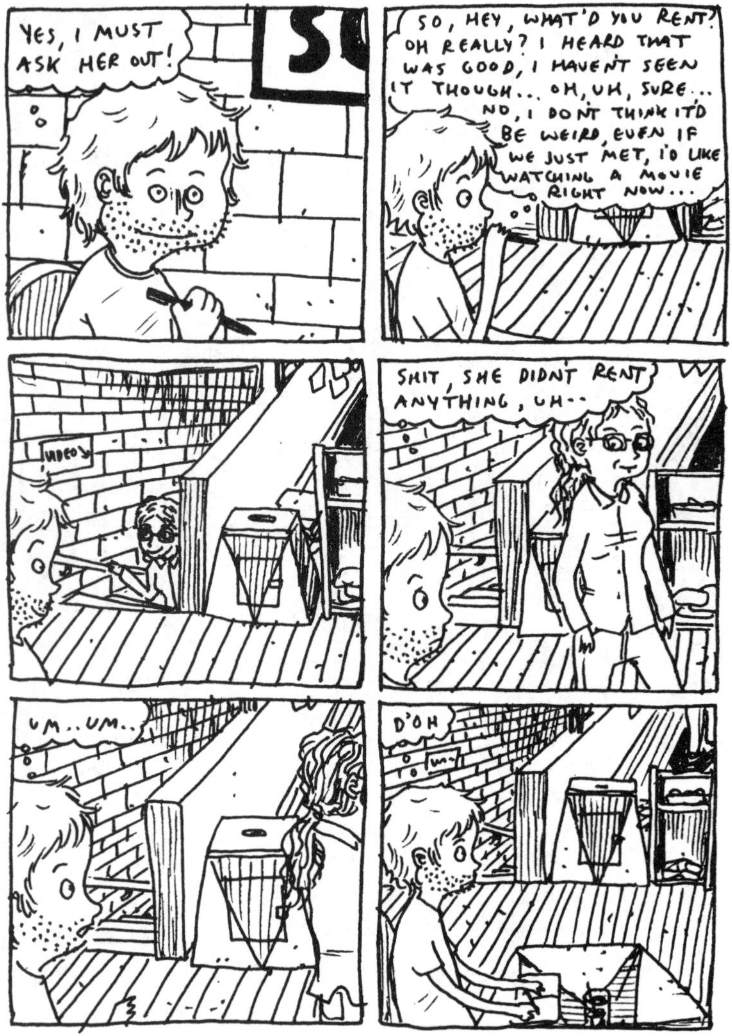
YES, I MUST ASK HER OUT!
SO, HEY, WHAT'D YOU RENT? OH REALLY? I HEARD THAT WAS GOOD, I HAVEN'T SEEN IT THOUGH... OH, UH, SURE... NO, I DON'T THINK IT'D BE WEIRD, EVEN IF WE JUST MET, I'D LIKE WATCHING A MOVIE RIGHT NOW...
VIDEOS
SHIT, SHE DIDN'T RENT ANYTHING, UH--
UM.. UM..
D'OH

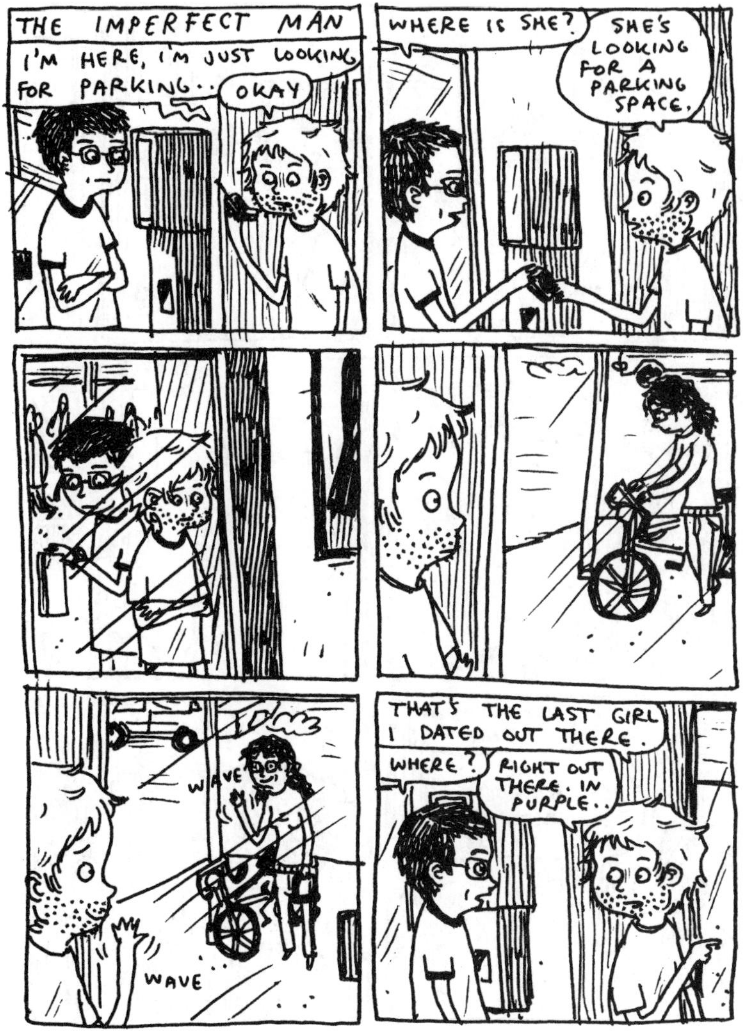
THE IMPERFECT MAN
I'M HERE, I'M JUST LOOKING FOR PARKING..
OKAY
WHERE IS SHE?
SHE'S LOOKING FOR A PARKING SPACE.
WAVE
WAVE
THAT'S THE LAST GIRL I DATED OUT THERE.
WHERE?
RIGHT OUT THERE. IN PURPLE..

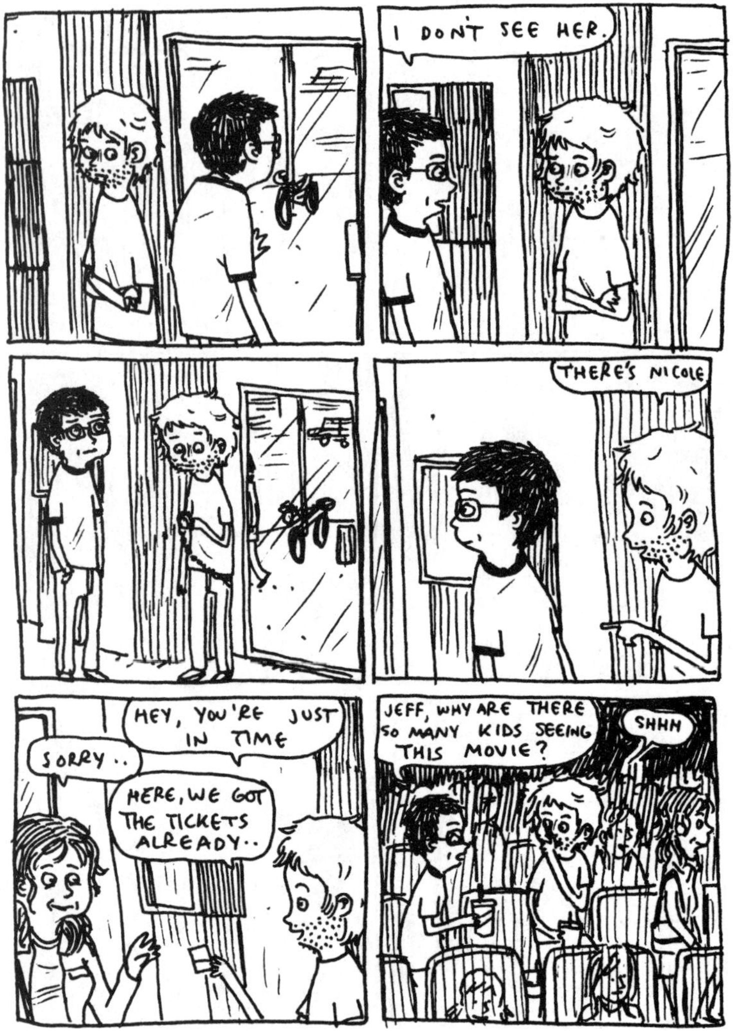
I DON'T SEE HER.
THERE'S NICOLE
HEY, YOU'RE JUST IN TIME
SORRY..
HERE, WE GOT THE TICKETS ALREADY..
JEFF, WHY ARE THERE SO MANY KIDS SEEING THIS MOVIE?
SHHH

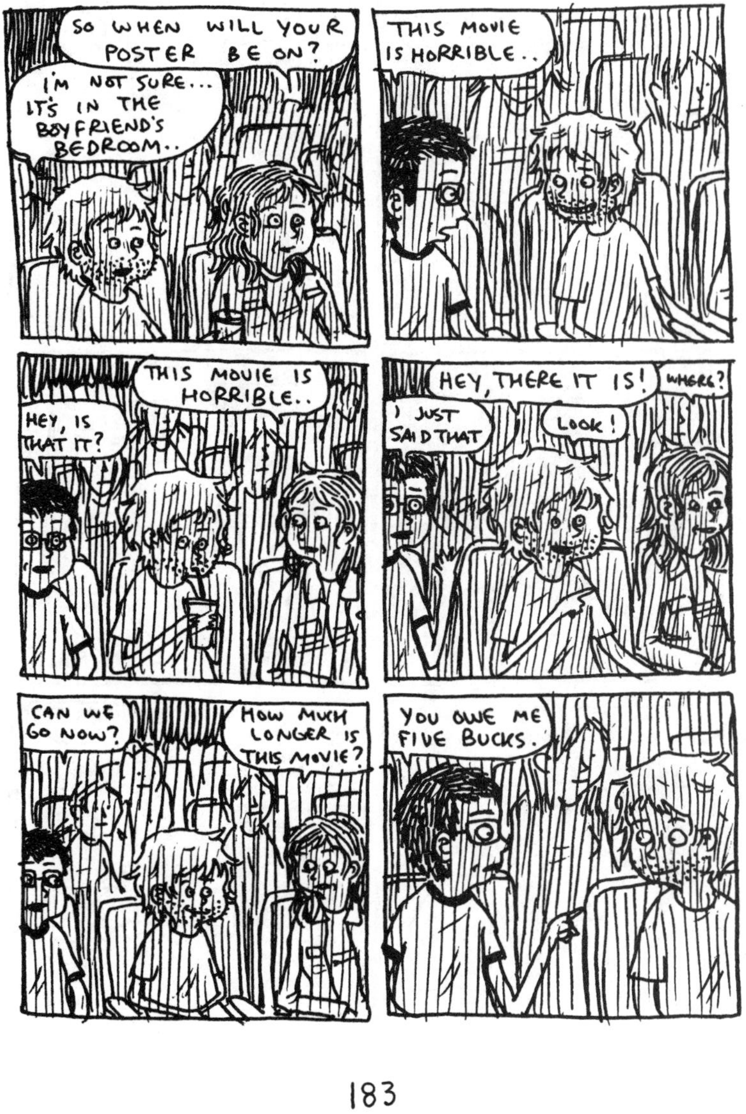
SO WHEN WILL YOUR POSTER BE ON?
I'M NOT SURE... IT'S IN THE BOYFRIEND'S BEDROOM..
THIS MOVIE IS HORRIBLE..
THIS MOVIE IS HORRIBLE..
HEY, IS THAT IT?
HEY, THERE IT IS!
WHERE?
I JUST SAID THAT
LOOK!
CAN WE GO NOW?
HOW MUCH LONGER IS THIS MOVIE?
YOU OWE ME FIVE BUCKS.

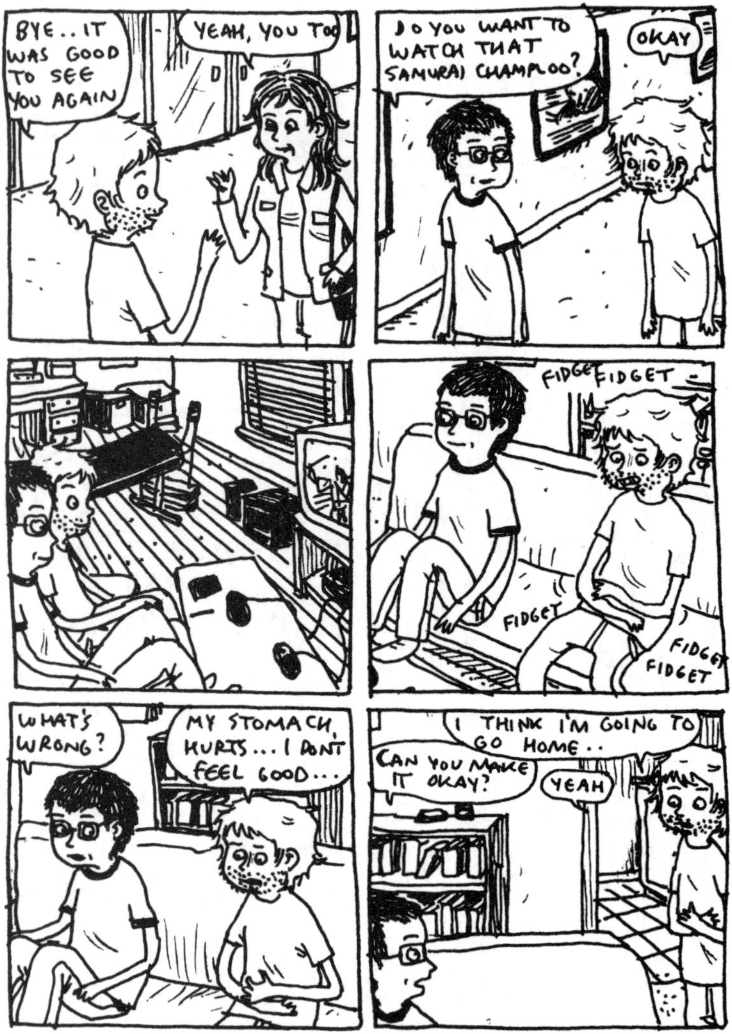
BYE.. IT WAS GOOD TO SEE YOU AGAIN
YEAH, YOU TOO
DO YOU WANT TO WATCH THAT SAMURAI CHAMPLOO?
OKAY
FIDGET FIDGET
FIDGET
FIDGET FIDGET
WHAT'S WRONG?
MY STOMACH HURTS... I DONT FEEL GOOD...
I THINK I'M GOING TO GO HOME..
CAN YOU MAKE IT OKAY?
YEAH

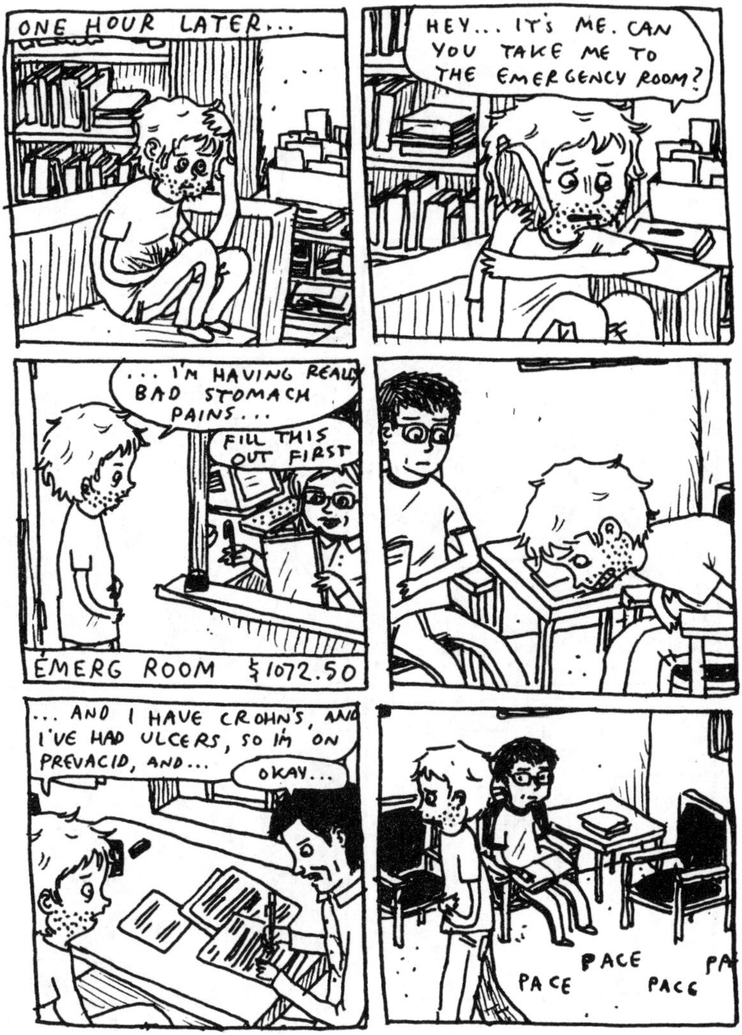
ONE HOUR LATER...
HEY... IT'S ME. CAN YOU TAKE ME TO THE EMERGENCY ROOM?
... I'M HAVING REALLY BAD STOMACH PAINS...
FILL THIS OUT FIRST
EMERG ROOM $1072.50
... AND I HAVE CROHN'S, AND I'VE HAD ULCERS, SO I'M ON PREVACID, AND...
OKAY...
PACE
PACE
PACE
PA

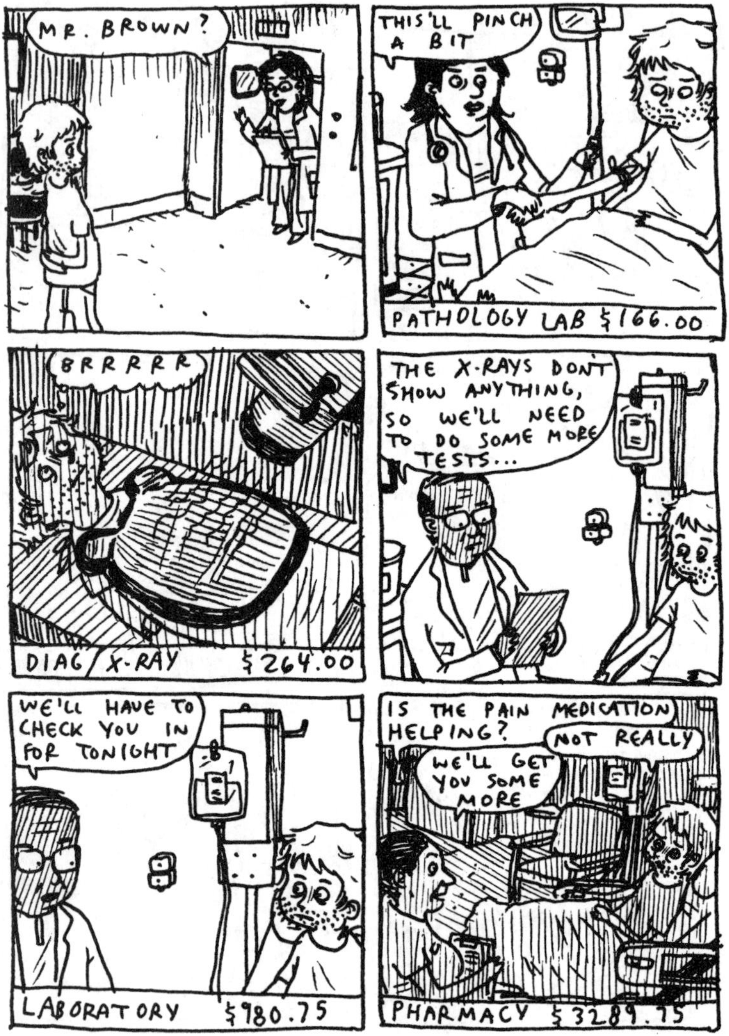
MR. BROWN?
THIS'LL PINCH A BIT
PATHOLOGY LAB $166.00
BRRRRR
DIAG X-RAY $264.00
THE X-RAYS DON'T SHOW ANYTHING, SO WE'LL NEED TO DO SOME MORE TESTS...
WE'LL HAVE TO CHECK YOU IN FOR TONIGHT
LABORATORY $980.75
IS THE PAIN MEDICATION HELPING?
NOT REALLY
WE'LL GET YOU SOME MORE
PHARMACY $3289.75

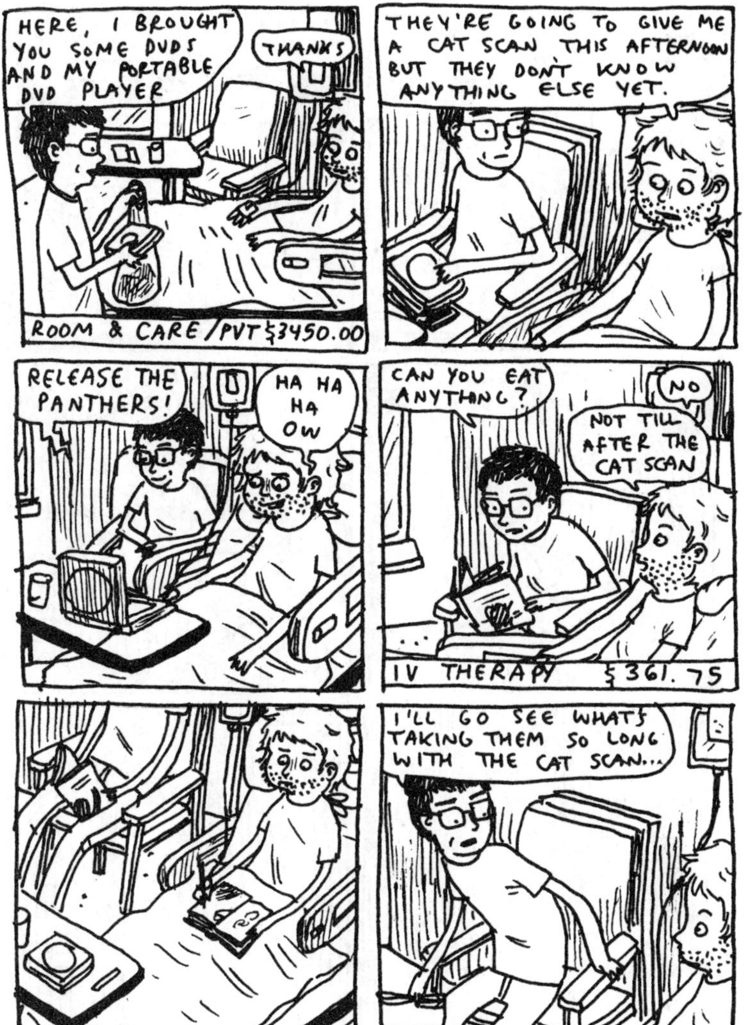
HERE, I BROUGHT YOU SOME DVDS AND MY PORTABLE DVD PLAYER
THANKS
ROOM & CARE / PVT $3450.00
THEY'RE GOING TO GIVE ME A CAT SCAN THIS AFTERNOON BUT THEY DON'T KNOW ANYTHING ELSE YET.
RELEASE THE PANTHERS!
HA HA HA OW
CAN YOU EAT ANYTHING?
NO
NOT TILL AFTER THE CAT SCAN
IV THERAPY $361.75
I'LL GO SEE WHAT'S TAKING THEM SO LONG WITH THE CAT SCAN...

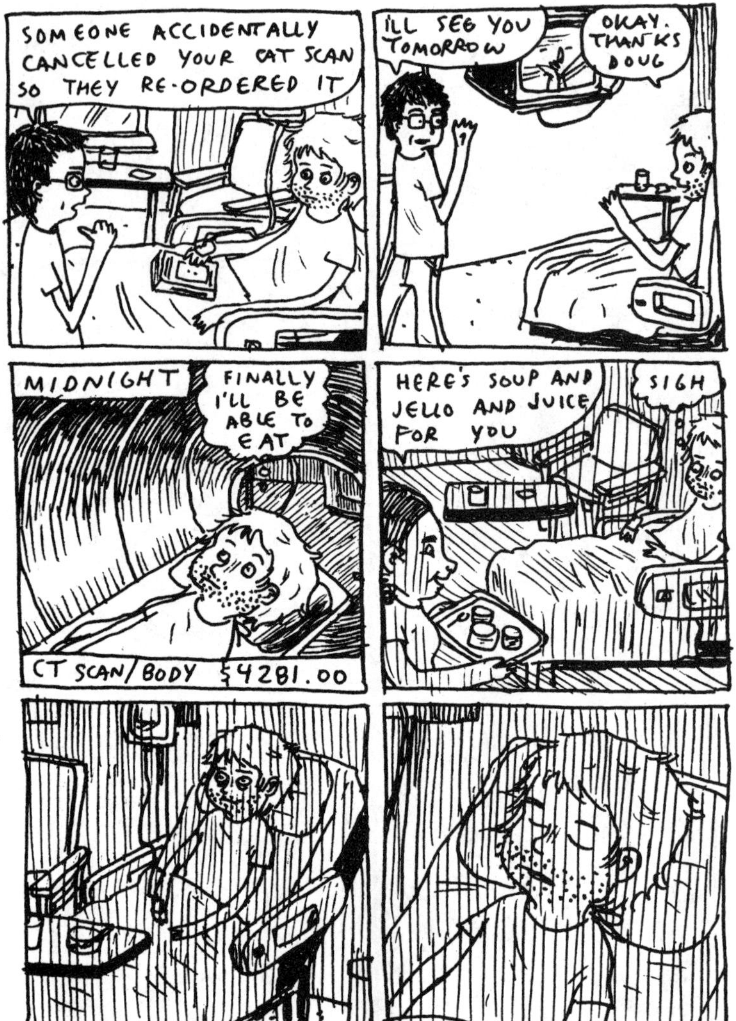
SOMEONE ACCIDENTALLY CANCELLED YOUR CAT SCAN SO THEY RE-ORDERED IT
I'LL SEE YOU TOMORROW
OKAY. THANKS DOUG
MIDNIGHT
FINALLY I'LL BE ABLE TO EAT
CT SCAN/BODY $4281.00
HERE'S SOUP AND JELLO AND JUICE FOR YOU
SIGH

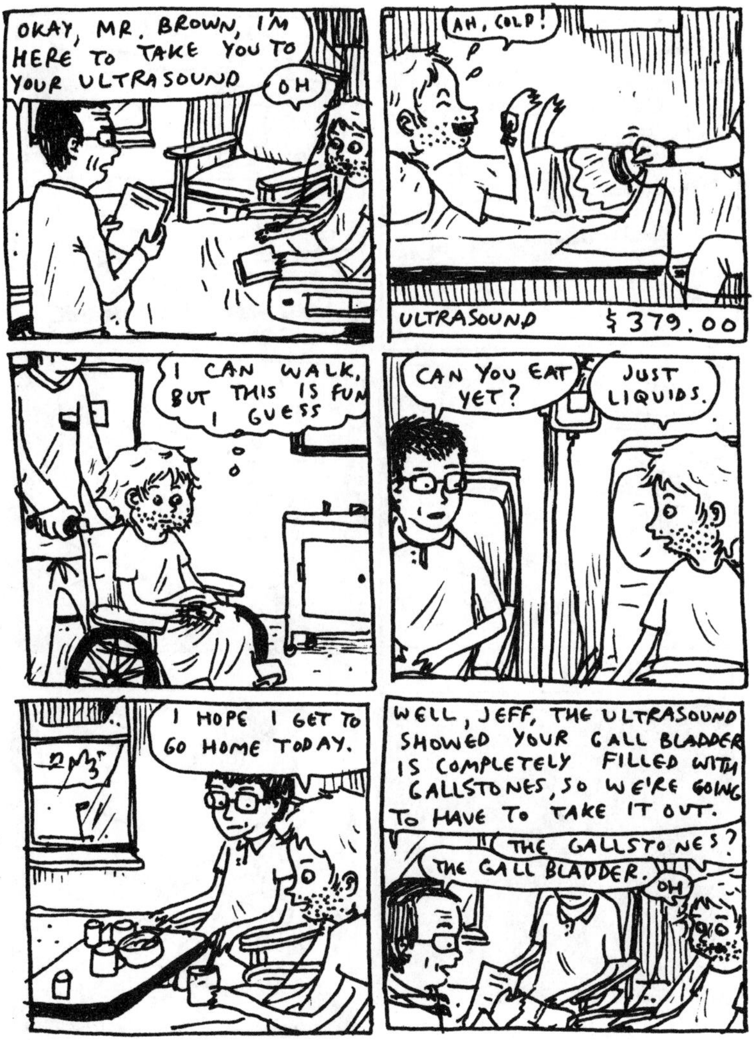
OKAY, MR. BROWN, I'M HERE TO TAKE YOU TO YOUR ULTRASOUND
OH
AH, COLD!
ULTRASOUND $379.00
I CAN WALK, BUT THIS IS FUN I GUESS
CAN YOU EAT YET?
JUST LIQUIDS.
I HOPE I GET TO GO HOME TODAY.
WELL, JEFF, THE ULTRASOUND SHOWED YOUR GALL BLADDER IS COMPLETELY FILLED WITH GALLSTONES, SO WE'RE GOING TO HAVE TO TAKE IT OUT.
THE GALLSTONES?
THE GALL BLADDER.
OH

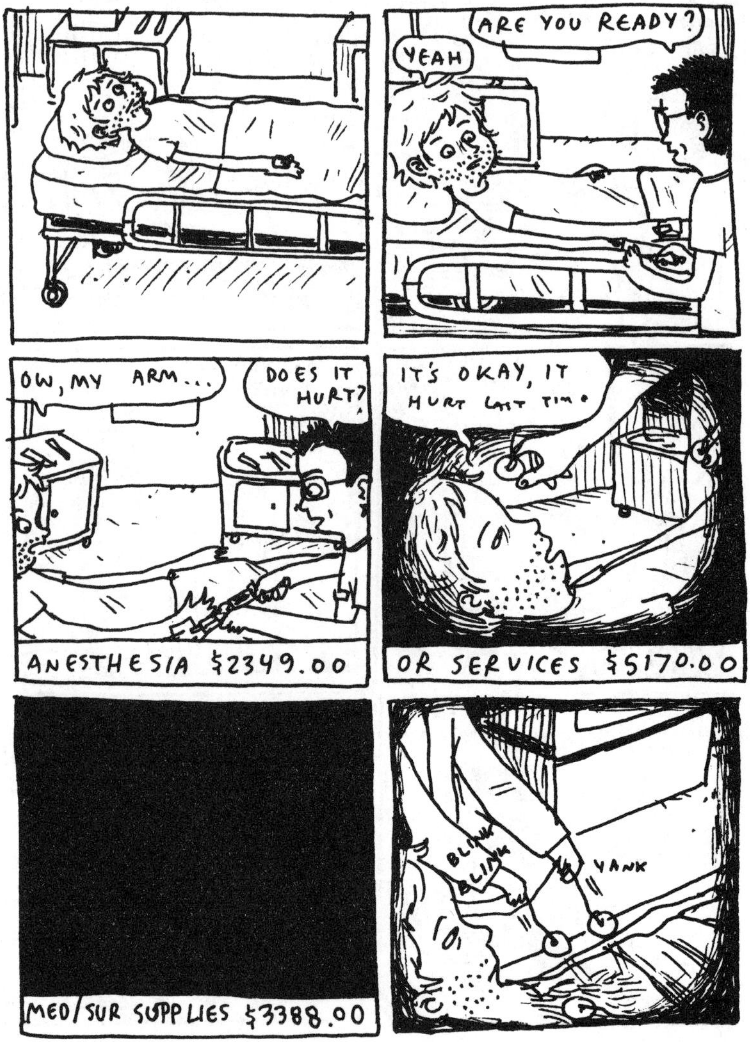
ARE YOU READY?
YEAH
OW, MY ARM...
DOES IT HURT?
ANESTHESIA $2349.00
IT'S OKAY, IT HURT LAST TIME.
OR SERVICES $5170.00
MED/SUR SUPPLIES $3388.00
BLINK BLINK
YANK

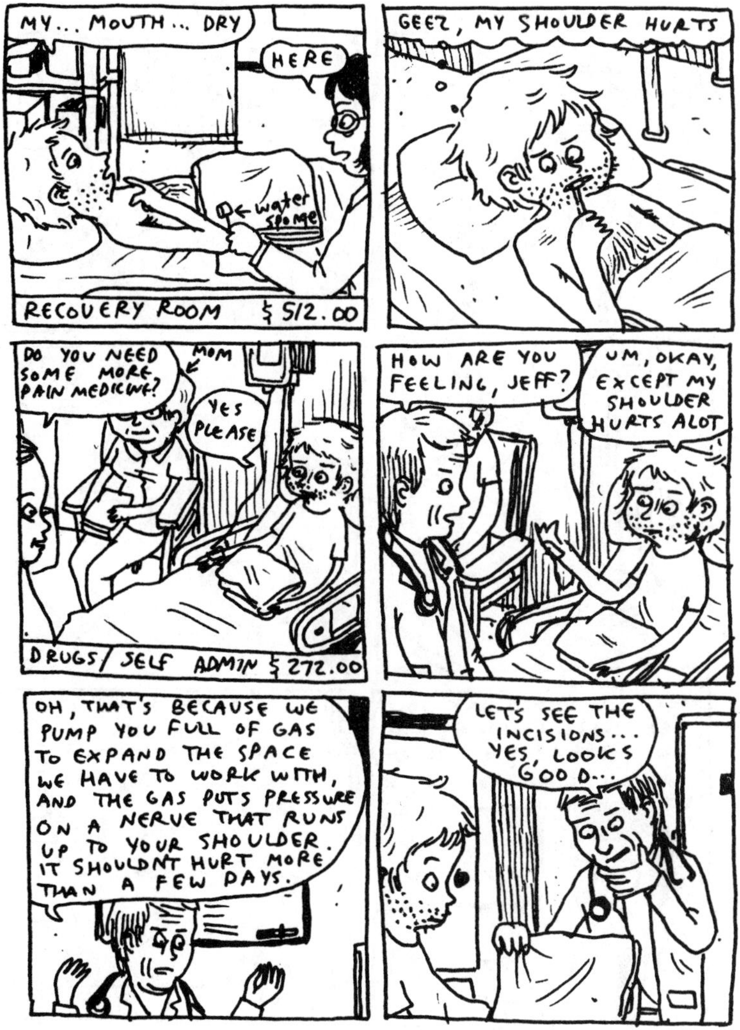
MY... MOUTH... DRY
HERE
← water sponge
RECOVERY ROOM $512.00
GEEZ, MY SHOULDER HURTS
DO YOU NEED SOME MORE PAIN MEDICINE?
MOM
YES PLEASE
DRUGS/ SELF ADMIN $272.00
HOW ARE YOU FEELING, JEFF?
UM, OKAY, EXCEPT MY SHOULDER HURTS ALOT
OH, THAT'S BECAUSE WE PUMP YOU FULL OF GAS TO EXPAND THE SPACE WE HAVE TO WORK WITH, AND THE GAS PUTS PRESSURE ON A NERVE THAT RUNS UP TO YOUR SHOULDER. IT SHOULDNT HURT MORE THAN A FEW DAYS.
LET'S SEE THE INCISIONS... YES, LOOKS GOOD...

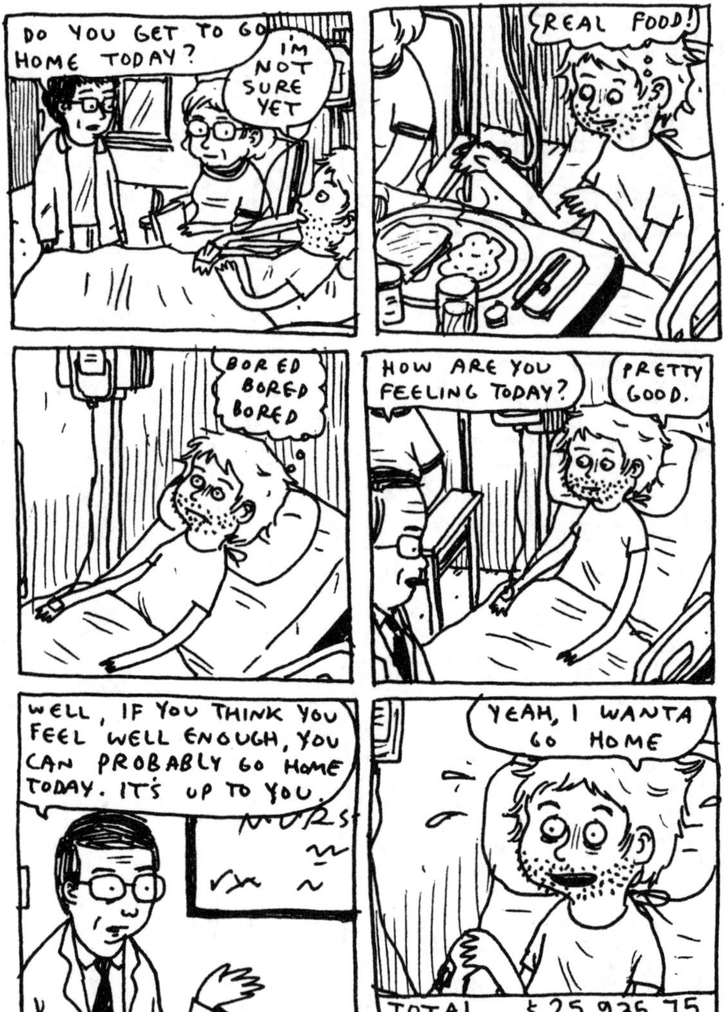
DO YOU GET TO GO HOME TODAY?
I'M NOT SURE YET
REAL FOOD!
BORED BORED BORED
HOW ARE YOU FEELING TODAY?
PRETTY GOOD.
WELL, IF YOU THINK YOU FEEL WELL ENOUGH, YOU CAN PROBABLY GO HOME TODAY. IT'S UP TO YOU.
YEAH, I WANTA GO HOME
TOTAL $25,935.75

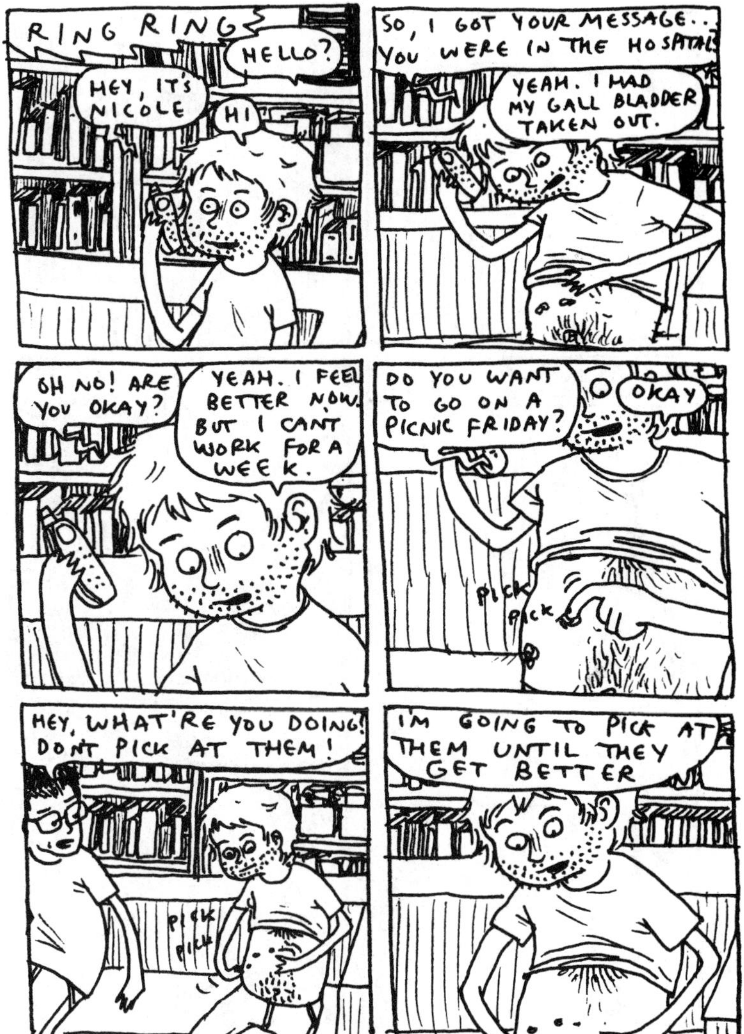
RING RING
HELLO?
HEY, IT'S NICOLE
HI
SO, I GOT YOUR MESSAGE... YOU WERE IN THE HOSPITAL?
YEAH. I HAD MY GALL BLADDER TAKEN OUT.
OH NO! ARE YOU OKAY?
YEAH. I FEEL BETTER NOW. BUT I CANT WORK FOR A WEEK.
DO YOU WANT TO GO ON A PICNIC FRIDAY?
OKAY
PICK
PICK
HEY, WHAT'RE YOU DOING! DON'T PICK AT THEM!
PICK
PICK
I'M GOING TO PICK AT THEM UNTIL THEY GET BETTER

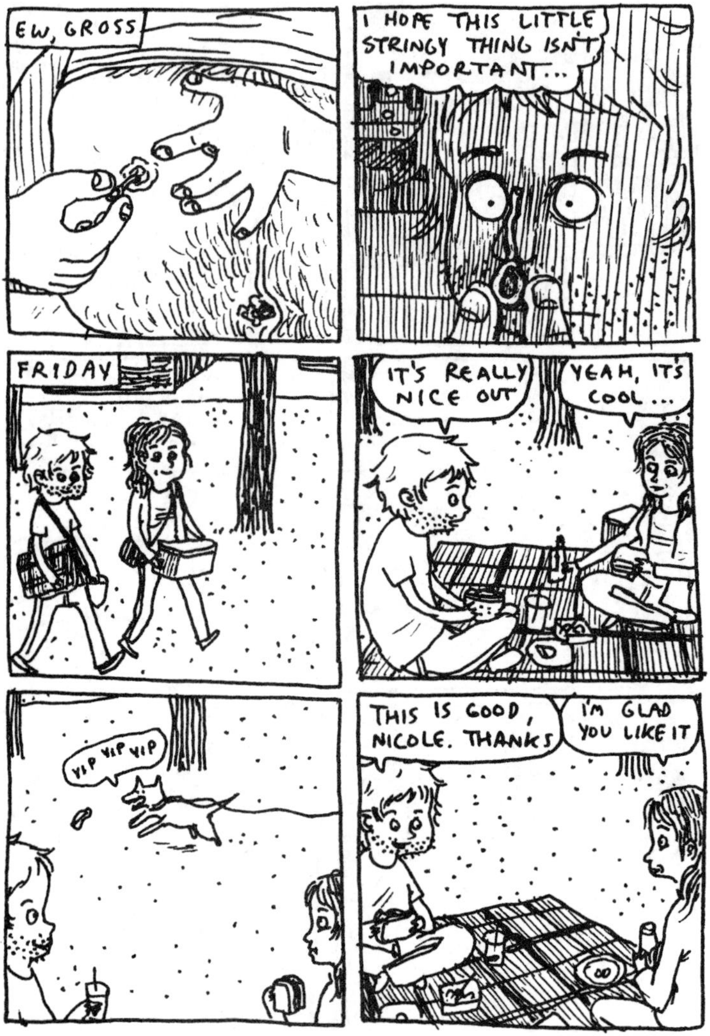
EW, GROSS
I HOPE THIS LITTLE STRINGY THING ISN'T IMPORTANT...
FRIDAY
IT'S REALLY NICE OUT
YEAH, IT'S COOL...
YIP YIP YIP
THIS IS GOOD, NICOLE. THANKS
I'M GLAD YOU LIKE IT

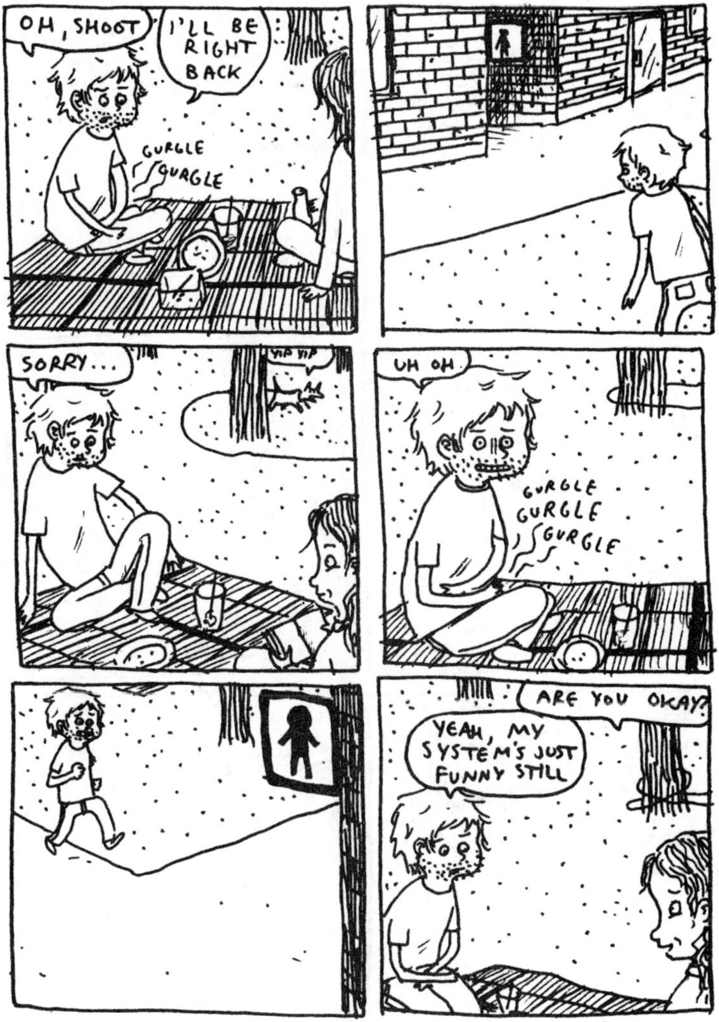
OH, SHOOT
I'LL BE RIGHT BACK
GURGLE
GURGLE
SORRY...
YIP YIP
UH OH
GURGLE
GURGLE
GURGLE
ARE YOU OKAY?
YEAH, MY SYSTEM'S JUST FUNNY STILL

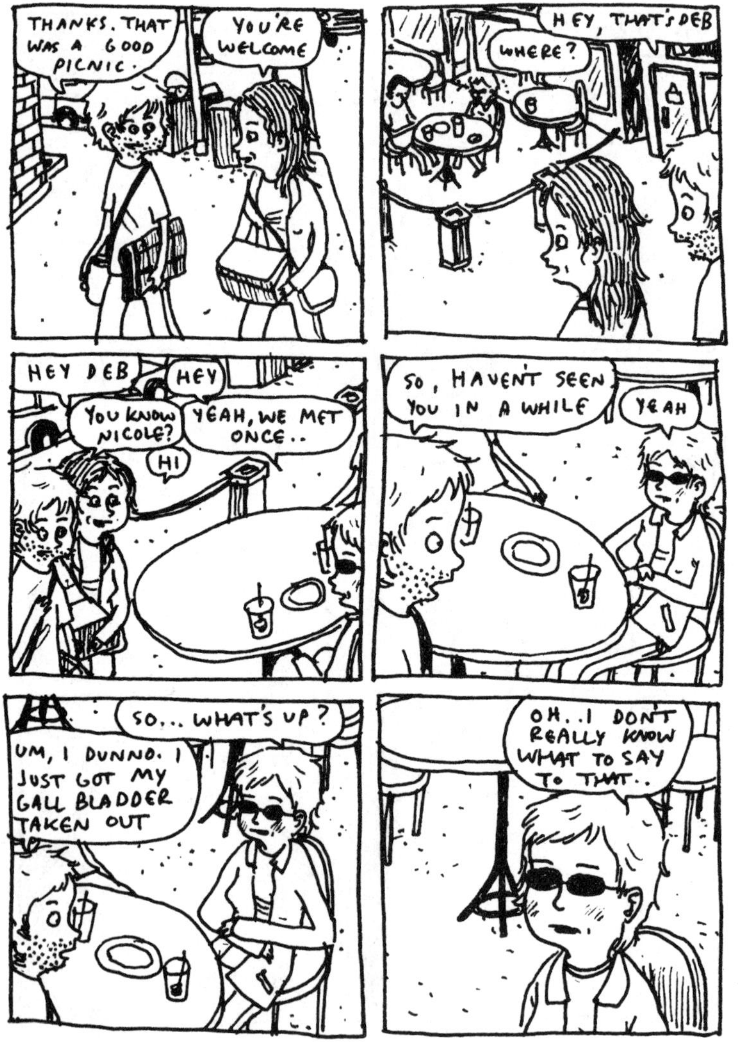
THANKS. THAT WAS A GOOD PICNIC.
YOU'RE WELCOME
HEY, THAT'S DEB
WHERE?
HEY DEB
HEY
YOU KNOW NICOLE?
YEAH, WE MET ONCE..
HI
SO, HAVEN'T SEEN YOU IN A WHILE
YEAH
SO... WHAT'S UP?
UM, I DUNNO. I JUST GOT MY GALL BLADDER TAKEN OUT
OH.. I DON'T REALLY KNOW WHAT TO SAY TO THAT..

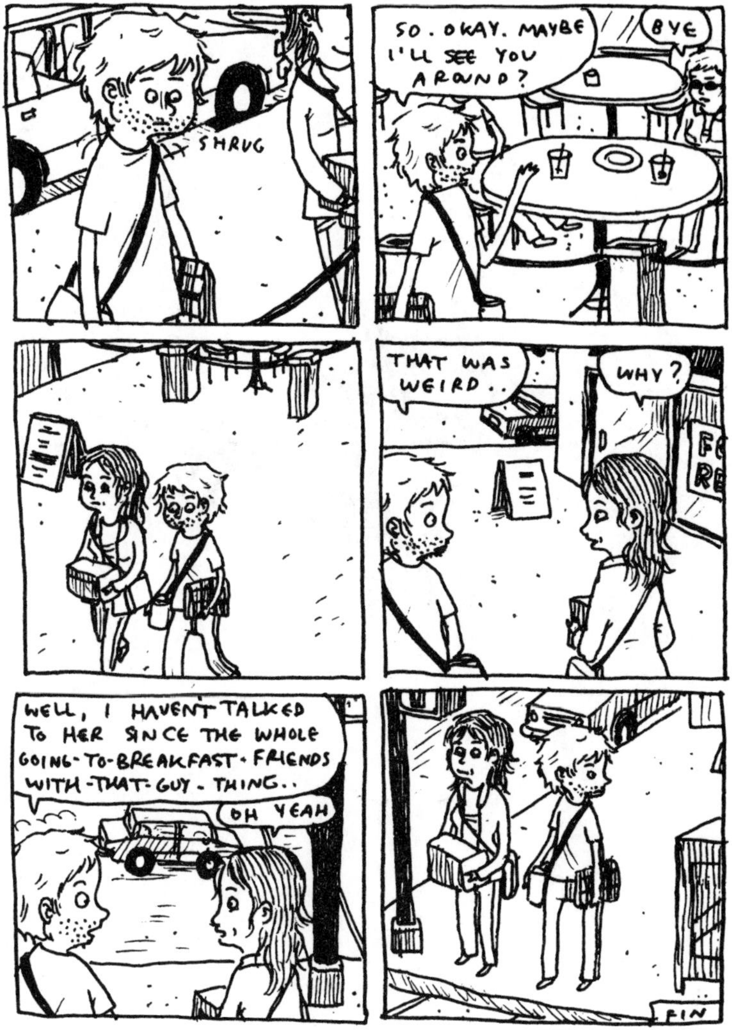
SHRUG
SO. OKAY. MAYBE I'LL SEE YOU AROUND?
BYE
THAT WAS WEIRD..
WHY?
FO
RE
WELL, I HAVEN'T TALKED TO HER SINCE THE WHOLE GOING-TO-BREAKFAST-FRIENDS WITH-THAT-GUY-THING..
OH YEAH
FIN

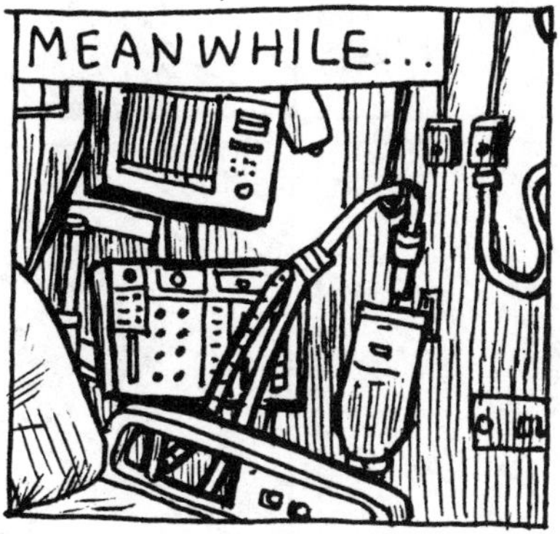
MEANWHILE...

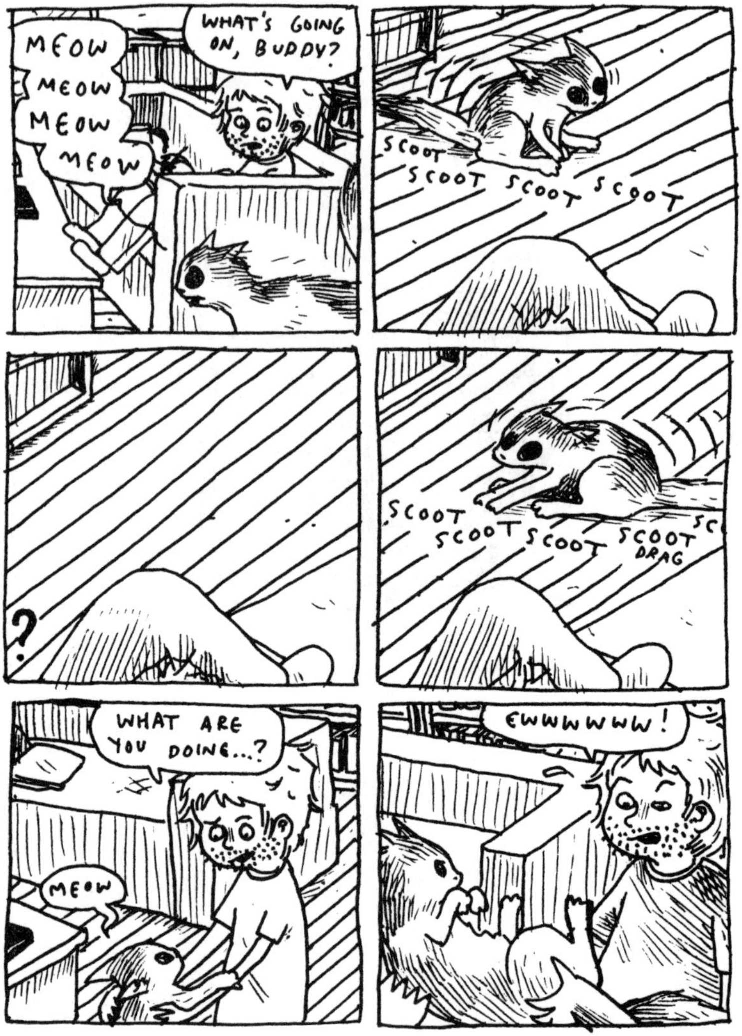
MEOW
MEOW
MEOW
MEOW
WHAT'S GOING ON, BUDDY?
SCOOT
SCOOT SCOOT SCOOT
?
SCOOT
SCOOT SCOOT SCOOT SC
DRAG
WHAT ARE YOU DOING...?
MEOW
EWWWWWW!

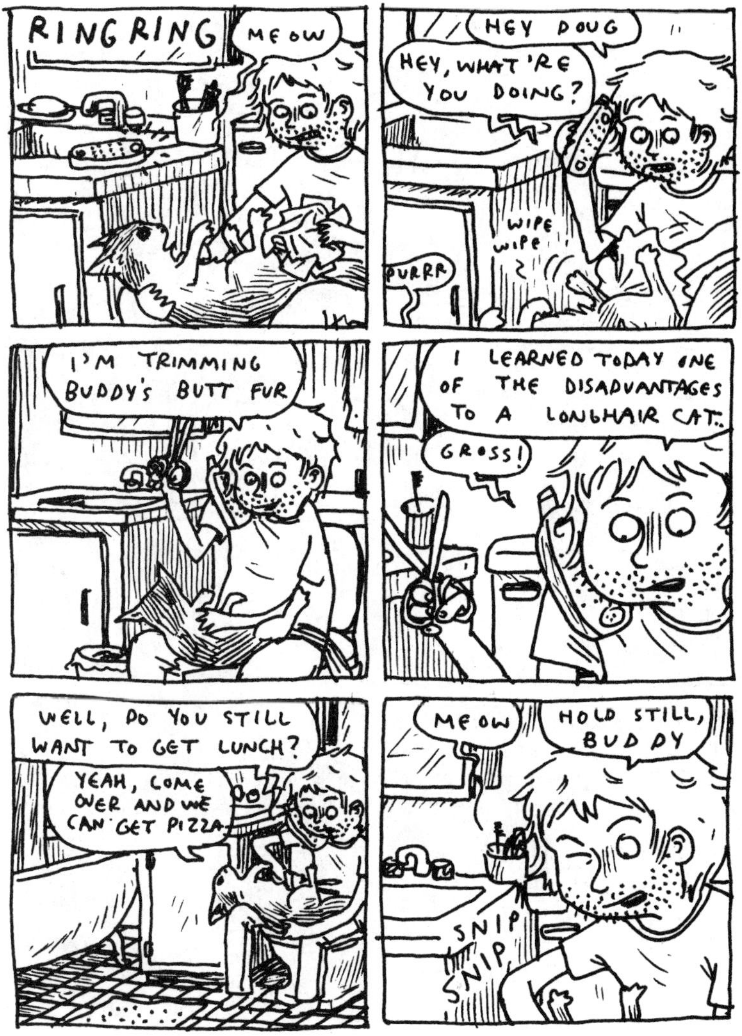
RING RING
MEOW
HEY DOUG
HEY, WHAT'RE YOU DOING?
WIPE WIPE
PURRR
I'M TRIMMING BUDDY'S BUTT FUR
I LEARNED TODAY ONE OF THE DISADVANTAGES TO A LONGHAIR CAT..
GROSS!
WELL, DO YOU STILL WANT TO GET LUNCH?
YEAH, COME OVER AND WE CAN GET PIZZA
MEOW
HOLD STILL, BUDDY
SNIP SNIP

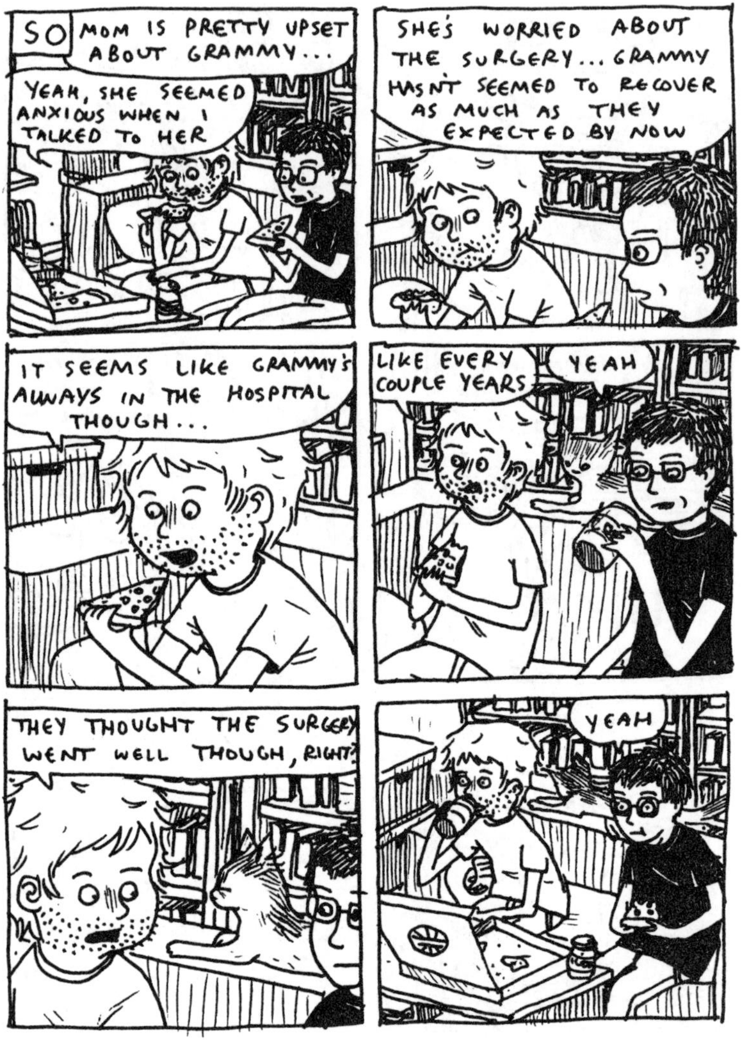
SO
MOM IS PRETTY UPSET ABOUT GRAMMY...
YEAH, SHE SEEMED ANXIOUS WHEN I TALKED TO HER
SHE'S WORRIED ABOUT THE SURGERY... GRAMMY HASN'T SEEMED TO RECOVER AS MUCH AS THEY EXPECTED BY NOW
IT SEEMS LIKE GRAMMY'S ALWAYS IN THE HOSPITAL THOUGH...
LIKE EVERY COUPLE YEARS
YEAH
THEY THOUGHT THE SURGERY WENT WELL THOUGH, RIGHT?
YEAH

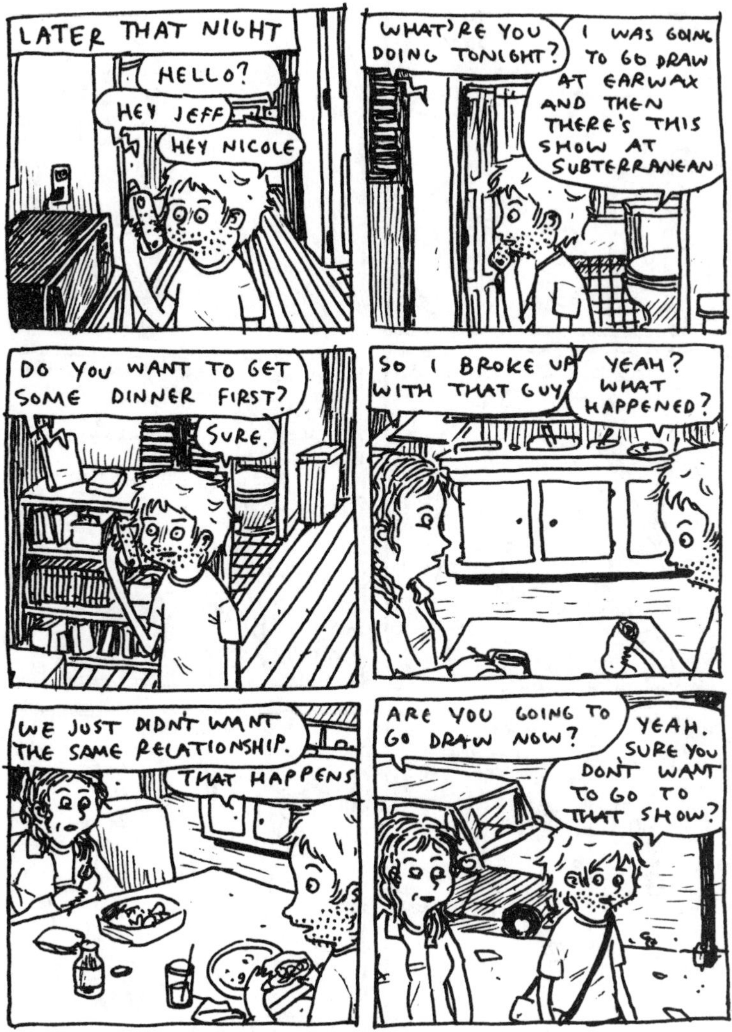
LATER THAT NIGHT
HELLO?
HEY JEFF
HEY NICOLE
WHAT'RE YOU DOING TONIGHT?
I WAS GOING TO GO DRAW AT EARWAX AND THEN THERE'S THIS SHOW AT SUBTERRANEAN
DO YOU WANT TO GET SOME DINNER FIRST?
SURE.
SO I BROKE UP WITH THAT GUY
YEAH? WHAT HAPPENED?
WE JUST DIDN'T WANT THE SAME RELATIONSHIP.
THAT HAPPENS
ARE YOU GOING TO GO DRAW NOW?
YEAH. SURE YOU DON'T WANT TO GO TO THAT SHOW?

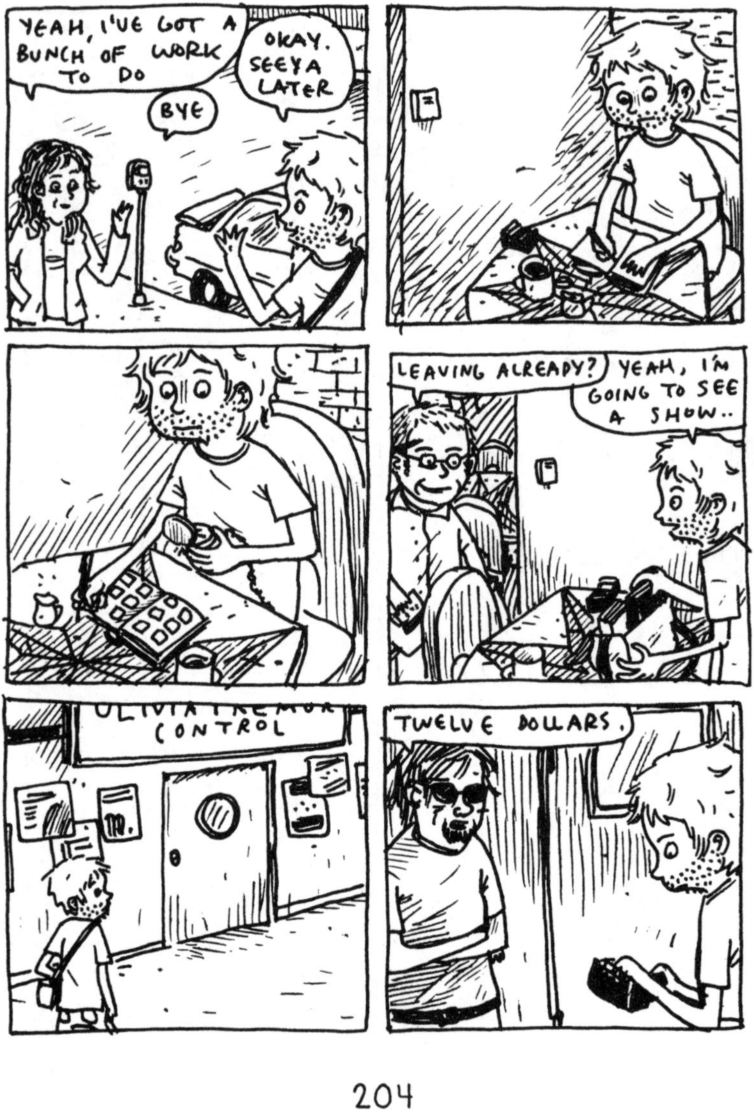
YEAH, I'VE GOT A BUNCH OF WORK TO DO
OKAY. SEEYA LATER
BYE
LEAVING ALREADY?
YEAH, I'M GOING TO SEE A SHOW..
CONTROL
TWELVE DOLLARS.

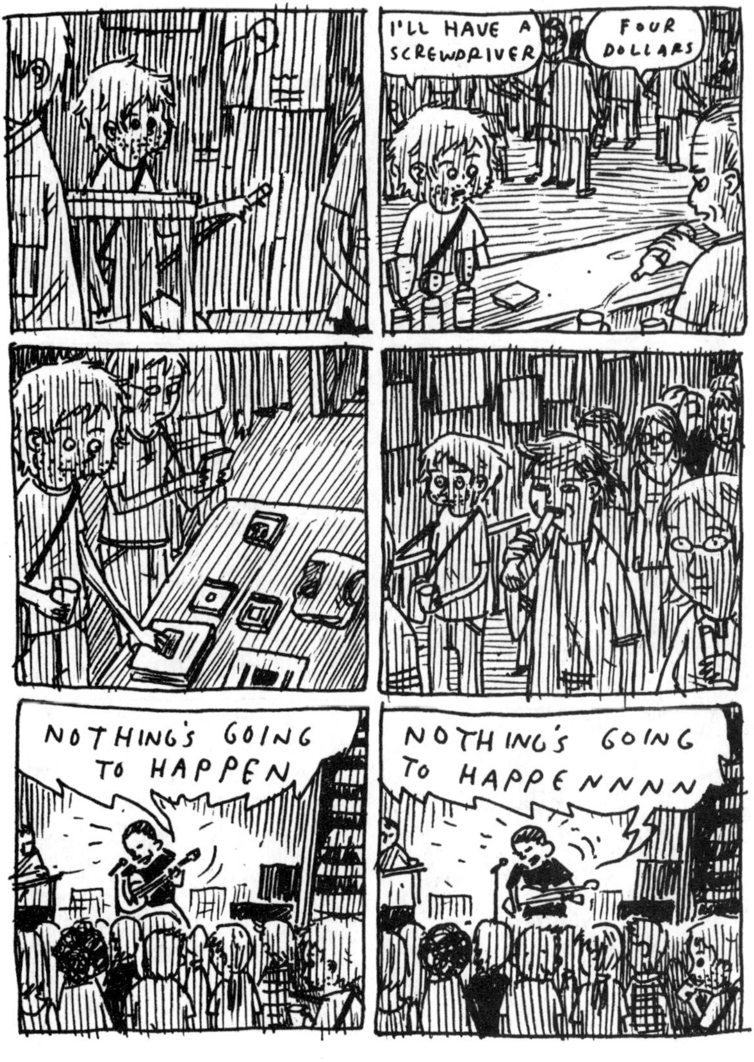
I'LL HAVE A SCREWDRIVER
FOUR DOLLARS
NOTHING'S GOING TO HAPPEN
NOTHING'S GOING TO HAPPENNNNN

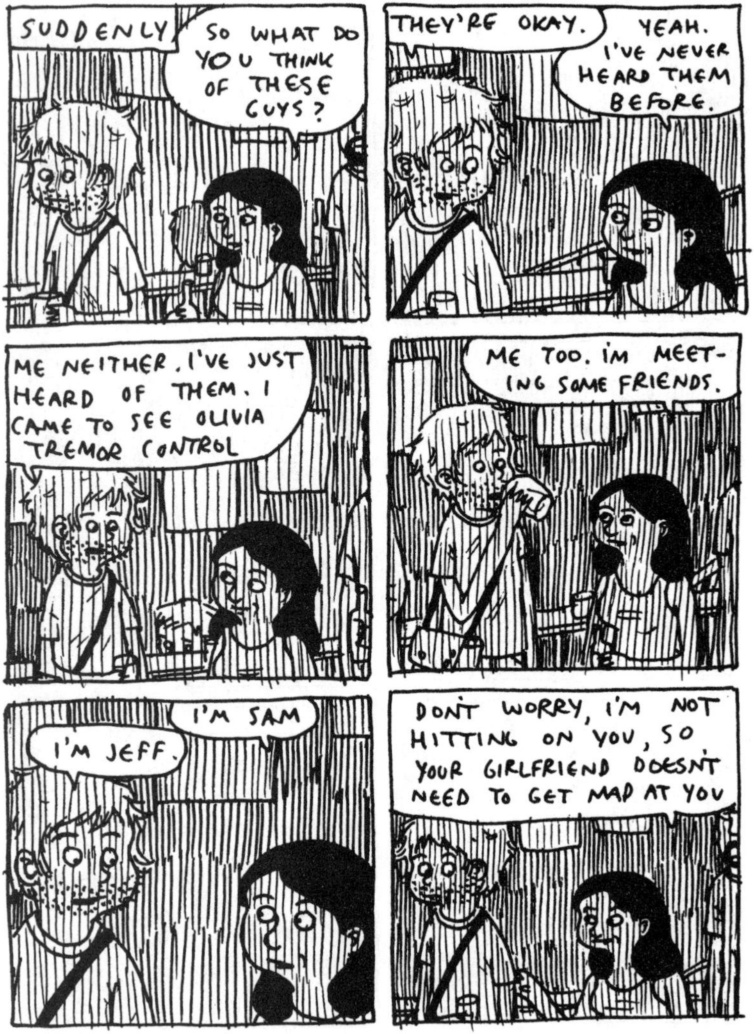
SUDDENLY
SO WHAT DO YOU THINK OF THESE GUYS?
THEY'RE OKAY.
YEAH. I'VE NEVER HEARD THEM BEFORE.
ME NEITHER. I'VE JUST HEARD OF THEM. I CAME TO SEE OLIVIA TREMOR CONTROL
ME TOO. I'M MEETING SOME FRIENDS.
I'M SAM
I'M JEFF.
DON'T WORRY, I'M NOT HITTING ON YOU, SO YOUR GIRLFRIEND DOESN'T NEED TO GET MAD AT YOU

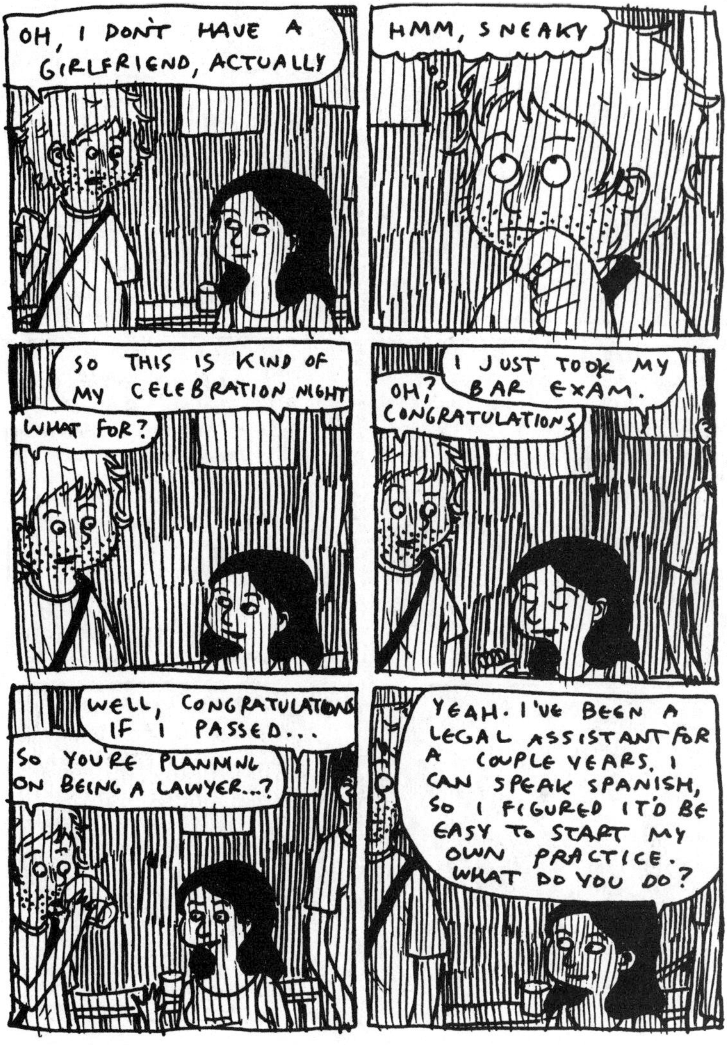
OH, I DON'T HAVE A GIRLFRIEND, ACTUALLY
HMM, SNEAKY
SO THIS IS KIND OF MY CELEBRATION NIGHT
WHAT FOR?
I JUST TOOK MY BAR EXAM.
OH? CONGRATULATIONS
WELL, CONGRATULATIONS IF I PASSED...
SO YOU'RE PLANNING ON BEING A LAWYER...?
YEAH. I'VE BEEN A LEGAL ASSISTANT FOR A COUPLE YEARS. I CAN SPEAK SPANISH, SO I FIGURED IT'D BE EASY TO START MY OWN PRACTICE. WHAT DO YOU DO?

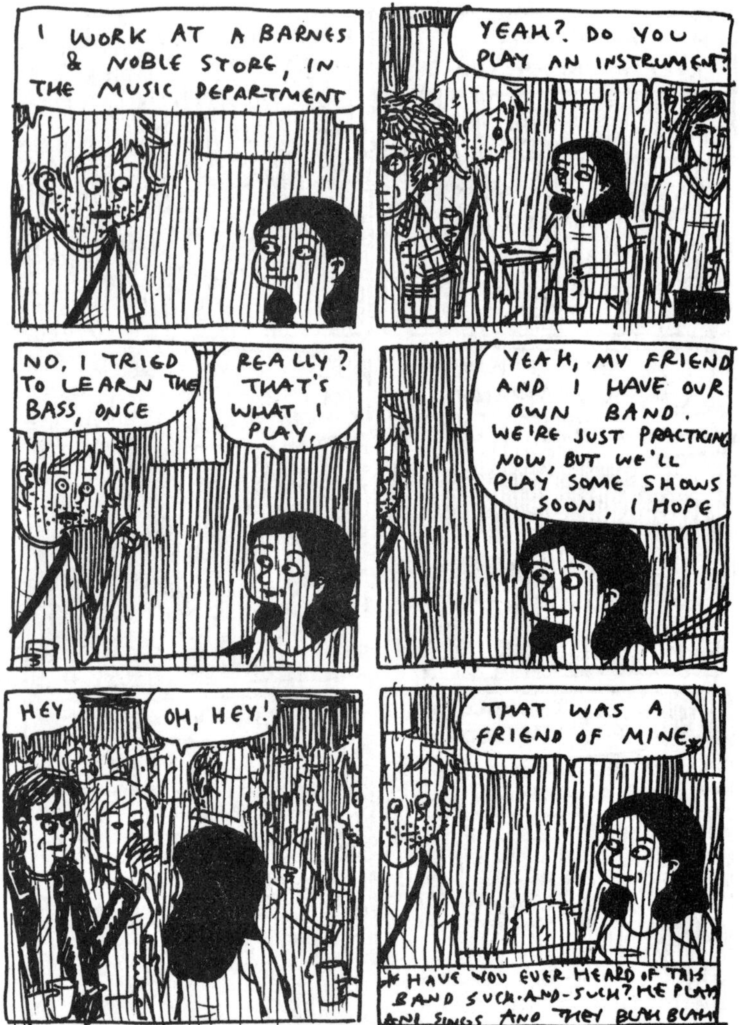
I WORK AT A BARNES & NOBLE STORE, IN THE MUSIC DEPARTMENT
YEAH? DO YOU PLAY AN INSTRUMENT?
NO, I TRIED TO LEARN THE BASS, ONCE
REALLY? THAT'S WHAT I PLAY.
YEAH, MY FRIEND AND I HAVE OUR OWN BAND. WE'RE JUST PRACTICING NOW, BUT WE'LL PLAY SOME SHOWS SOON, I HOPE
HEY
OH, HEY!
THAT WAS A FRIEND OF MINE*
*HAVE YOU EVER HEARD OF THIS BAND SUCH-AND-SUCH? HE PLAYS AND SINGS AND THEY BLAH BLAH

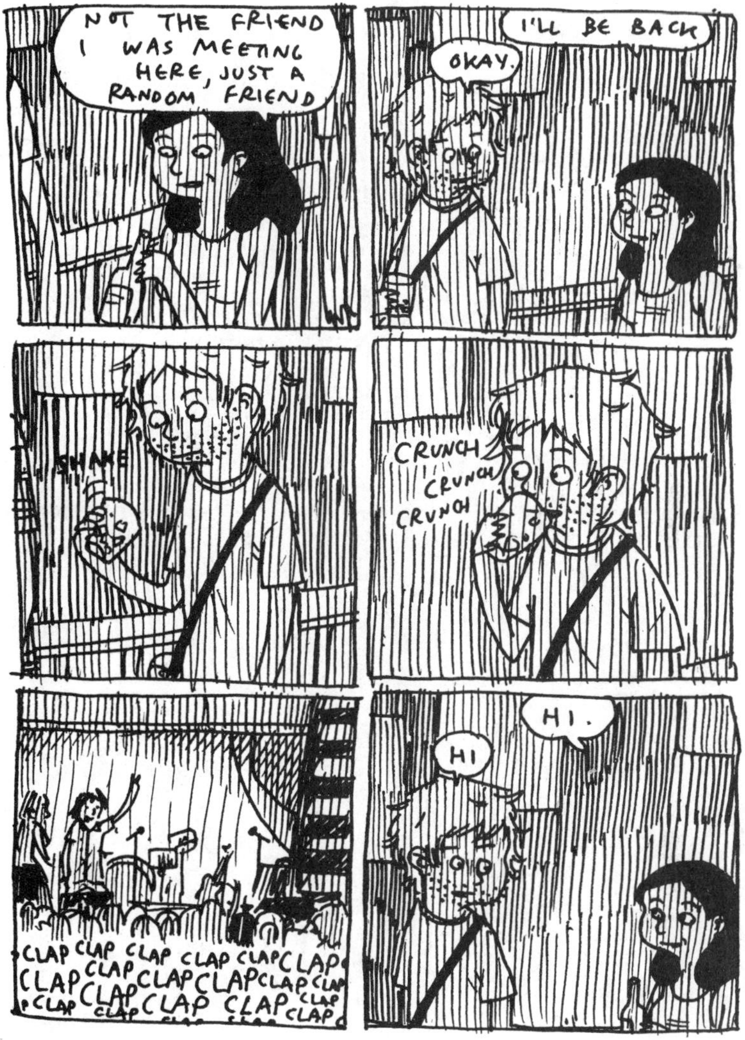
NOT THE FRIEND I WAS MEETING HERE, JUST A RANDOM FRIEND
I'LL BE BACK
OKAY.
SHAKE
CRUNCH
CRUNCH
CRUNCH
CLAP CLAP CLAP CLAP CLAP CLAP
CLAP CLAP CLAP CLAP CLAP
CLAP CLAP CLAP CLAP CLAP
HI.
HI

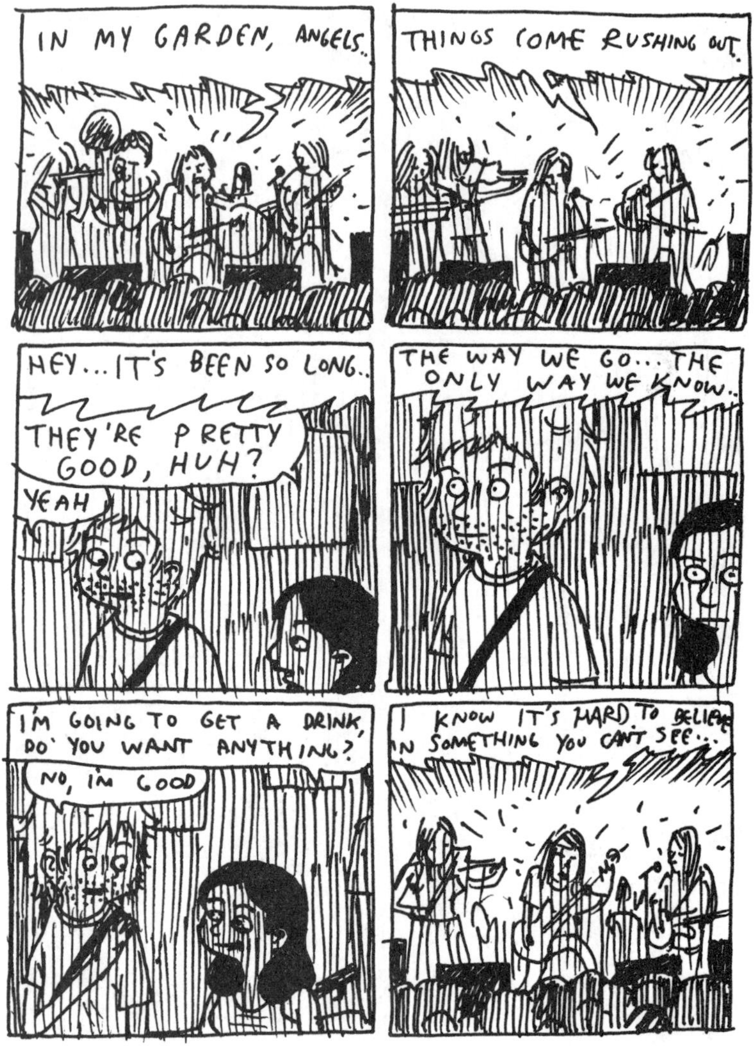
IN MY GARDEN, ANGELS..
THINGS COME RUSHING OUT.
HEY... IT'S BEEN SO LONG..
THEY'RE PRETTY GOOD, HUH?
YEAH
THE WAY WE GO... THE ONLY WAY WE KNOW..
I'M GOING TO GET A DRINK, DO YOU WANT ANYTHING?
NO, I'M GOOD
I KNOW IT'S HARD TO BELIEVE IN SOMETHING YOU CAN'T SEE...

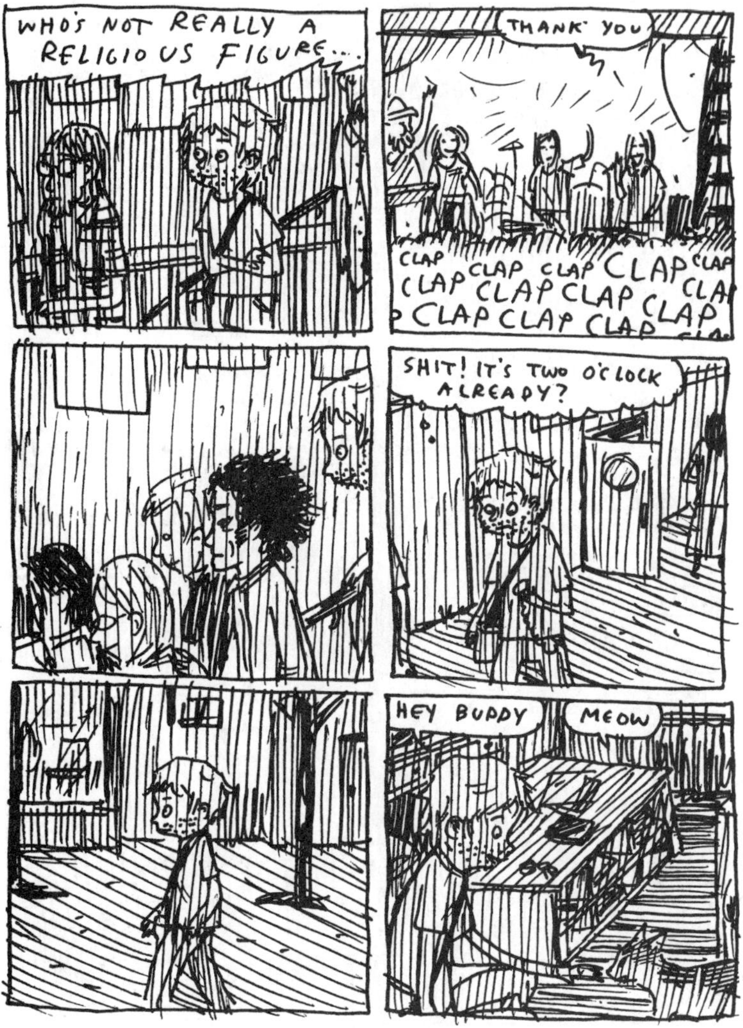
WHO'S NOT REALLY A RELIGIOUS FIGURE...
THANK YOU
CLAP CLAP CLAP CLAP
CLAP CLAP CLAP CLAP
CLAP CLAP CLAP CLAP
SHIT! IT'S TWO O'CLOCK ALREADY?
HEY BUDDY
MEOW

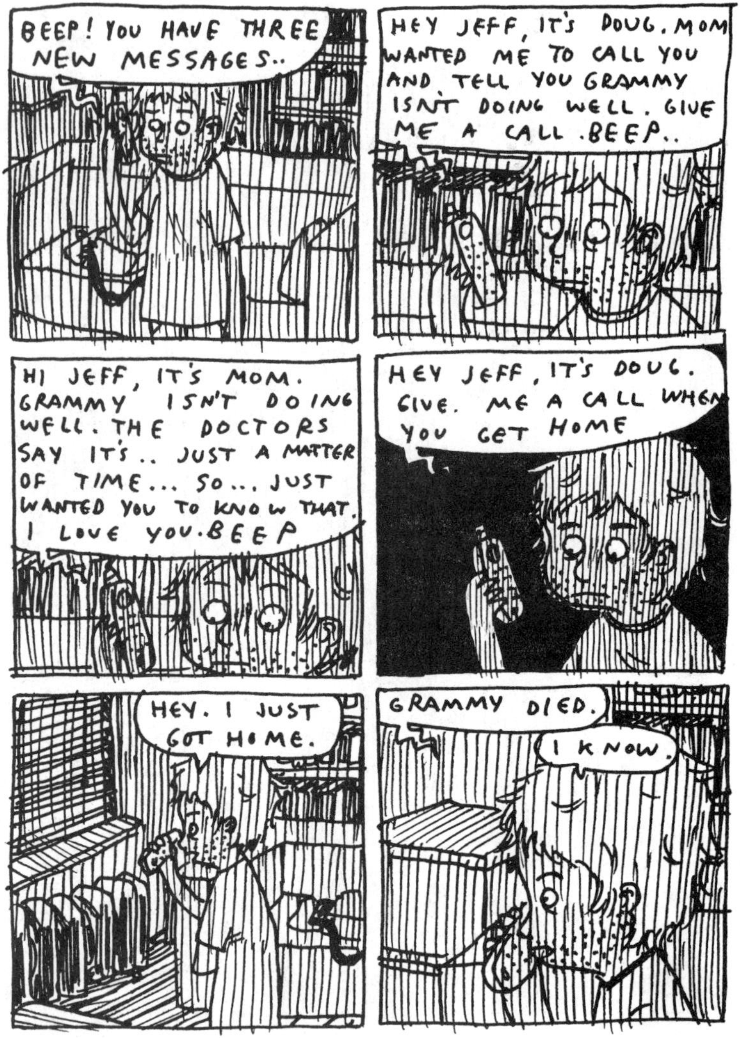
BEEP! YOU HAVE THREE NEW MESSAGES..
HEY JEFF, IT'S DOUG. MOM WANTED ME TO CALL YOU AND TELL YOU GRAMMY ISN'T DOING WELL. GIVE ME A CALL. BEEP..
HI JEFF, IT'S MOM. GRAMMY ISN'T DOING WELL. THE DOCTORS SAY IT'S.. JUST A MATTER OF TIME... SO... JUST WANTED YOU TO KNOW THAT. I LOVE YOU. BEEP
HEY JEFF, IT'S DOUG. GIVE. ME A CALL WHEN YOU GET HOME
HEY. I JUST GOT HOME.
GRAMMY DIED.
I KNOW.

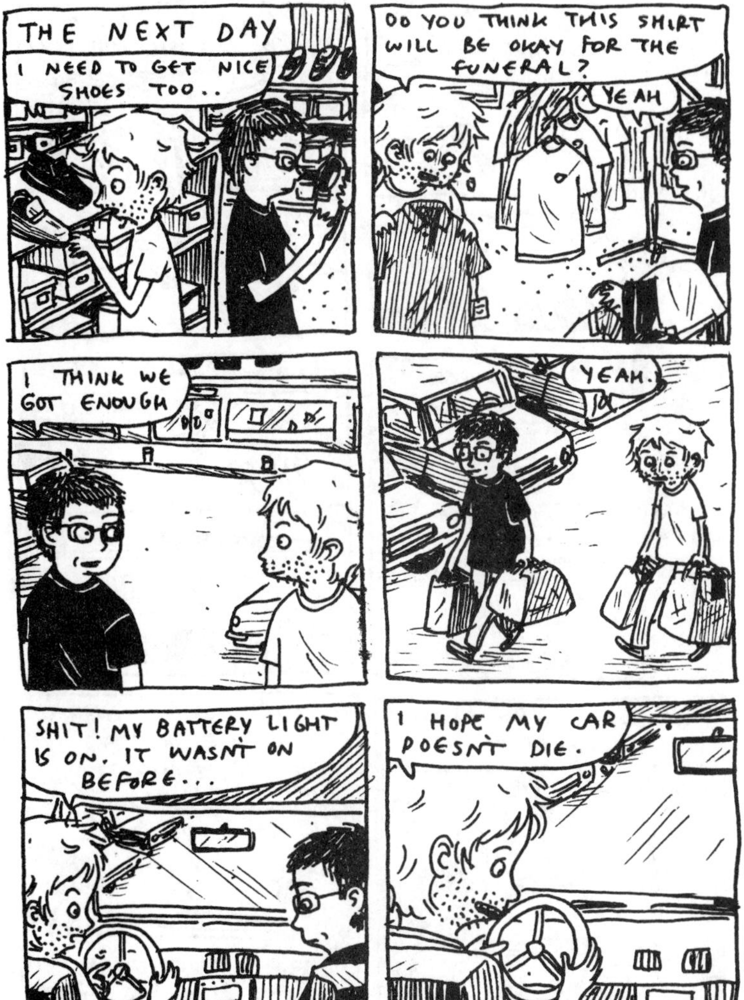
THE NEXT DAY
I NEED TO GET NICE SHOES TOO..
DO YOU THINK THIS SHIRT WILL BE OKAY FOR THE FUNERAL?
YEAH
I THINK WE GOT ENOUGH
YEAH.
SHIT! MY BATTERY LIGHT IS ON. IT WASN'T ON BEFORE...
I HOPE MY CAR DOESN'T DIE.

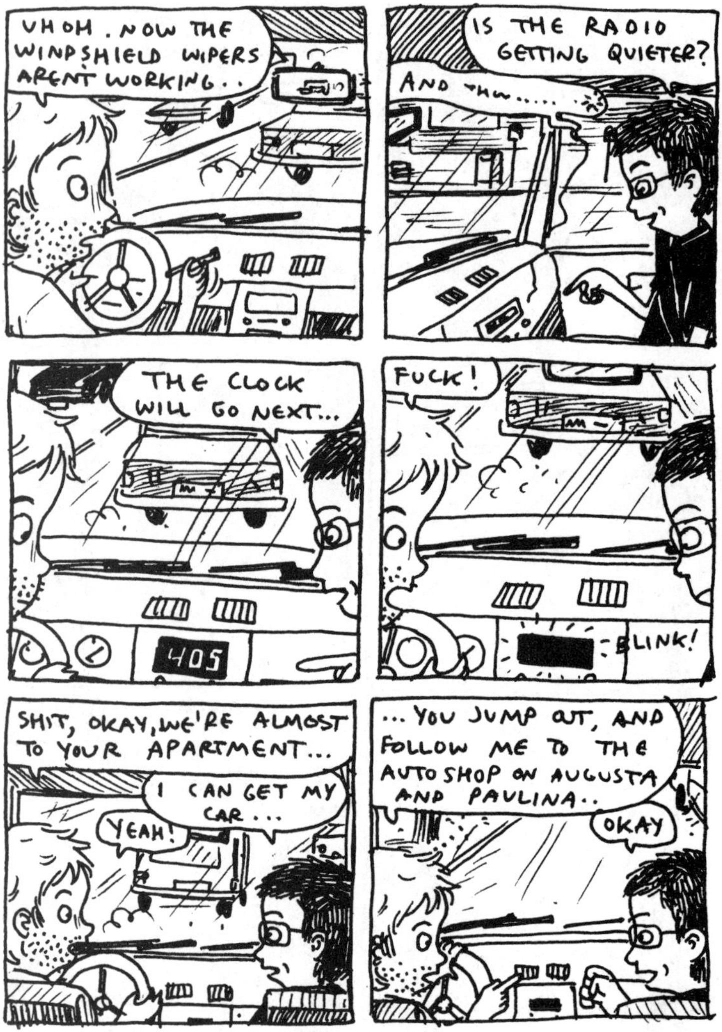
UH OH. NOW THE WINDSHIELD WIPERS AREN'T WORKING..
IS THE RADIO GETTING QUIETER?
AND THW.....
THE CLOCK WILL GO NEXT...
405
FUCK!
BLINK!
SHIT, OKAY, WE'RE ALMOST TO YOUR APARTMENT...
I CAN GET MY CAR...
YEAH!
...YOU JUMP OUT, AND FOLLOW ME TO THE AUTO SHOP ON AUGUSTA AND PAULINA..
OKAY

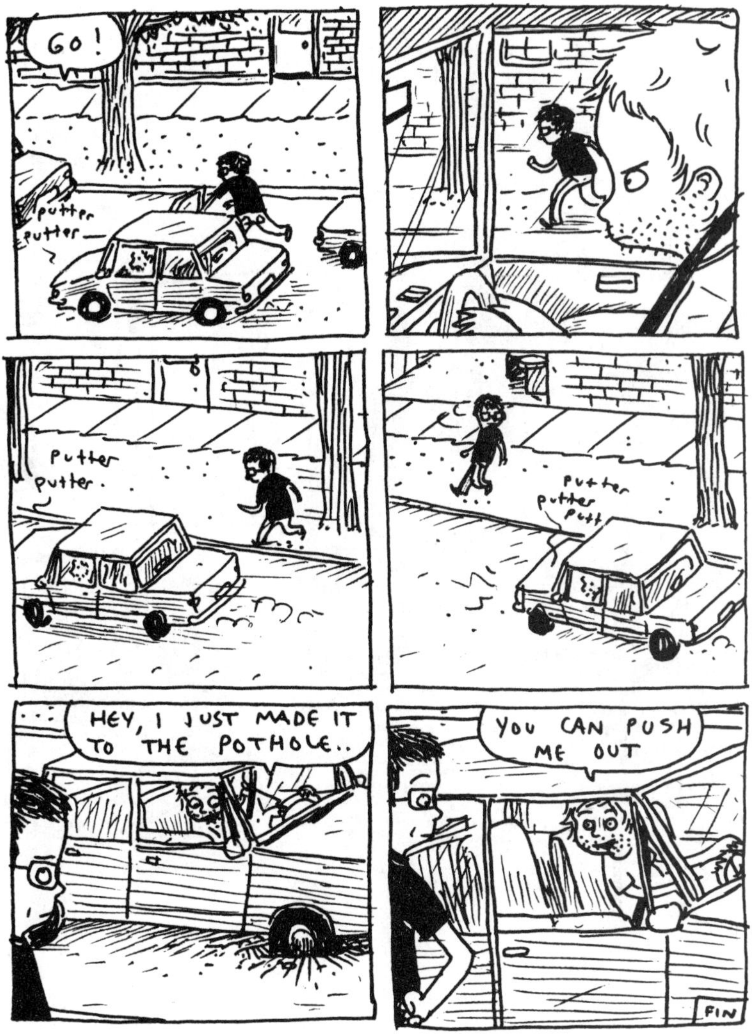
GO!
putter
putter
putter
putter.
putter
putter
putt
HEY, I JUST MADE IT TO THE POTHOLE..
YOU CAN PUSH ME OUT
FIN

THE CALM BEFORE THE STORM

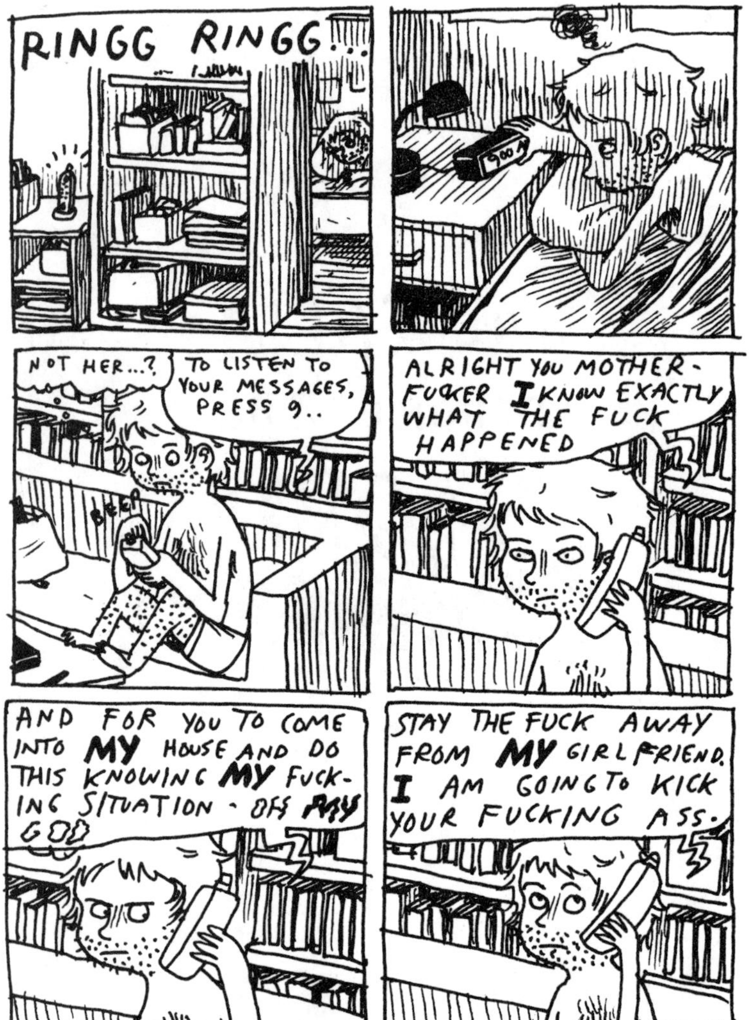

RINGG RINGG...
NOT HER...?
TO LISTEN TO YOUR MESSAGES, PRESS 9..
ALRIGHT YOU MOTHER-FUCKER I KNOW EXACTLY WHAT THE FUCK HAPPENED
AND FOR YOU TO COME INTO MY HOUSE AND DO THIS KNOWING MY FUCKING SITUATION - OH MY GOD
STAY THE FUCK AWAY FROM MY GIRLFRIEND. I AM GOING TO KICK YOUR FUCKING ASS.

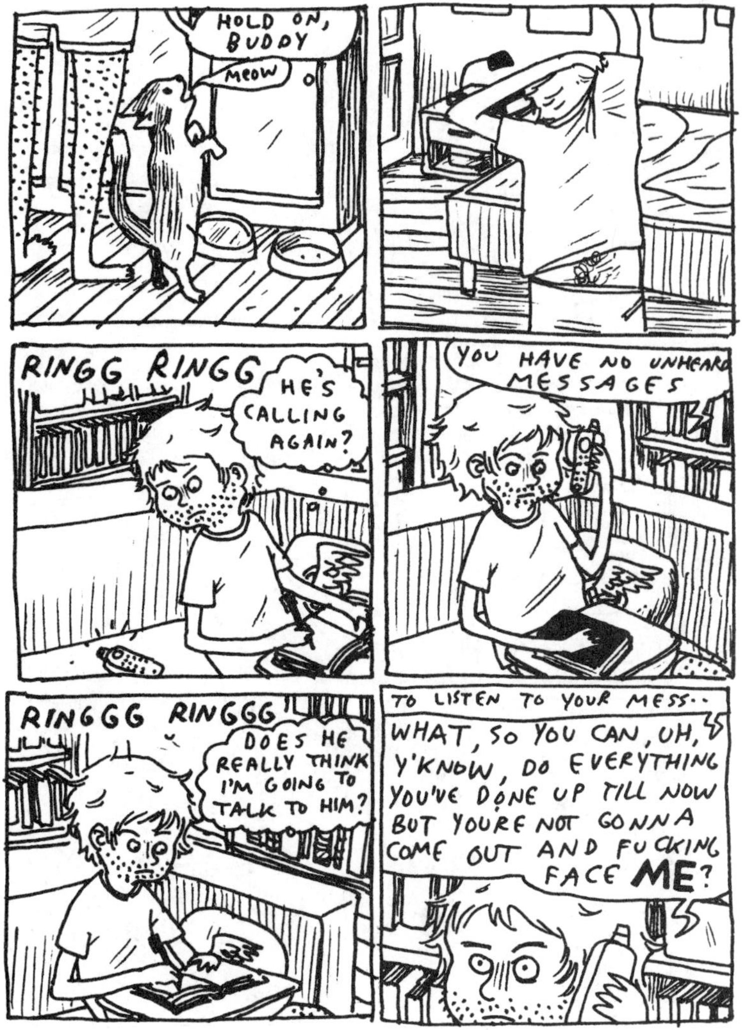
HOLD ON, BUDDY
MEOW
RINGG RINGG
HE'S CALLING AGAIN?
YOU HAVE NO UNHEARD MESSAGES
RINGGG RINGGG
DOES HE REALLY THINK I'M GOING TO TALK TO HIM?
TO LISTEN TO YOUR MESS··
WHAT, SO YOU CAN, UH, Y'KNOW, DO EVERYTHING YOU'VE DONE UP TILL NOW BUT YOURE NOT GONNA COME OUT AND FUCKING FACE ME?

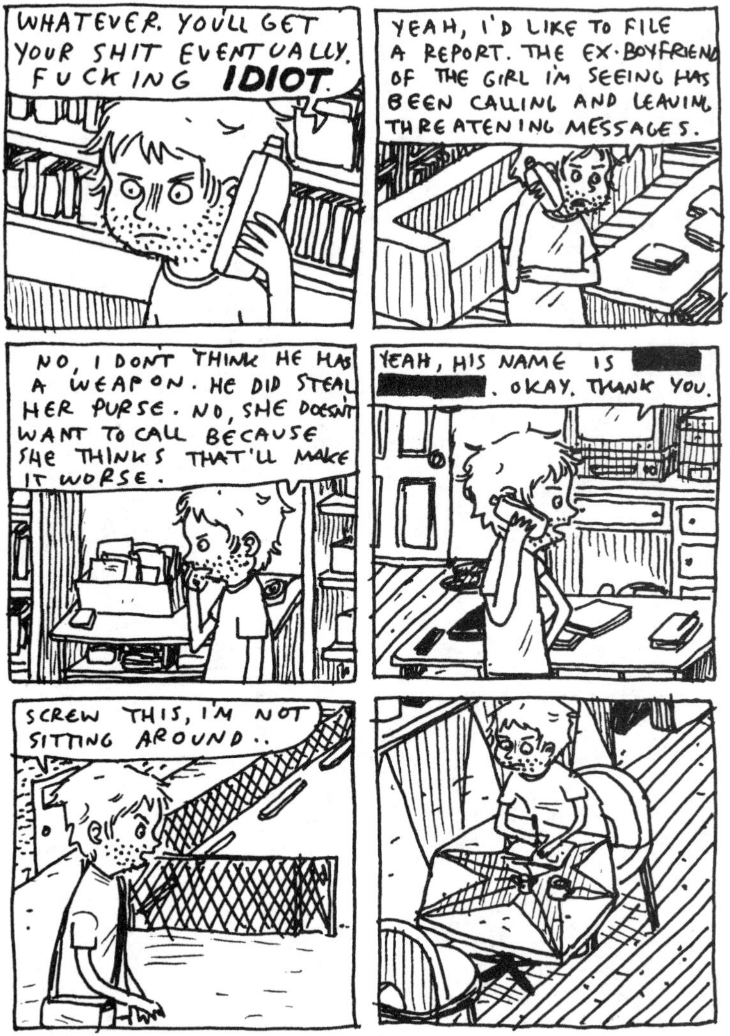
WHATEVER. YOU'LL GET YOUR SHIT EVENTUALLY. FUCKING **IDIOT**.
YEAH, I'D LIKE TO FILE A REPORT. THE EX-BOYFRIEND OF THE GIRL I'M SEEING HAS BEEN CALLING AND LEAVING THREATENING MESSAGES.
NO, I DON'T THINK HE HAS A WEAPON. HE DID STEAL HER PURSE. NO, SHE DOESN'T WANT TO CALL BECAUSE SHE THINKS THAT'LL MAKE IT WORSE.
YEAH, HIS NAME IS [redacted]. OKAY. THANK YOU.
SCREW THIS, I'M NOT SITTING AROUND..

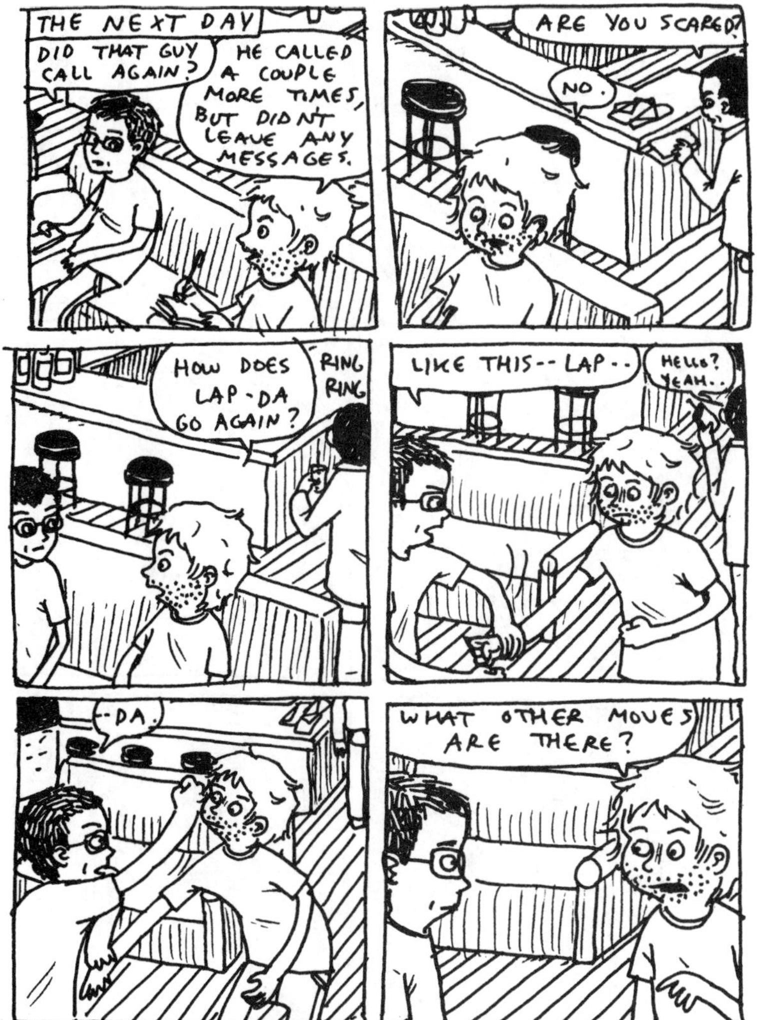
THE NEXT DAY
DID THAT GUY CALL AGAIN?
HE CALLED A COUPLE MORE TIMES, BUT DIDN'T LEAVE ANY MESSAGES.
ARE YOU SCARED?
NO.
HOW DOES LAP-DA GO AGAIN?
RING RING
LIKE THIS-- LAP--
HELLO? YEAH..
--DA.
WHAT OTHER MOVES ARE THERE?

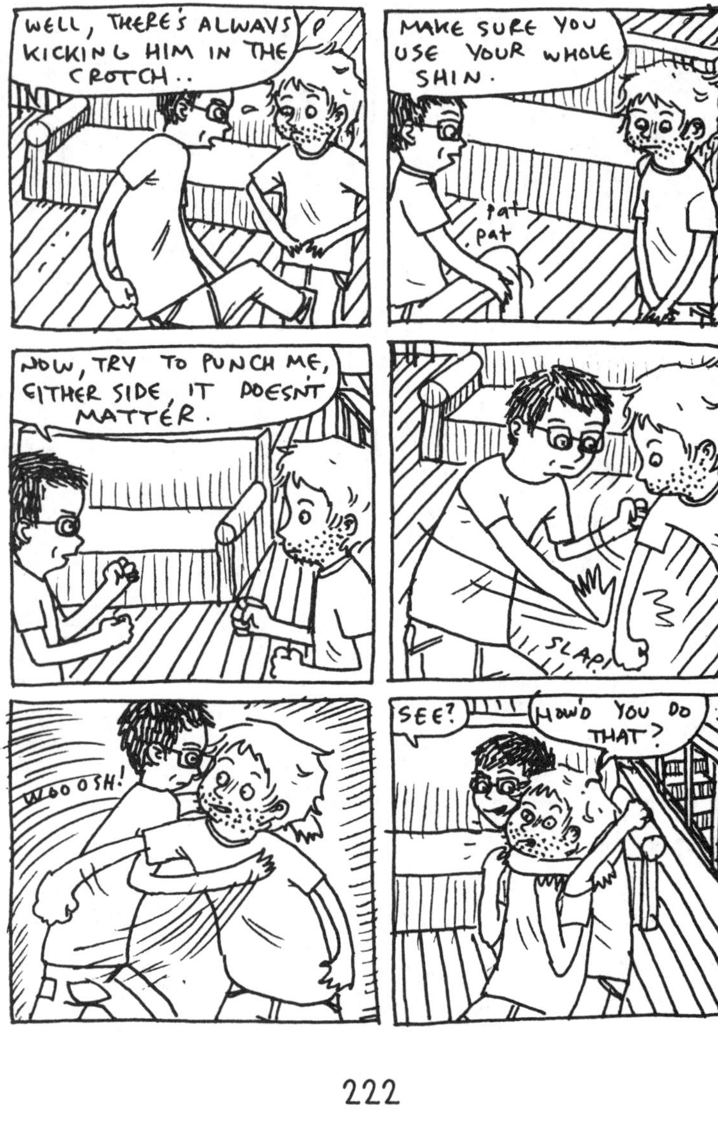
WELL, THERE'S ALWAYS KICKING HIM IN THE CROTCH..
MAKE SURE YOU USE YOUR WHOLE SHIN.
pat pat
NOW, TRY TO PUNCH ME, EITHER SIDE, IT DOESN'T MATTER.
SLAP!
WOOOSH!
SEE?
HOW'D YOU DO THAT?

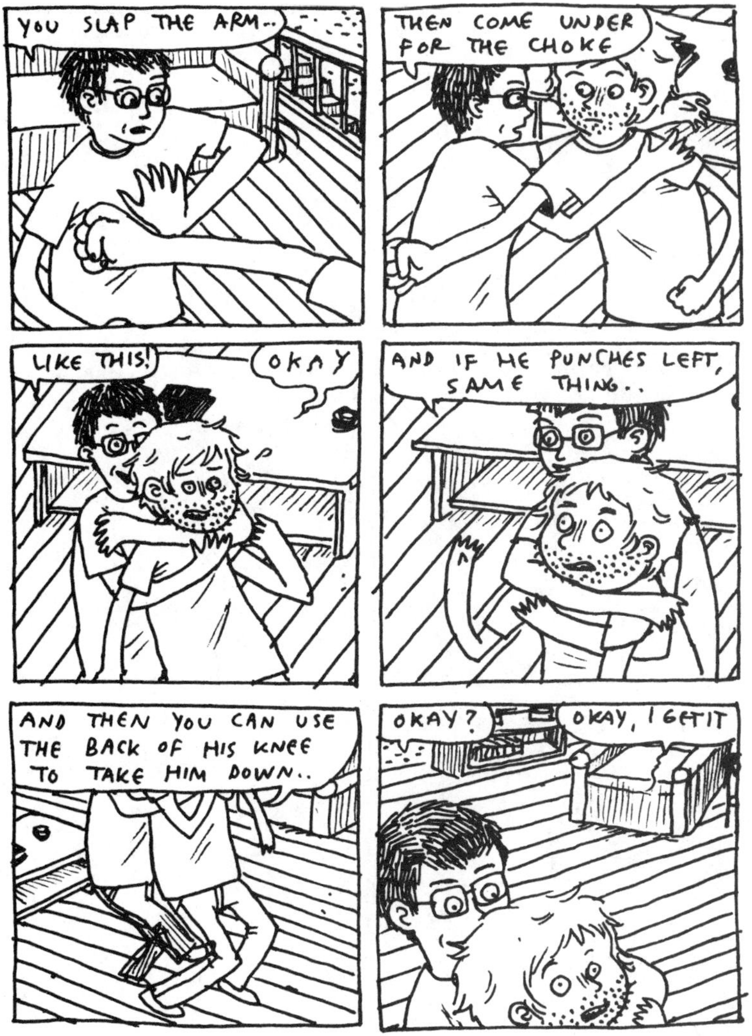
YOU SLAP THE ARM..
THEN COME UNDER FOR THE CHOKE
LIKE THIS!
OKAY
AND IF HE PUNCHES LEFT, SAME THING..
AND THEN YOU CAN USE THE BACK OF HIS KNEE TO TAKE HIM DOWN..
OKAY?
OKAY, I GET IT

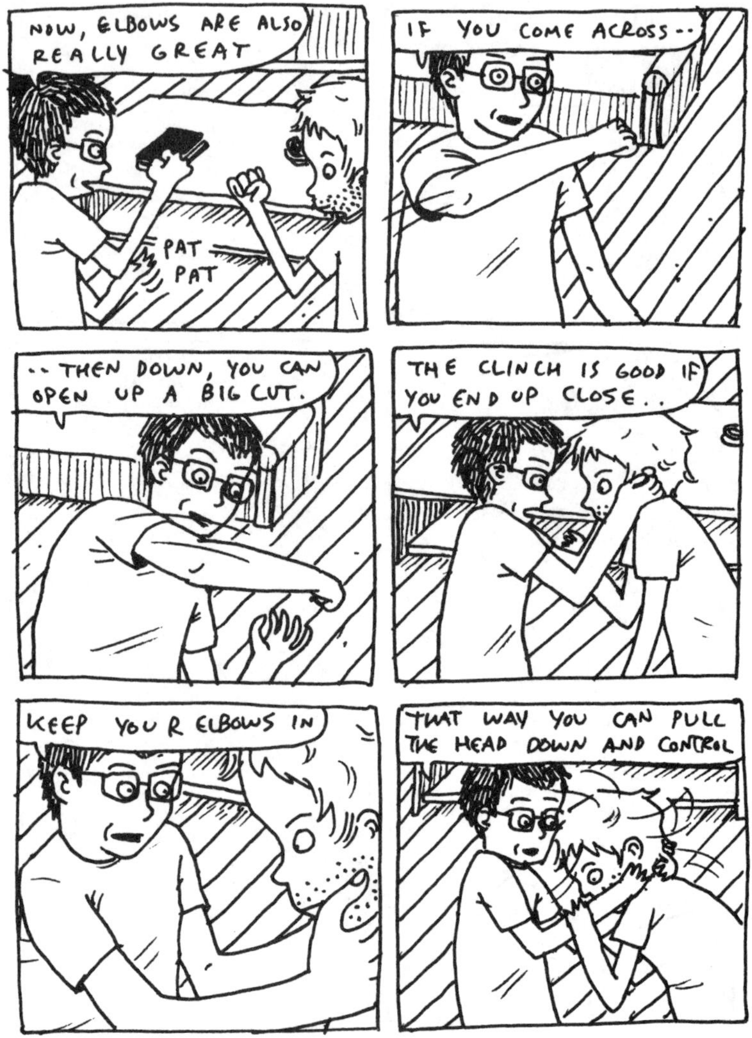
NOW, ELBOWS ARE ALSO REALLY GREAT
PAT PAT
IF YOU COME ACROSS--
--THEN DOWN, YOU CAN OPEN UP A BIG CUT.
THE CLINCH IS GOOD IF YOU END UP CLOSE..
KEEP YOUR ELBOWS IN
THAT WAY YOU CAN PULL THE HEAD DOWN AND CONTROL

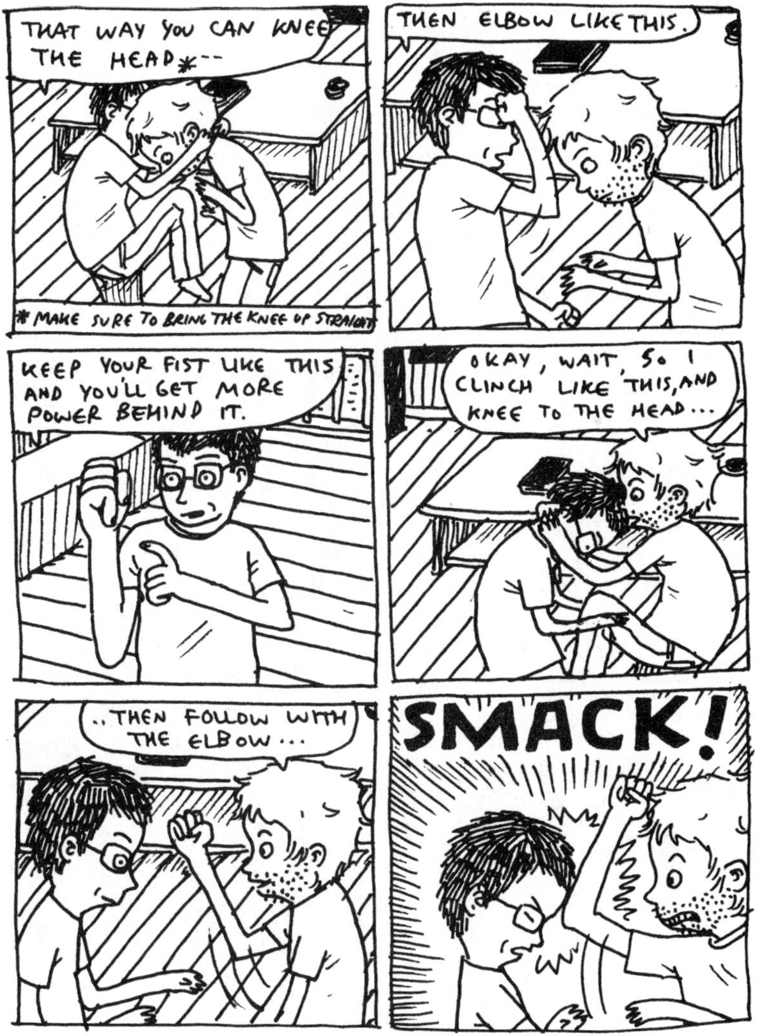
THAT WAY YOU CAN KNEE THE HEAD*--
* MAKE SURE TO BRING THE KNEE UP STRAIGHT
THEN ELBOW LIKE THIS.
KEEP YOUR FIST LIKE THIS AND YOU'LL GET MORE POWER BEHIND IT.
OKAY, WAIT, SO I CLINCH LIKE THIS, AND KNEE TO THE HEAD...
..THEN FOLLOW WITH THE ELBOW...
SMACK!

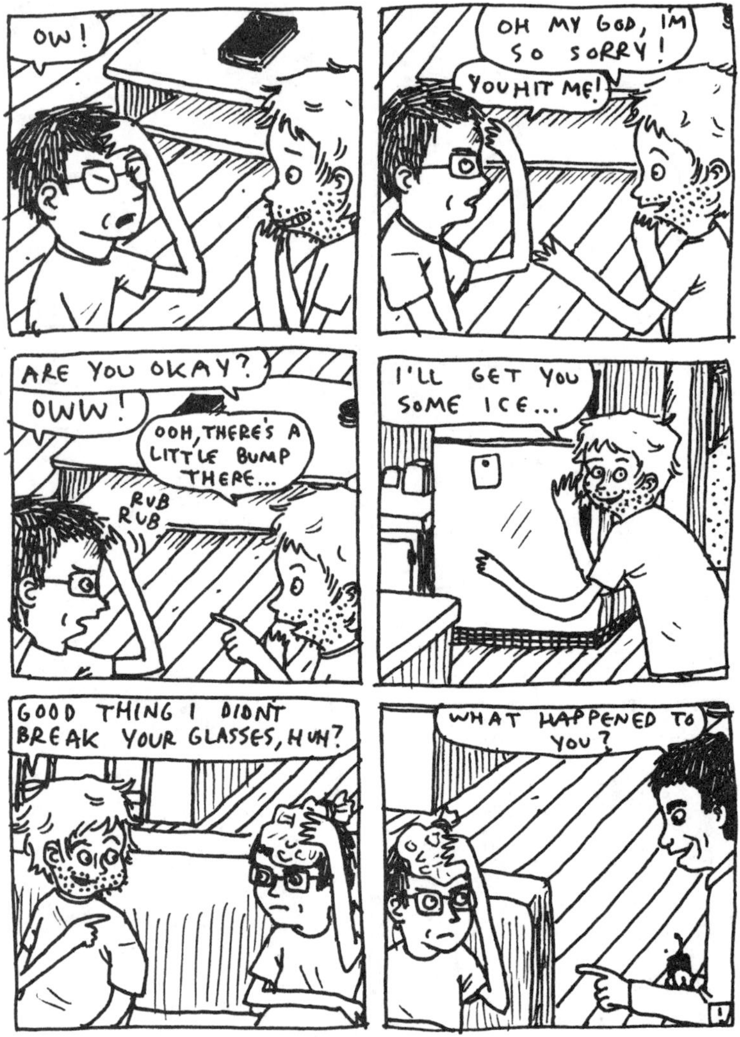
OW!
OH MY GOD, I'M SO SORRY!
YOU HIT ME!
ARE YOU OKAY?
OWW!
OOH, THERE'S A LITTLE BUMP THERE...
RUB RUB
I'LL GET YOU SOME ICE...
GOOD THING I DIDNT BREAK YOUR GLASSES, HUH?
WHAT HAPPENED TO YOU?

THE UNPLANNED POTENTIAL OF LIFE

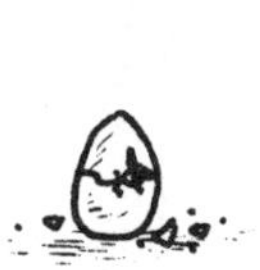

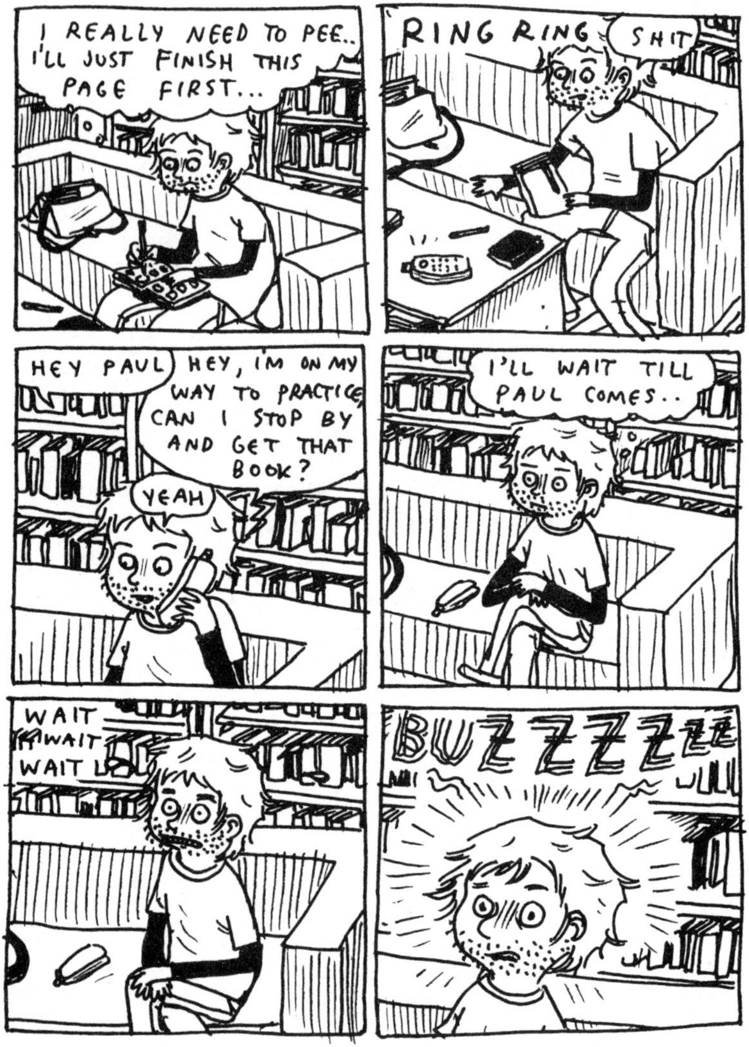
I REALLY NEED TO PEE..
I'LL JUST FINISH THIS PAGE FIRST...
RING RING
SHIT
HEY PAUL
HEY, I'M ON MY WAY TO PRACTICE, CAN I STOP BY AND GET THAT BOOK?
YEAH
I'LL WAIT TILL PAUL COMES..
WAIT
WAIT
WAIT
BUZZZZZZZ

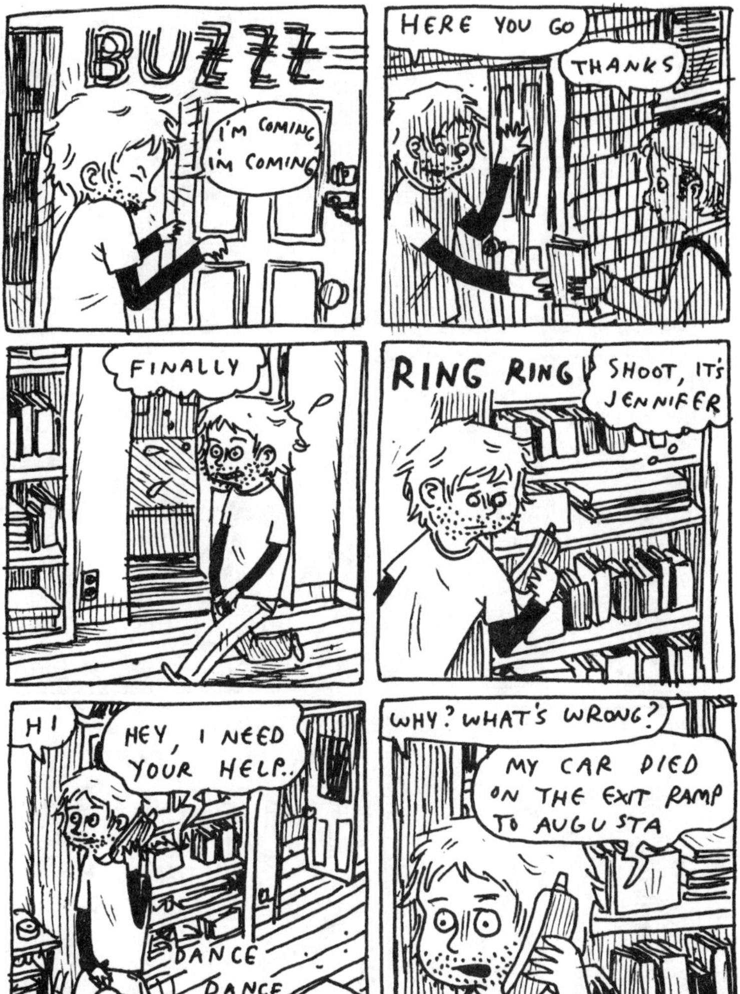
BUZZZ
I'M COMING I'M COMING
HERE YOU GO
THANKS
FINALLY
RING RING
SHOOT, IT'S JENNIFER
HI
HEY, I NEED YOUR HELP..
DANCE
DANCE
WHY? WHAT'S WRONG?
MY CAR DIED ON THE EXIT RAMP TO AUGUSTA

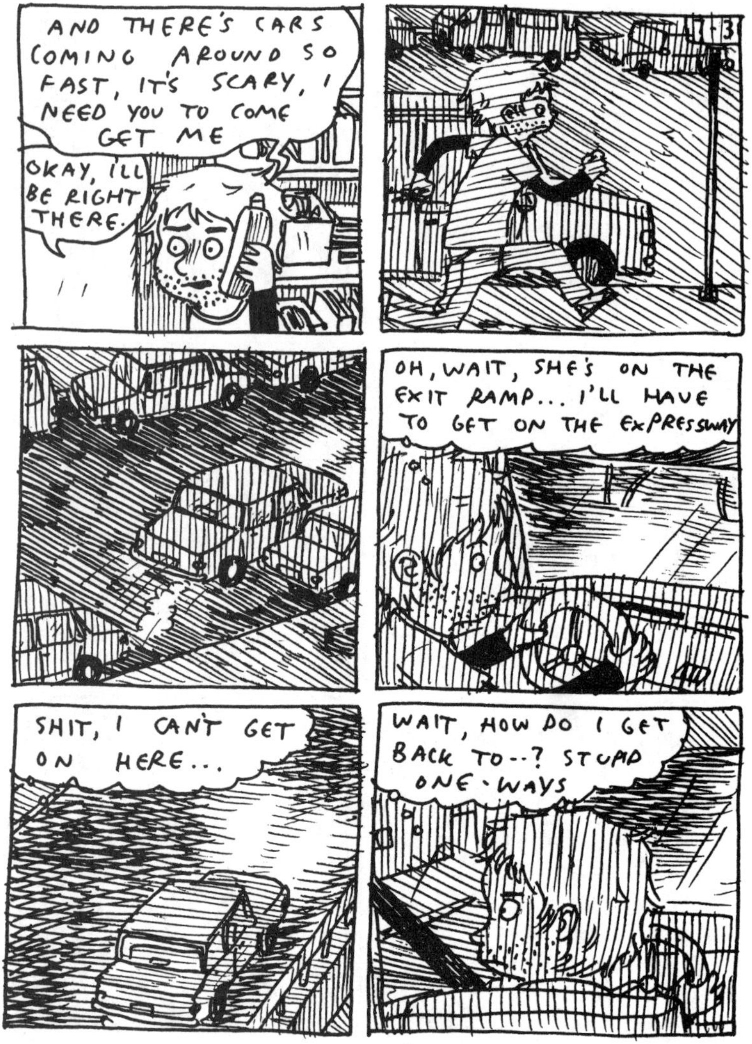
AND THERE'S CARS COMING AROUND SO FAST, IT'S SCARY, I NEED YOU TO COME GET ME
OKAY, I'LL BE RIGHT THERE.
7-3
OH, WAIT, SHE'S ON THE EXIT RAMP... I'LL HAVE TO GET ON THE EXPRESSWAY
SHIT, I CAN'T GET ON HERE...
WAIT, HOW DO I GET BACK TO--? STUPID ONE-WAYS

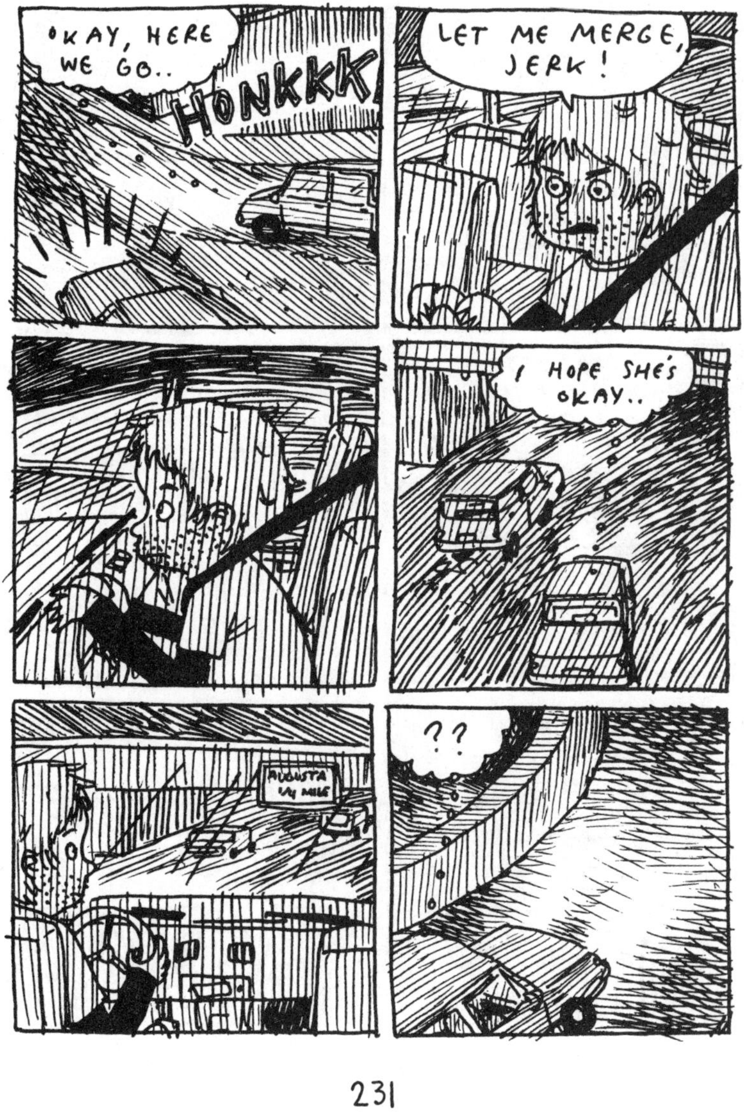
OKAY, HERE WE GO..
HONKKK
LET ME MERGE, JERK!
I HOPE SHE'S OKAY..
AUGUSTA 1/4 MILE
??

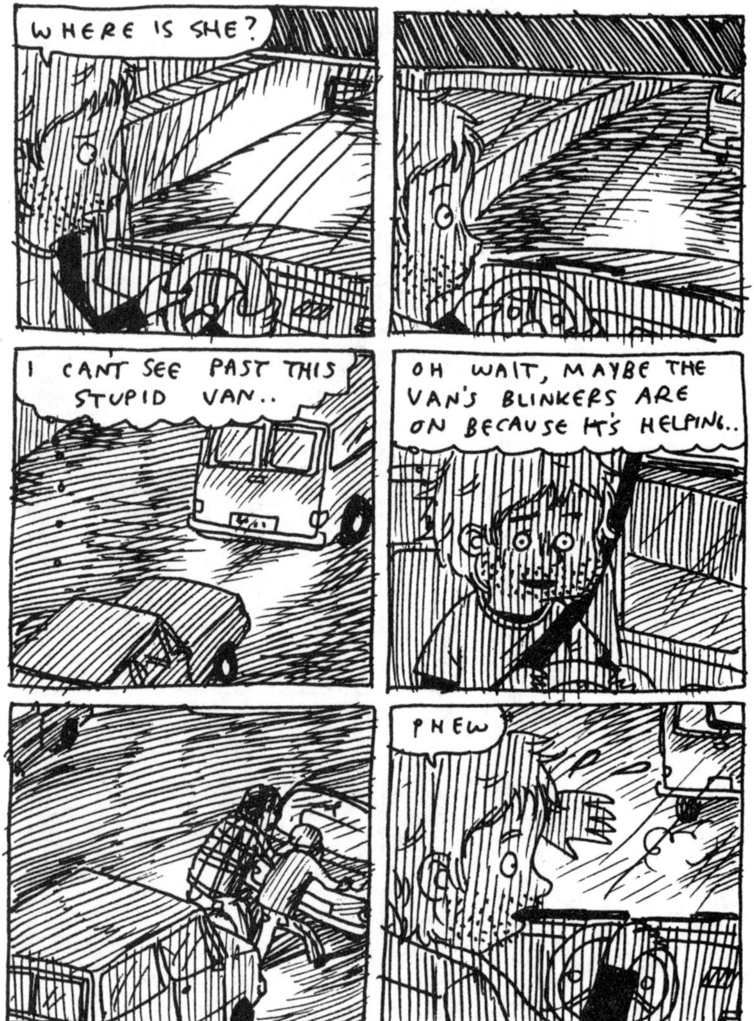
WHERE IS SHE?
I CANT SEE PAST THIS STUPID VAN..
OH WAIT, MAYBE THE VAN'S BLINKERS ARE ON BECAUSE IT'S HELPING..
PHEW

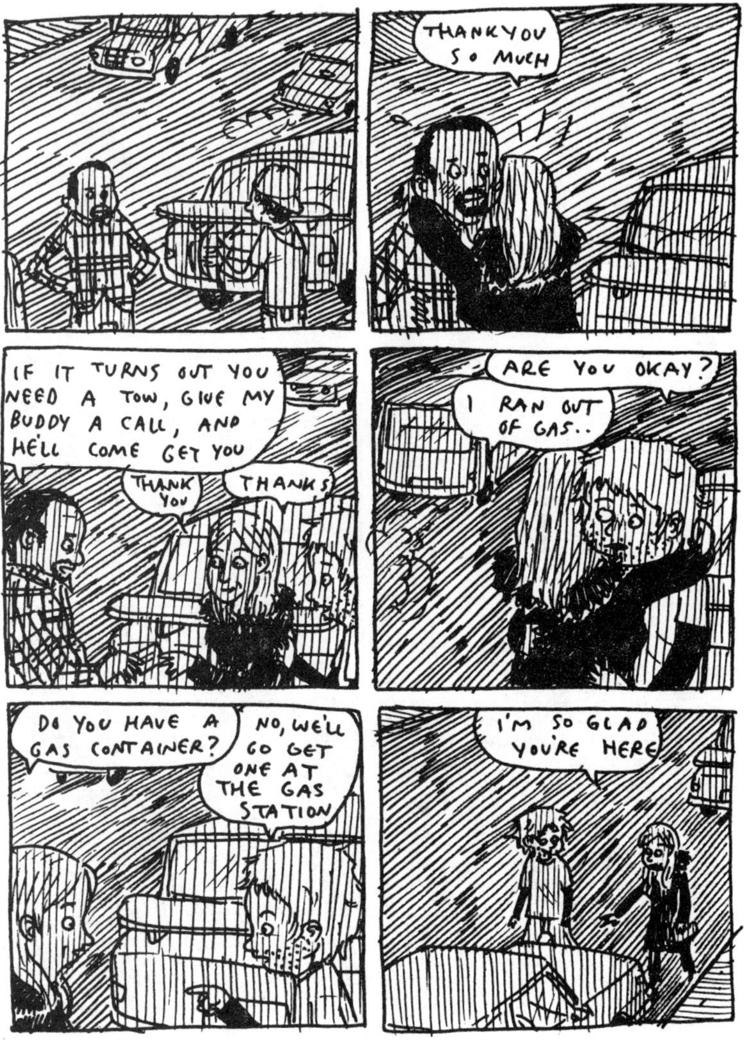
THANKYOU SO MUCH
IF IT TURNS OUT YOU NEED A TOW, GIVE MY BUDDY A CALL, AND HE'LL COME GET YOU
THANK YOU
THANKS
ARE YOU OKAY?
I RAN OUT OF GAS..
DO YOU HAVE A GAS CONTAINER?
NO, WE'LL GO GET ONE AT THE GAS STATION
I'M SO GLAD YOU'RE HERE

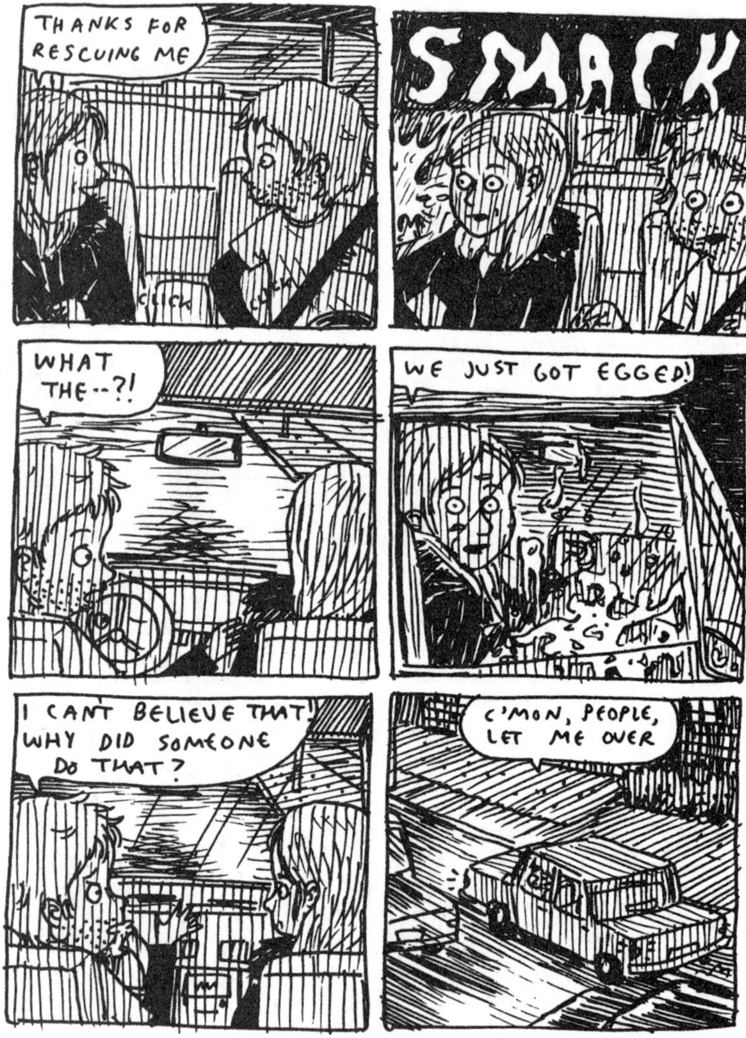
THANKS FOR RESCUING ME
CLICK
SMACK
WHAT THE--?!
WE JUST GOT EGGED!
I CAN'T BELIEVE THAT! WHY DID SOMEONE DO THAT?
C'MON, PEOPLE, LET ME OVER

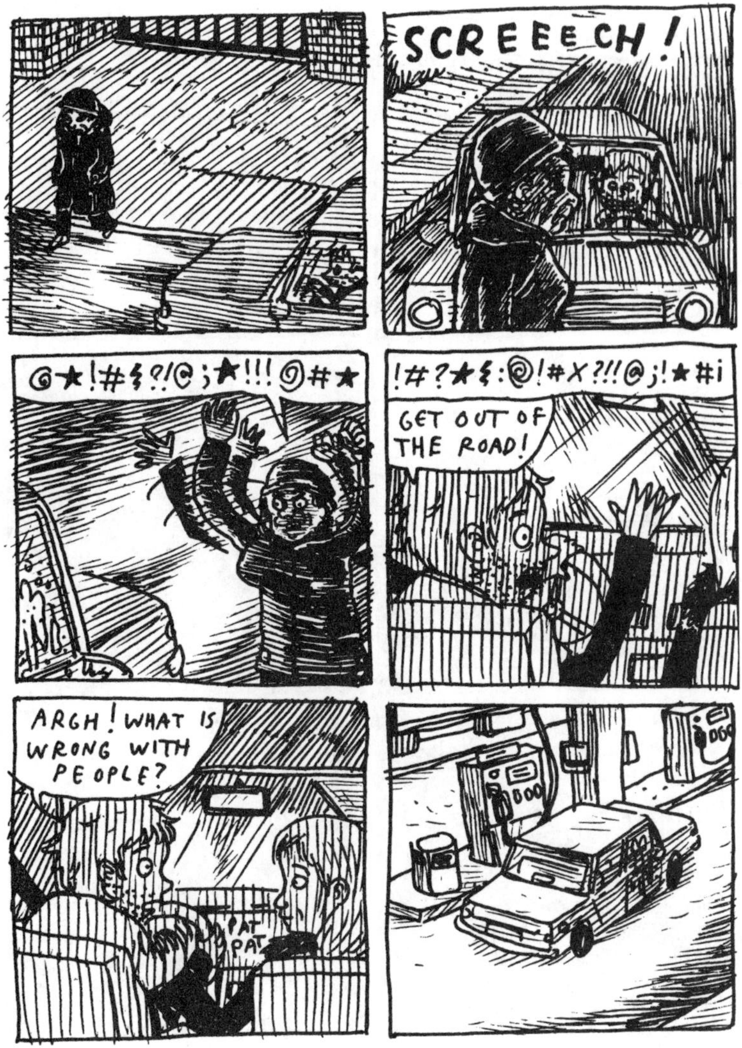
SCREEECH!
GET OUT OF THE ROAD!
ARGH! WHAT IS WRONG WITH PEOPLE?
PAT PAT

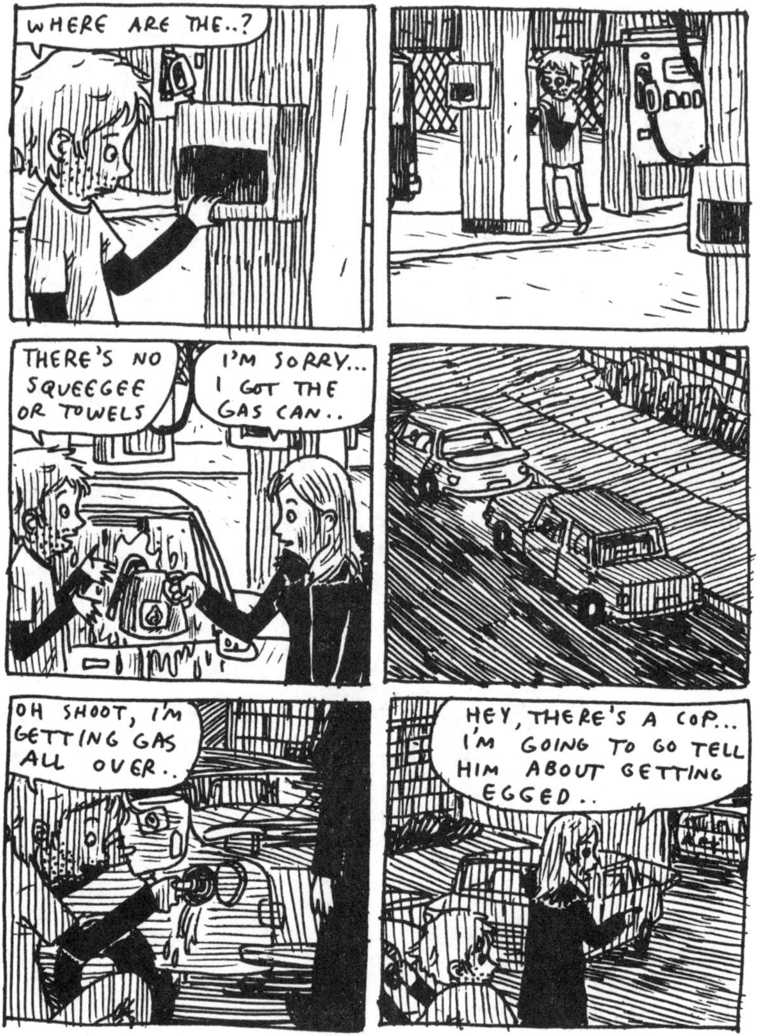
WHERE ARE THE..?
THERE'S NO SQUEEGEE OR TOWELS
I'M SORRY... I GOT THE GAS CAN..
OH SHOOT, I'M GETTING GAS ALL OVER..
HEY, THERE'S A COP... I'M GOING TO GO TELL HIM ABOUT GETTING EGGED..

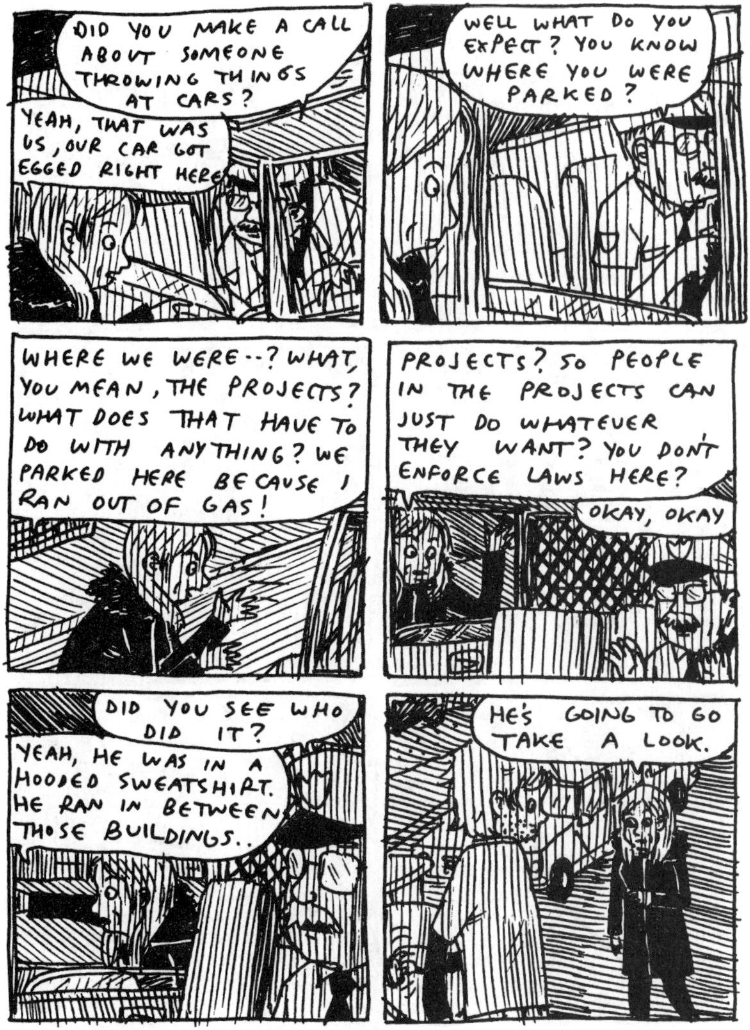
DID YOU MAKE A CALL ABOUT SOMEONE THROWING THINGS AT CARS?
YEAH, THAT WAS US, OUR CAR GOT EGGED RIGHT HERE.
WELL WHAT DO YOU EXPECT? YOU KNOW WHERE YOU WERE PARKED?
WHERE WE WERE--? WHAT, YOU MEAN, THE PROJECTS? WHAT DOES THAT HAVE TO DO WITH ANYTHING? WE PARKED HERE BECAUSE I RAN OUT OF GAS!
PROJECTS? SO PEOPLE IN THE PROJECTS CAN JUST DO WHATEVER THEY WANT? YOU DON'T ENFORCE LAWS HERE?
OKAY, OKAY
DID YOU SEE WHO DID IT?
YEAH, HE WAS IN A HOODED SWEATSHIRT. HE RAN IN BETWEEN THOSE BUILDINGS..
HE'S GOING TO GO TAKE A LOOK.

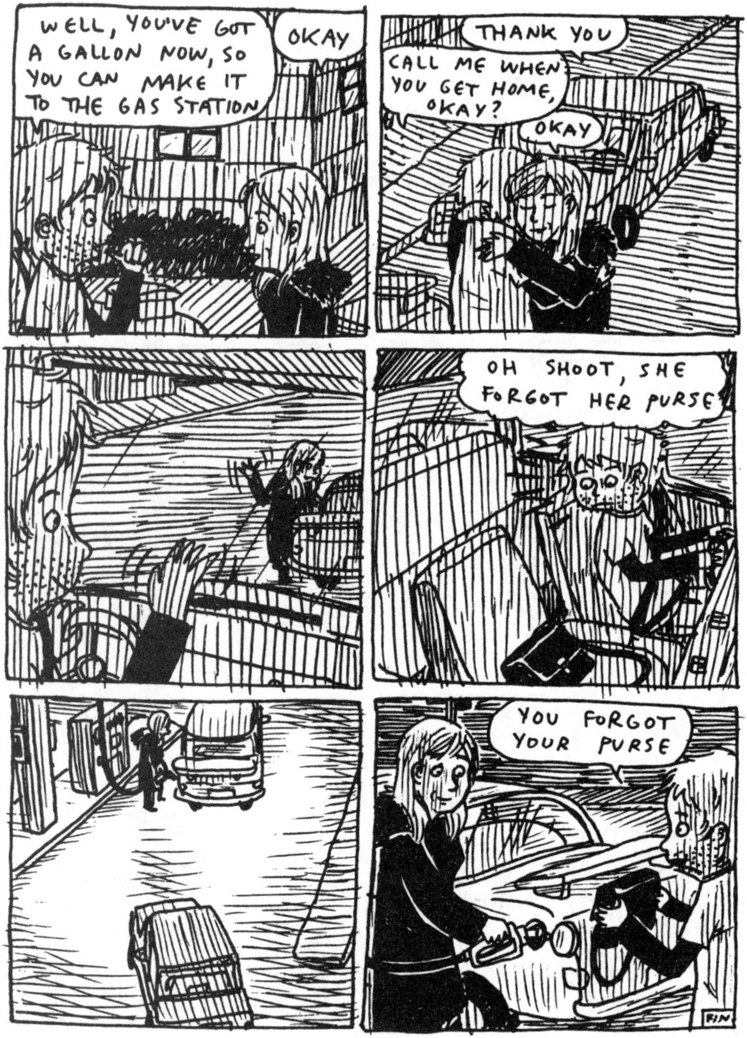
WELL, YOU'VE GOT A GALLON NOW, SO YOU CAN MAKE IT TO THE GAS STATION
OKAY
THANK YOU
CALL ME WHEN YOU GET HOME, OKAY?
OKAY
OH SHOOT, SHE FORGOT HER PURSE
YOU FORGOT YOUR PURSE
FIN

LITTLE THINGS

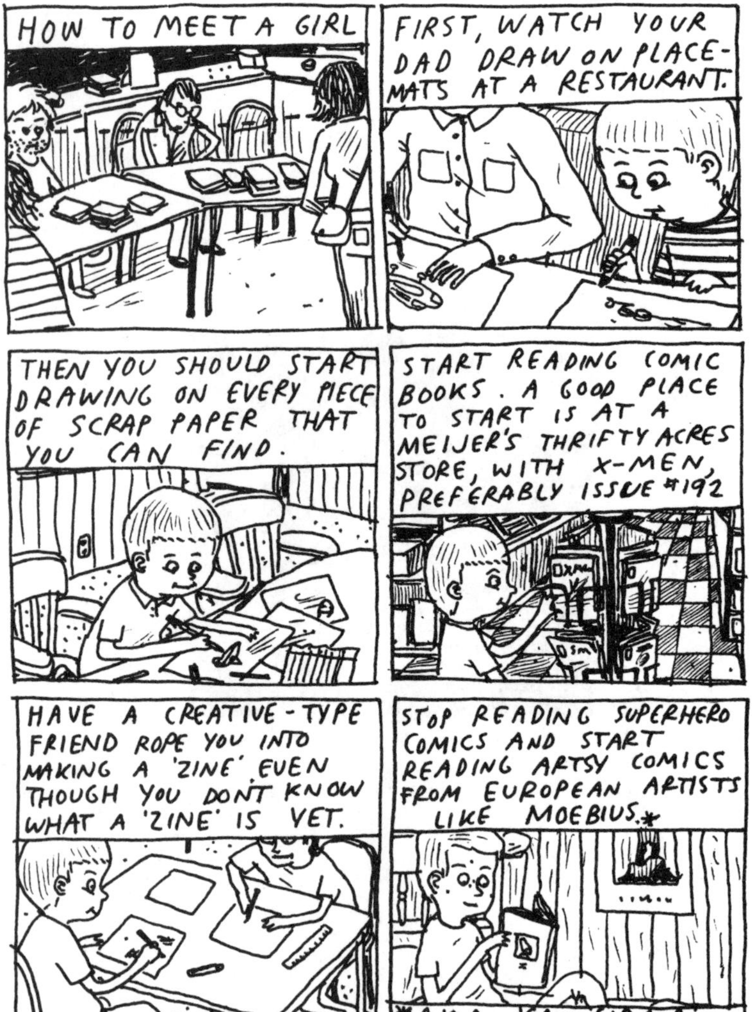
HOW TO MEET A GIRL
FIRST, WATCH YOUR DAD DRAW ON PLACE-MATS AT A RESTAURANT.
THEN YOU SHOULD START DRAWING ON EVERY PIECE OF SCRAP PAPER THAT YOU CAN FIND.
START READING COMIC BOOKS. A GOOD PLACE TO START IS AT A MEIJER'S THRIFTY ACRES STORE, WITH X-MEN, PREFERABLY ISSUE #192
HAVE A CREATIVE-TYPE FRIEND ROPE YOU INTO MAKING A 'ZINE' EVEN THOUGH YOU DON'T KNOW WHAT A 'ZINE' IS YET.
STOP READING SUPERHERO COMICS AND START READING ARTSY COMICS FROM EUROPEAN ARTISTS LIKE MOEBIUS.*
*A.K.A. JEAN GIRAUD

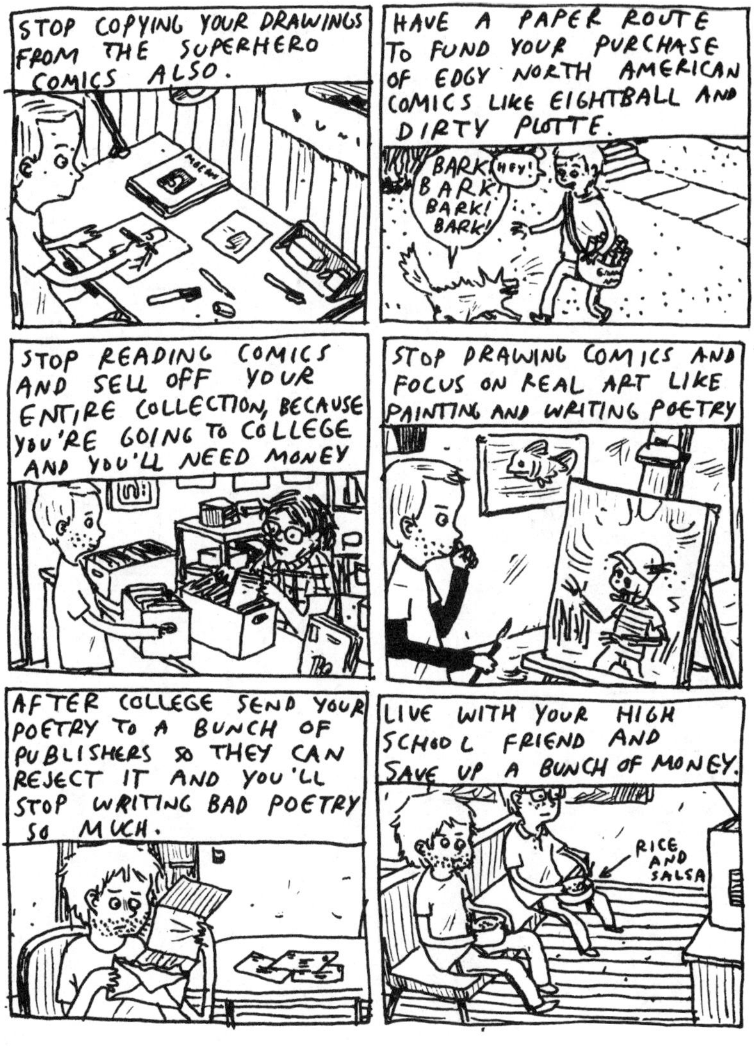
STOP COPYING YOUR DRAWINGS FROM THE SUPERHERO COMICS ALSO.
HAVE A PAPER ROUTE TO FUND YOUR PURCHASE OF EDGY NORTH AMERICAN COMICS LIKE EIGHTBALL AND DIRTY PLOTTE.
BARK! BARK! BARK! BARK!
HEY!
STOP READING COMICS AND SELL OFF YOUR ENTIRE COLLECTION, BECAUSE YOU'RE GOING TO COLLEGE AND YOU'LL NEED MONEY
STOP DRAWING COMICS AND FOCUS ON REAL ART LIKE PAINTING AND WRITING POETRY
AFTER COLLEGE SEND YOUR POETRY TO A BUNCH OF PUBLISHERS SO THEY CAN REJECT IT AND YOU'LL STOP WRITING BAD POETRY SO MUCH.
LIVE WITH YOUR HIGH SCHOOL FRIEND AND SAVE UP A BUNCH OF MONEY.
RICE AND SALSA

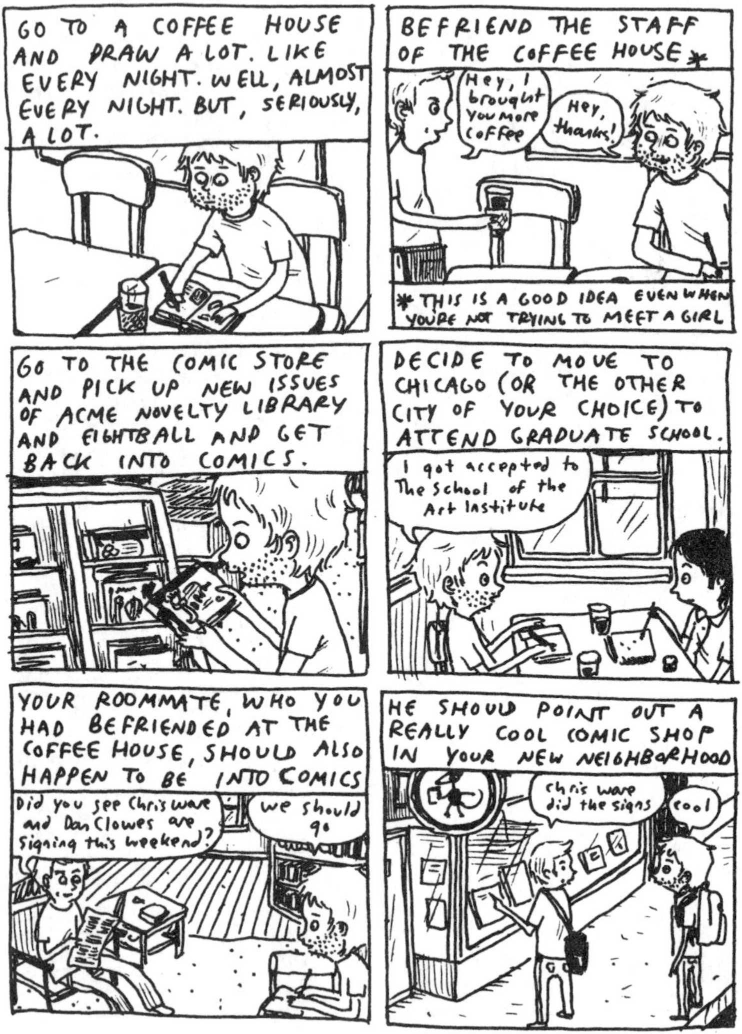
GO TO A COFFEE HOUSE AND DRAW A LOT. LIKE EVERY NIGHT. WELL, ALMOST EVERY NIGHT. BUT, SERIOUSLY, A LOT.
BEFRIEND THE STAFF OF THE COFFEE HOUSE*
Hey, I brought you more coffee
Hey, thanks!
* THIS IS A GOOD IDEA EVEN WHEN YOU'RE NOT TRYING TO MEET A GIRL
GO TO THE COMIC STORE AND PICK UP NEW ISSUES OF ACME NOVELTY LIBRARY AND EIGHTBALL AND GET BACK INTO COMICS.
DECIDE TO MOVE TO CHICAGO (OR THE OTHER CITY OF YOUR CHOICE) TO ATTEND GRADUATE SCHOOL.
I got accepted to The School of the Art Institute
YOUR ROOMMATE, WHO YOU HAD BEFRIENDED AT THE COFFEE HOUSE, SHOULD ALSO HAPPEN TO BE INTO COMICS
Did you see Chris Ware and Dan Clowes are signing this weekend?
we should go
HE SHOULD POINT OUT A REALLY COOL COMIC SHOP IN YOUR NEW NEIGHBORHOOD
chris ware did the signs
cool

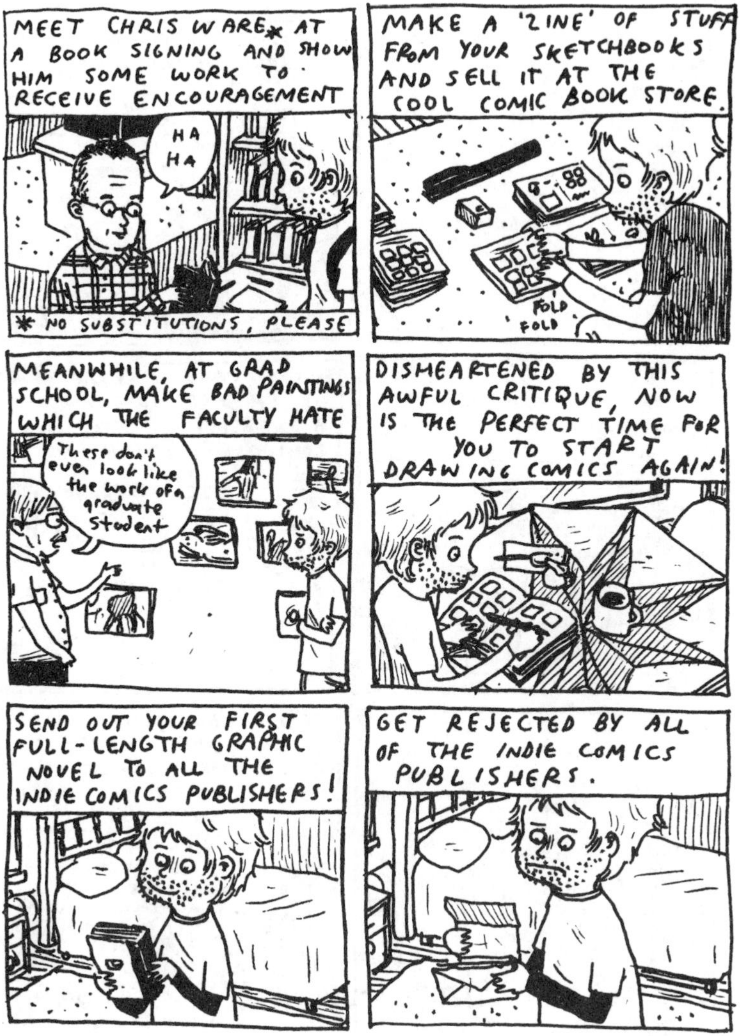
MEET CHRIS WARE* AT A BOOK SIGNING AND SHOW HIM SOME WORK TO RECEIVE ENCOURAGEMENT
HA HA
* NO SUBSTITUTIONS, PLEASE
MAKE A 'ZINE' OF STUFF FROM YOUR SKETCHBOOKS AND SELL IT AT THE COOL COMIC BOOK STORE.
FOLD FOLD
MEANWHILE, AT GRAD SCHOOL, MAKE BAD PAINTINGS WHICH THE FACULTY HATE
These don't even look like the work of a graduate student
DISHEARTENED BY THIS AWFUL CRITIQUE, NOW IS THE PERFECT TIME FOR YOU TO START DRAWING COMICS AGAIN!
SEND OUT YOUR FIRST FULL-LENGTH GRAPHIC NOVEL TO ALL THE INDIE COMICS PUBLISHERS!
GET REJECTED BY ALL OF THE INDIE COMICS PUBLISHERS.

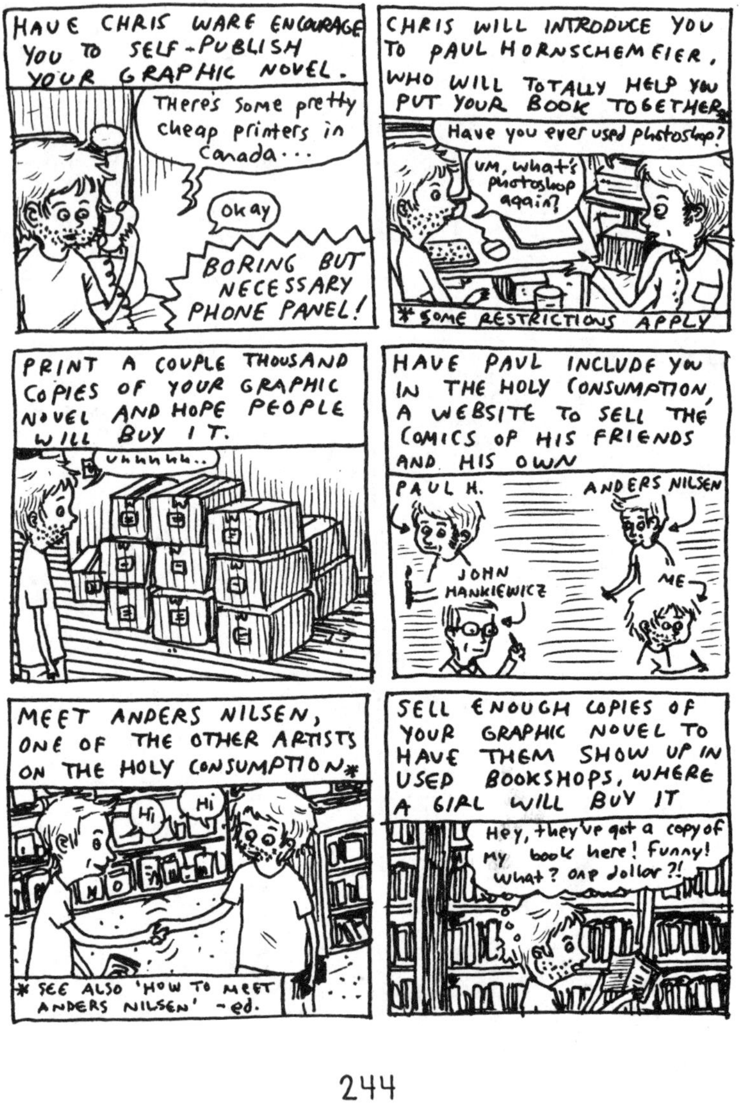
HAVE CHRIS WARE ENCOURAGE YOU TO SELF-PUBLISH YOUR GRAPHIC NOVEL.
There's some pretty cheap printers in Canada...
okay
BORING BUT NECESSARY PHONE PANEL!
CHRIS WILL INTRODUCE YOU TO PAUL HORNSCHEMEIER, WHO WILL TOTALLY HELP YOU PUT YOUR BOOK TOGETHER*
Have you ever used photoshop?
UM, what's photoshop again?
* SOME RESTRICTIONS APPLY
PRINT A COUPLE THOUSAND COPIES OF YOUR GRAPHIC NOVEL AND HOPE PEOPLE WILL BUY IT.
uhhhhh..
HAVE PAUL INCLUDE YOU IN THE HOLY CONSUMPTION, A WEBSITE TO SELL THE COMICS OF HIS FRIENDS AND HIS OWN
PAUL H.
ANDERS NILSEN
JOHN HANKIEWICZ
ME
MEET ANDERS NILSEN, ONE OF THE OTHER ARTISTS ON THE HOLY CONSUMPTION*
Hi
Hi
* SEE ALSO 'HOW TO MEET ANDERS NILSEN' -ed.
SELL ENOUGH COPIES OF YOUR GRAPHIC NOVEL TO HAVE THEM SHOW UP IN USED BOOKSHOPS, WHERE A GIRL WILL BUY IT
Hey, they've got a copy of my book here! Funny! what? one dollar?!

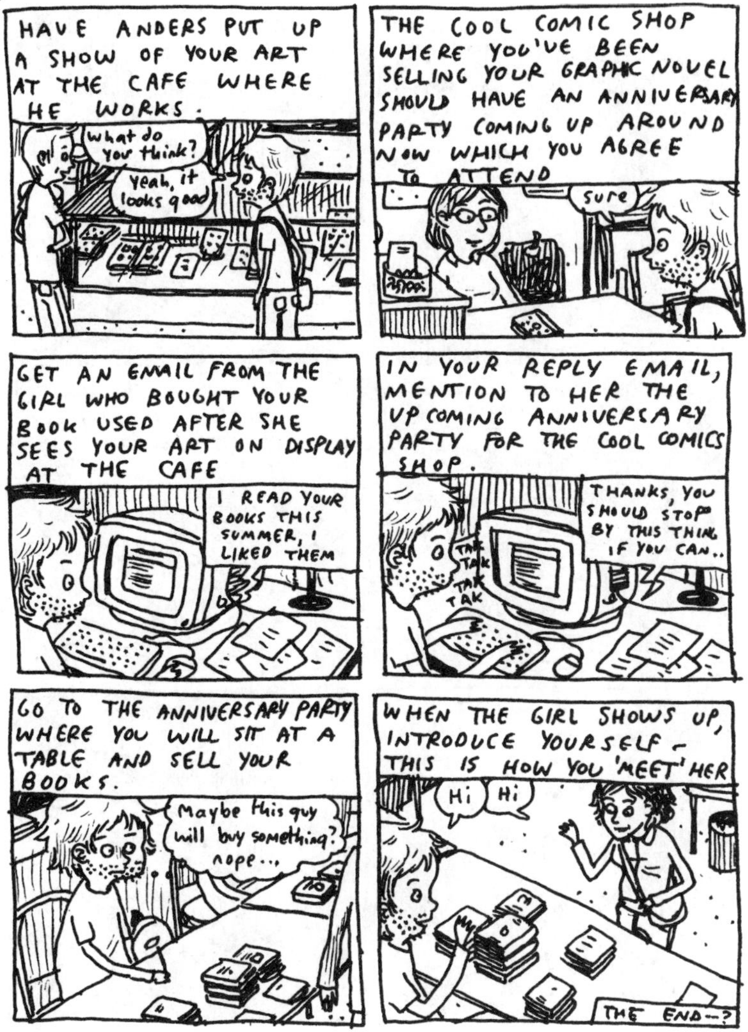
HAVE ANDERS PUT UP A SHOW OF YOUR ART AT THE CAFE WHERE HE WORKS.
what do you think?
yeah, it looks good
THE COOL COMIC SHOP WHERE YOU'VE BEEN SELLING YOUR GRAPHIC NOVEL SHOULD HAVE AN ANNIVERSARY PARTY COMING UP AROUND NOW WHICH YOU AGREE TO ATTEND
sure
GET AN EMAIL FROM THE GIRL WHO BOUGHT YOUR BOOK USED AFTER SHE SEES YOUR ART ON DISPLAY AT THE CAFE
I READ YOUR BOOKS THIS SUMMER, I LIKED THEM
IN YOUR REPLY EMAIL, MENTION TO HER THE UPCOMING ANNIVERSARY PARTY FOR THE COOL COMICS SHOP.
THANKS, YOU SHOULD STOP BY THIS THING IF YOU CAN..
TAK TAK TAK TAK
GO TO THE ANNIVERSARY PARTY WHERE YOU WILL SIT AT A TABLE AND SELL YOUR BOOKS.
Maybe this guy will buy something? nope...
WHEN THE GIRL SHOWS UP, INTRODUCE YOURSELF - THIS IS HOW YOU 'MEET' HER
Hi
Hi
THE END--?

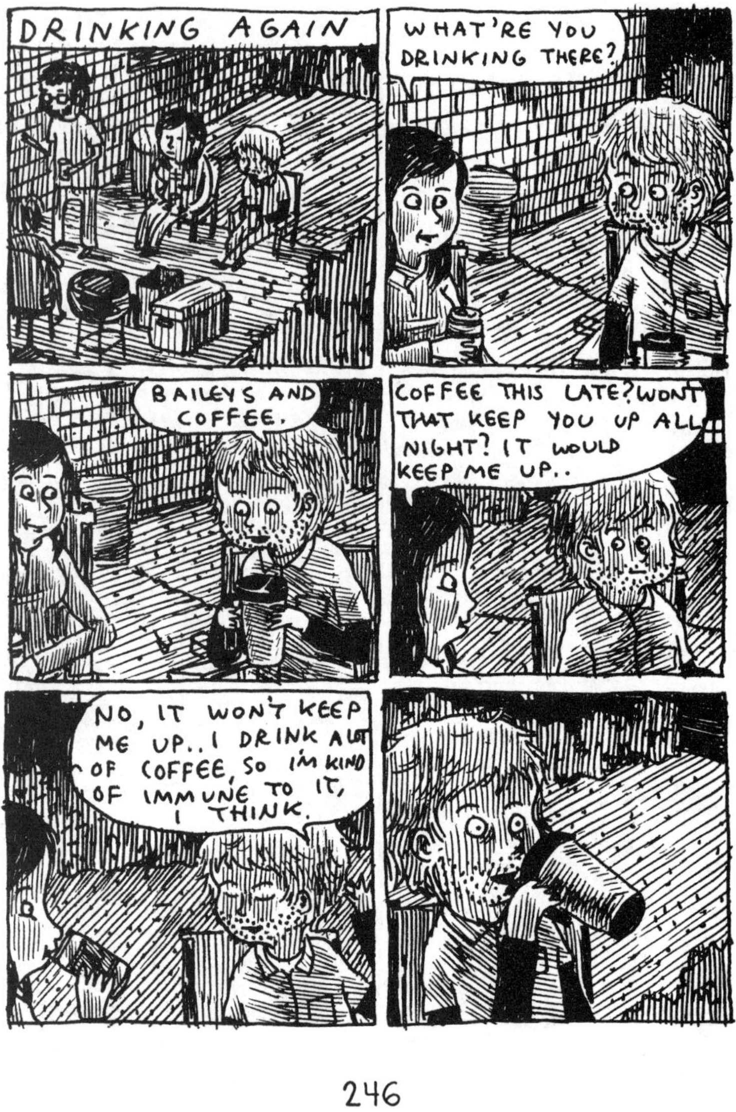
DRINKING AGAIN
WHAT'RE YOU DRINKING THERE?
BAILEYS AND COFFEE.
COFFEE THIS LATE? WONT THAT KEEP YOU UP ALL NIGHT? IT WOULD KEEP ME UP..
NO, IT WON'T KEEP ME UP.. I DRINK A LOT OF COFFEE, SO I'M KIND OF IMMUNE TO IT, I THINK.

YAWN
SHIT
148
217
BLEEACHHHK
306
352

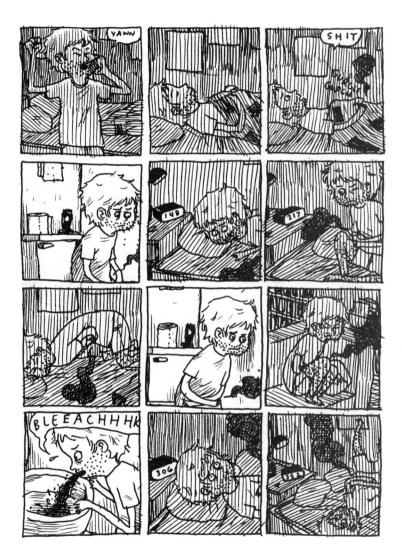

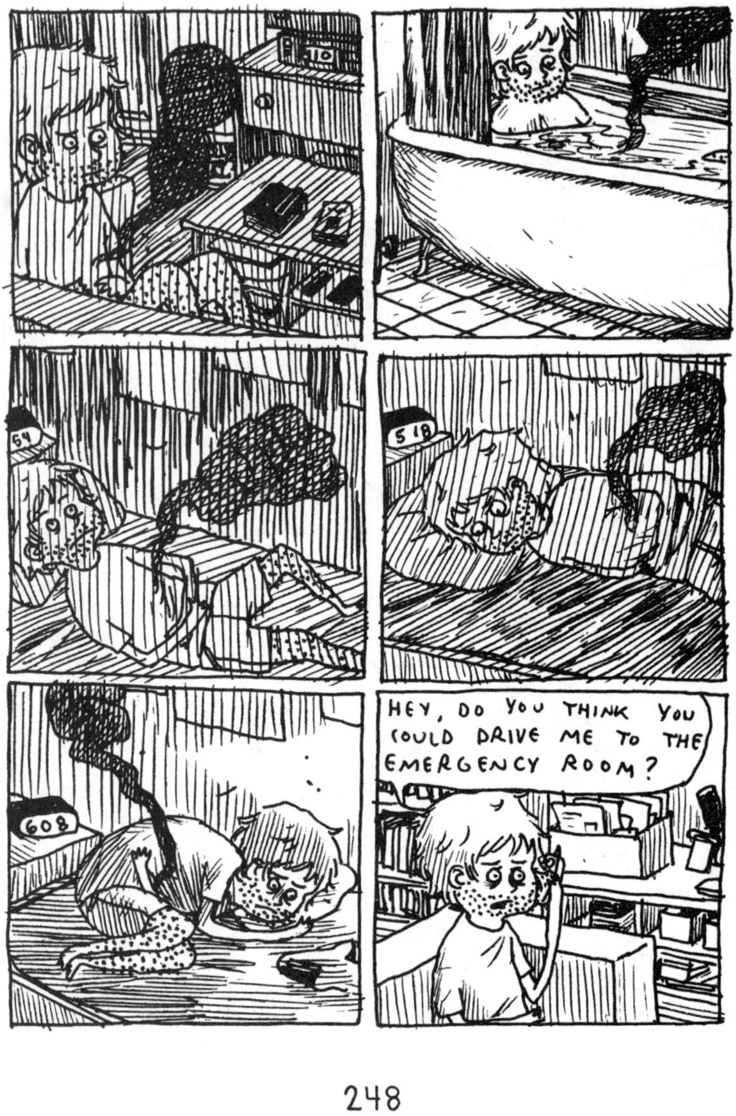
HEY, DO YOU THINK YOU COULD DRIVE ME TO THE EMERGENCY ROOM?

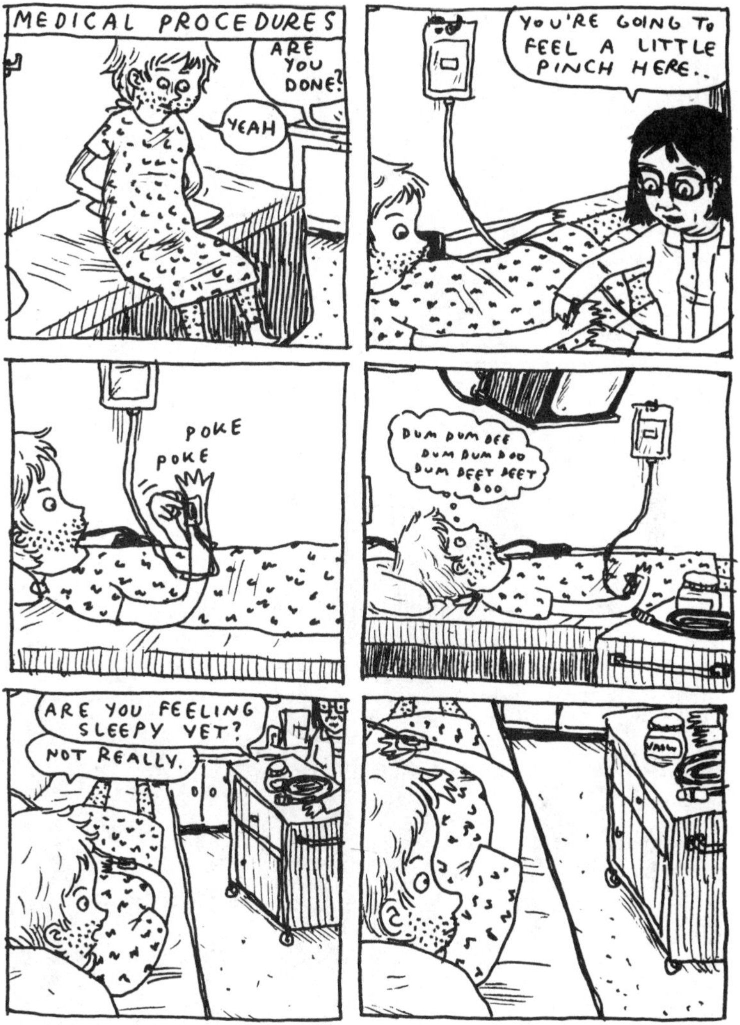

MEDICAL PROCEDURES
ARE YOU DONE?
YEAH
YOU'RE GOING TO FEEL A LITTLE PINCH HERE..
POKE
POKE
DUM DUM DEE DUM DUM DOO DUM DEET DEET DOO
ARE YOU FEELING SLEEPY YET?
NOT REALLY.

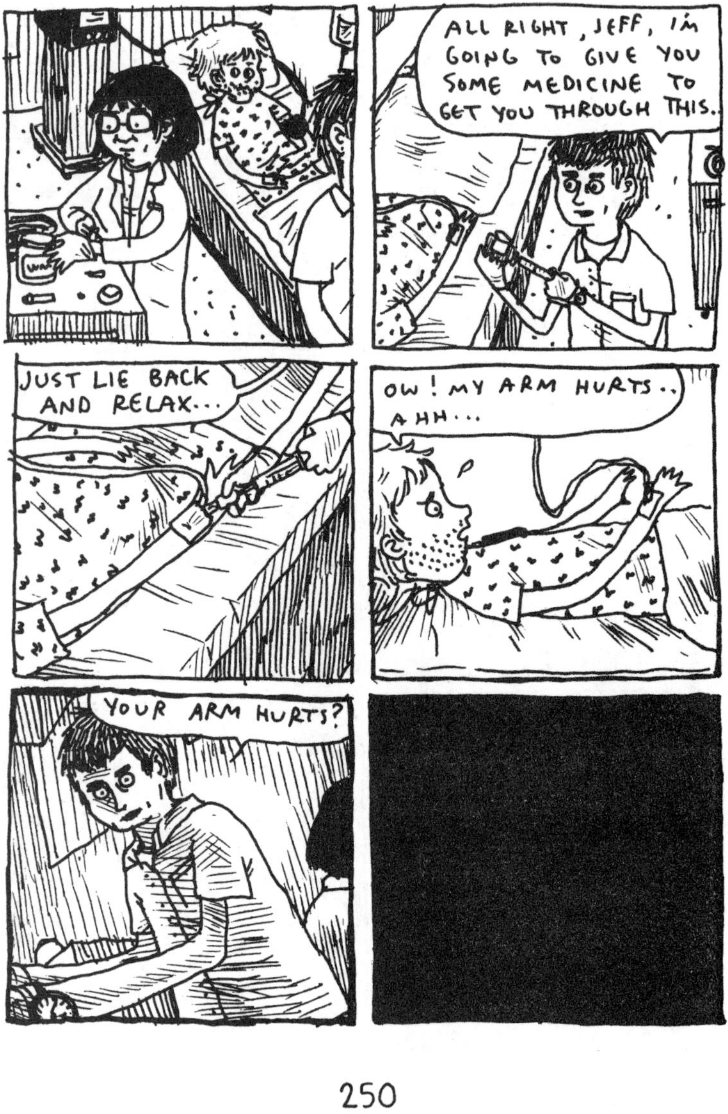
ALL RIGHT, JEFF, I'M GOING TO GIVE YOU SOME MEDICINE TO GET YOU THROUGH THIS.
JUST LIE BACK AND RELAX...
OW! MY ARM HURTS.. AHH...
YOUR ARM HURTS?

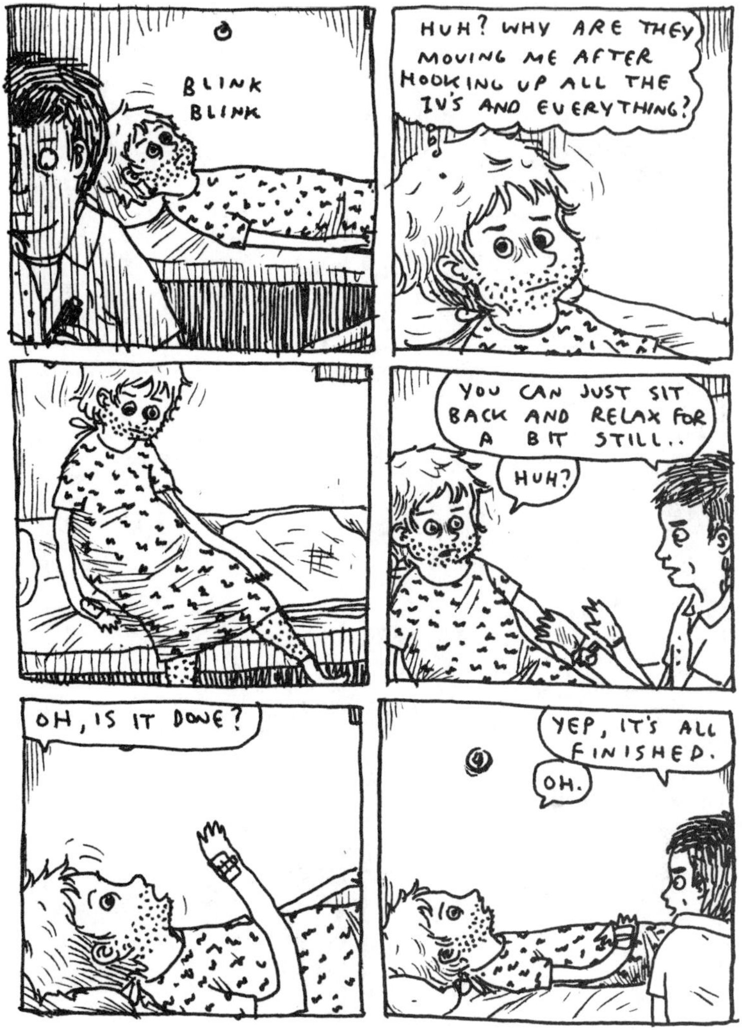
BLINK
BLINK
HUH? WHY ARE THEY MOVING ME AFTER HOOKING UP ALL THE IV'S AND EVERYTHING?
YOU CAN JUST SIT BACK AND RELAX FOR A BIT STILL..
HUH?
OH, IS IT DONE?
YEP, IT'S ALL FINISHED.
OH.

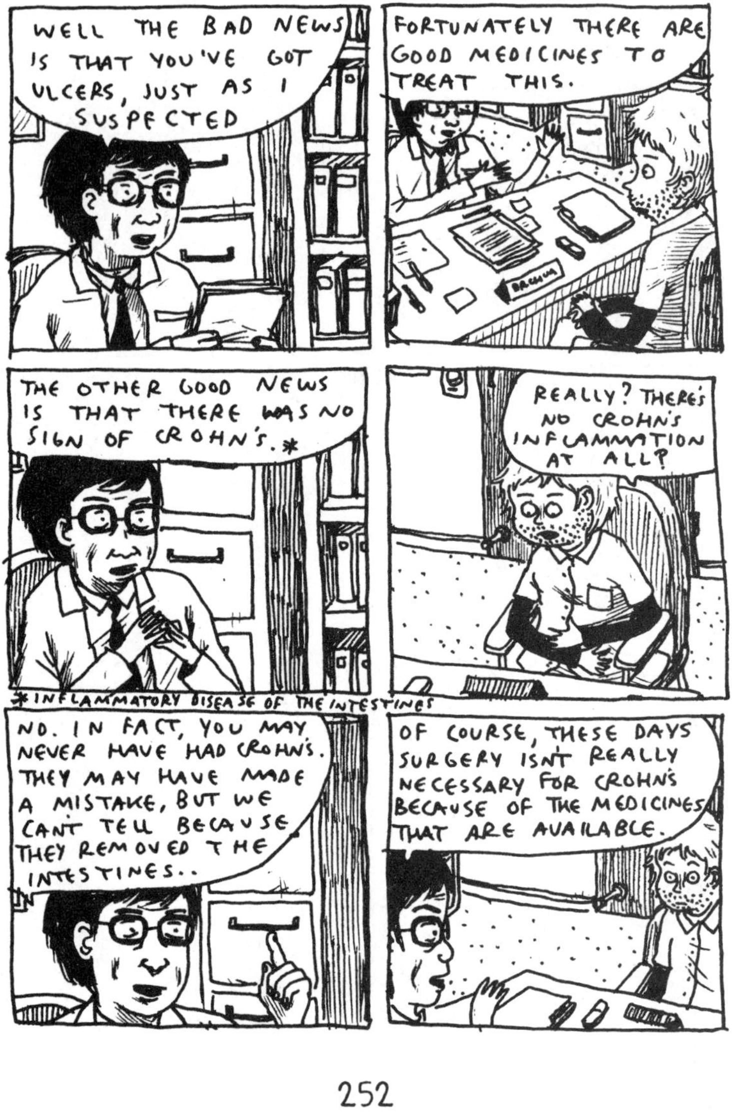
WELL THE BAD NEWS IS THAT YOU'VE GOT ULCERS, JUST AS I SUSPECTED
FORTUNATELY THERE ARE GOOD MEDICINES TO TREAT THIS.
THE OTHER GOOD NEWS IS THAT THERE WAS NO SIGN OF CROHN'S.*
REALLY? THERE'S NO CROHN'S INFLAMMATION AT ALL?
*INFLAMMATORY DISEASE OF THE INTESTINES
NO. IN FACT, YOU MAY NEVER HAVE HAD CROHN'S. THEY MAY HAVE MADE A MISTAKE, BUT WE CANT TELL BECAUSE THEY REMOVED THE INTESTINES..
OF COURSE, THESE DAYS SURGERY ISN'T REALLY NECESSARY FOR CROHN'S BECAUSE OF THE MEDICINES THAT ARE AVAILABLE.

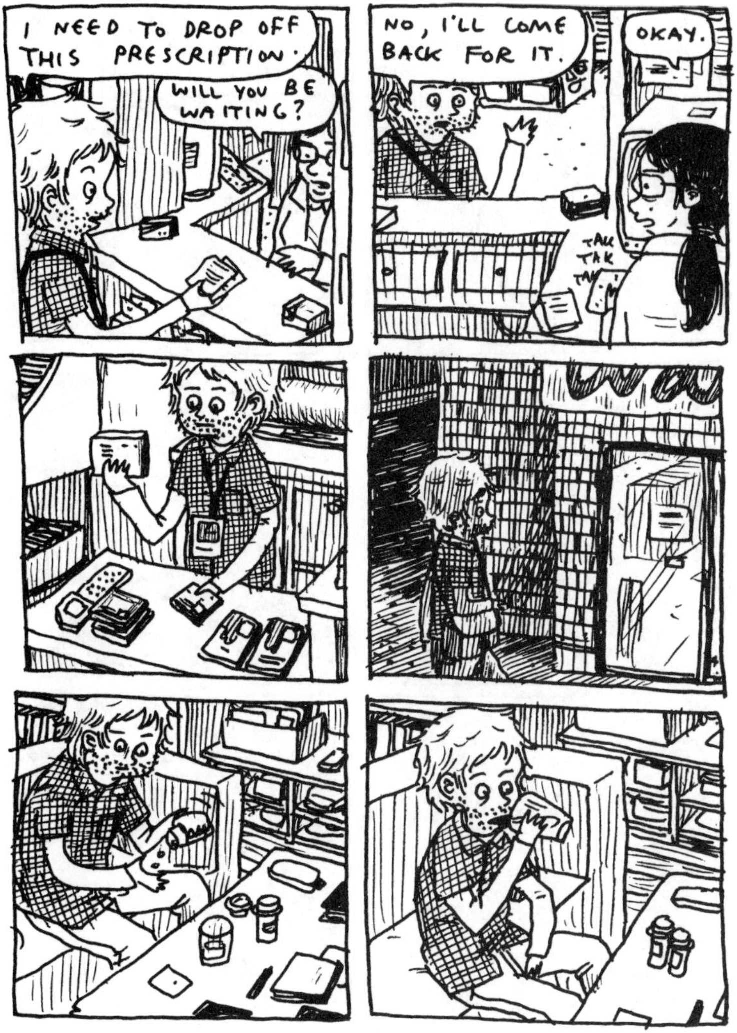
I NEED TO DROP OFF THIS PRESCRIPTION.
WILL YOU BE WAITING?
NO, I'LL COME BACK FOR IT.
OKAY.
TAK
TAK

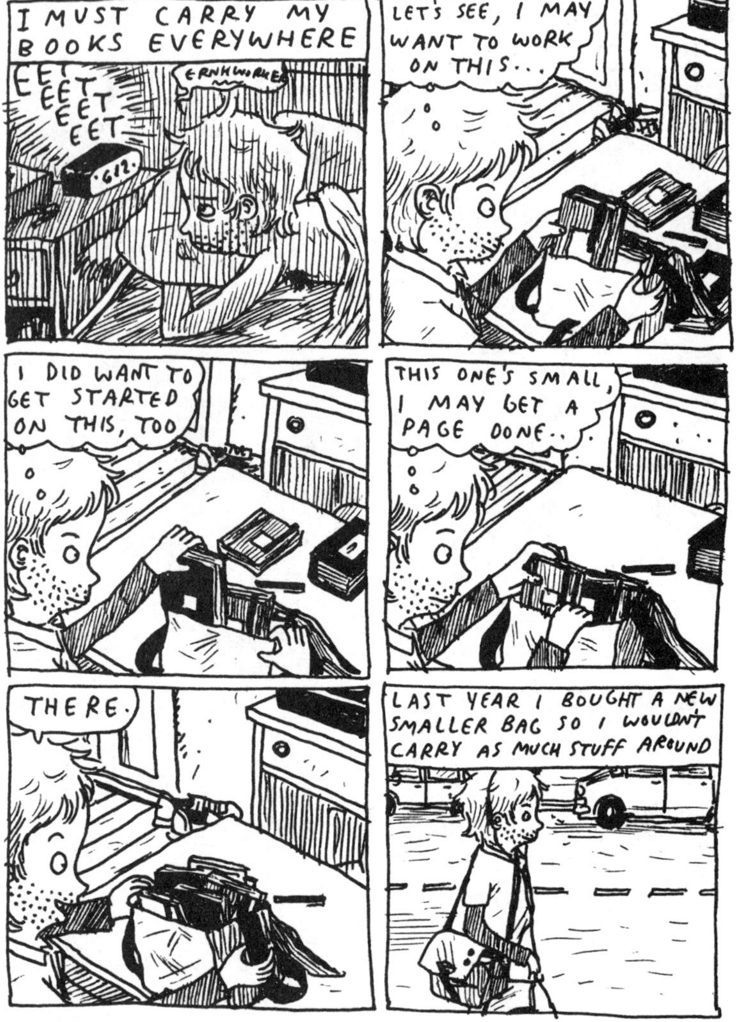
I MUST CARRY MY BOOKS EVERYWHERE
EEET EEET EEET EEET
ERNHWORKE
6:12
LET'S SEE, I MAY WANT TO WORK ON THIS...
I DID WANT TO GET STARTED ON THIS, TOO
THIS ONE'S SMALL, I MAY GET A PAGE DONE..
THERE.
LAST YEAR I BOUGHT A NEW SMALLER BAG SO I WOULDN'T CARRY AS MUCH STUFF AROUND

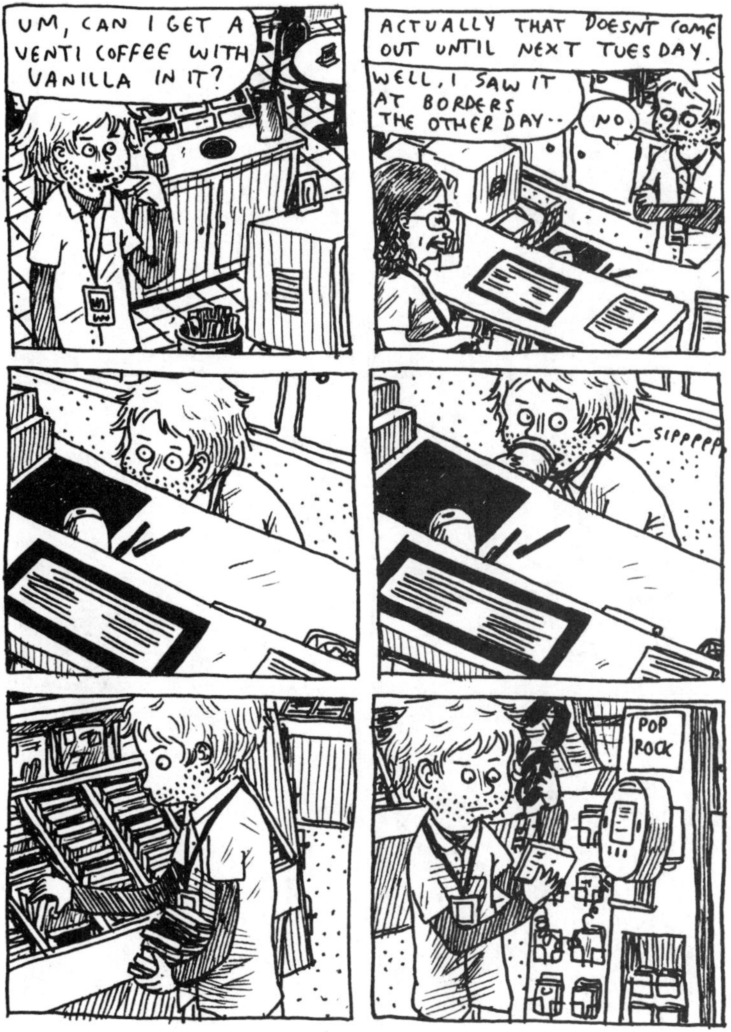
UM, CAN I GET A VENTI COFFEE WITH VANILLA IN IT?
ACTUALLY THAT DOESN'T COME OUT UNTIL NEXT TUESDAY.
WELL, I SAW IT AT BORDERS THE OTHER DAY..
NO.
SIPPPPP
POP ROCK

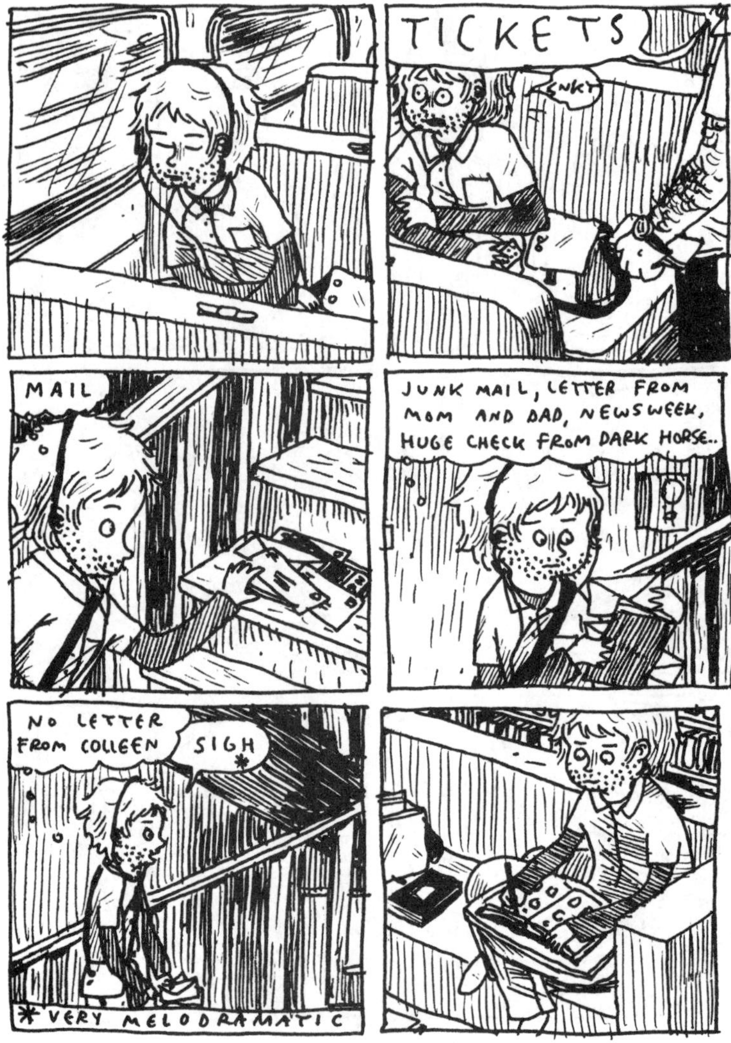
TICKETS
SNKT
MAIL
JUNK MAIL, LETTER FROM MOM AND DAD, NEWSWEEK, HUGE CHECK FROM DARK HORSE..
NO LETTER FROM COLLEEN
SIGH *
* VERY MELODRAMATIC

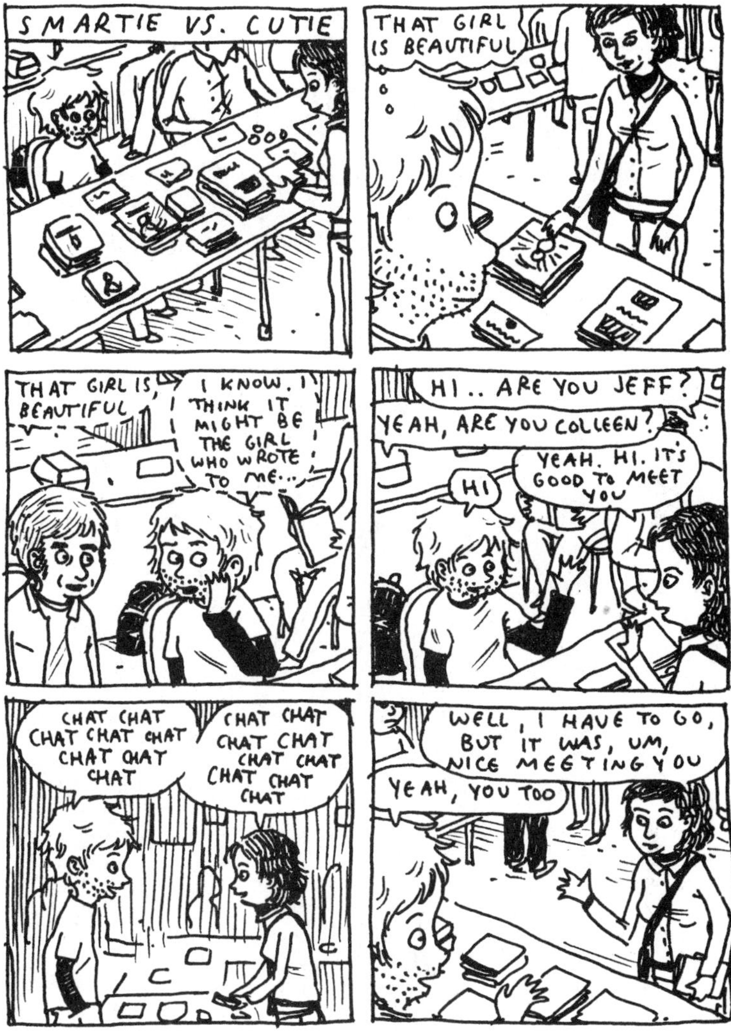
SMARTIE VS. CUTIE
THAT GIRL IS BEAUTIFUL
THAT GIRL IS, BEAUTIFUL
I KNOW. I THINK IT MIGHT BE THE GIRL WHO WROTE TO ME...
HI.. ARE YOU JEFF?
YEAH, ARE YOU COLLEEN?
HI
YEAH. HI. IT'S GOOD TO MEET YOU
CHAT CHAT CHAT CHAT CHAT CHAT CHAT CHAT
CHAT CHAT CHAT CHAT CHAT CHAT CHAT CHAT CHAT
WELL, I HAVE TO GO, BUT IT WAS, UM, NICE MEETING YOU
YEAH, YOU TOO

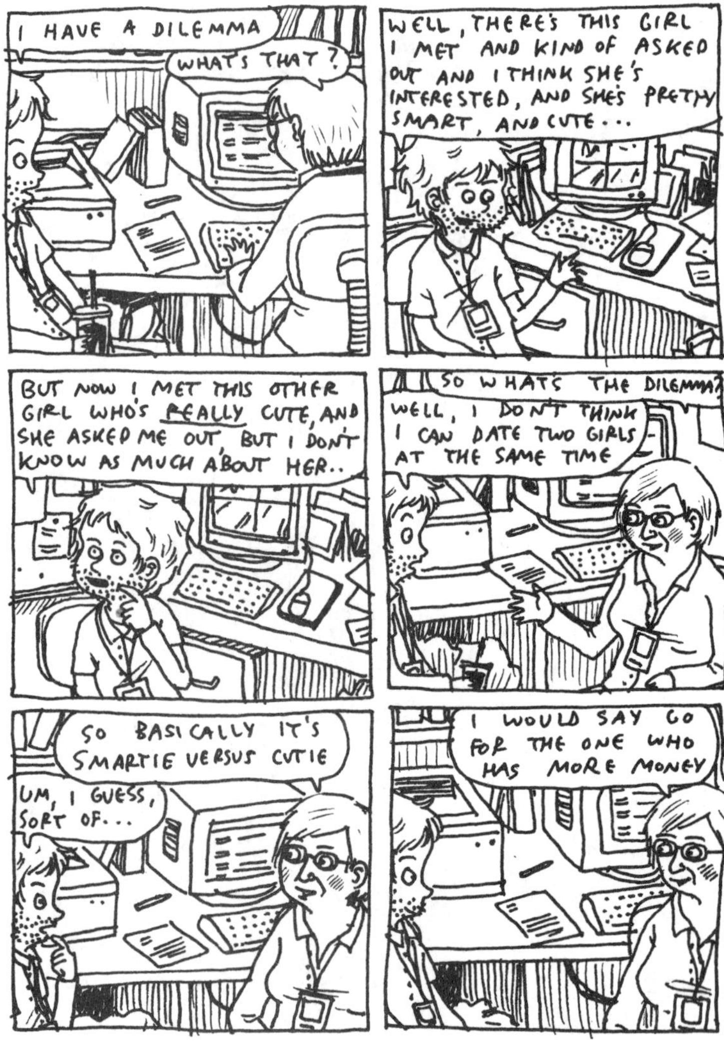
I HAVE A DILEMMA
WHAT'S THAT?
WELL, THERE'S THIS GIRL I MET AND KIND OF ASKED OUT AND I THINK SHE'S INTERESTED, AND SHE'S PRETTY SMART, AND CUTE...
BUT NOW I MET THIS OTHER GIRL WHO'S REALLY CUTE, AND SHE ASKED ME OUT, BUT I DON'T KNOW AS MUCH ABOUT HER..
SO WHATS THE DILEMMA?
WELL, I DON'T THINK I CAN DATE TWO GIRLS AT THE SAME TIME
SO BASICALLY IT'S SMARTIE VERSUS CUTIE
UM, I GUESS, SORT OF...
I WOULD SAY GO FOR THE ONE WHO HAS MORE MONEY

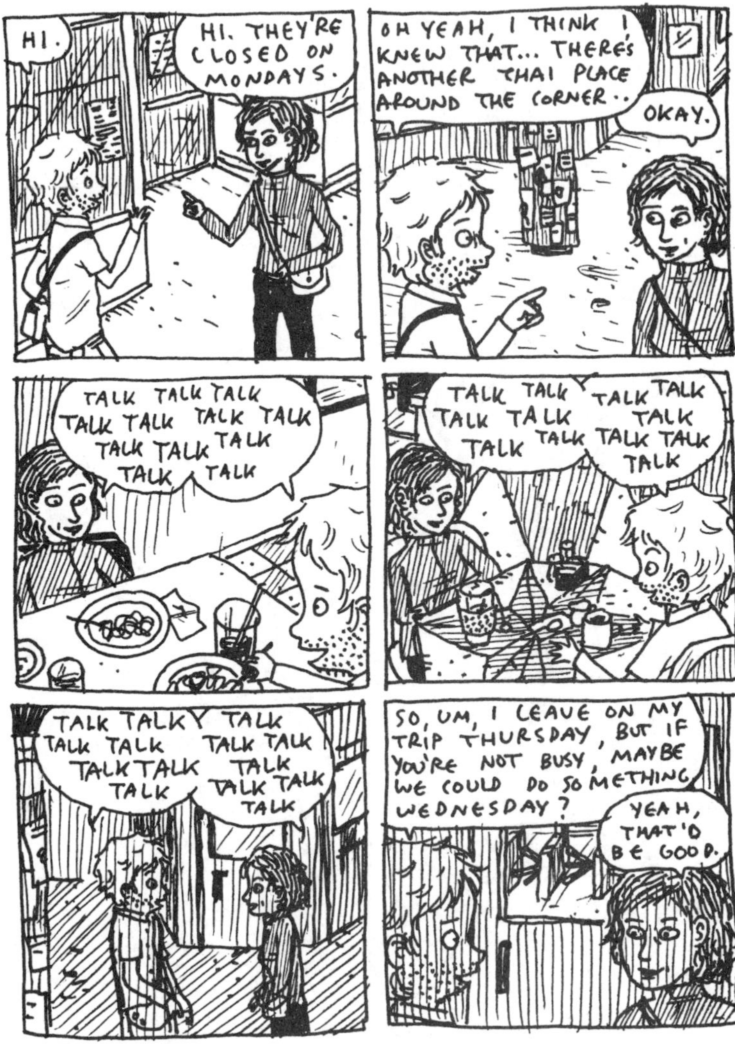
HI.
HI. THEY'RE CLOSED ON MONDAYS.
OH YEAH, I THINK I KNEW THAT... THERE'S ANOTHER THAI PLACE AROUND THE CORNER..
OKAY.
TALK TALK TALK TALK TALK TALK TALK TALK TALK TALK TALK TALK
TALK TALK TALK TALK TALK TALK TALK TALK TALK TALK TALK TALK TALK
TALK TALK TALK TALK TALK TALK TALK TALK TALK TALK TALK TALK TALK
SO, UM, I LEAVE ON MY TRIP THURSDAY, BUT IF YOU'RE NOT BUSY, MAYBE WE COULD DO SOMETHING WEDNESDAY?
YEAH, THAT'D BE GOOD.

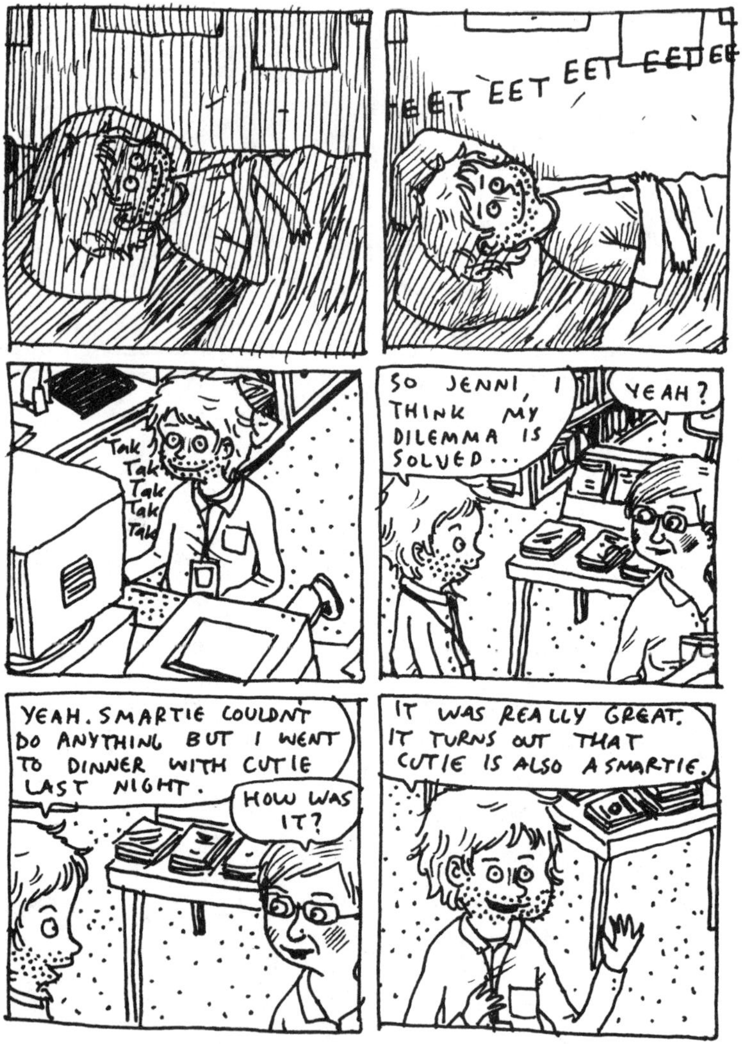
EET EET EET EET EE
Tak Tak Tak Tak Tak
SO JENNI, I THINK MY DILEMMA IS SOLVED...
YEAH?
YEAH. SMARTIE COULDNT DO ANYTHING BUT I WENT TO DINNER WITH CUTIE LAST NIGHT.
HOW WAS IT?
IT WAS REALLY GREAT. IT TURNS OUT THAT CUTIE IS ALSO A SMARTIE.

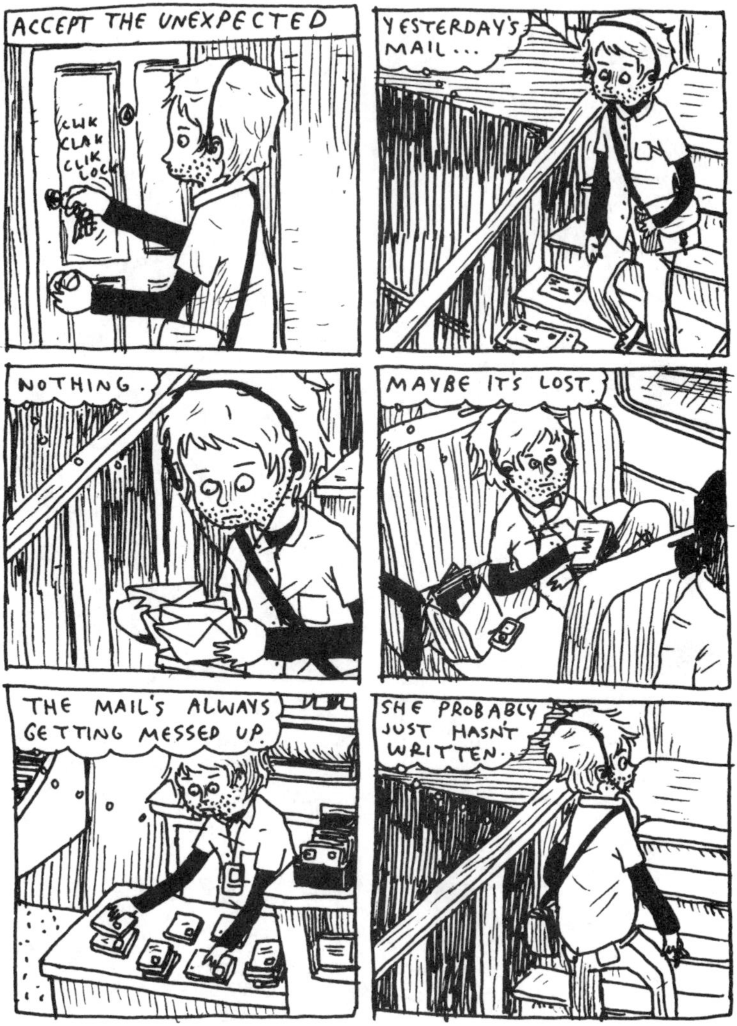
ACCEPT THE UNEXPECTED
CLIK
CLAK
CLIK
LOCK
YESTERDAY'S MAIL...
NOTHING.
MAYBE IT'S LOST.
THE MAIL'S ALWAYS GETTING MESSED UP.
SHE PROBABLY JUST HASN'T WRITTEN.

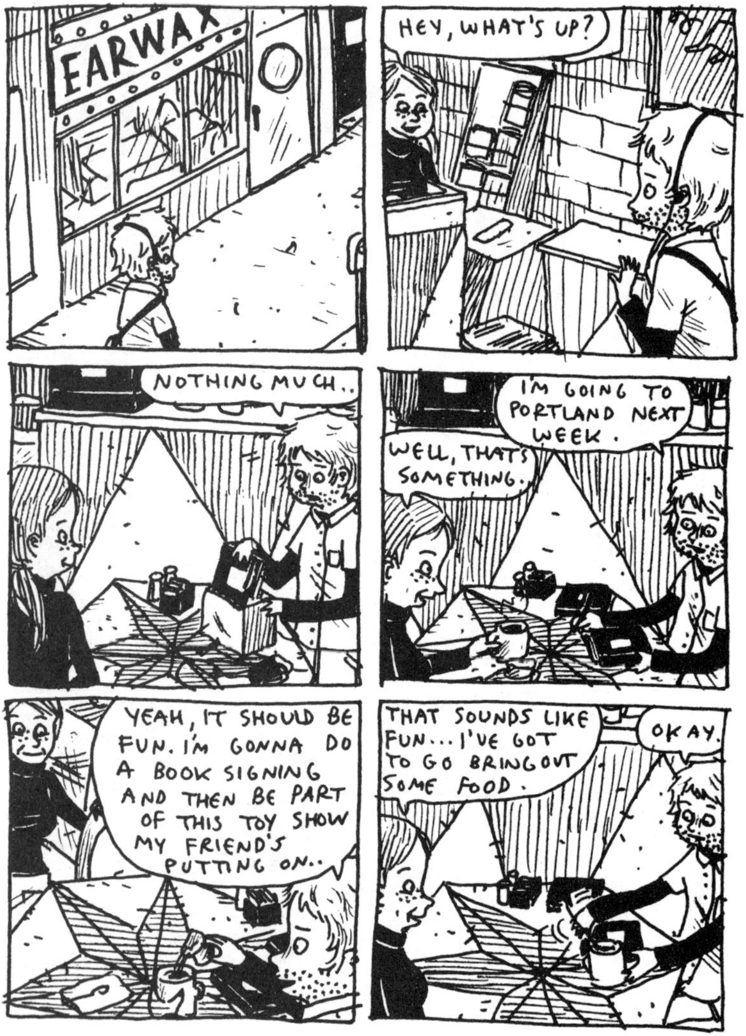
EARWAX
HEY, WHAT'S UP?
NOTHING MUCH..
I'M GOING TO PORTLAND NEXT WEEK.
WELL, THAT'S SOMETHING.
YEAH, IT SHOULD BE FUN. I'M GONNA DO A BOOK SIGNING AND THEN BE PART OF THIS TOY SHOW MY FRIEND'S PUTTING ON..
THAT SOUNDS LIKE FUN... I'VE GOT TO GO BRING OUT SOME FOOD.
OKAY.

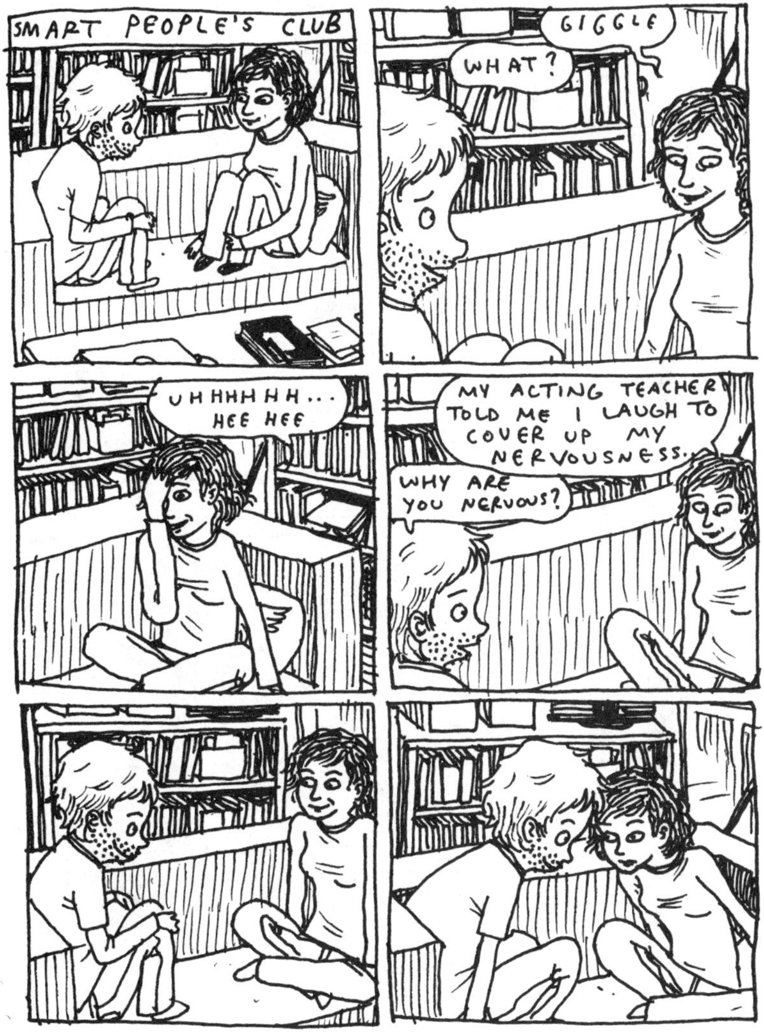
SMART PEOPLE'S CLUB
GIGGLE
WHAT?
UHHHHHH... HEE HEE
MY ACTING TEACHER TOLD ME I LAUGH TO COVER UP MY NERVOUSNESS...
WHY ARE YOU NERVOUS?

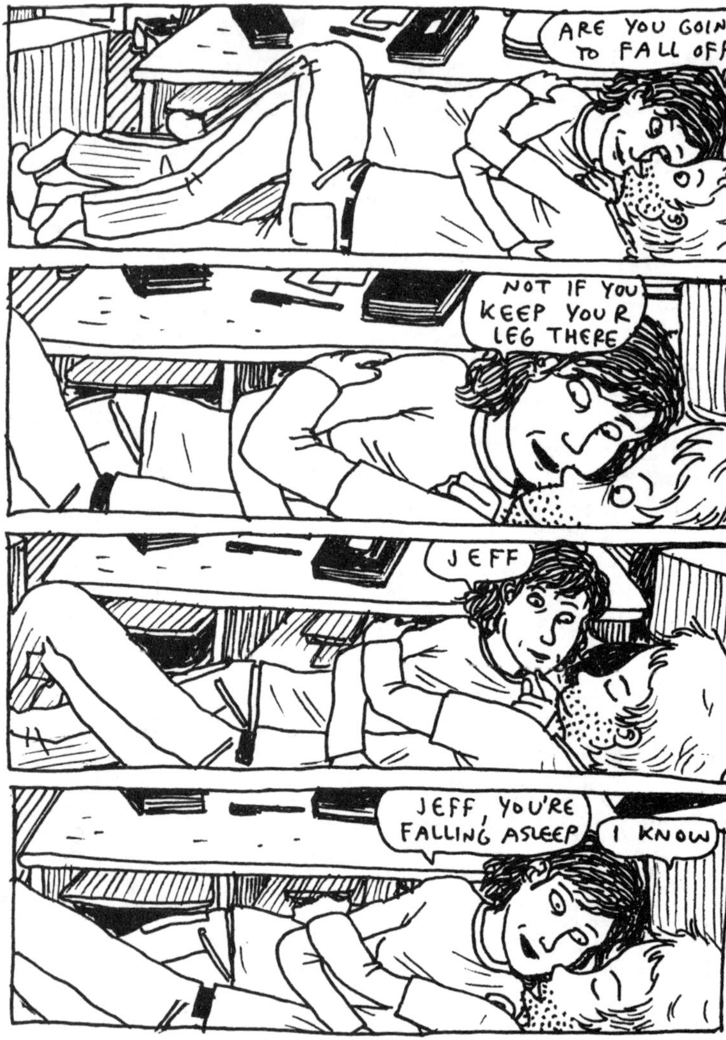
ARE YOU GOING TO FALL OFF?
NOT IF YOU KEEP YOUR LEG THERE
JEFF
JEFF, YOU'RE FALLING ASLEEP
I KNOW

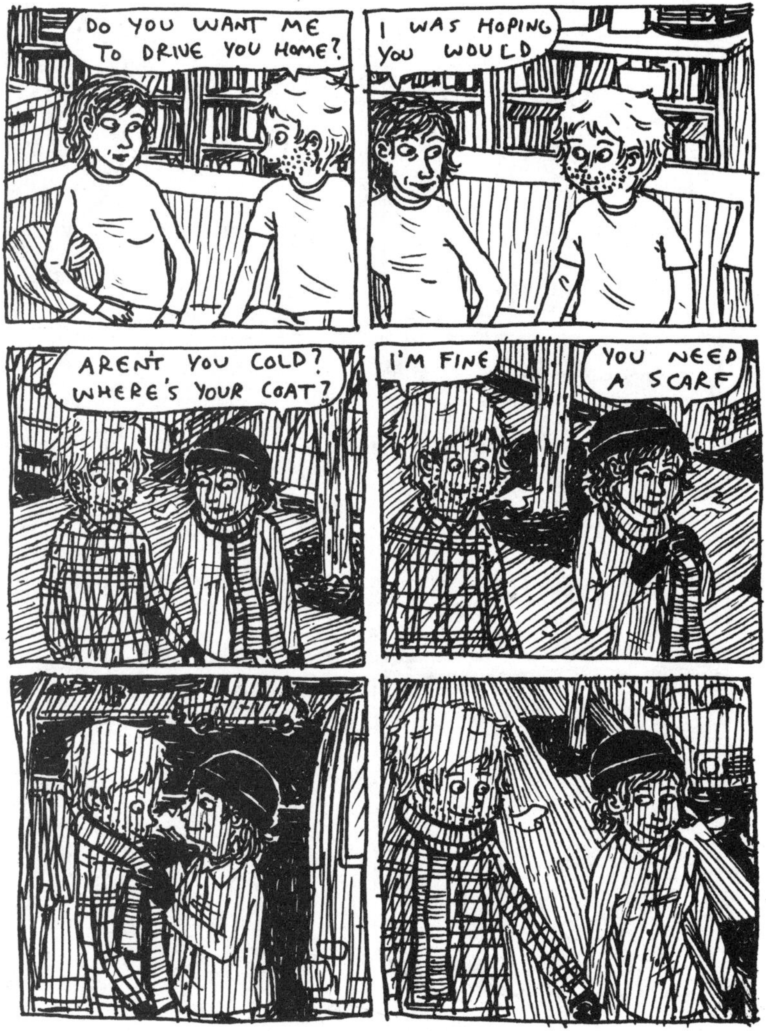
DO YOU WANT ME TO DRIVE YOU HOME?
I WAS HOPING YOU WOULD
AREN'T YOU COLD? WHERE'S YOUR COAT?
I'M FINE
YOU NEED A SCARF

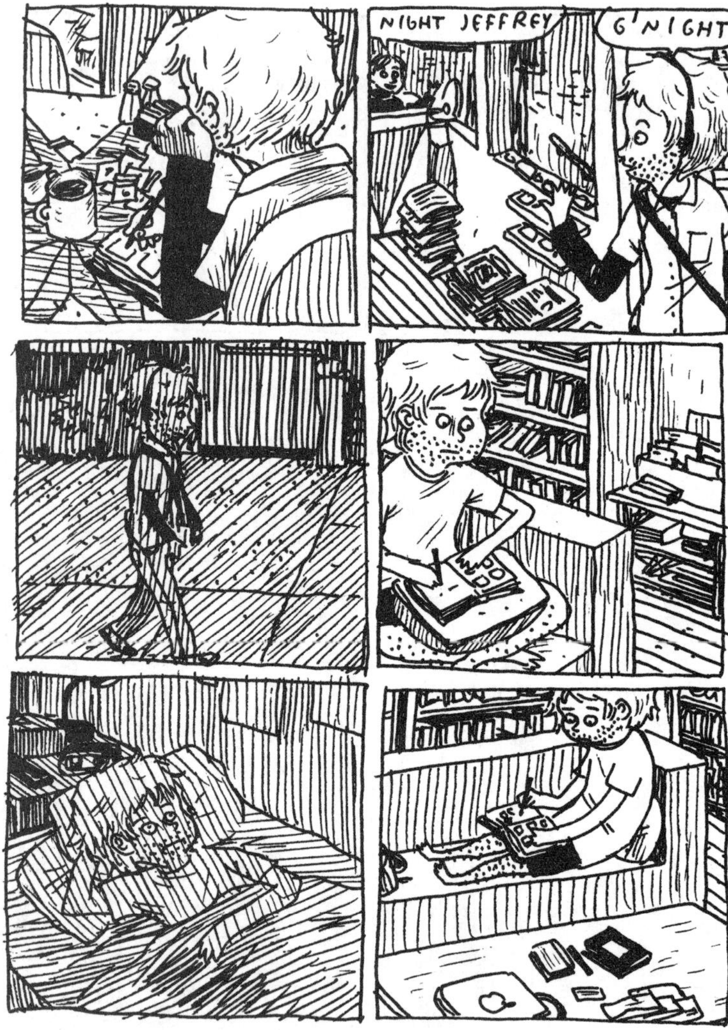
NIGHT JEFFREY
G'NIGHT

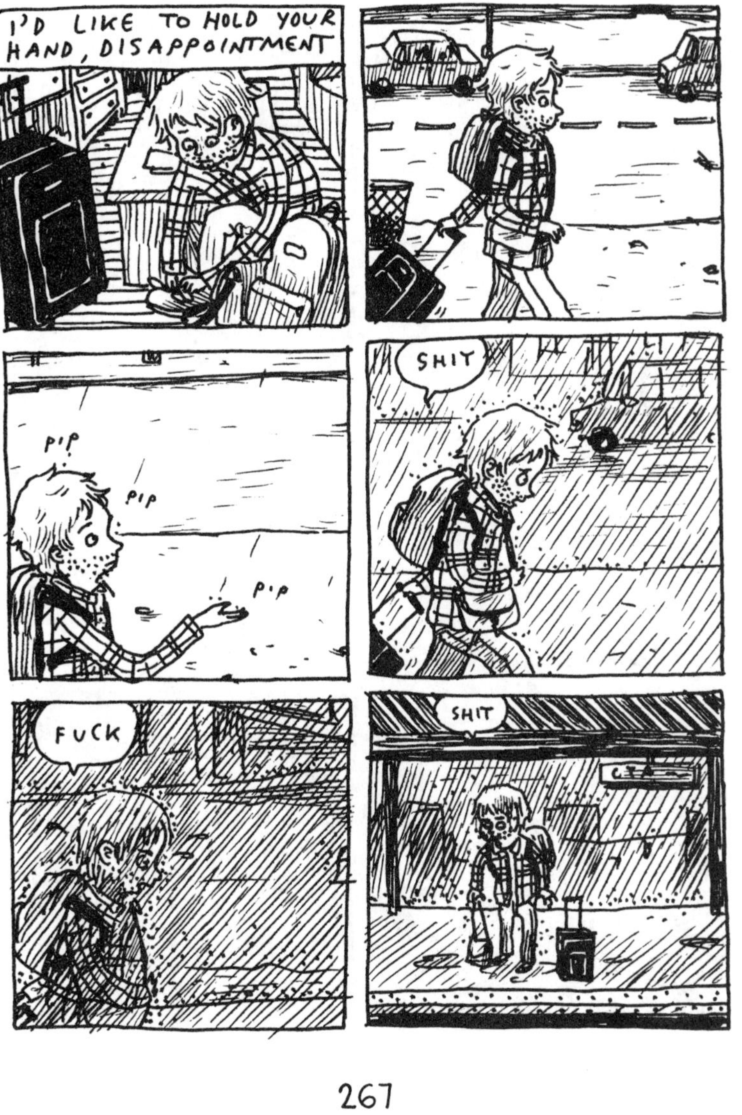
I'D LIKE TO HOLD YOUR HAND, DISAPPOINTMENT
PIP
PIP
PIP
SHIT
FUCK
SHIT

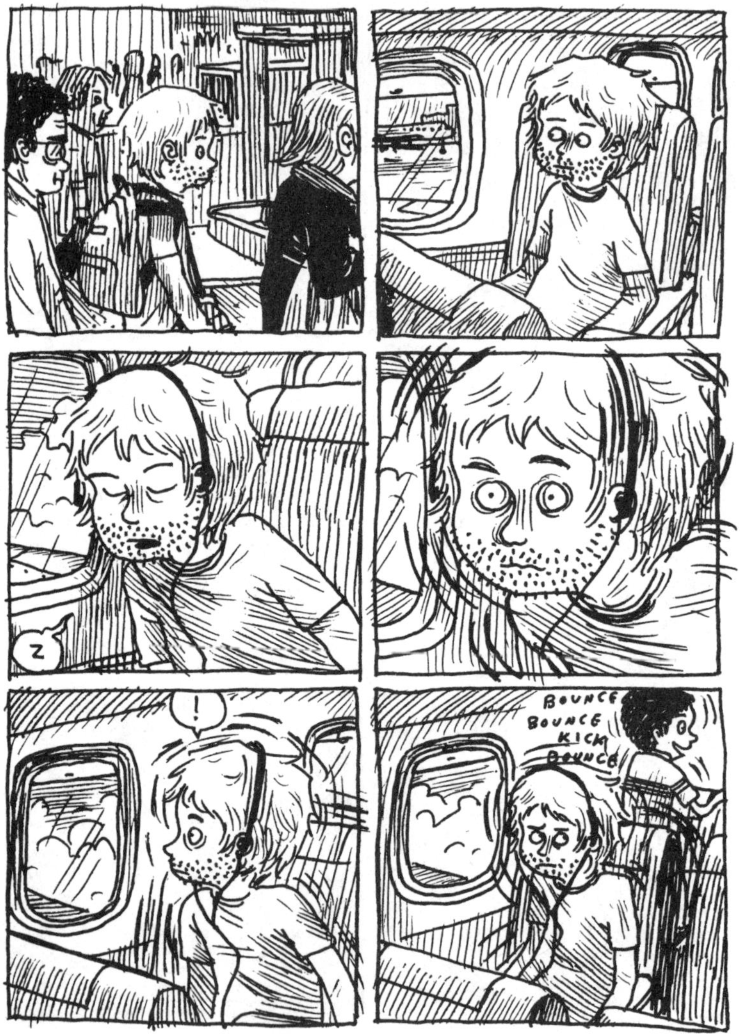

z
!
BOUNCE
BOUNCE
KICK
BOUNCE

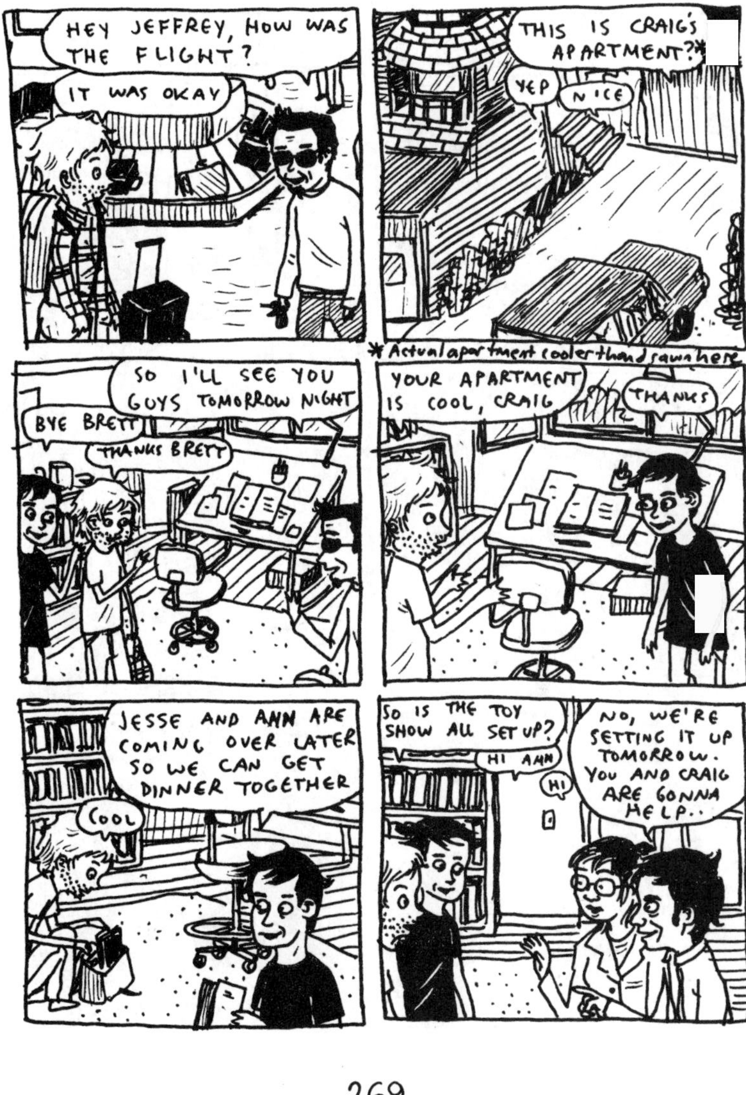
HEY JEFFREY, HOW WAS THE FLIGHT?
IT WAS OKAY
THIS IS CRAIG'S APARTMENT?*
YEP
NICE
*Actual apartment cooler than drawn here
SO I'LL SEE YOU GUYS TOMORROW NIGHT
BYE BRETT
THANKS BRETT
YOUR APARTMENT IS COOL, CRAIG
THANKS
JESSE AND ANN ARE COMING OVER LATER SO WE CAN GET DINNER TOGETHER
COOL
SO IS THE TOY SHOW ALL SET UP?
HI ANN
HI
NO, WE'RE SETTING IT UP TOMORROW. YOU AND CRAIG ARE GONNA HELP..

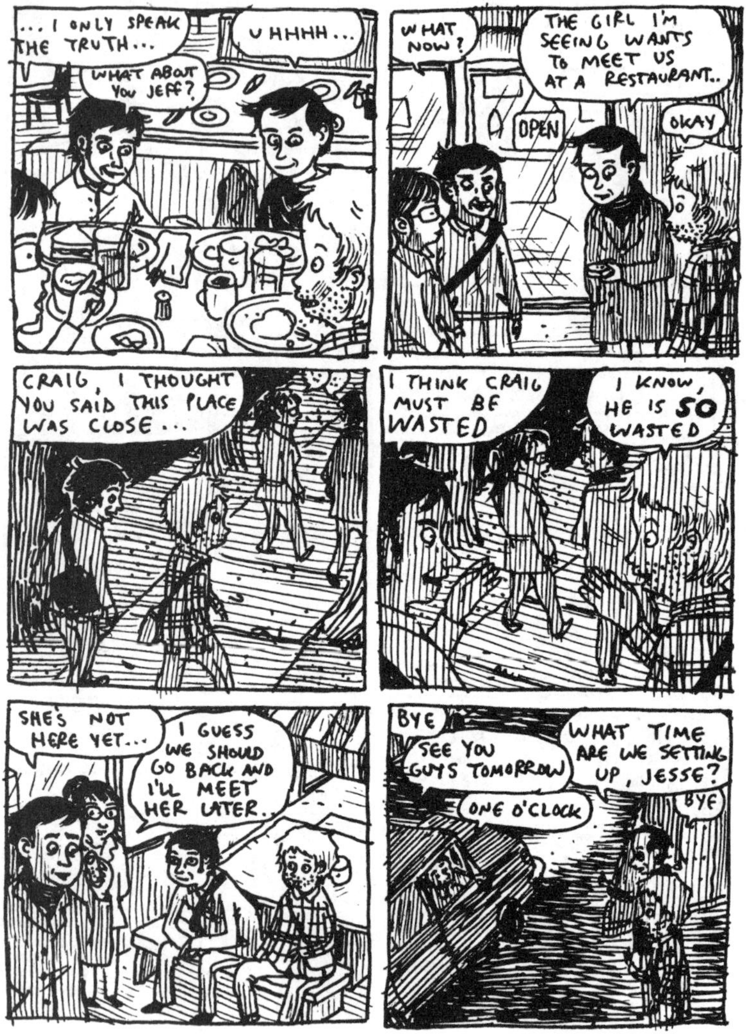

...I ONLY SPEAK THE TRUTH...
WHAT ABOUT YOU JEFF?
UHHHH...
WHAT NOW?
THE GIRL I'M SEEING WANTS TO MEET US AT A RESTAURANT..
OPEN
OKAY
CRAIG, I THOUGHT YOU SAID THIS PLACE WAS CLOSE...
I THINK CRAIG MUST BE WASTED
I KNOW, HE IS SO WASTED
SHE'S NOT HERE YET...
I GUESS WE SHOULD GO BACK AND I'LL MEET HER LATER..
BYE
SEE YOU GUYS TOMORROW
WHAT TIME ARE WE SETTING UP, JESSE?
ONE O'CLOCK
BYE

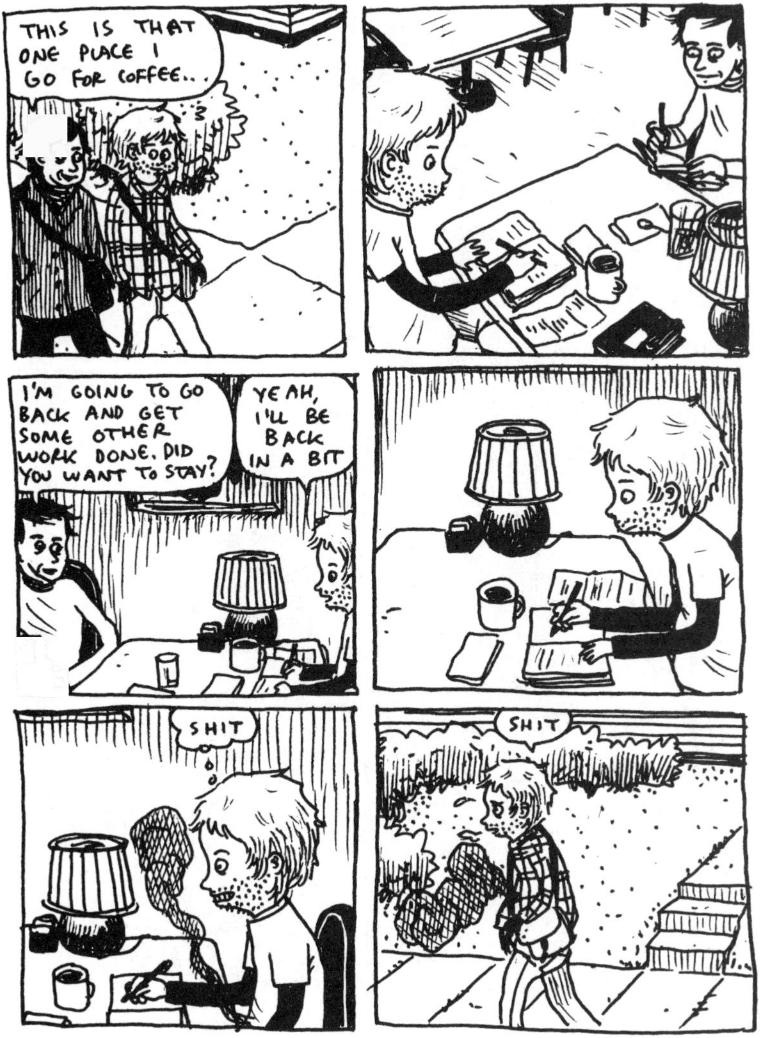
THIS IS THAT ONE PLACE I GO FOR COFFEE..
I'M GOING TO GO BACK AND GET SOME OTHER WORK DONE. DID YOU WANT TO STAY?
YEAH, I'LL BE BACK IN A BIT
SHIT
SHIT

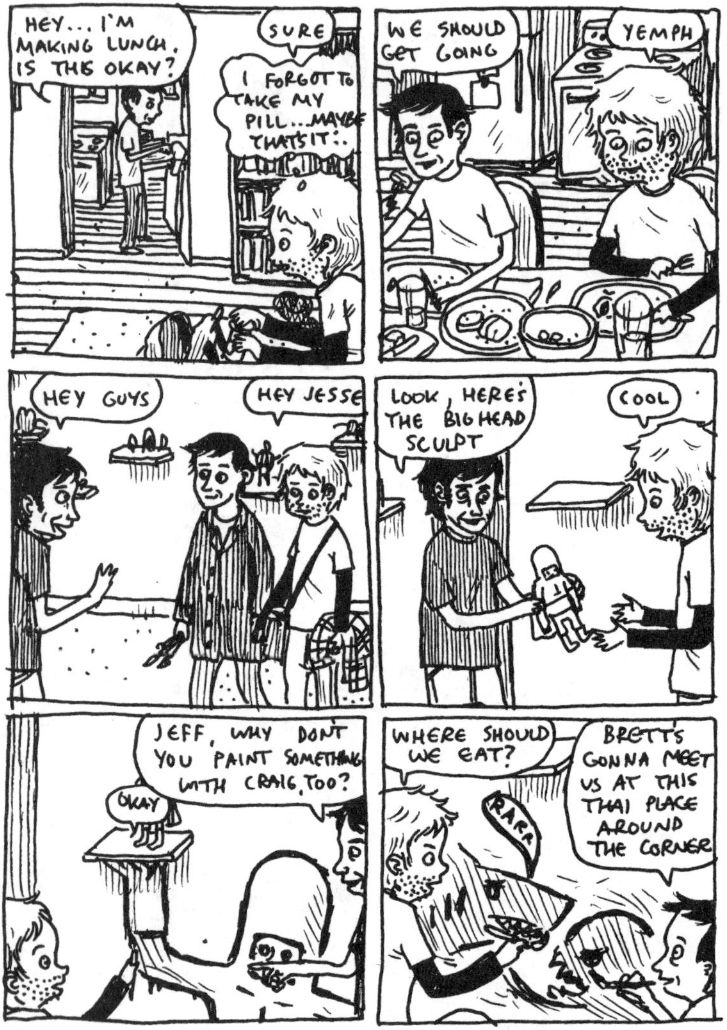
HEY... I'M MAKING LUNCH. IS THIS OKAY?
SURE
I FORGOT TO TAKE MY PILL... MAYBE THAT'S IT..
WE SHOULD GET GOING
YEMPH
HEY GUYS
HEY JESSE
LOOK, HERE'S THE BIG HEAD SCULPT
COOL
JEFF, WHY DON'T YOU PAINT SOMETHING WITH CRAIG, TOO?
OKAY
WHERE SHOULD WE EAT?
BRETT'S GONNA MEET US AT THIS THAI PLACE AROUND THE CORNER
RARR

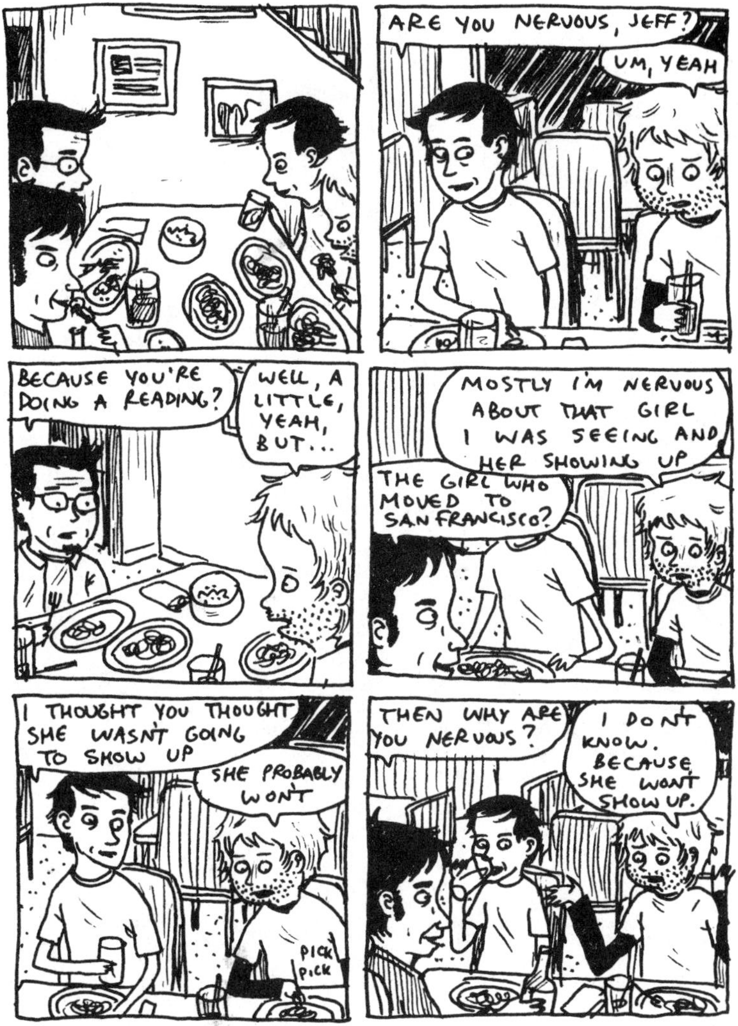
ARE YOU NERVOUS, JEFF?
UM, YEAH
BECAUSE YOU'RE DOING A READING?
WELL, A LITTLE, YEAH, BUT...
MOSTLY I'M NERVOUS ABOUT THAT GIRL I WAS SEEING AND HER SHOWING UP
THE GIRL WHO MOVED TO SAN FRANCISCO?
I THOUGHT YOU THOUGHT SHE WASN'T GOING TO SHOW UP
SHE PROBABLY WON'T
PICK PICK
THEN WHY ARE YOU NERVOUS?
I DON'T KNOW. BECAUSE SHE WON'T SHOW UP.

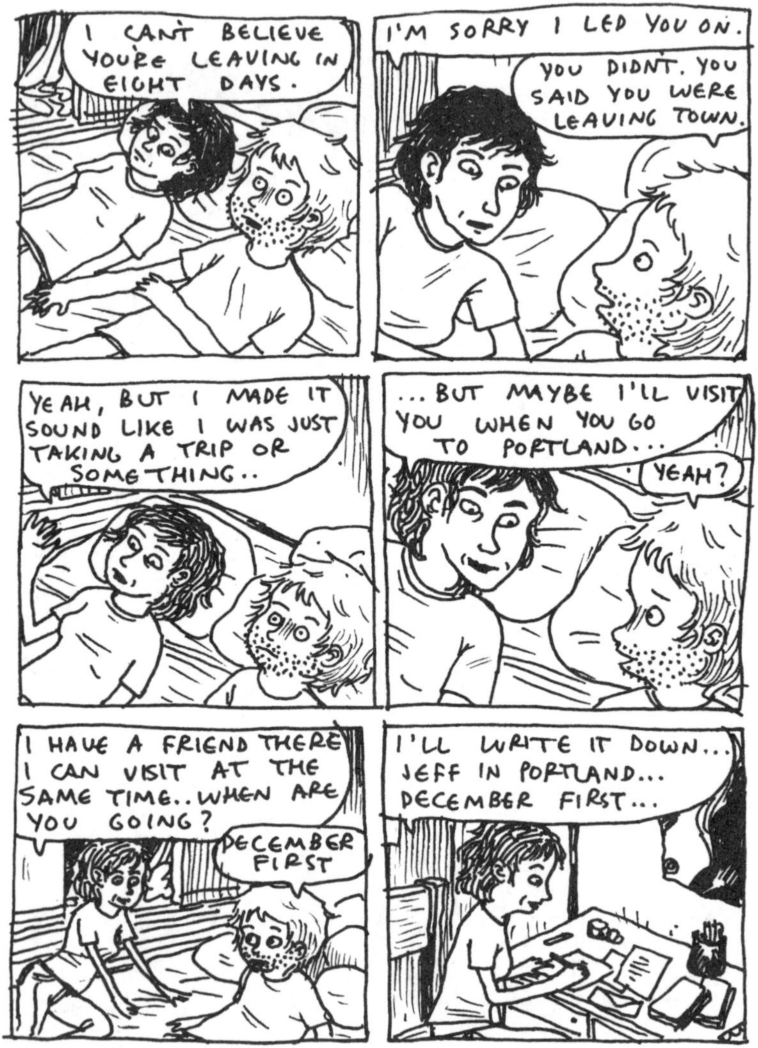
I CAN'T BELIEVE YOU'RE LEAVING IN EIGHT DAYS.
I'M SORRY I LED YOU ON.
YOU DIDN'T. YOU SAID YOU WERE LEAVING TOWN.
YEAH, BUT I MADE IT SOUND LIKE I WAS JUST TAKING A TRIP OR SOMETHING..
...BUT MAYBE I'LL VISIT YOU WHEN YOU GO TO PORTLAND...
YEAH?
I HAVE A FRIEND THERE I CAN VISIT AT THE SAME TIME..WHEN ARE YOU GOING?
DECEMBER FIRST
I'LL WRITE IT DOWN... JEFF IN PORTLAND... DECEMBER FIRST...

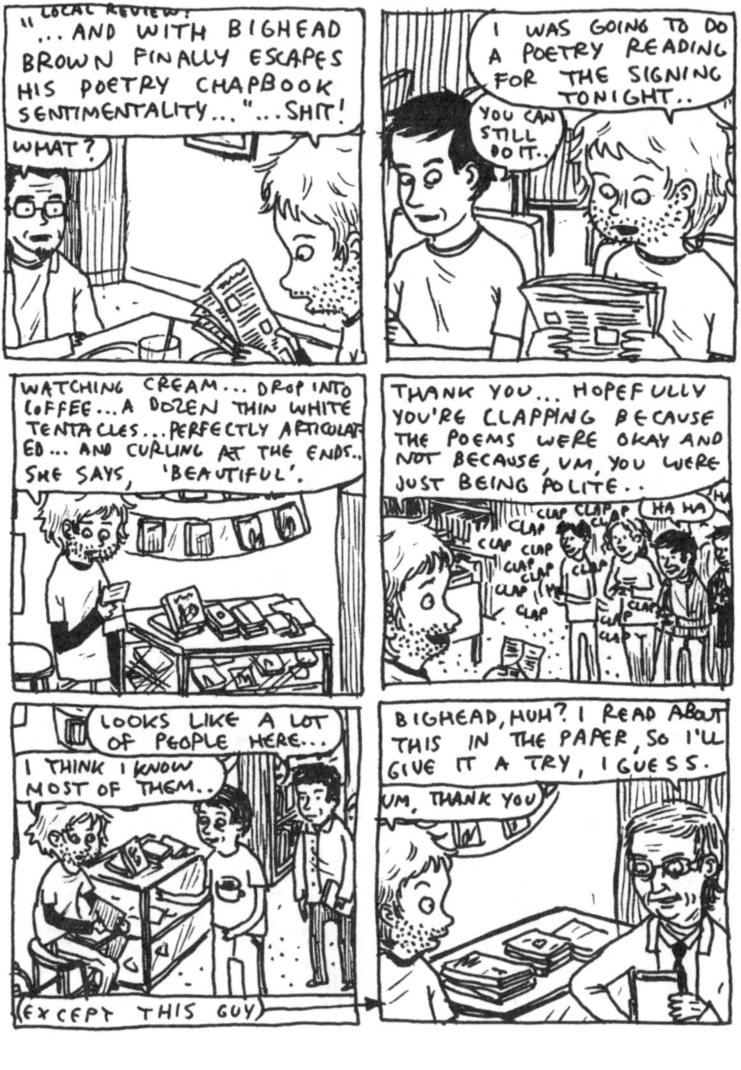
"LOCAL REVIEW! "... AND WITH BIGHEAD BROWN FINALLY ESCAPES HIS POETRY CHAPBOOK SENTIMENTALITY..."...SHIT!
WHAT?
I WAS GOING TO DO A POETRY READING FOR THE SIGNING TONIGHT..
YOU CAN STILL DO IT..
WATCHING CREAM... DROP INTO COFFEE... A DOZEN THIN WHITE TENTACLES... PERFECTLY ARTICULATED... AND CURLING AT THE ENDS.. SHE SAYS, 'BEAUTIFUL'.
THANK YOU... HOPEFULLY YOU'RE CLAPPING BECAUSE THE POEMS WERE OKAY AND NOT BECAUSE, UM, YOU WERE JUST BEING POLITE..
CLAP CLAP CLAP CLAP CLAP CLAP CLAP CLAP CLAP CLAP CLAP CLAP CLAP CLAP CLAP
HA HA
LOOKS LIKE A LOT OF PEOPLE HERE..
I THINK I KNOW MOST OF THEM..
(EXCEPT THIS GUY)
BIGHEAD, HUH? I READ ABOUT THIS IN THE PAPER, SO I'LL GIVE IT A TRY, I GUESS.
UM, THANK YOU

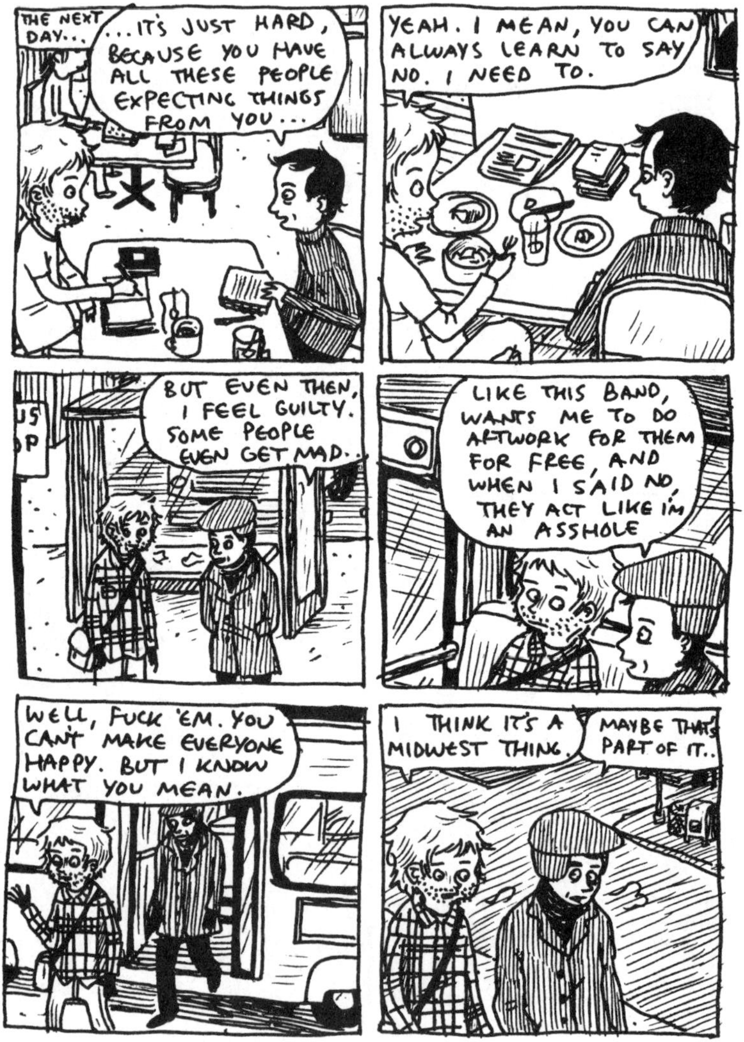
THE NEXT DAY...
...IT'S JUST HARD, BECAUSE YOU HAVE ALL THESE PEOPLE EXPECTING THINGS FROM YOU...
YEAH. I MEAN, YOU CAN ALWAYS LEARN TO SAY NO. I NEED TO.
BUT EVEN THEN, I FEEL GUILTY. SOME PEOPLE EVEN GET MAD...
LIKE THIS BAND, WANTS ME TO DO ARTWORK FOR THEM FOR FREE, AND WHEN I SAID NO, THEY ACT LIKE I'M AN ASSHOLE
WELL, FUCK 'EM. YOU CAN'T MAKE EVERYONE HAPPY. BUT I KNOW WHAT YOU MEAN.
I THINK IT'S A MIDWEST THING.
MAYBE THAT'S PART OF IT..

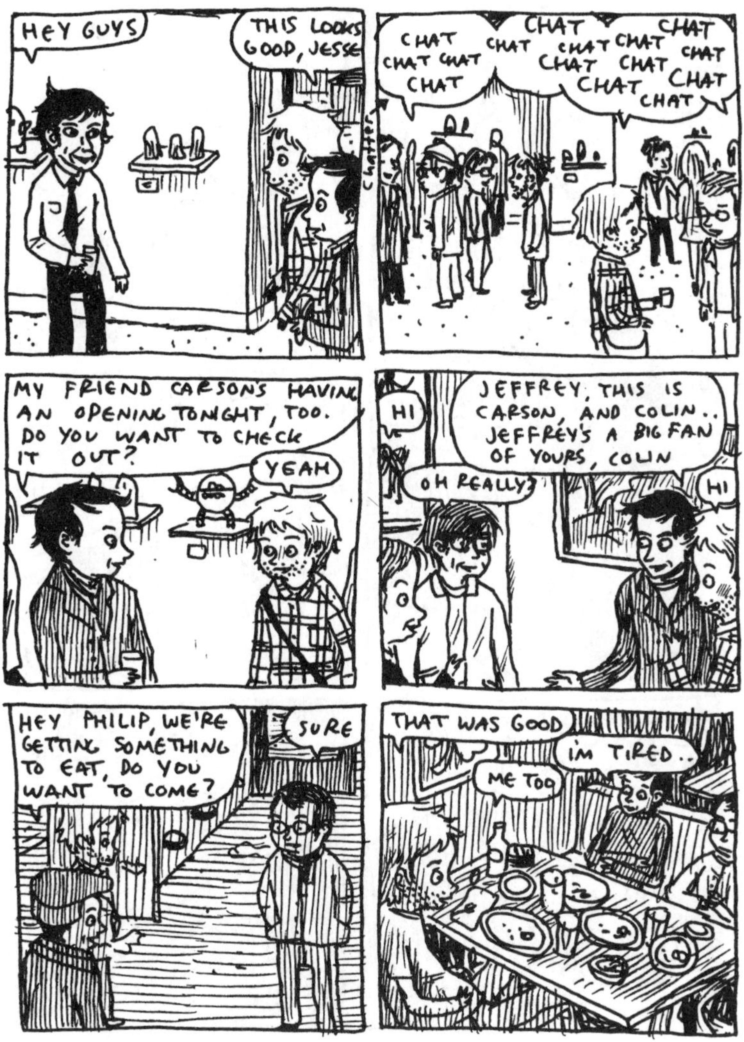
HEY GUYS
THIS LOOKS GOOD, JESSE
chatter
CHAT CHAT CHAT CHAT
CHAT
CHAT CHAT CHAT CHAT CHAT CHAT CHAT CHAT CHAT CHAT CHAT CHAT CHAT
MY FRIEND CARSON'S HAVING AN OPENING TONIGHT, TOO. DO YOU WANT TO CHECK IT OUT?
YEAH
HI
JEFFREY, THIS IS CARSON, AND COLIN.. JEFFREY'S A BIG FAN OF YOURS, COLIN
OH REALLY?
HI
HEY PHILIP, WE'RE GETTING SOMETHING TO EAT, DO YOU WANT TO COME?
SURE
THAT WAS GOOD
I'M TIRED..
ME TOO

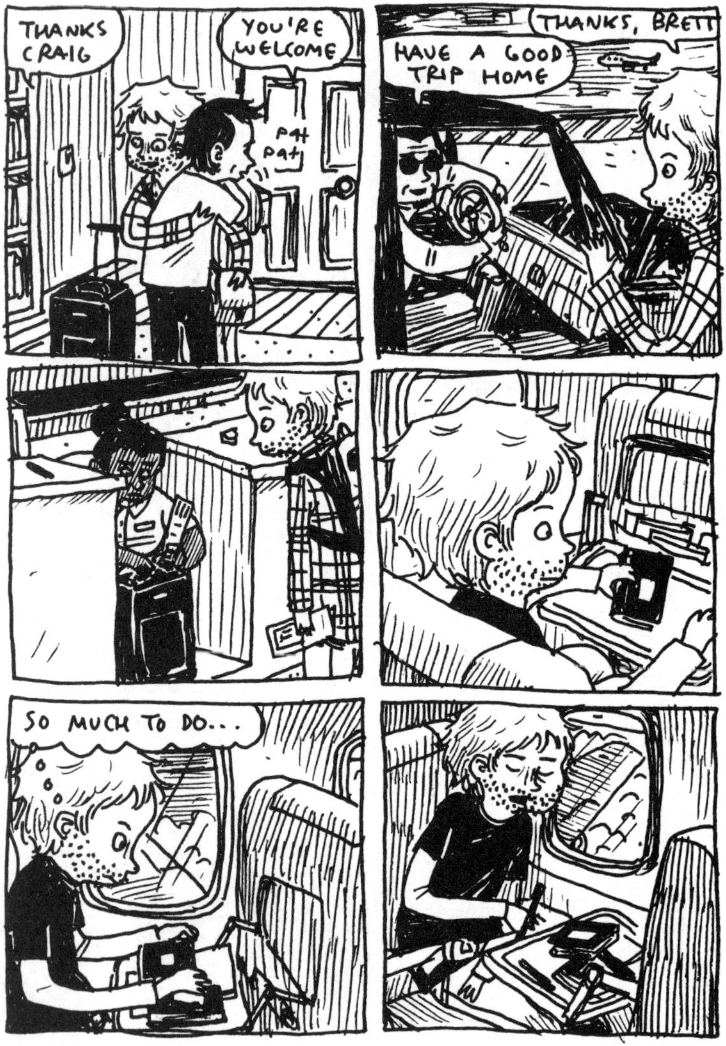
THANKS CRAIG
YOU'RE WELCOME
pat pat
THANKS, BRETT
HAVE A GOOD TRIP HOME
SO MUCH TO DO...

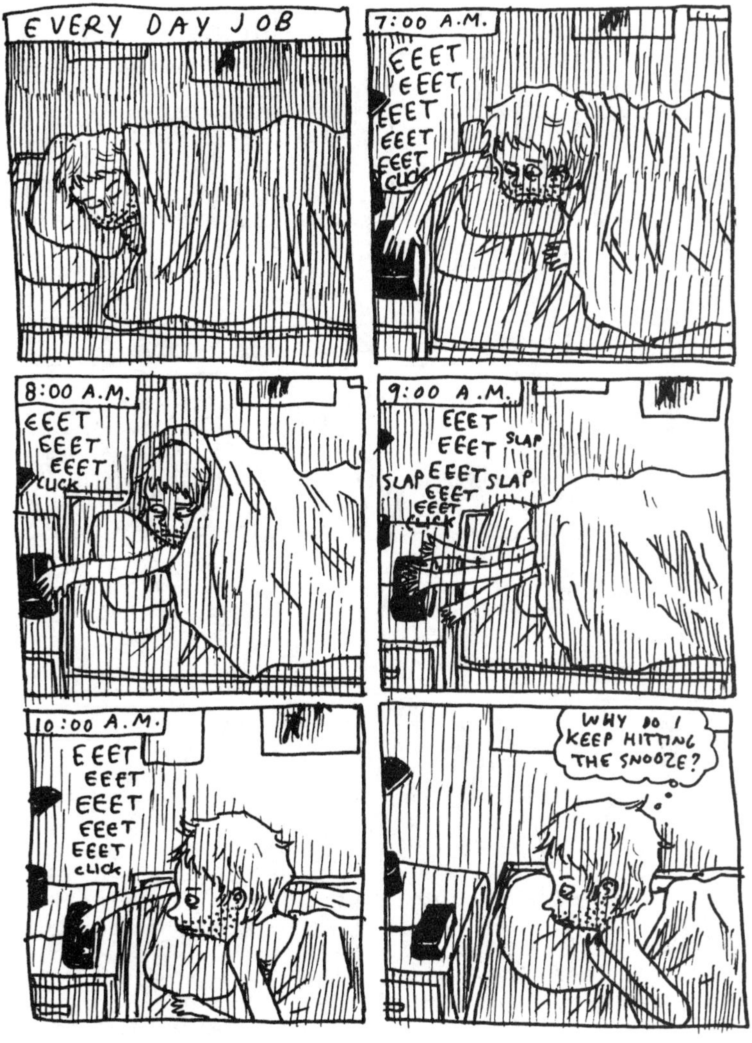
EVERY DAY JOB
7:00 A.M.
EEET EEET EEET EEET EEET CLICK
8:00 A.M.
EEET EEET EEET CLICK
9:00 A.M.
EEET EEET SLAP SLAP EEET SLAP EEET EEET CLICK
10:00 A.M.
EEET EEET EEET EEET EEET CLICK
WHY DO I KEEP HITTING THE SNOOZE?

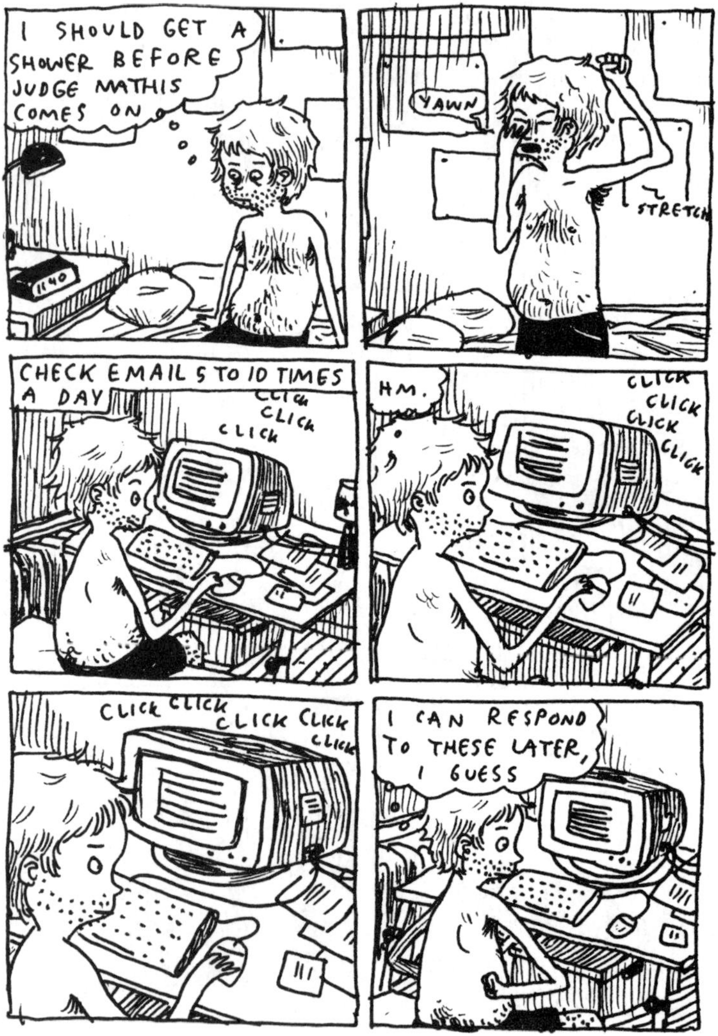
I SHOULD GET A SHOWER BEFORE JUDGE MATHIS COMES ON
1140
YAWN
STRETCH
CHECK EMAIL 5 TO 10 TIMES A DAY
CLICK
CLICK
CLICK
HM.
CLICK
CLICK
CLICK
CLICK
CLICK CLICK CLICK CLICK CLICK
I CAN RESPOND TO THESE LATER, I GUESS

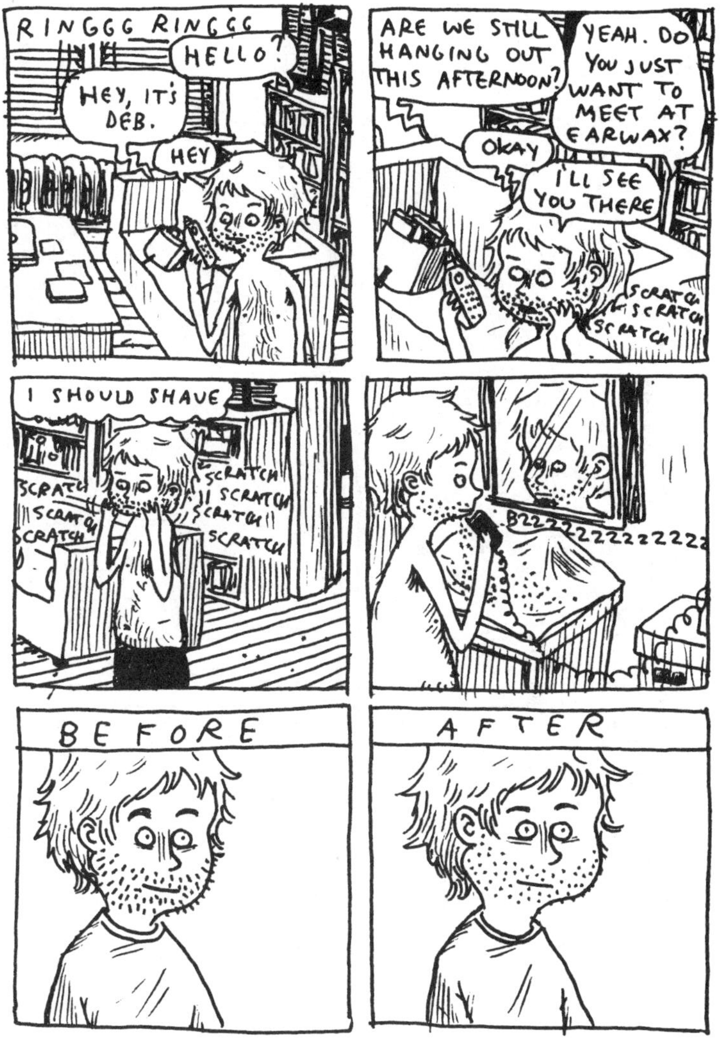
RINGGG RINGGG
HELLO?
HEY, IT'S DEB.
HEY
ARE WE STILL HANGING OUT THIS AFTERNOON?
YEAH. DO YOU JUST WANT TO MEET AT EARWAX?
OKAY
I'LL SEE YOU THERE
SCRATCH SCRATCH SCRATCH
I SHOULD SHAVE
SCRATCH SCRATCH SCRATCH
SCRATCH SCRATCH SCRATCH SCRATCH
BZZZZZZZZZZZZZZZ
BEFORE
AFTER

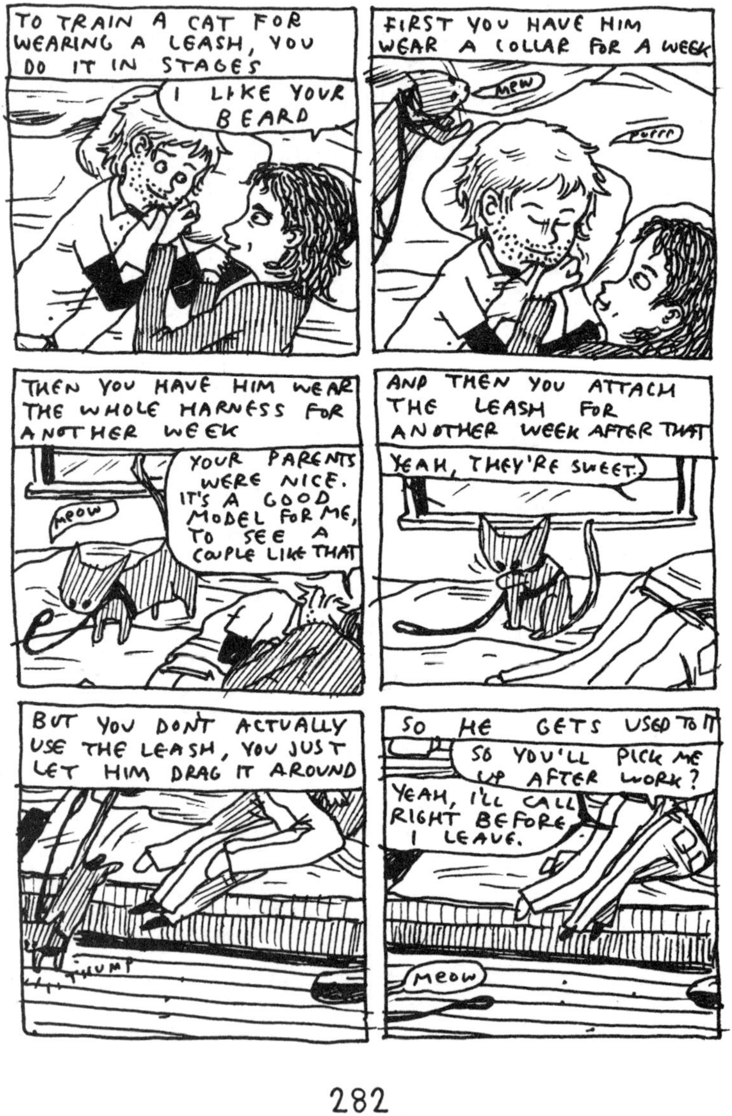
TO TRAIN A CAT FOR WEARING A LEASH, YOU DO IT IN STAGES
I LIKE YOUR BEARD
FIRST YOU HAVE HIM WEAR A COLLAR FOR A WEEK
MEW
PURRR
THEN YOU HAVE HIM WEAR THE WHOLE HARNESS FOR ANOTHER WEEK
YOUR PARENTS WERE NICE. IT'S A GOOD MODEL FOR ME, TO SEE A COUPLE LIKE THAT
MEOW
AND THEN YOU ATTACH THE LEASH FOR ANOTHER WEEK AFTER THAT
YEAH, THEY'RE SWEET.
BUT YOU DONT ACTUALLY USE THE LEASH, YOU JUST LET HIM DRAG IT AROUND
THUMP
SO HE GETS USED TO IT
SO YOU'LL PICK ME UP AFTER WORK?
YEAH, I'LL CALL RIGHT BEFORE I LEAVE.
MEOW

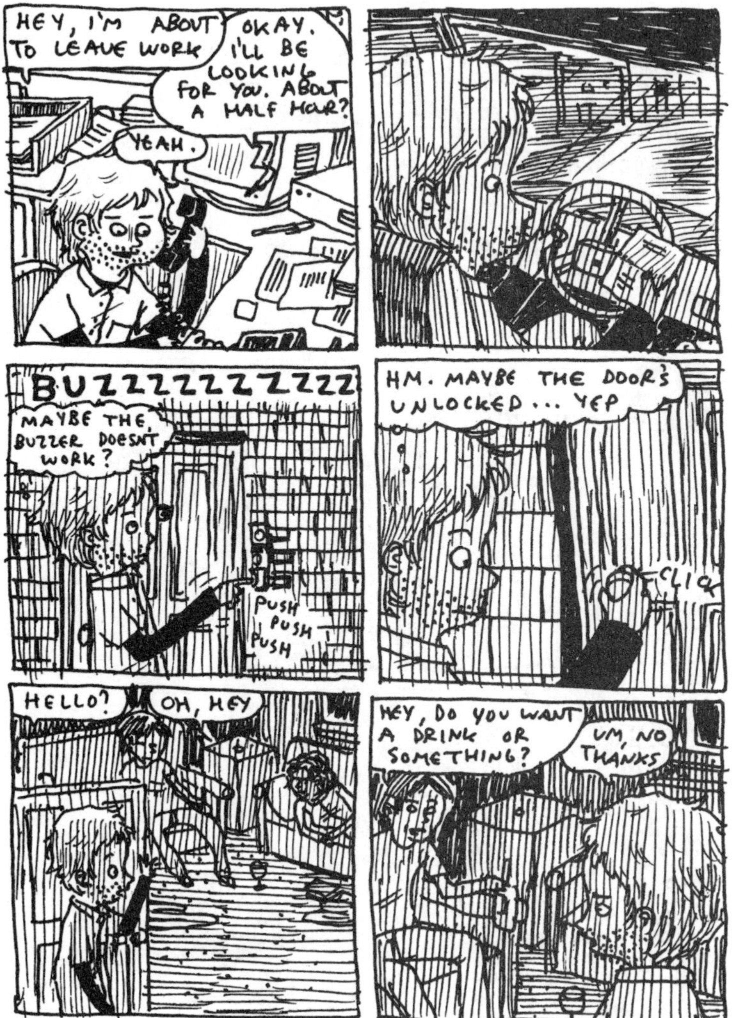
HEY, I'M ABOUT TO LEAVE WORK
OKAY. I'LL BE LOOKING FOR YOU. ABOUT A HALF HOUR?
YEAH.
BUZZZZZZZZZZ
MAYBE THE BUZZER DOESN'T WORK?
PUSH PUSH PUSH
HM. MAYBE THE DOOR'S UNLOCKED... YEP
CLICK
HELLO?
OH, HEY
HEY, DO YOU WANT A DRINK OR SOMETHING?
UM, NO THANKS

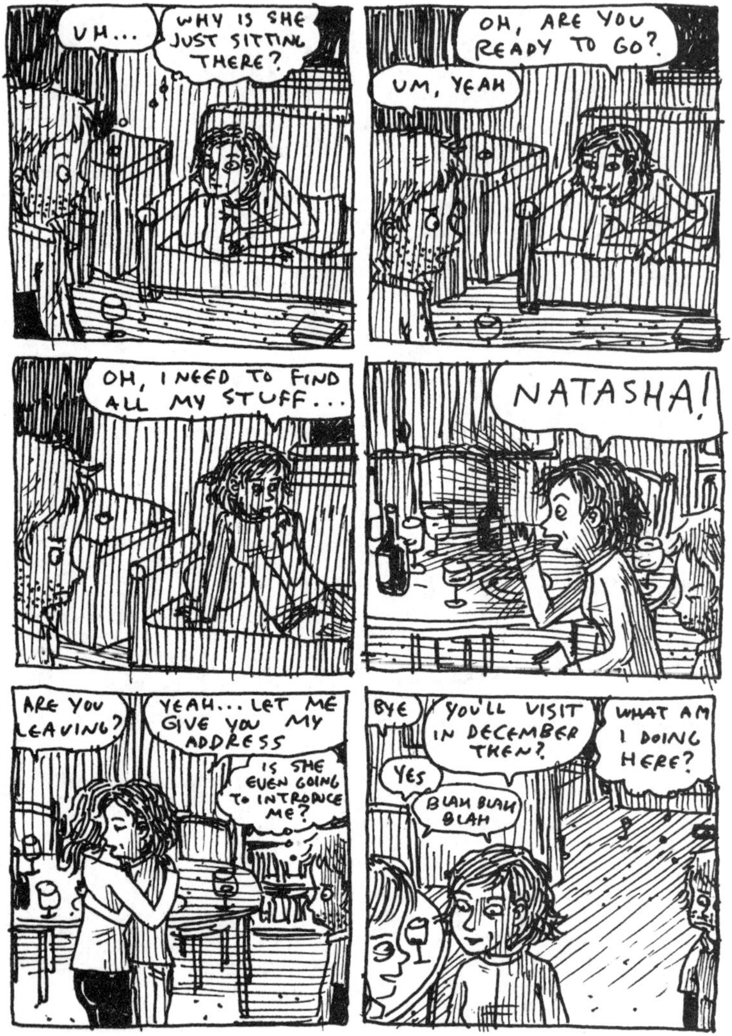
UH...
WHY IS SHE JUST SITTING THERE?
OH, ARE YOU READY TO GO?
UM, YEAH
OH, I NEED TO FIND ALL MY STUFF...
NATASHA!
ARE YOU LEAVING?
YEAH... LET ME GIVE YOU MY ADDRESS
IS SHE EVEN GOING TO INTRODUCE ME?
BYE
YOU'LL VISIT IN DECEMBER THEN?
YES
BLAH BLAH BLAH
WHAT AM I DOING HERE?

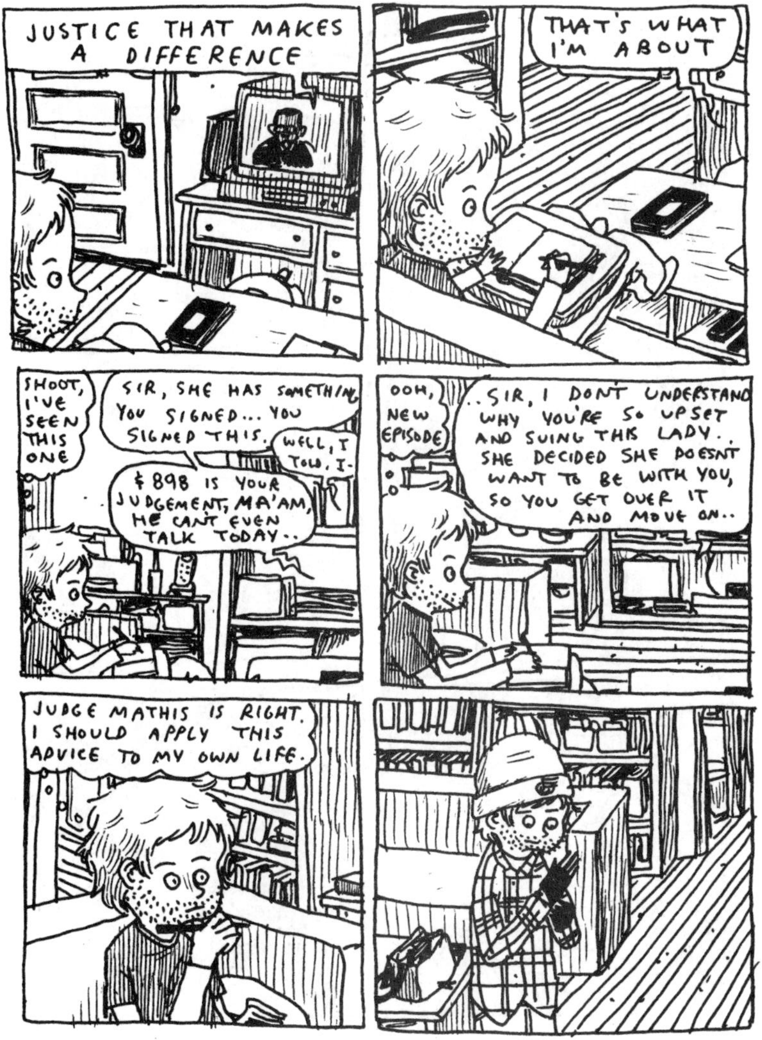
JUSTICE THAT MAKES A DIFFERENCE
THAT'S WHAT I'M ABOUT
SHOOT, I'VE SEEN THIS ONE
SIR, SHE HAS SOMETHING YOU SIGNED... YOU SIGNED THIS.
WELL, I TOLD, I-
$898 IS YOUR JUDGEMENT, MA'AM, HE CAN'T EVEN TALK TODAY..
OOH, NEW EPISODE
..SIR, I DONT UNDERSTAND WHY YOU'RE SO UPSET AND SUING THIS LADY.. SHE DECIDED SHE DOESNT WANT TO BE WITH YOU, SO YOU GET OVER IT AND MOVE ON..
JUDGE MATHIS IS RIGHT. I SHOULD APPLY THIS ADVICE TO MY OWN LIFE.

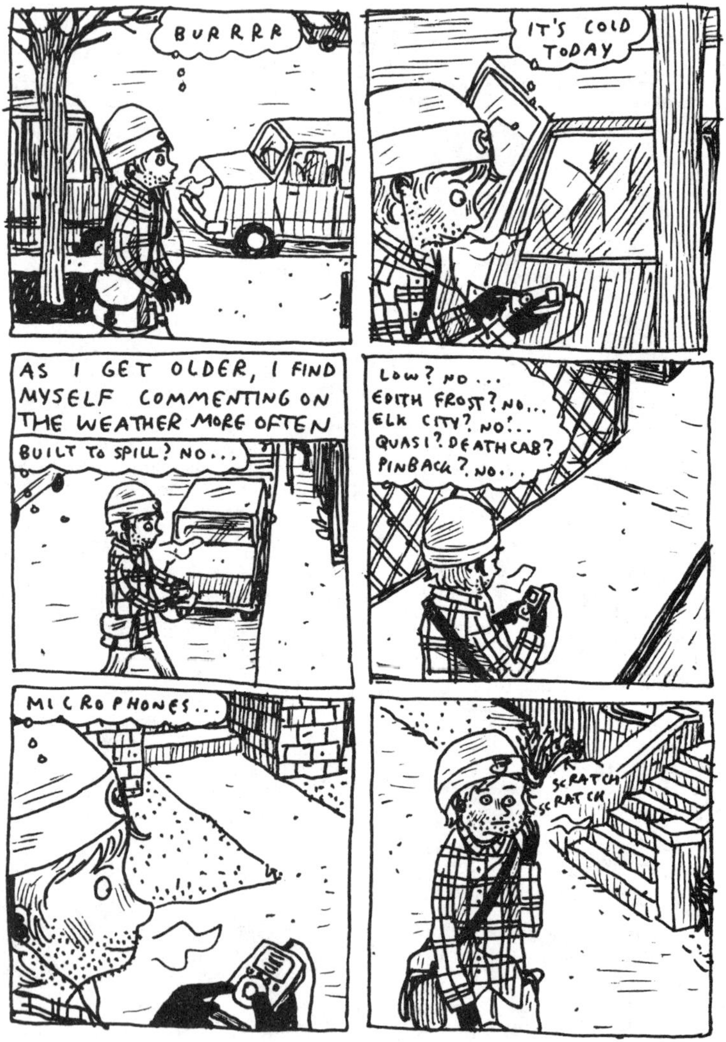
BURRRR
IT'S COLD TODAY
AS I GET OLDER, I FIND MYSELF COMMENTING ON THE WEATHER MORE OFTEN
BUILT TO SPILL? NO...
LOW? NO...
EDITH FROST? NO...
ELK CITY? NO!...
QUASI? DEATH CAB?
PINBACK? NO...
MICROPHONES...
SCRATCH
SCRATCH

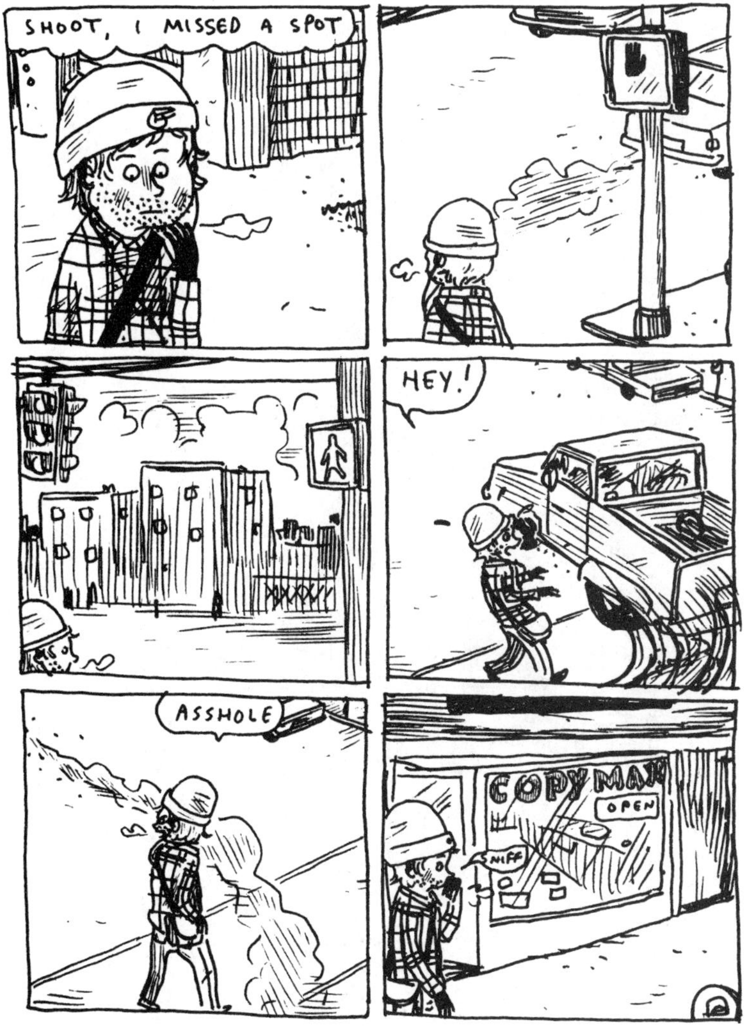
SHOOT, I MISSED A SPOT
HEY!
ASSHOLE
COPY MA
OPEN
SNIFF

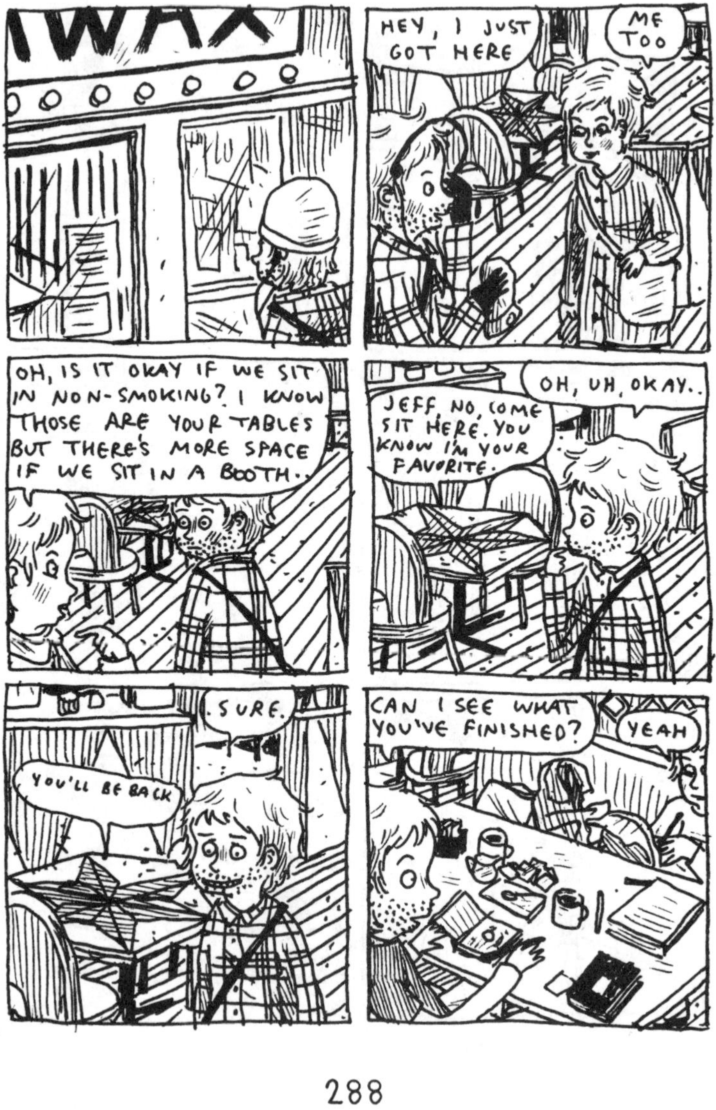
IWAX
HEY, I JUST GOT HERE
ME TOO
OH, IS IT OKAY IF WE SIT IN NON-SMOKING? I KNOW THOSE ARE YOUR TABLES BUT THERE'S MORE SPACE IF WE SIT IN A BOOTH..
JEFF, NO, COME SIT HERE. YOU KNOW I'M YOUR FAVORITE.
OH, UH, OKAY..
YOU'LL BE BACK
.SURE.
CAN I SEE WHAT YOU'VE FINISHED?
YEAH

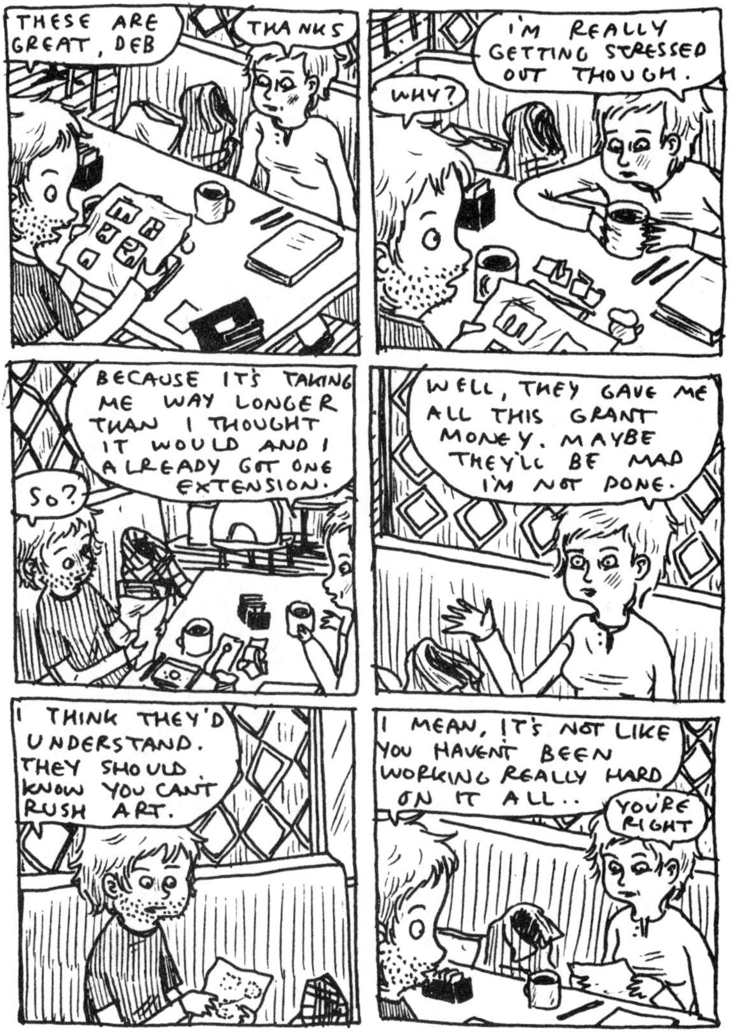
THESE ARE GREAT, DEB
THANKS
I'M REALLY GETTING STRESSED OUT THOUGH.
WHY?
BECAUSE IT'S TAKING ME WAY LONGER THAN I THOUGHT IT WOULD AND I ALREADY GOT ONE EXTENSION.
SO?
WELL, THEY GAVE ME ALL THIS GRANT MONEY. MAYBE THEY'LL BE MAD I'M NOT DONE.
I THINK THEY'D UNDERSTAND. THEY SHOULD KNOW YOU CAN'T RUSH ART.
I MEAN, IT'S NOT LIKE YOU HAVEN'T BEEN WORKING REALLY HARD ON IT ALL..
YOU'RE RIGHT

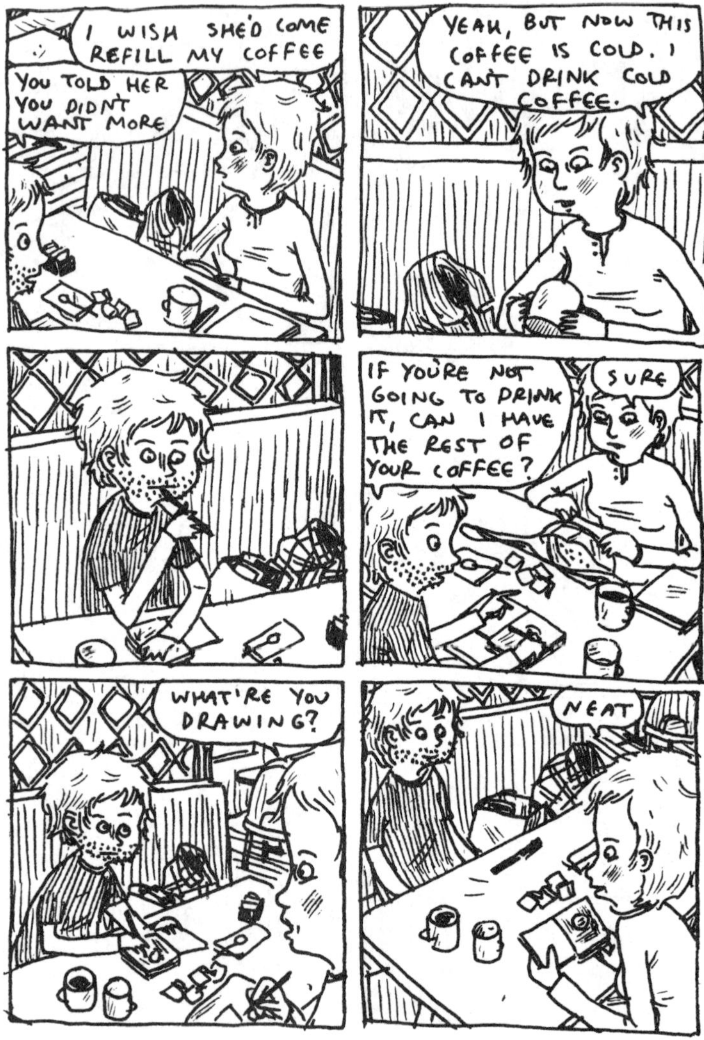
I WISH SHE'D COME REFILL MY COFFEE
YOU TOLD HER YOU DIDN'T WANT MORE
YEAH, BUT NOW THIS COFFEE IS COLD. I CAN'T DRINK COLD COFFEE.
IF YOU'RE NOT GOING TO DRINK IT, CAN I HAVE THE REST OF YOUR COFFEE?
SURE
WHAT'RE YOU DRAWING?
NEAT

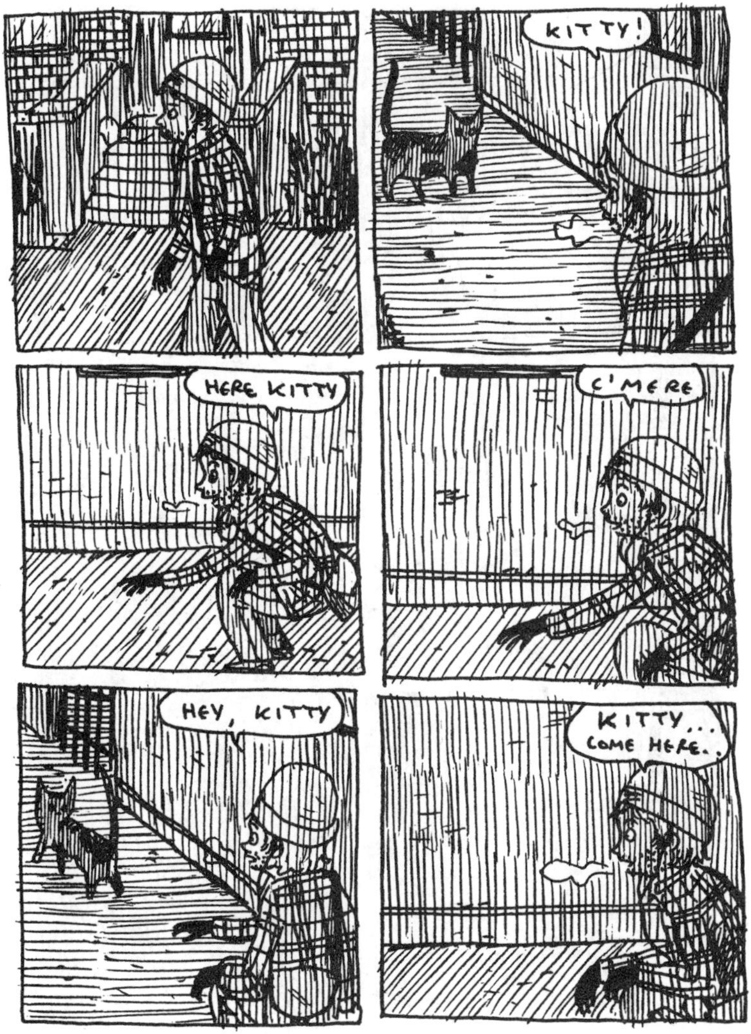
KITTY!
HERE KITTY
C'MERE
HEY, KITTY
KITTY...
COME HERE..

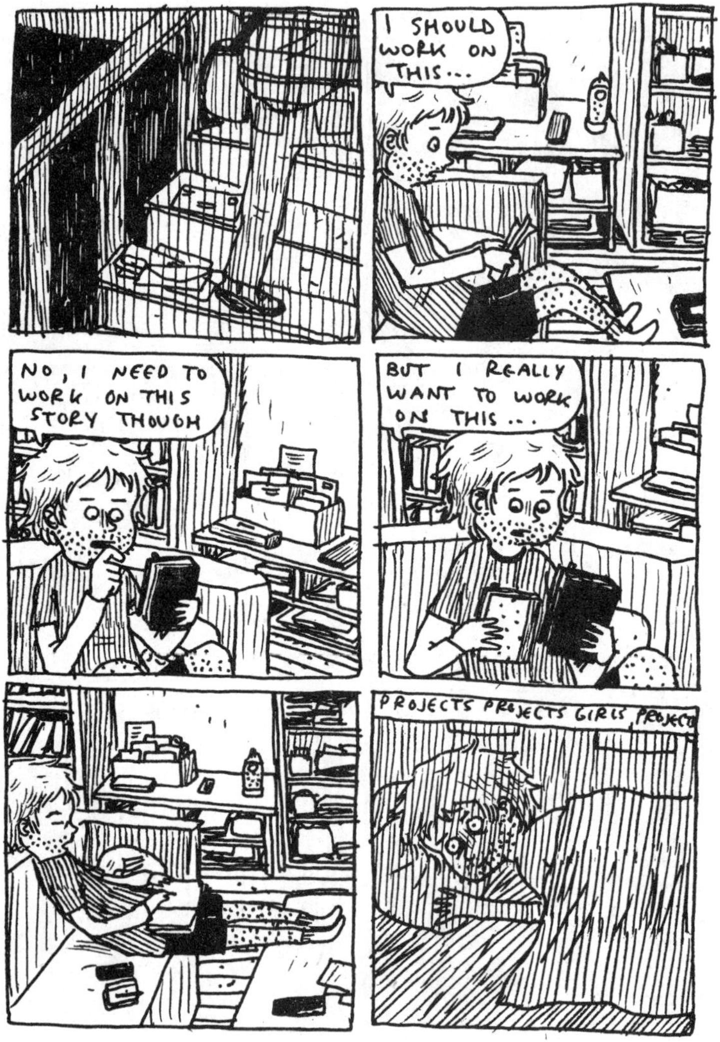
I SHOULD WORK ON THIS...
NO, I NEED TO WORK ON THIS STORY THOUGH
BUT I REALLY WANT TO WORK ON THIS...
PROJECTS PROJECTS GIRLS PROJECTS

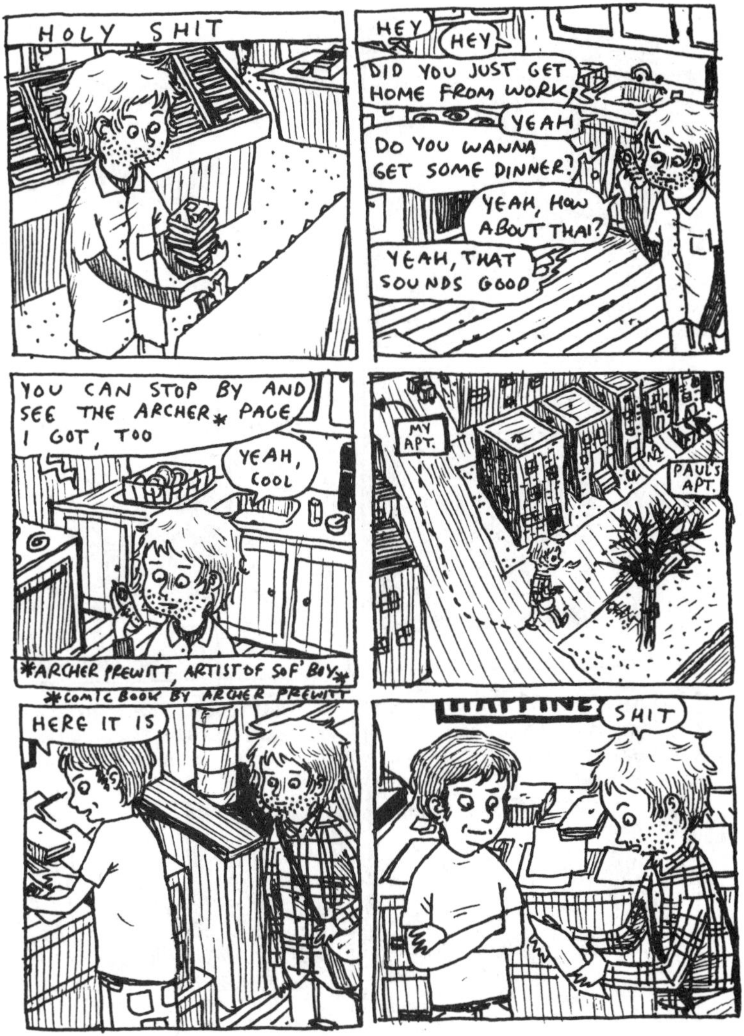
HOLY SHIT
HEY
HEY
DID YOU JUST GET HOME FROM WORK?
YEAH
DO YOU WANNA GET SOME DINNER?
YEAH, HOW ABOUT THAI?
YEAH, THAT SOUNDS GOOD
YOU CAN STOP BY AND SEE THE ARCHER* PAGE* I GOT, TOO
YEAH, COOL
ARCHER PREWITT, ARTIST OF SOF' BOY
*COMIC BOOK BY ARCHER PREWITT
MY APT.
PAUL'S APT.
HERE IT IS
SHIT

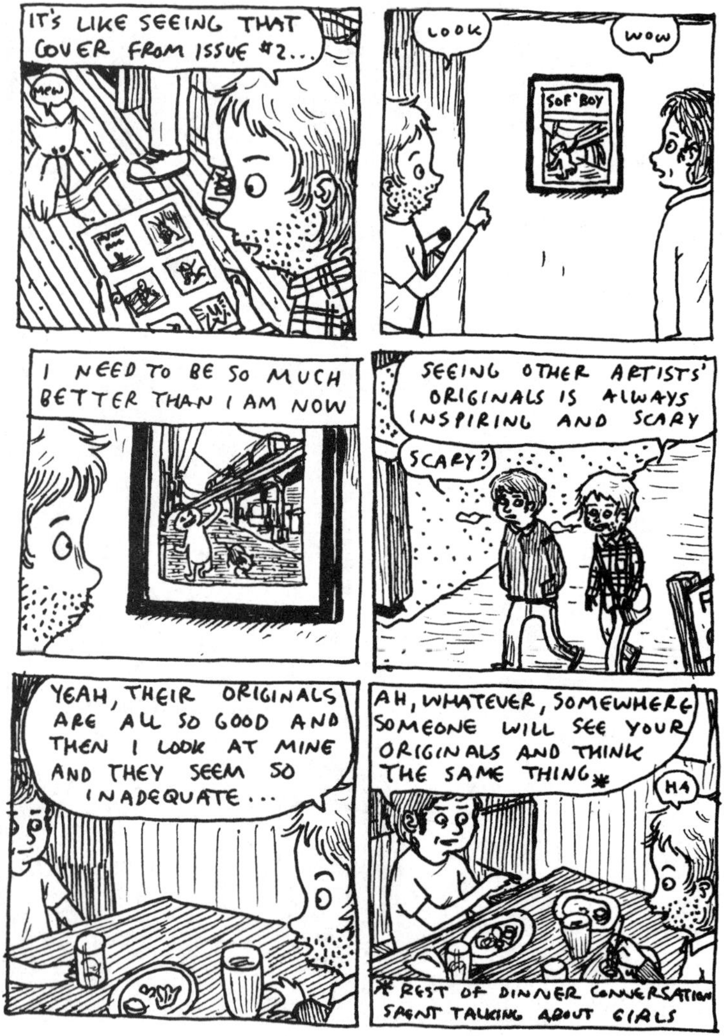
IT'S LIKE SEEING THAT COVER FROM ISSUE #2...
MEW
LOOK
WOW
SOF' BOY
I NEED TO BE SO MUCH BETTER THAN I AM NOW
SEEING OTHER ARTISTS' ORIGINALS IS ALWAYS INSPIRING AND SCARY
SCARY?
YEAH, THEIR ORIGINALS ARE ALL SO GOOD AND THEN I LOOK AT MINE AND THEY SEEM SO INADEQUATE...
AH, WHATEVER, SOMEWHERE SOMEONE WILL SEE YOUR ORIGINALS AND THINK THE SAME THING*
HA
* REST OF DINNER CONVERSATION SPENT TALKING ABOUT GIRLS

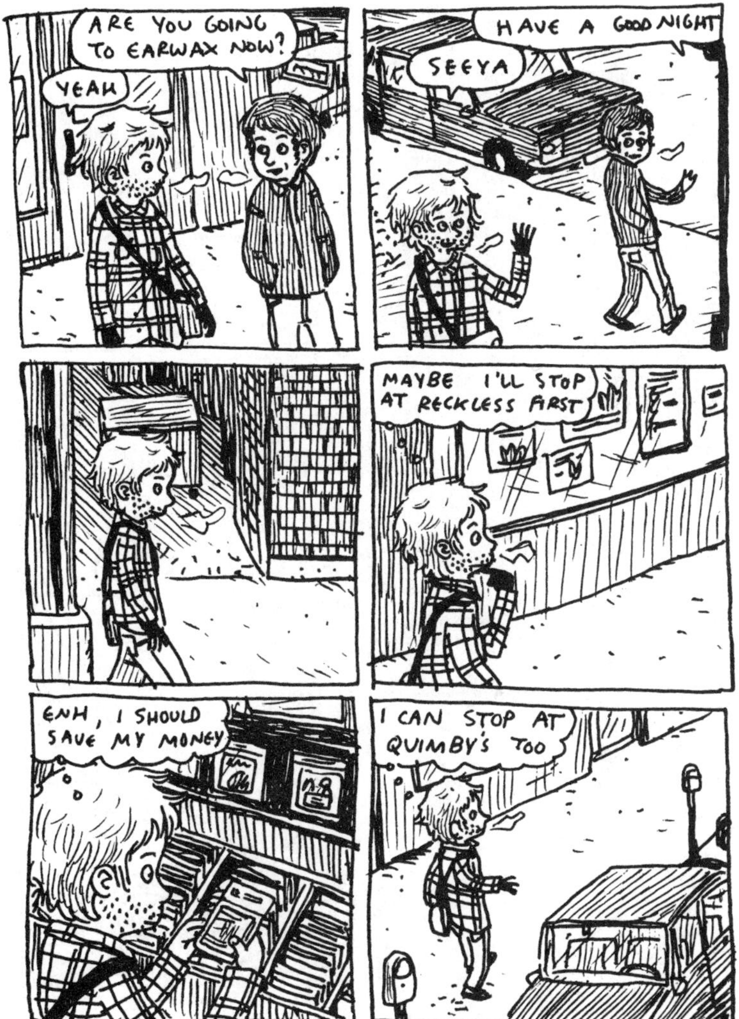
ARE YOU GOING TO EARWAX NOW?
YEAH
HAVE A GOOD NIGHT
SEEYA
MAYBE I'LL STOP AT RECKLESS FIRST
ENH, I SHOULD SAVE MY MONEY
I CAN STOP AT QUIMBY'S TOO

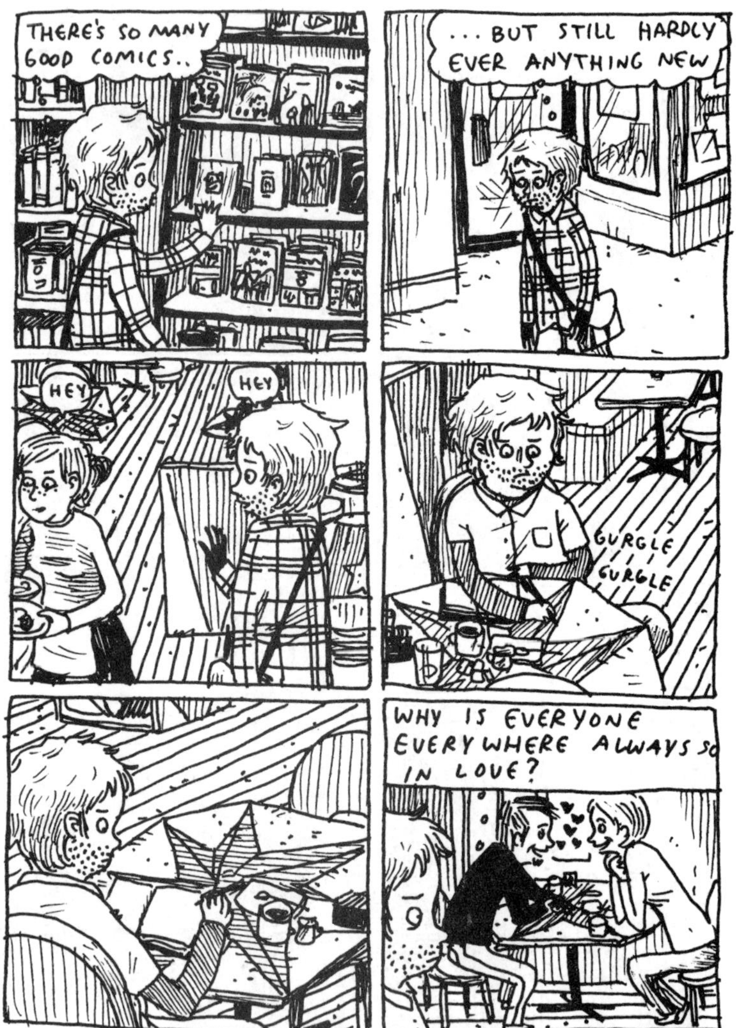

THERE'S SO MANY GOOD COMICS..
...BUT STILL HARDLY EVER ANYTHING NEW
HEY
HEY
GURGLE GURGLE
WHY IS EVERYONE EVERYWHERE ALWAYS SO IN LOVE?

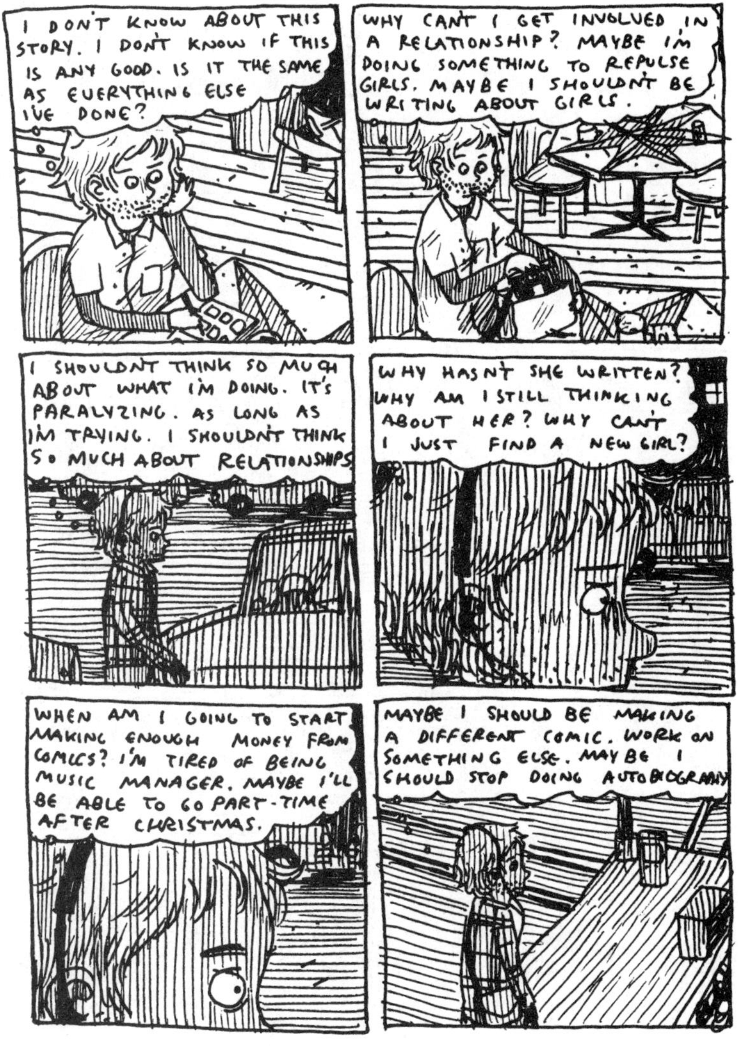
I DON'T KNOW ABOUT THIS STORY. I DON'T KNOW IF THIS IS ANY GOOD. IS IT THE SAME AS EVERYTHING ELSE I'VE DONE?
WHY CAN'T I GET INVOLVED IN A RELATIONSHIP? MAYBE I'M DOING SOMETHING TO REPULSE GIRLS. MAYBE I SHOULDN'T BE WRITING ABOUT GIRLS.
I SHOULDN'T THINK SO MUCH ABOUT WHAT I'M DOING. IT'S PARALYZING. AS LONG AS I'M TRYING. I SHOULDN'T THINK SO MUCH ABOUT RELATIONSHIPS
WHY HASN'T SHE WRITTEN? WHY AM I STILL THINKING ABOUT HER? WHY CAN'T I JUST FIND A NEW GIRL?
WHEN AM I GOING TO START MAKING ENOUGH MONEY FROM COMICS? I'M TIRED OF BEING MUSIC MANAGER. MAYBE I'LL BE ABLE TO GO PART-TIME AFTER CHRISTMAS.
MAYBE I SHOULD BE MAKING A DIFFERENT COMIC. WORK ON SOMETHING ELSE. MAYBE I SHOULD STOP DOING AUTOBIOGRAPHY

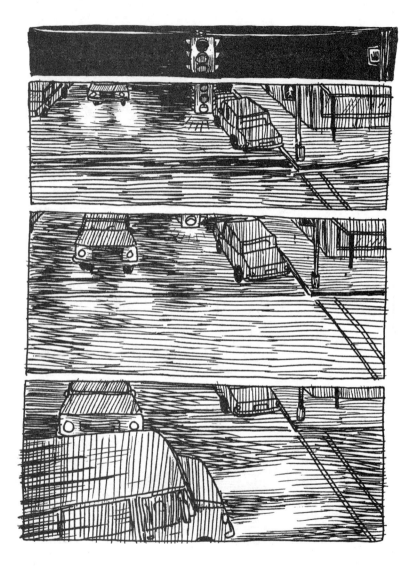

298

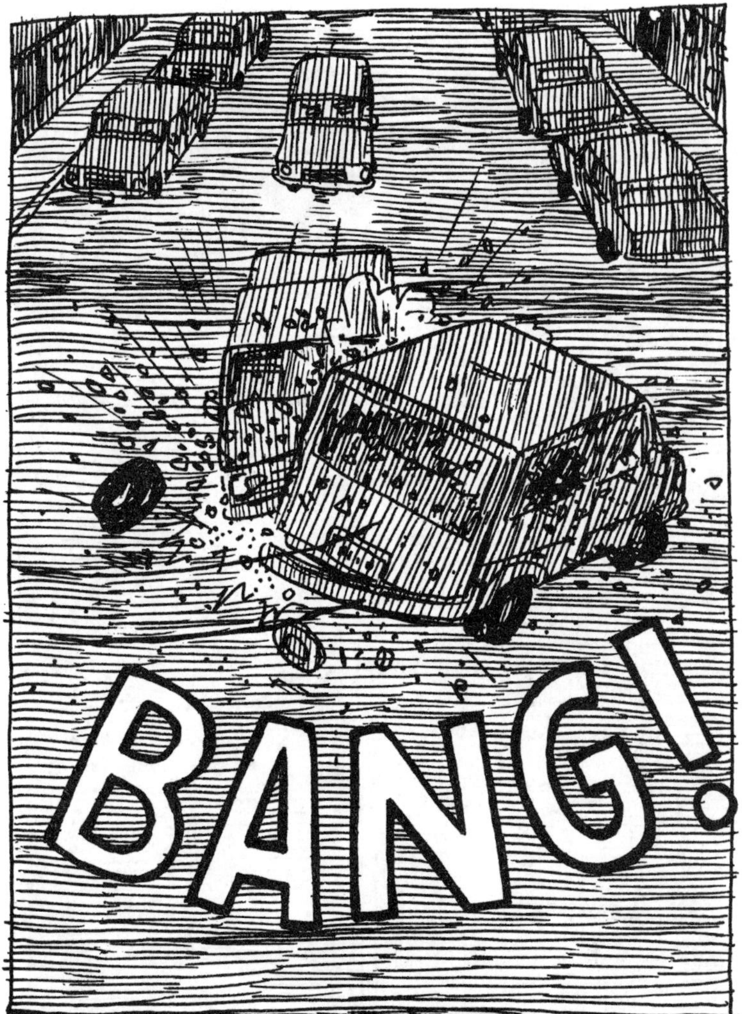
BANG!

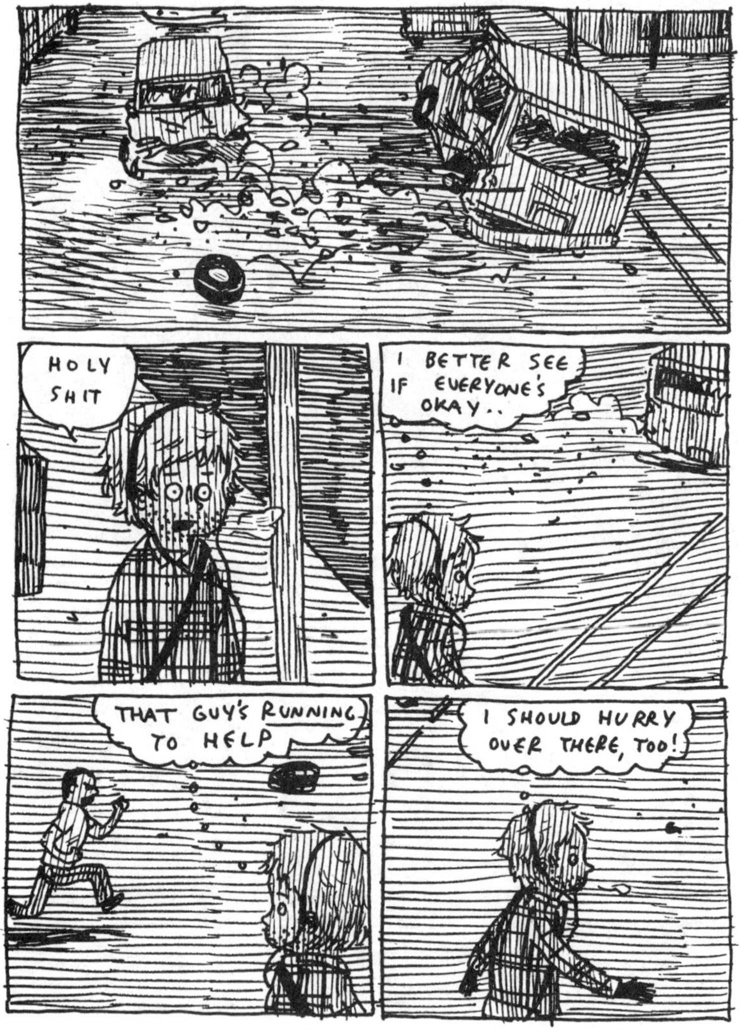
HOLY SHIT
I BETTER SEE IF EVERYONE'S OKAY..
THAT GUY'S RUNNING TO HELP
I SHOULD HURRY OVER THERE, TOO!

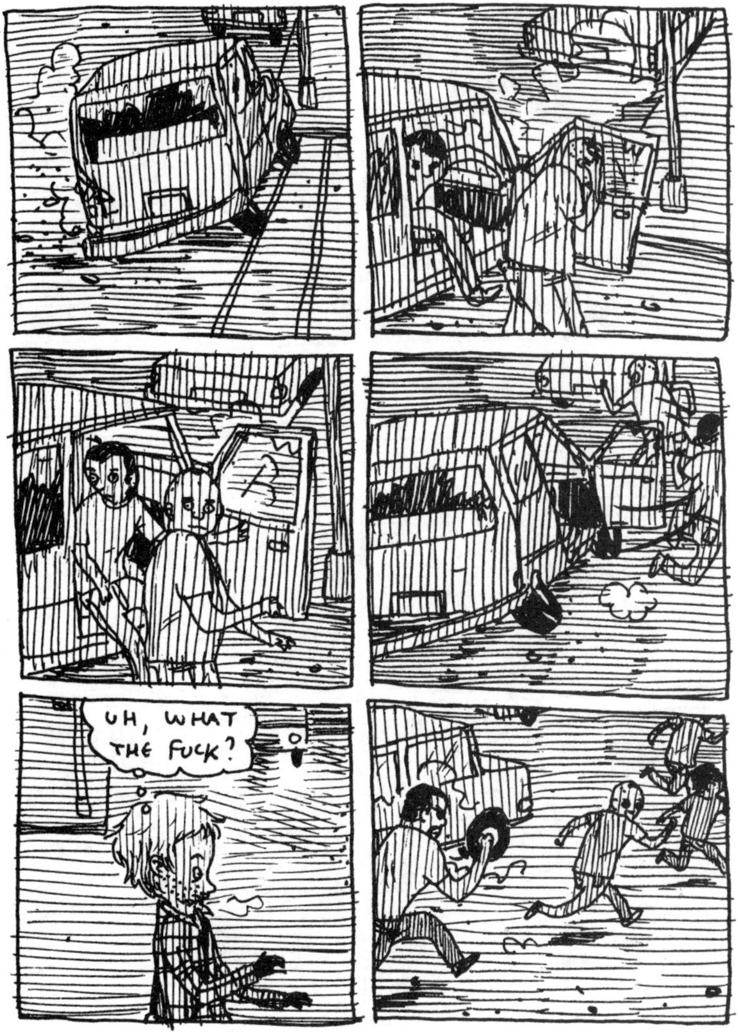
UH, WHAT THE FUCK?

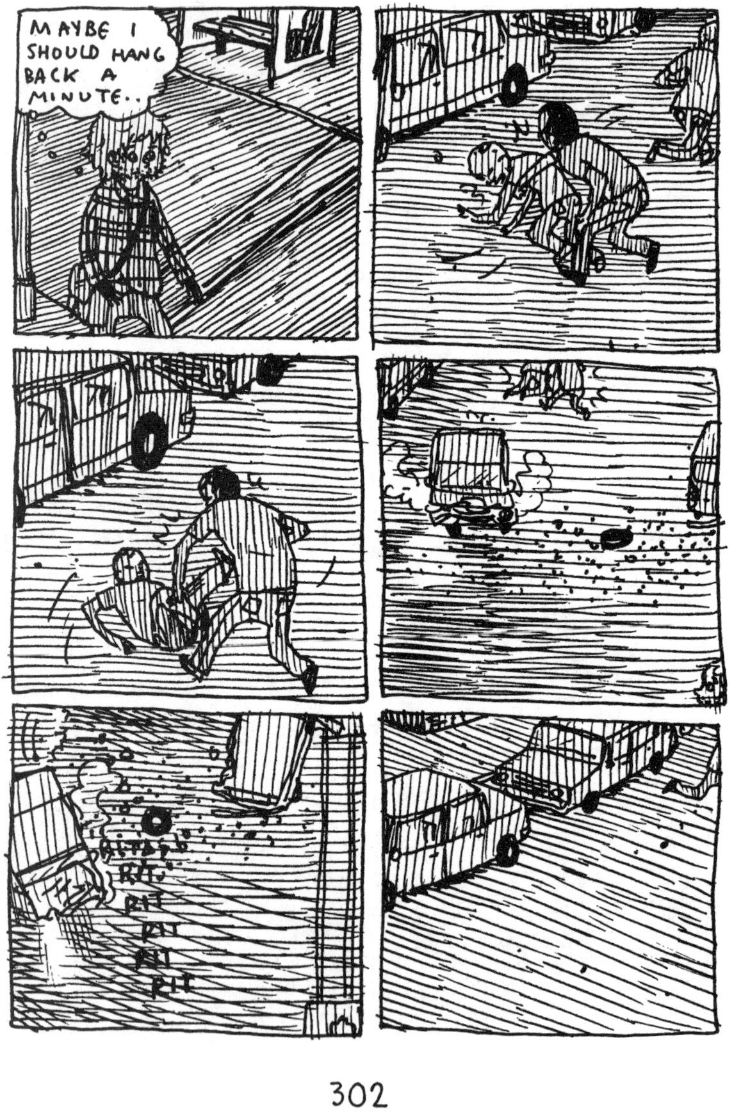
MAYBE I SHOULD HANG BACK A MINUTE..
RIT
RIT
RIT
RIT
RIT

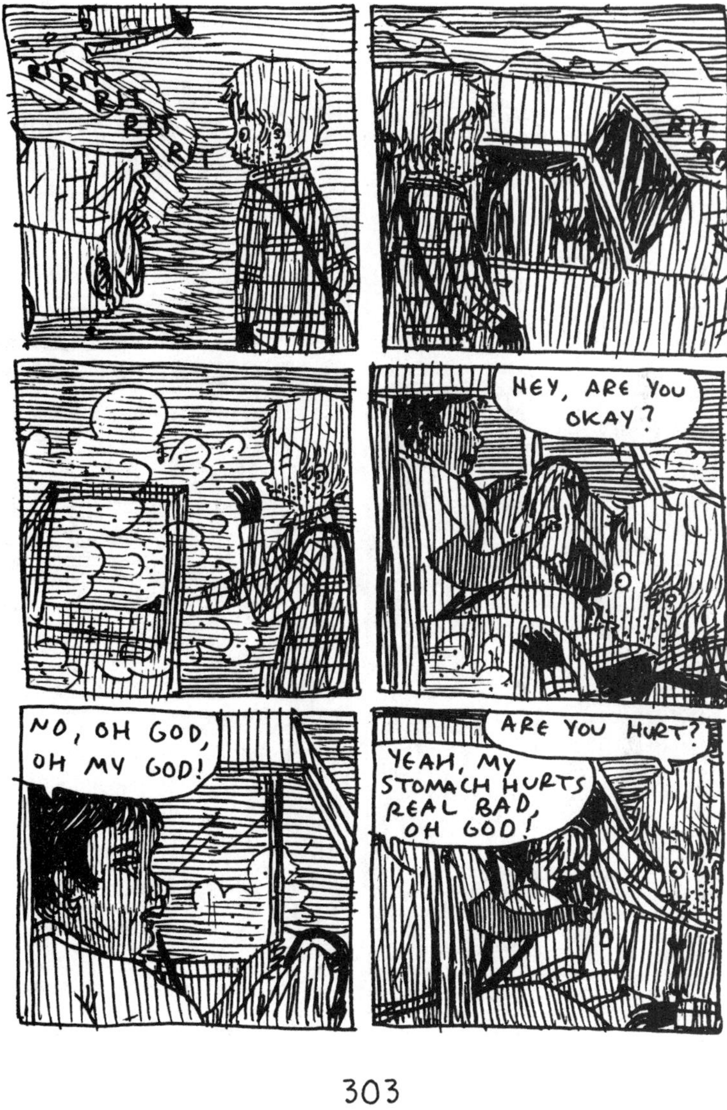
RIT RIT RIT RIT
RIT
HEY, ARE YOU OKAY?
NO, OH GOD, OH MY GOD!
ARE YOU HURT?
YEAH, MY STOMACH HURTS REAL BAD, OH GOD!

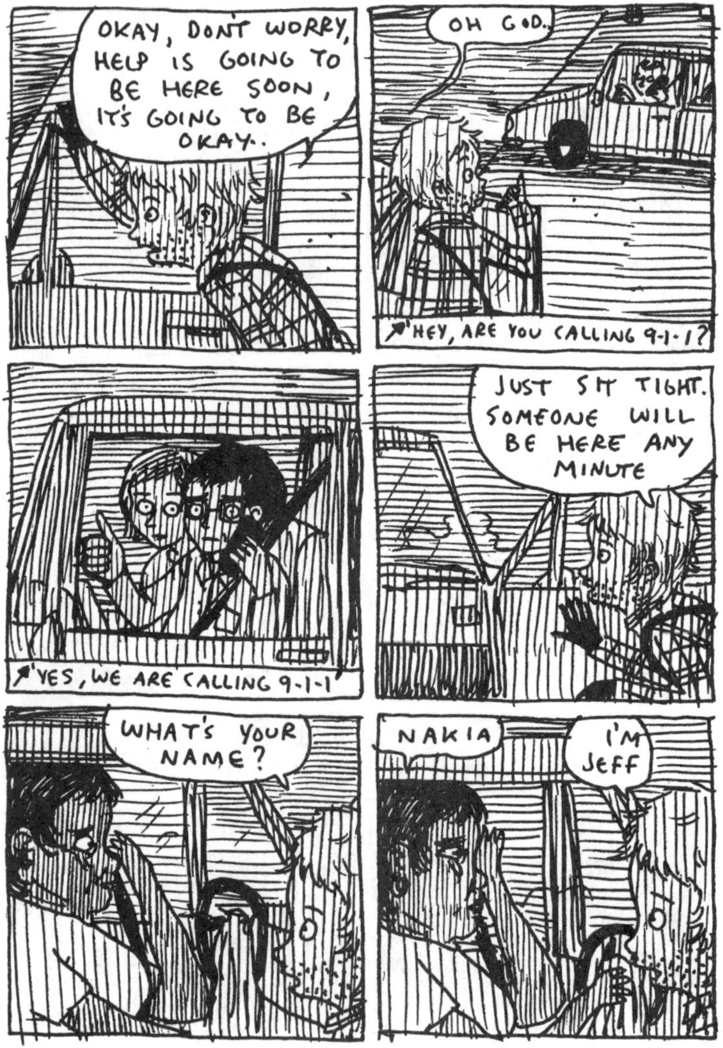
OKAY, DON'T WORRY, HELP IS GOING TO BE HERE SOON, IT'S GOING TO BE OKAY..
OH GOD..
"HEY, ARE YOU CALLING 9-1-1?
"YES, WE ARE CALLING 9-1-1"
JUST SIT TIGHT. SOMEONE WILL BE HERE ANY MINUTE
WHAT'S YOUR NAME?
NAKIA
I'M JEFF

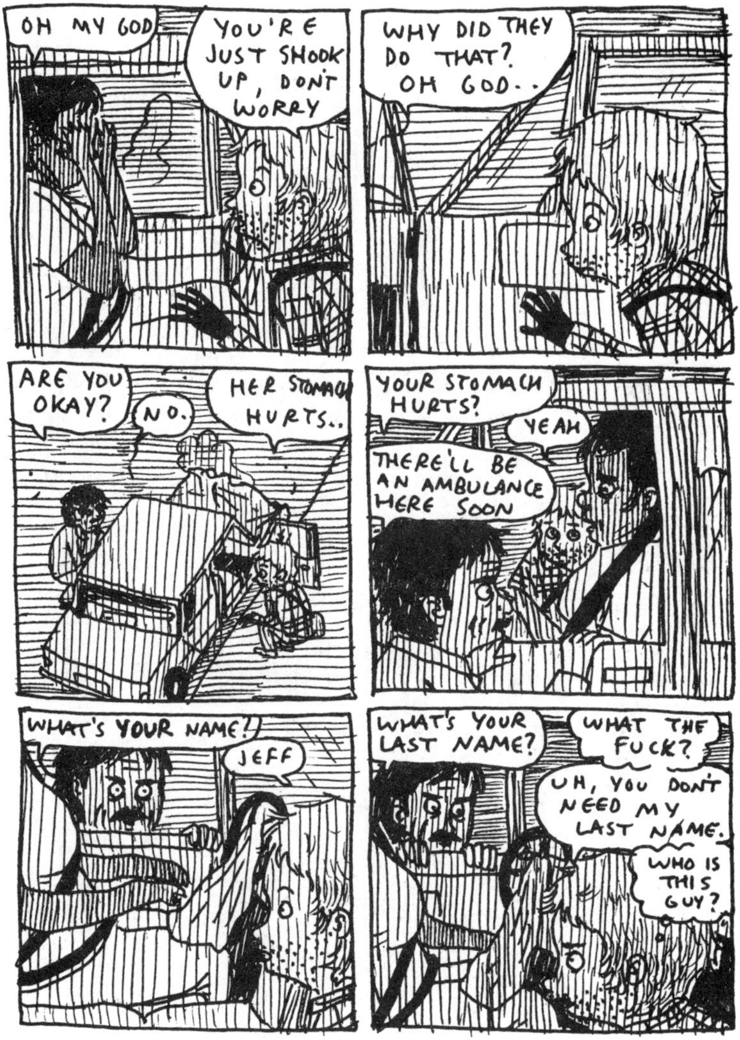
OH MY GOD
YOU'RE JUST SHOOK UP, DON'T WORRY
WHY DID THEY DO THAT? OH GOD..
ARE YOU OKAY?
NO.
HER STOMACH HURTS..
YOUR STOMACH HURTS?
YEAH
THERE'LL BE AN AMBULANCE HERE SOON
WHAT'S YOUR NAME?
JEFF
WHAT'S YOUR LAST NAME?
WHAT THE FUCK?
UH, YOU DON'T NEED MY LAST NAME.
WHO IS THIS GUY?

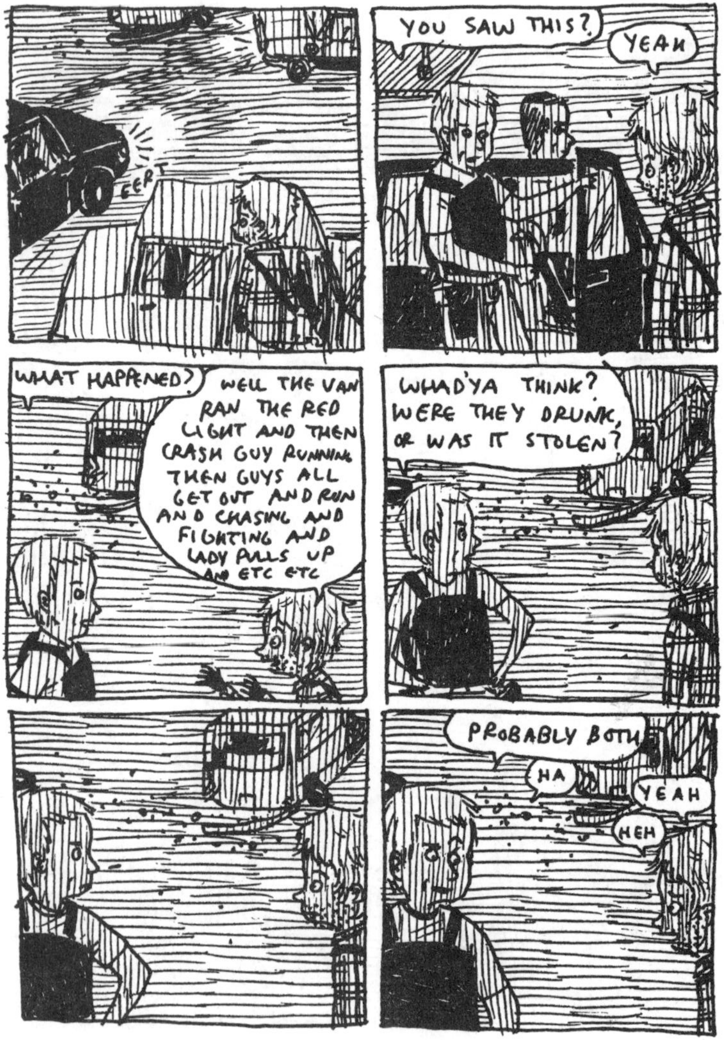
EERT
YOU SAW THIS?
YEAH
WHAT HAPPENED?
WELL THE VAN RAN THE RED LIGHT AND THEN CRASH GUY RUNNING THEN GUYS ALL GET OUT AND RUN AND CHASING AND FIGHTING AND LADY PULLS UP AN ETC ETC
WHAD'YA THINK? WERE THEY DRUNK, OR WAS IT STOLEN?
PROBABLY BOTH
HA
YEAH
HEH

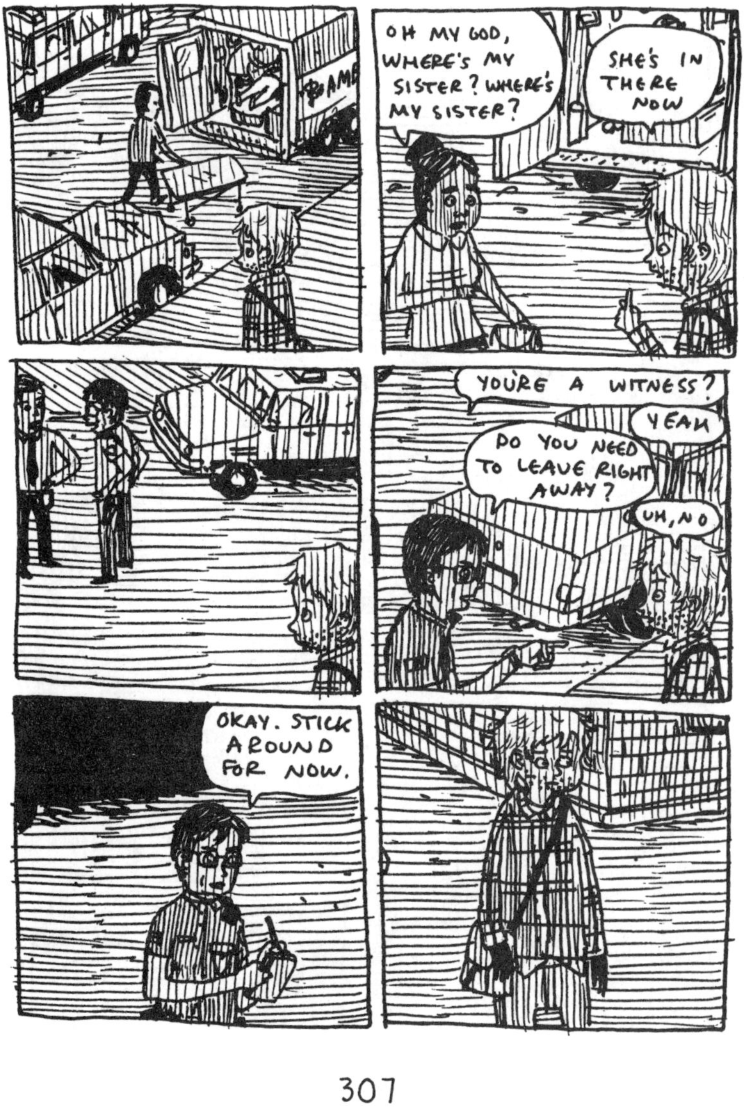
OH MY GOD, WHERE'S MY SISTER? WHERE'S MY SISTER?
SHE'S IN THERE NOW
YOU'RE A WITNESS?
YEAH
DO YOU NEED TO LEAVE RIGHT AWAY?
UH, NO
OKAY. STICK AROUND FOR NOW.

HEY!
HOLY SHIT
...THE DRIVER?
....DRUNK..
...GANG BANGERS..
..CHASING...
YOU'RE A WITNESS? COME WITH ME A MINUTE
YEAH.
OKAY.
NAME? WHERE DO YOU LIVE? WHAT'S YOUR PHONE NUMBER? WHAT DID YOU SEE? OKAY, YOU CAN GO.
BLAH BLAH BLAH VAN BLAH GUYS RUN BLAH BLAH BLAH

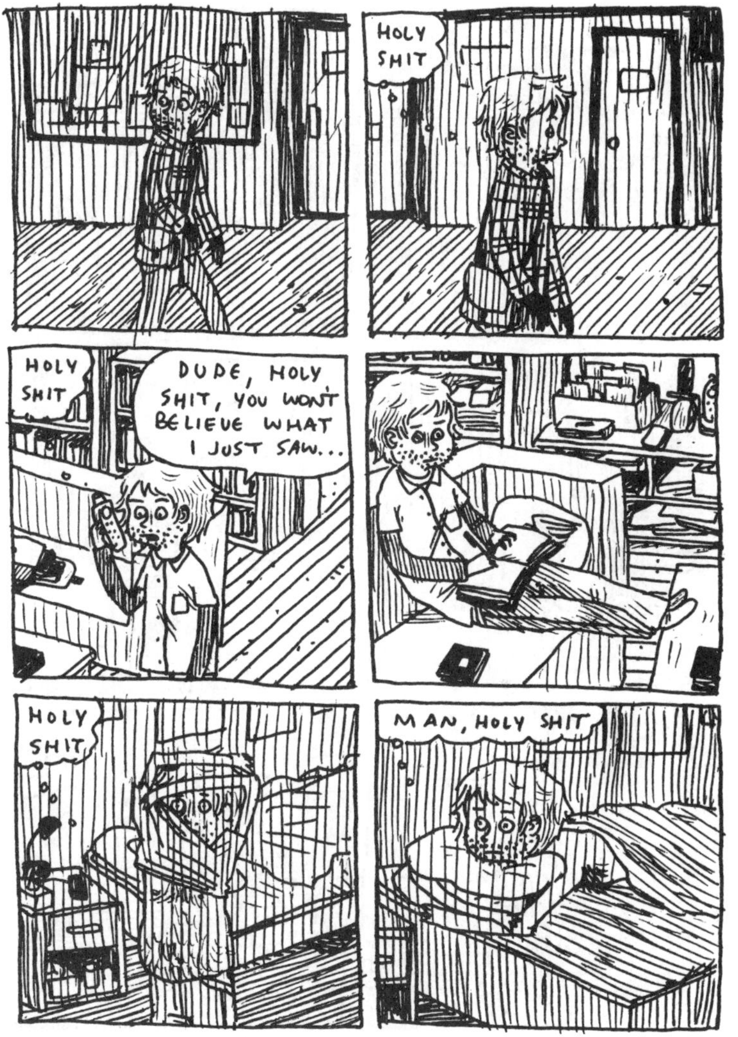
HOLY SHIT
HOLY SHIT
DUDE, HOLY SHIT, YOU WON'T BELIEVE WHAT I JUST SAW...
HOLY SHIT
MAN, HOLY SHIT

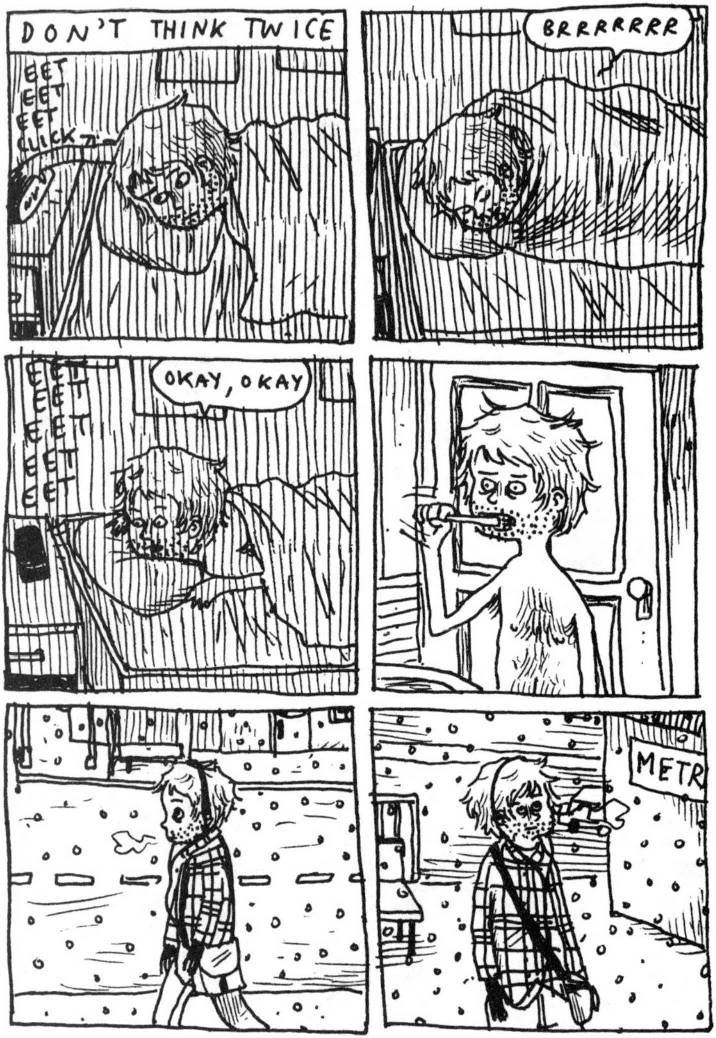
DON'T THINK TWICE
EET
EET
EET
CLICK
BRRRRRRR
EET
EET
EET
EET
EET
OKAY, OKAY
METR

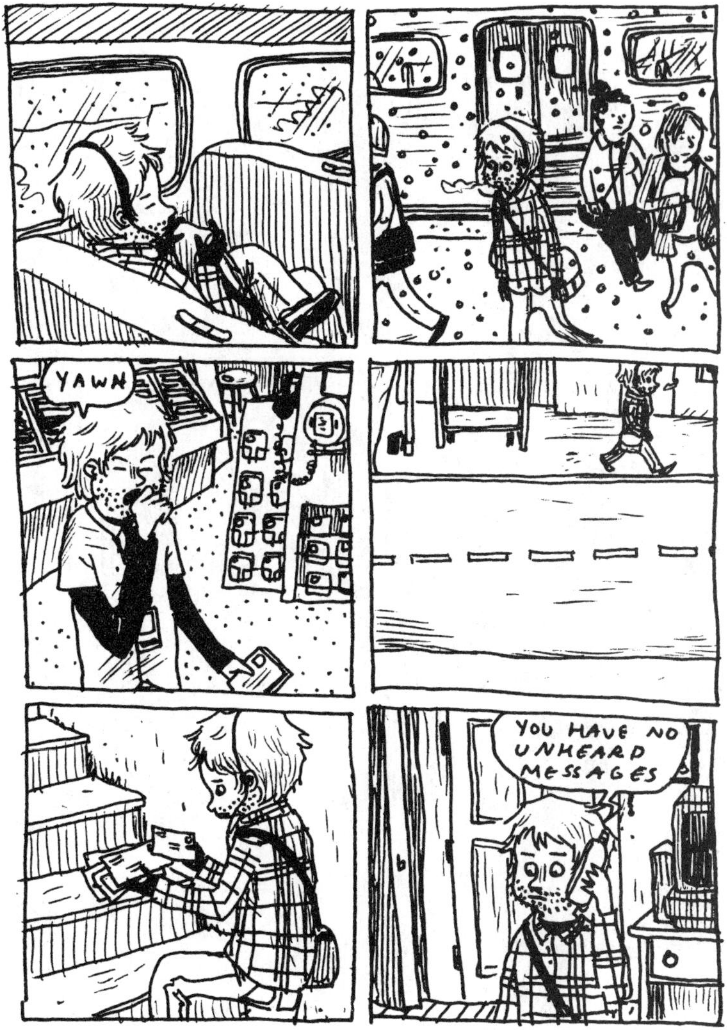
YAWN
YOU HAVE NO UNHEARD MESSAGES

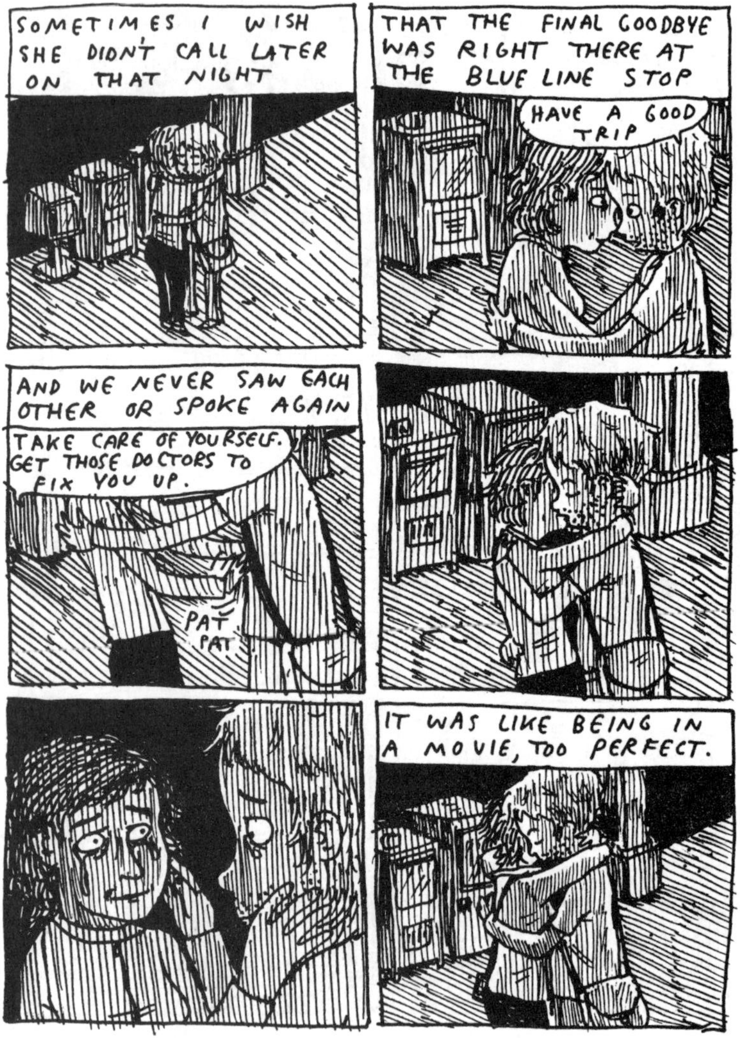
SOMETIMES I WISH SHE DIDN'T CALL LATER ON THAT NIGHT
THAT THE FINAL GOODBYE WAS RIGHT THERE AT THE BLUE LINE STOP
HAVE A GOOD TRIP
AND WE NEVER SAW EACH OTHER OR SPOKE AGAIN
TAKE CARE OF YOURSELF. GET THOSE DOCTORS TO FIX YOU UP.
PAT PAT
IT WAS LIKE BEING IN A MOVIE, TOO PERFECT.

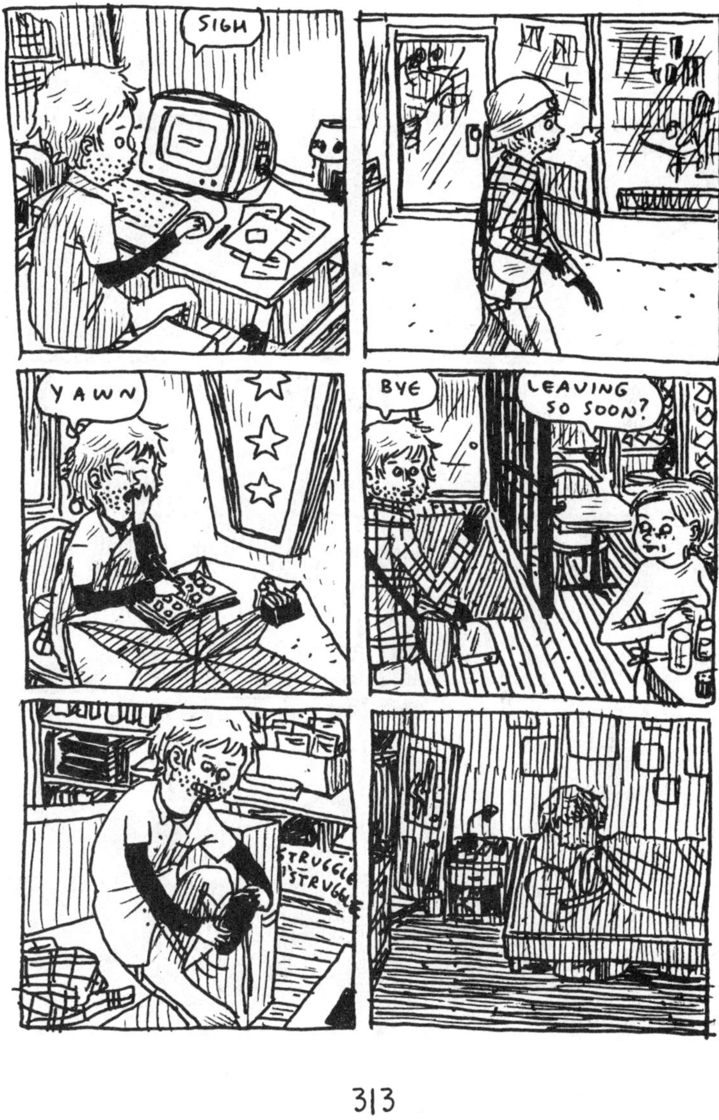
SIGH
YAWN
BYE
LEAVING SO SOON?
STRUGGLE
STRUGGLE

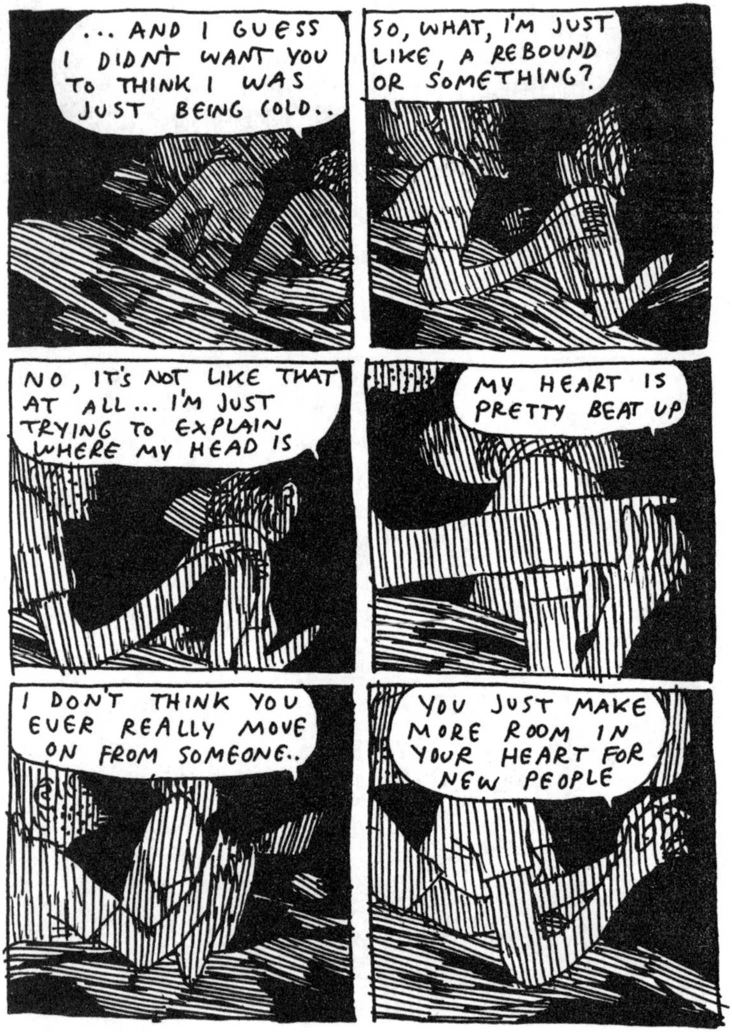
... AND I GUESS I DIDN'T WANT YOU TO THINK I WAS JUST BEING COLD..
SO, WHAT, I'M JUST LIKE, A REBOUND OR SOMETHING?
NO, IT'S NOT LIKE THAT AT ALL... I'M JUST TRYING TO EXPLAIN WHERE MY HEAD IS
MY HEART IS PRETTY BEAT UP
I DON'T THINK YOU EVER REALLY MOVE ON FROM SOMEONE..
YOU JUST MAKE MORE ROOM IN YOUR HEART FOR NEW PEOPLE

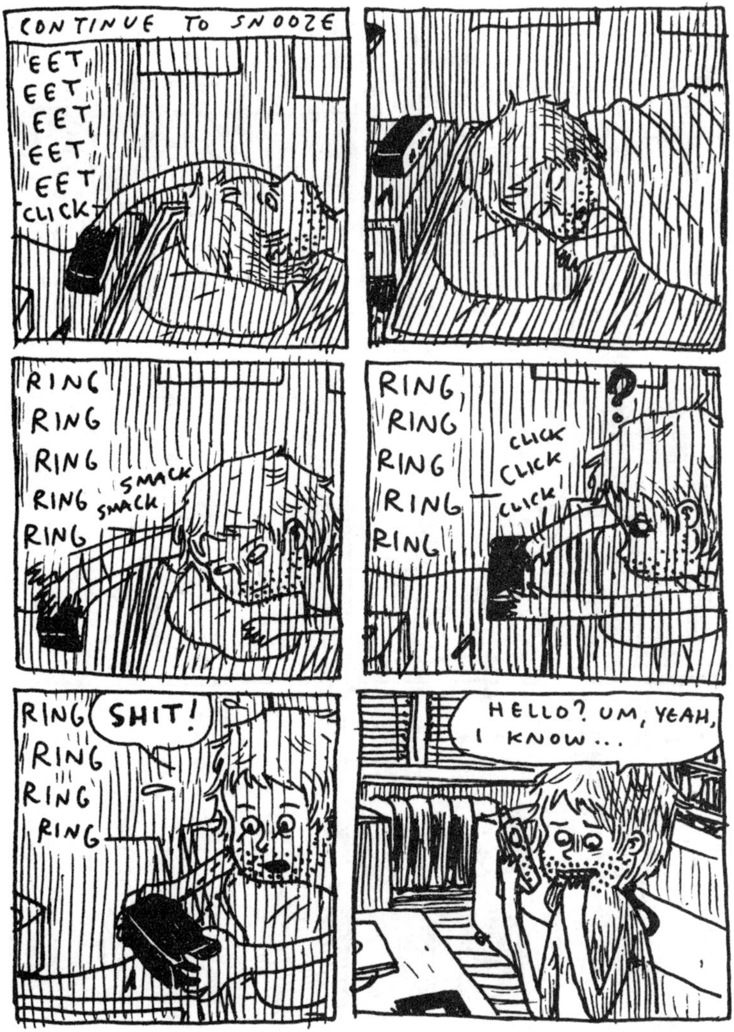
CONTINUE TO SNOOZE
EET
EET
EET
EET
EET
CLICK
RING
RING
RING
RING
RING
SMACK
SMACK
RING
RING
RING
RING
RING
CLICK
CLICK
CLICK
RING
SHIT!
RING
RING
RING
HELLO? UM, YEAH, I KNOW...

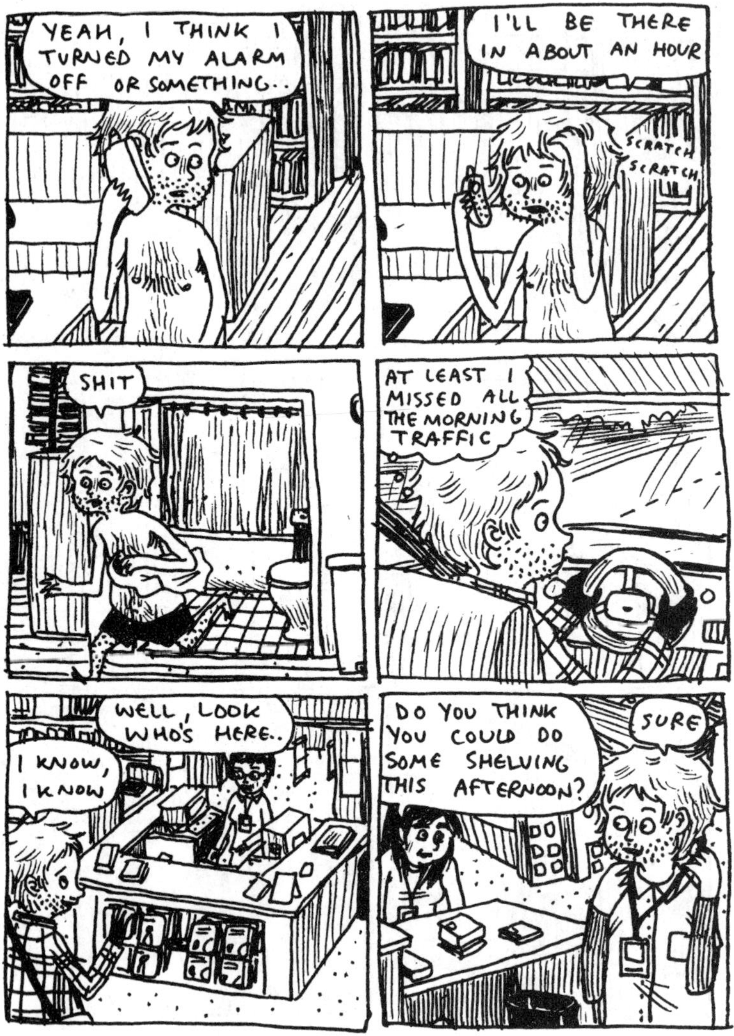
YEAH, I THINK I TURNED MY ALARM OFF OR SOMETHING..
I'LL BE THERE IN ABOUT AN HOUR
SCRATCH SCRATCH
SHIT
AT LEAST I MISSED ALL THE MORNING TRAFFIC
WELL, LOOK WHO'S HERE..
I KNOW, I KNOW
DO YOU THINK YOU COULD DO SOME SHELVING THIS AFTERNOON?
SURE

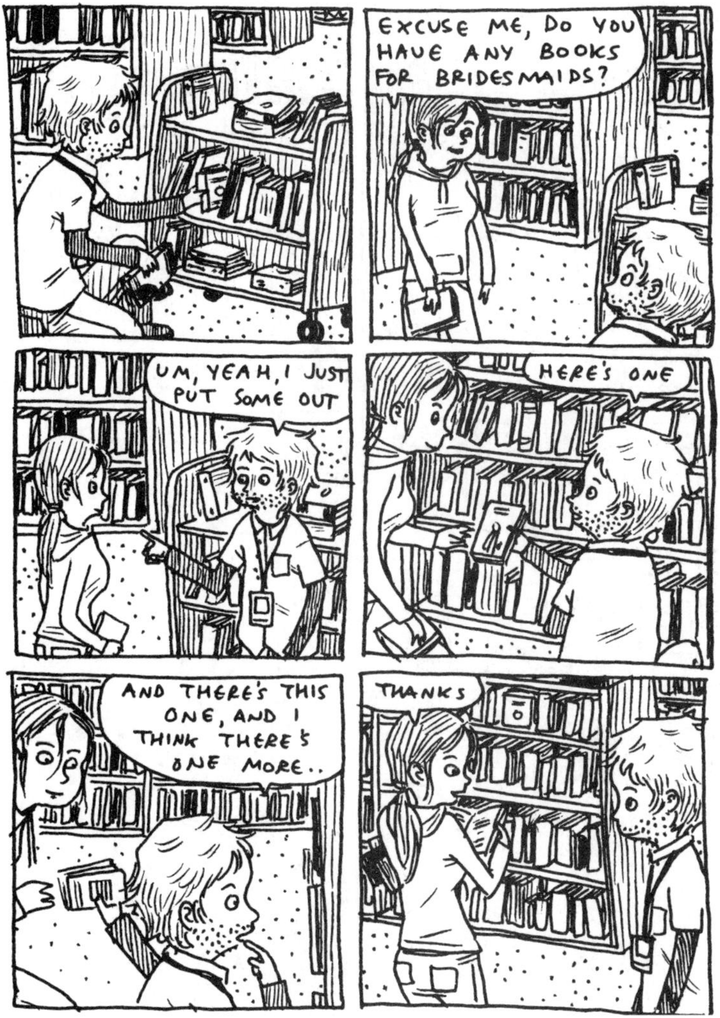
EXCUSE ME, DO YOU HAVE ANY BOOKS FOR BRIDESMAIDS?
UM, YEAH, I JUST PUT SOME OUT
HERE'S ONE
AND THERE'S THIS ONE, AND I THINK THERE'S ONE MORE..
THANKS

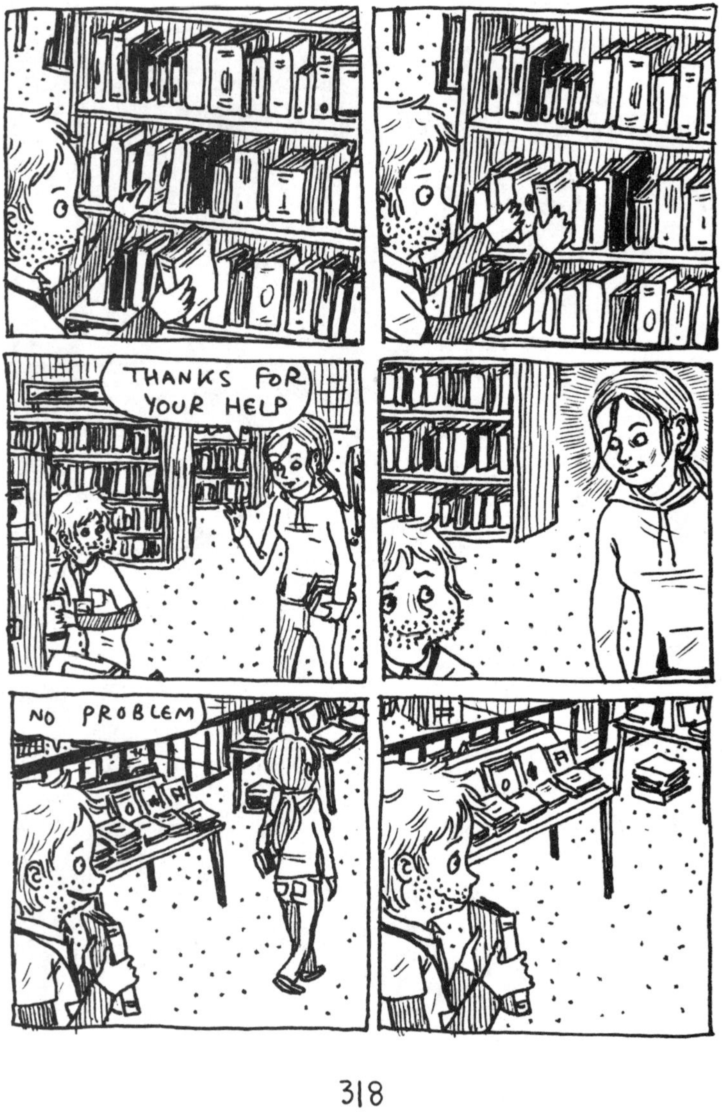
THANKS FOR YOUR HELP
NO PROBLEM

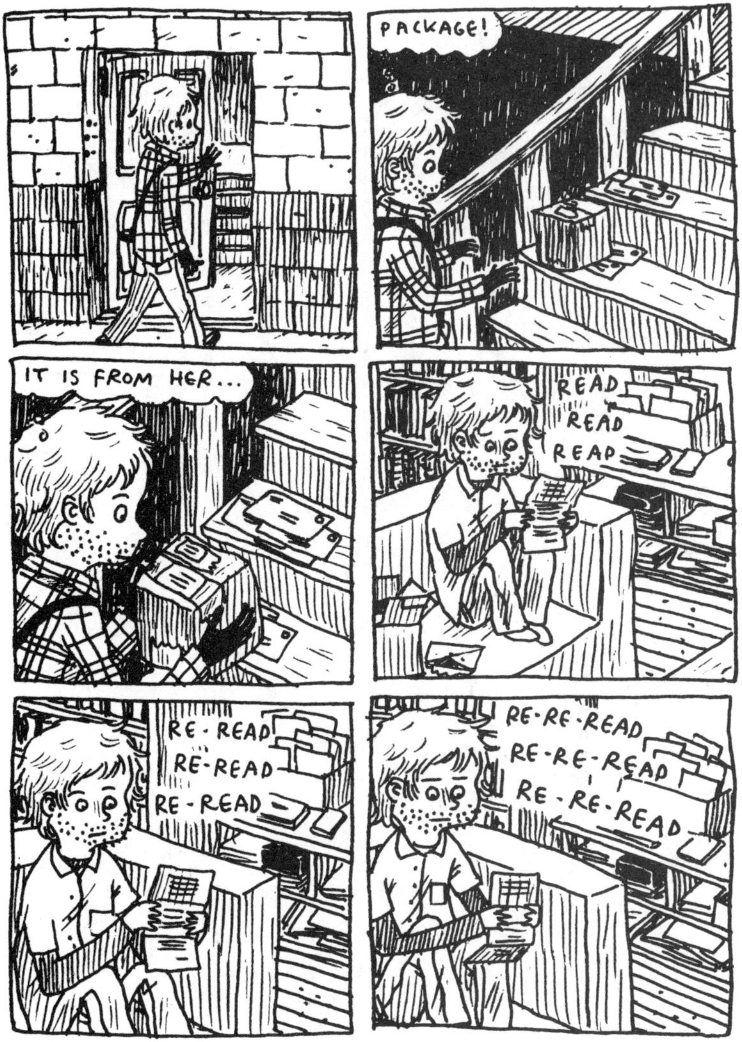
PACKAGE!
IT IS FROM HER...
READ
READ
READ
RE-READ
RE-READ
RE-READ
RE-RE-READ
RE-RE-READ
RE-RE-READ

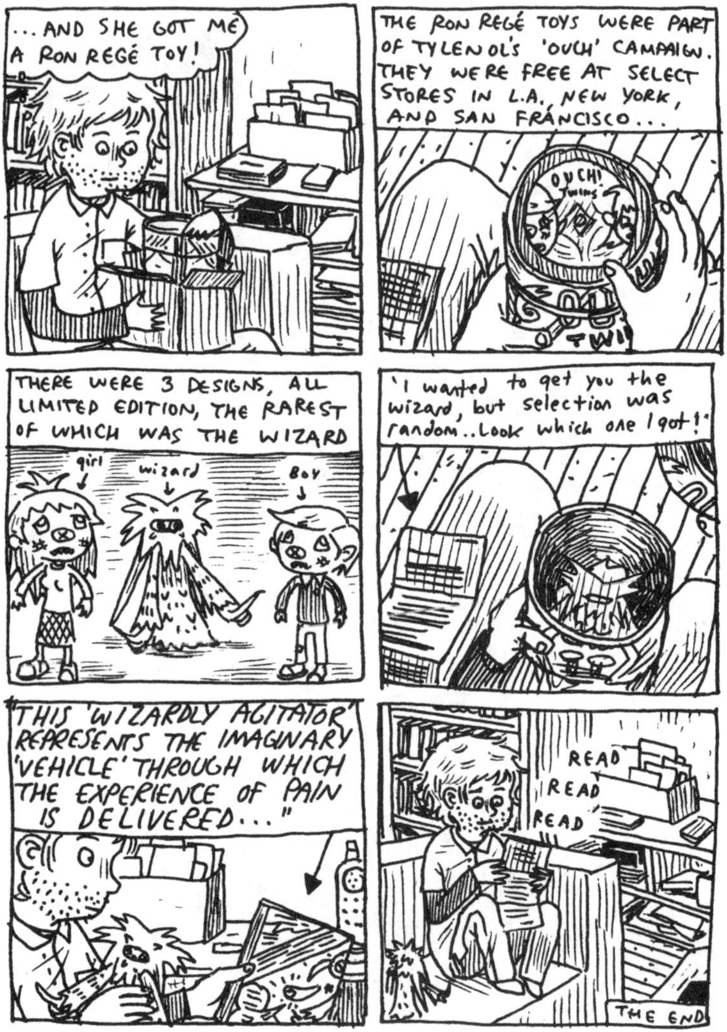
...AND SHE GOT ME A RON REGÉ TOY!
THE RON REGÉ TOYS WERE PART OF TYLENOL'S 'OUCH' CAMPAIGN. THEY WERE FREE AT SELECT STORES IN L.A., NEW YORK, AND SAN FRANCISCO...
OUCH!
THERE WERE 3 DESIGNS, ALL LIMITED EDITION, THE RAREST OF WHICH WAS THE WIZARD
girl
wizard
BOY
'I wanted to get you the wizard, but selection was random.. Look which one I got!'
"THIS 'WIZARDLY AGITATOR' REPRESENTS THE IMAGINARY 'VEHICLE' THROUGH WHICH THE EXPERIENCE OF PAIN IS DELIVERED..."
READ
READ
READ
THE END

A
TINY
PIECE
OF
MYSELF

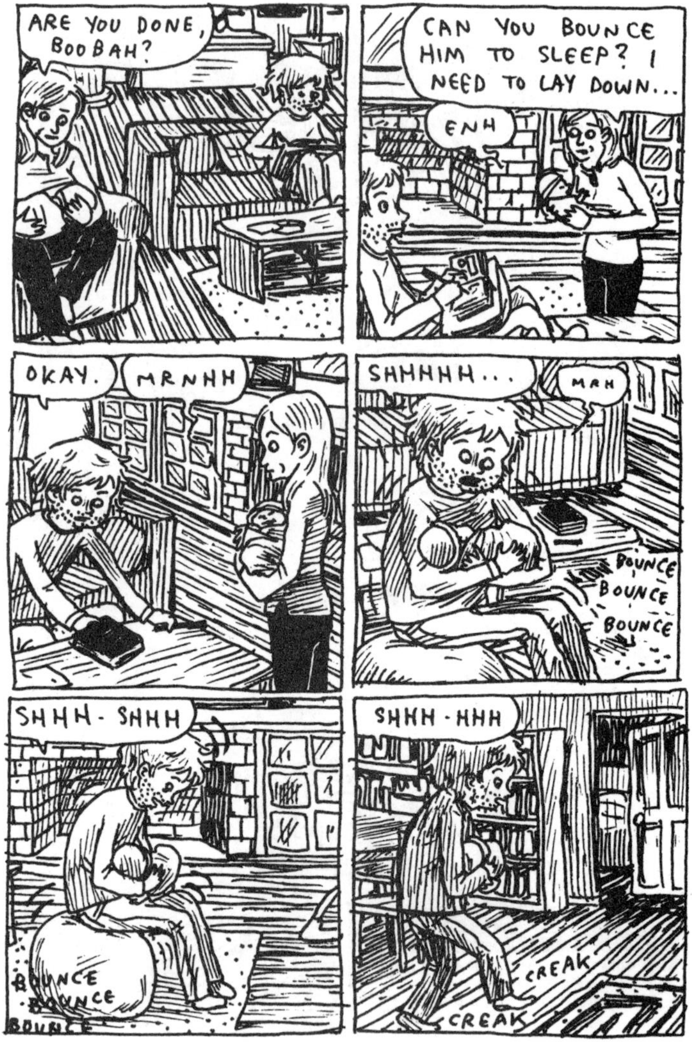
ARE YOU DONE, BOOBAH?
CAN YOU BOUNCE HIM TO SLEEP? I NEED TO LAY DOWN...
ENH
OKAY.
MRNHH
SHHHHH...
MRH
BOUNCE
BOUNCE
BOUNCE
SHHH-SHHH
BOUNCE
BOUNCE
SHHH-HHH
CREAK
CREAK

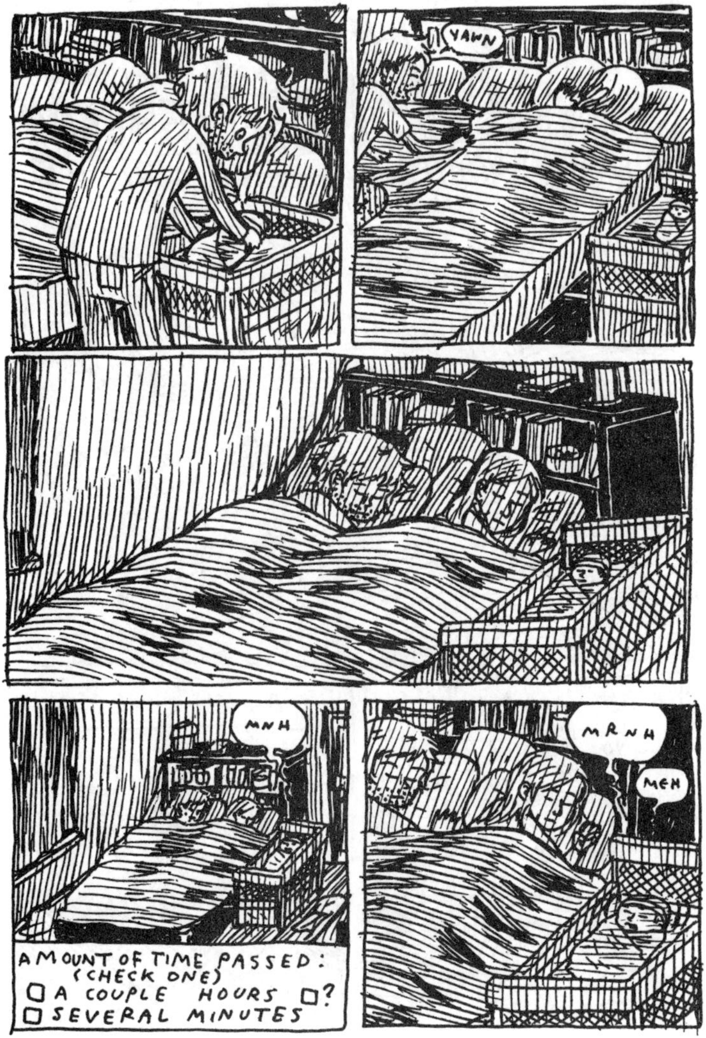
YAWN
MNH
AMOUNT OF TIME PASSED:
(CHECK ONE)
A COUPLE HOURS
?
SEVERAL MINUTES
MRNH
MEH

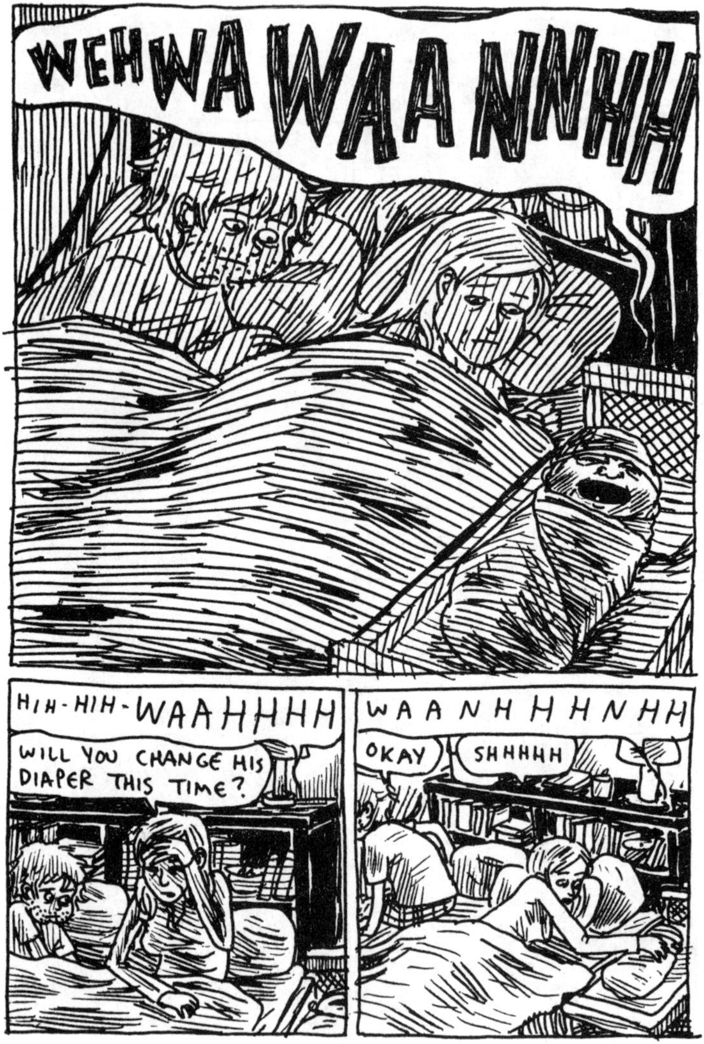
WEHWAWAANNHH
HIH-HIH-WAAHHHH
WILL YOU CHANGE HIS DIAPER THIS TIME?
WAANHHHNHH
OKAY
SHHHHH

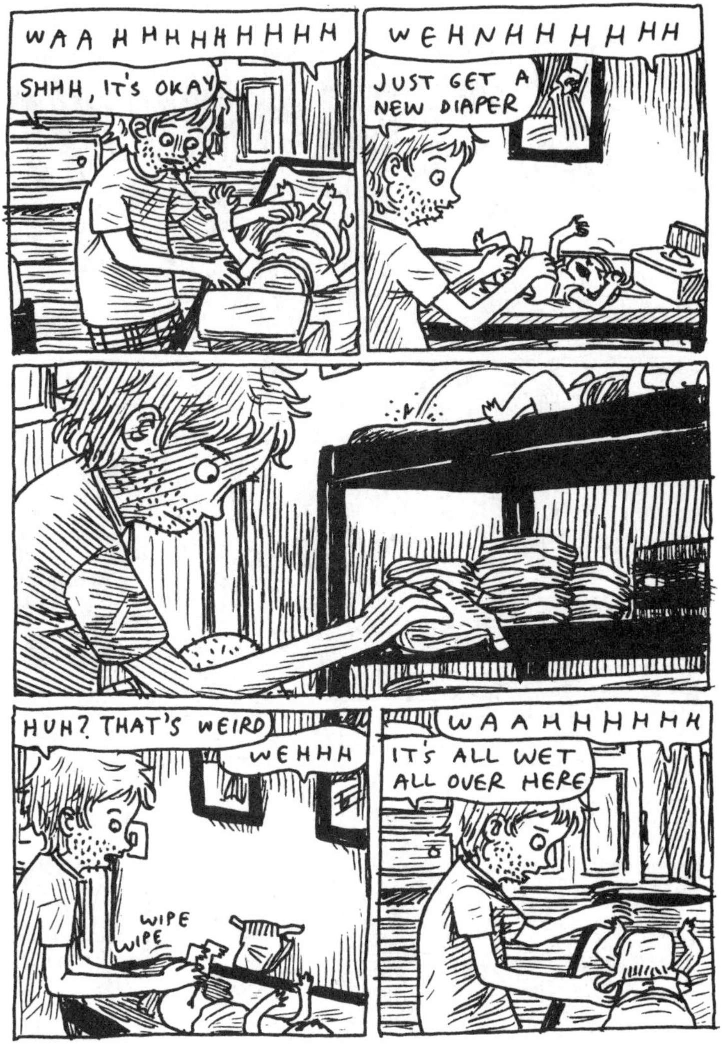
WAAHHHHHHHHH
SHHH, IT'S OKAY
WEHNHHHHHHH
JUST GET A NEW DIAPER
HUH? THAT'S WEIRD
WEHHH
WIPE
WIPE
WAAHHHHHHH
IT'S ALL WET ALL OVER HERE

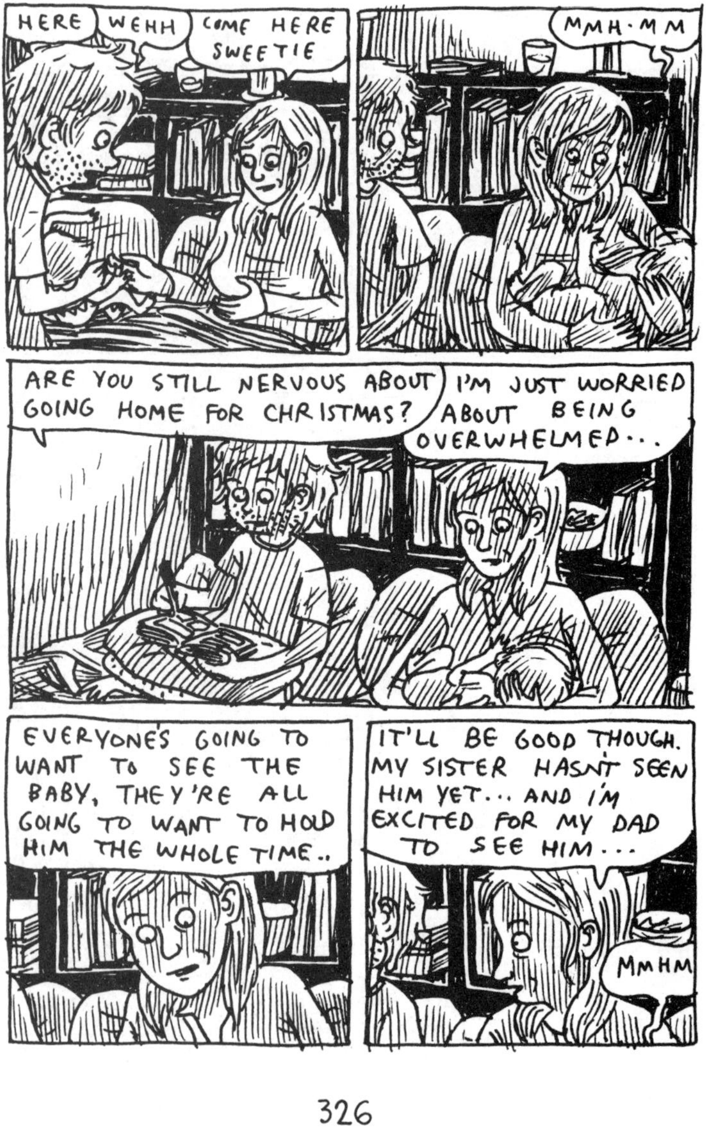
HERE
WEHH
COME HERE SWEETIE
MMH·MM
ARE YOU STILL NERVOUS ABOUT GOING HOME FOR CHRISTMAS?
I'M JUST WORRIED ABOUT BEING OVERWHELMED...
EVERYONE'S GOING TO WANT TO SEE THE BABY, THEY'RE ALL GOING TO WANT TO HOLD HIM THE WHOLE TIME..
IT'LL BE GOOD THOUGH. MY SISTER HASN'T SEEN HIM YET... AND I'M EXCITED FOR MY DAD TO SEE HIM...
MMHM

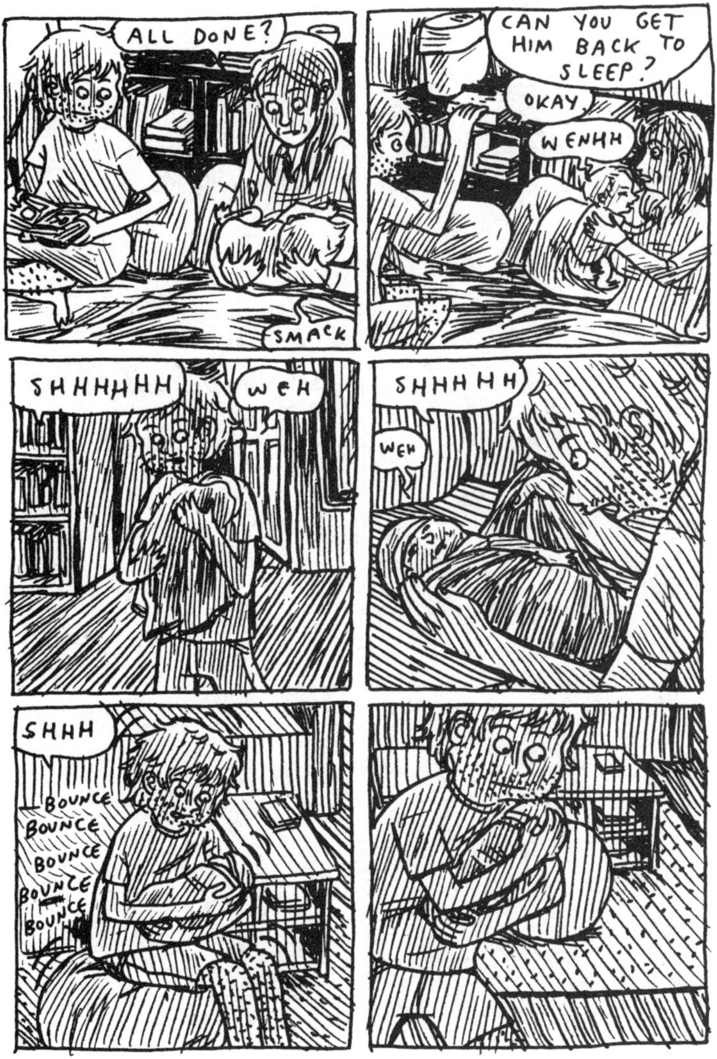
ALL DONE?
SMACK
CAN YOU GET HIM BACK TO SLEEP?
OKAY.
WENHH
SHHHHHH
WEH
SHHHHH
WEH
SHHH
BOUNCE
BOUNCE
BOUNCE
BOUNCE
BOUNCE

WAAHHHH
SHHHH
SHHHHHHH
WEHH
SHHHH
SHHHH

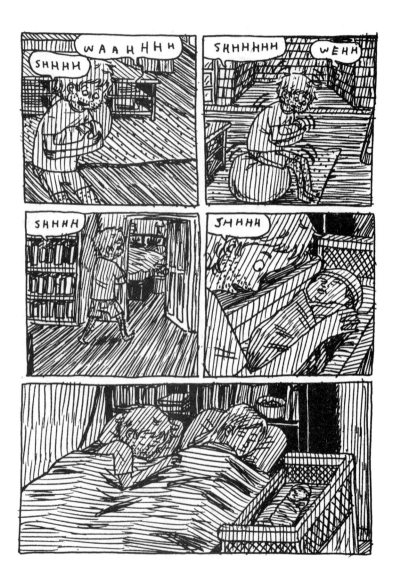

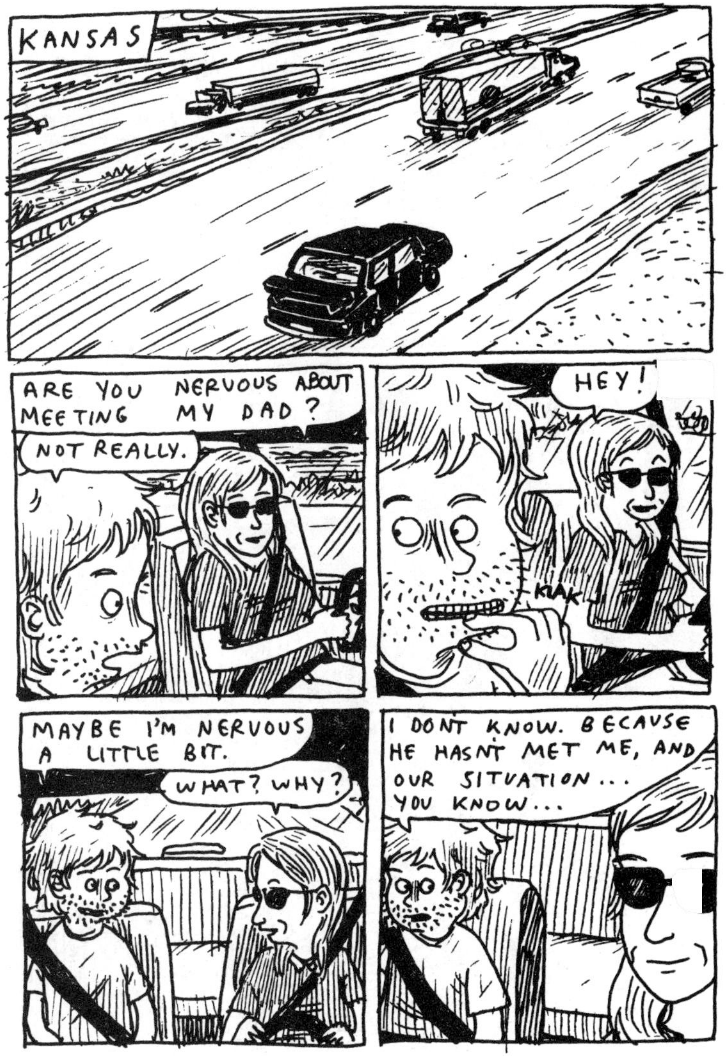
KANSAS
ARE YOU NERVOUS ABOUT MEETING MY DAD?
NOT REALLY.
HEY!
KLAK
MAYBE I'M NERVOUS A LITTLE BIT.
WHAT? WHY?
I DONT KNOW. BECAUSE HE HASNT MET ME, AND OUR SITUATION... YOU KNOW...

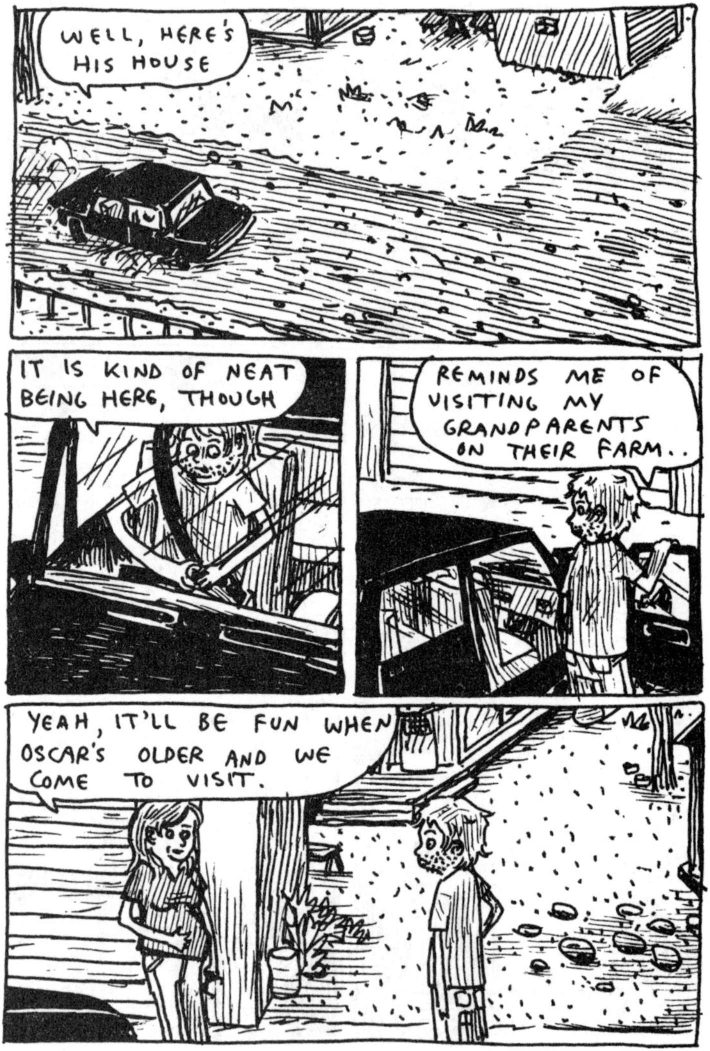
WELL, HERE'S HIS HOUSE
IT IS KIND OF NEAT BEING HERE, THOUGH
REMINDS ME OF VISITING MY GRANDPARENTS ON THEIR FARM..
YEAH, IT'LL BE FUN WHEN OSCAR'S OLDER AND WE COME TO VISIT.

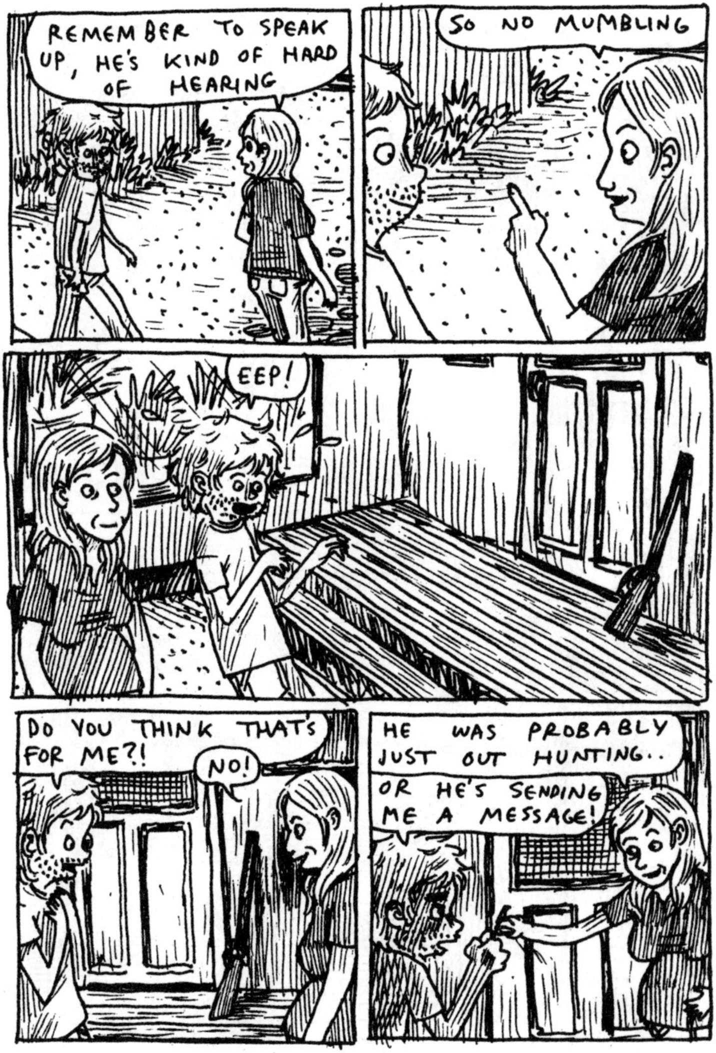
REMEMBER TO SPEAK UP, HE'S KIND OF HARD OF HEARING
SO NO MUMBLING
EEP!
DO YOU THINK THAT'S FOR ME?!
NO!
HE WAS PROBABLY JUST OUT HUNTING..
OR HE'S SENDING ME A MESSAGE!

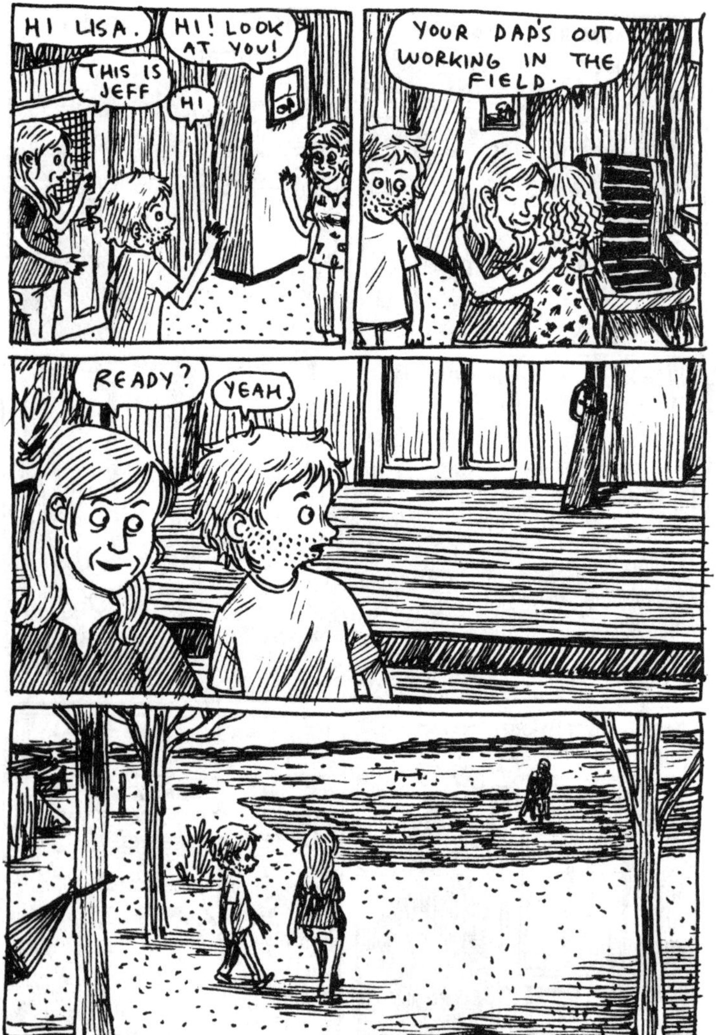
HI LISA.
HI! LOOK AT YOU!
THIS IS JEFF
HI
YOUR DAD'S OUT WORKING IN THE FIELD.
READY?
YEAH.

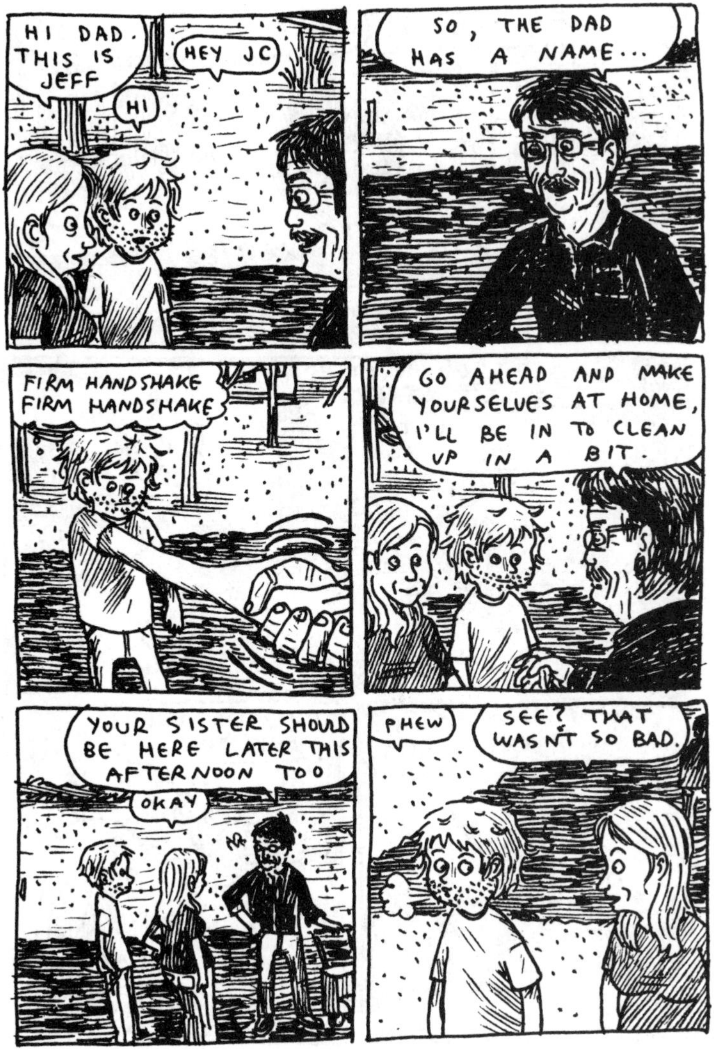
HI DAD. THIS IS JEFF
HEY JC
HI
SO, THE DAD HAS A NAME...
FIRM HANDSHAKE FIRM HANDSHAKE
GO AHEAD AND MAKE YOURSELVES AT HOME, I'LL BE IN TO CLEAN UP IN A BIT.
YOUR SISTER SHOULD BE HERE LATER THIS AFTERNOON TOO
OKAY
PHEW
SEE? THAT WASN'T SO BAD.

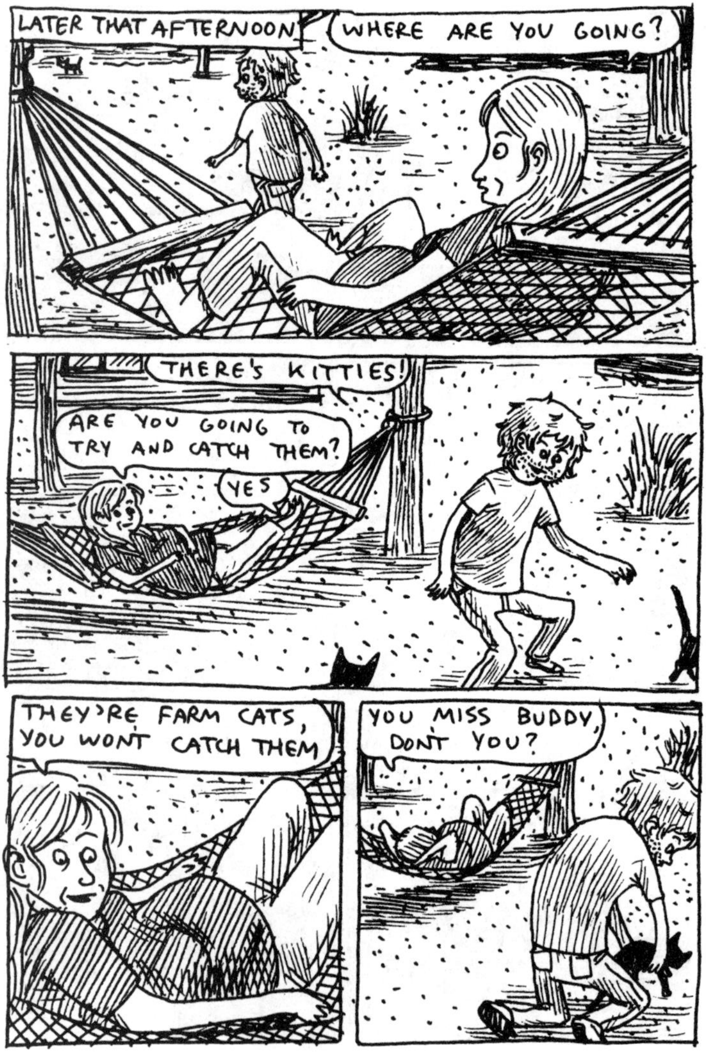
LATER THAT AFTERNOON
WHERE ARE YOU GOING?
THERE'S KITTIES!
ARE YOU GOING TO TRY AND CATCH THEM?
YES
THEY'RE FARM CATS, YOU WONT CATCH THEM
YOU MISS BUDDY, DONT YOU?

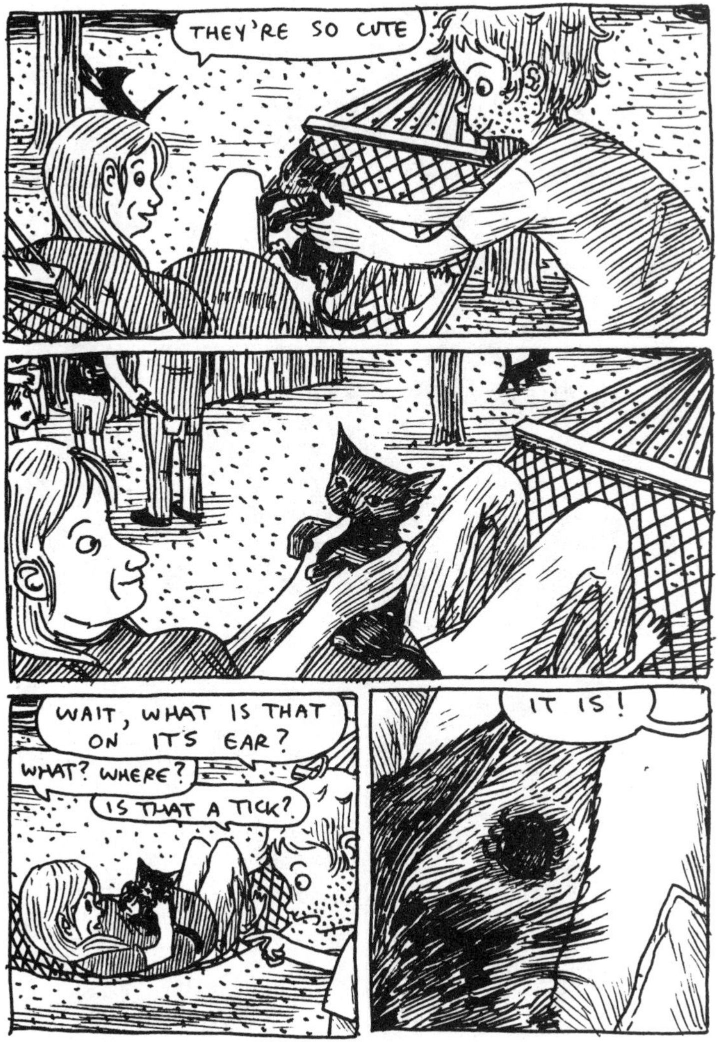
THEY'RE SO CUTE
WAIT, WHAT IS THAT ON IT'S EAR?
WHAT? WHERE?
IS THAT A TICK?
IT IS!

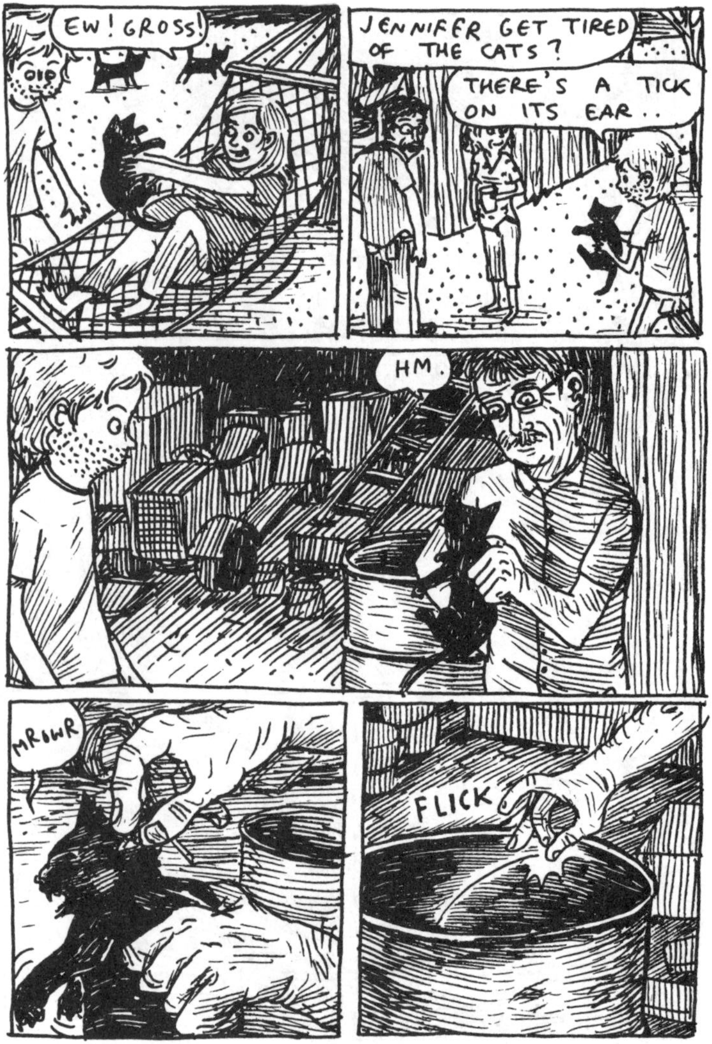
EW! GROSS!
JENNIFER GET TIRED OF THE CATS?
THERE'S A TICK ON ITS EAR..
HM.
MROWR
FLICK

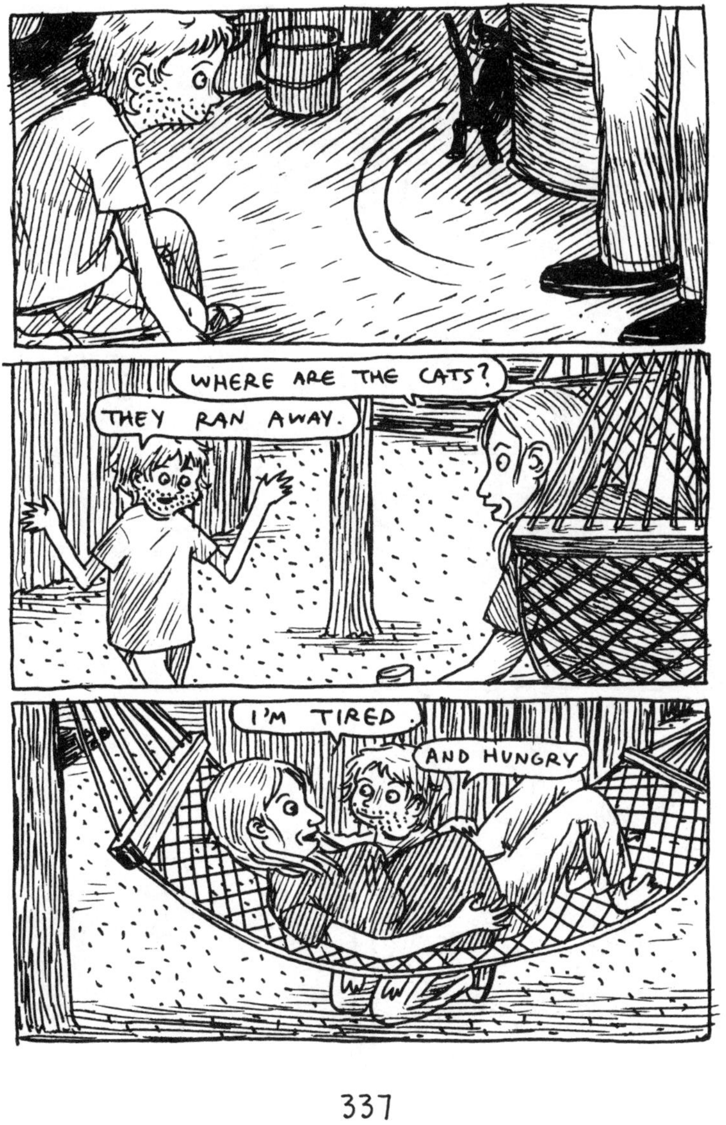
WHERE ARE THE CATS?
THEY RAN AWAY.
I'M TIRED.
AND HUNGRY

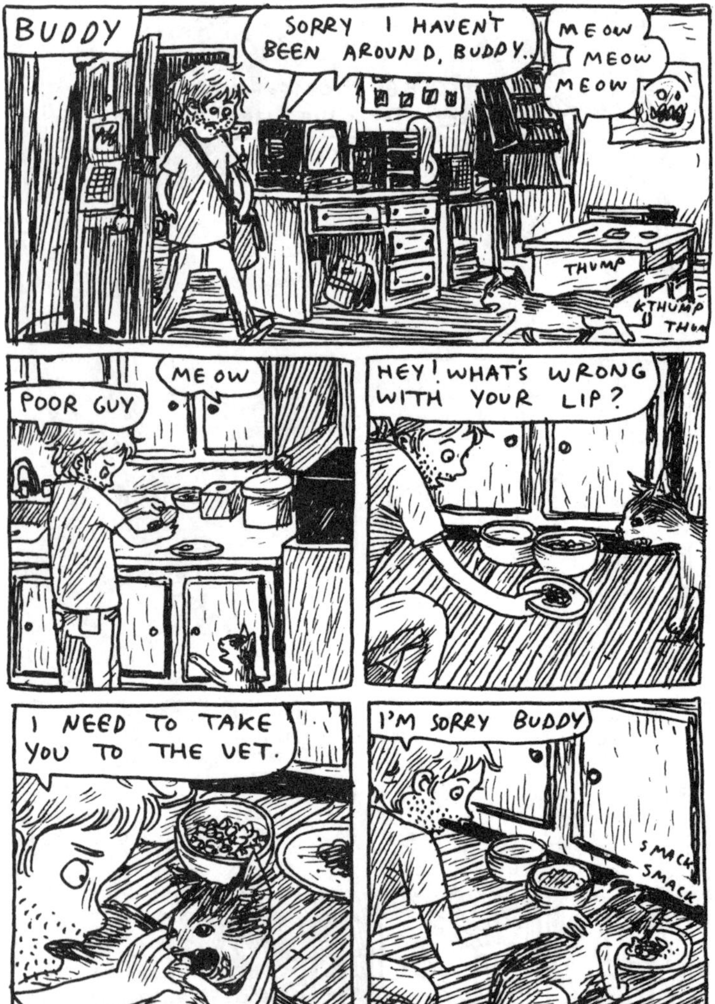
BUDDY
SORRY I HAVEN'T BEEN AROUND, BUDDY..
MEOW MEOW MEOW
THUMP
KTHUMP
POOR GUY
MEOW
HEY! WHAT'S WRONG WITH YOUR LIP?
I NEED TO TAKE YOU TO THE VET.
I'M SORRY BUDDY
SMACK
SMACK

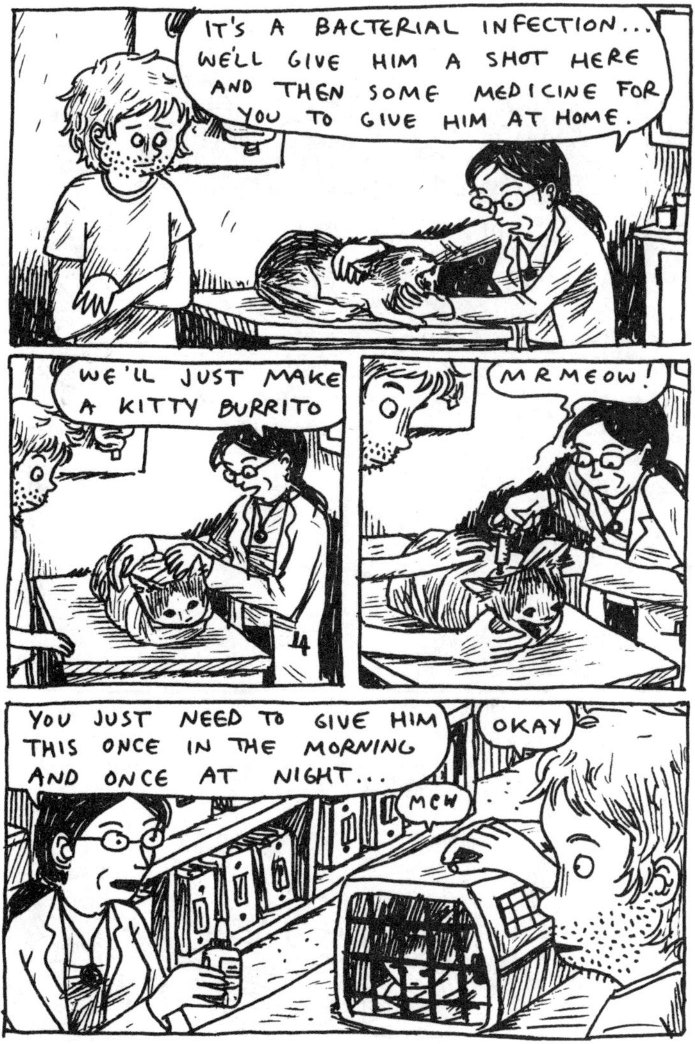
IT'S A BACTERIAL INFECTION... WE'LL GIVE HIM A SHOT HERE AND THEN SOME MEDICINE FOR YOU TO GIVE HIM AT HOME.
WE'LL JUST MAKE A KITTY BURRITO
MRMEOW!
YOU JUST NEED TO GIVE HIM THIS ONCE IN THE MORNING AND ONCE AT NIGHT...
OKAY
MEW

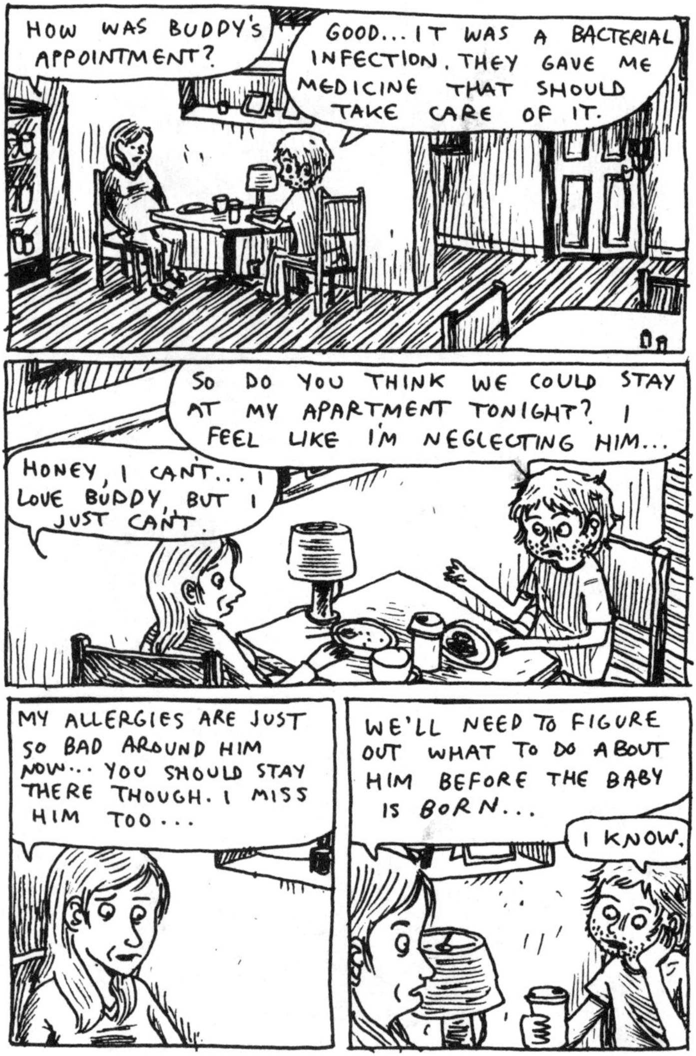
HOW WAS BUDDY'S APPOINTMENT?
GOOD... IT WAS A BACTERIAL INFECTION. THEY GAVE ME MEDICINE THAT SHOULD TAKE CARE OF IT.
SO DO YOU THINK WE COULD STAY AT MY APARTMENT TONIGHT? I FEEL LIKE I'M NEGLECTING HIM...
HONEY, I CAN'T... I LOVE BUDDY, BUT I JUST CAN'T.
MY ALLERGIES ARE JUST SO BAD AROUND HIM NOW... YOU SHOULD STAY THERE THOUGH. I MISS HIM TOO...
WE'LL NEED TO FIGURE OUT WHAT TO DO ABOUT HIM BEFORE THE BABY IS BORN...
I KNOW.

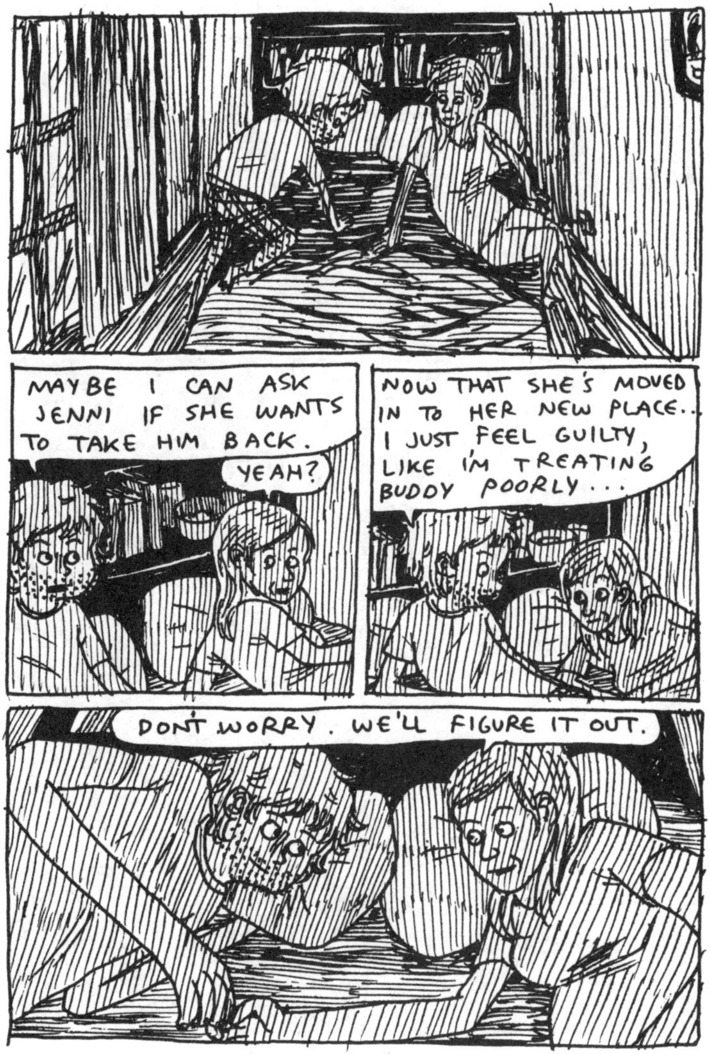
MAYBE I CAN ASK JENNI IF SHE WANTS TO TAKE HIM BACK.
YEAH?
NOW THAT SHE'S MOVED IN TO HER NEW PLACE.. I JUST FEEL GUILTY, LIKE I'M TREATING BUDDY POORLY...
DON'T WORRY. WE'LL FIGURE IT OUT.

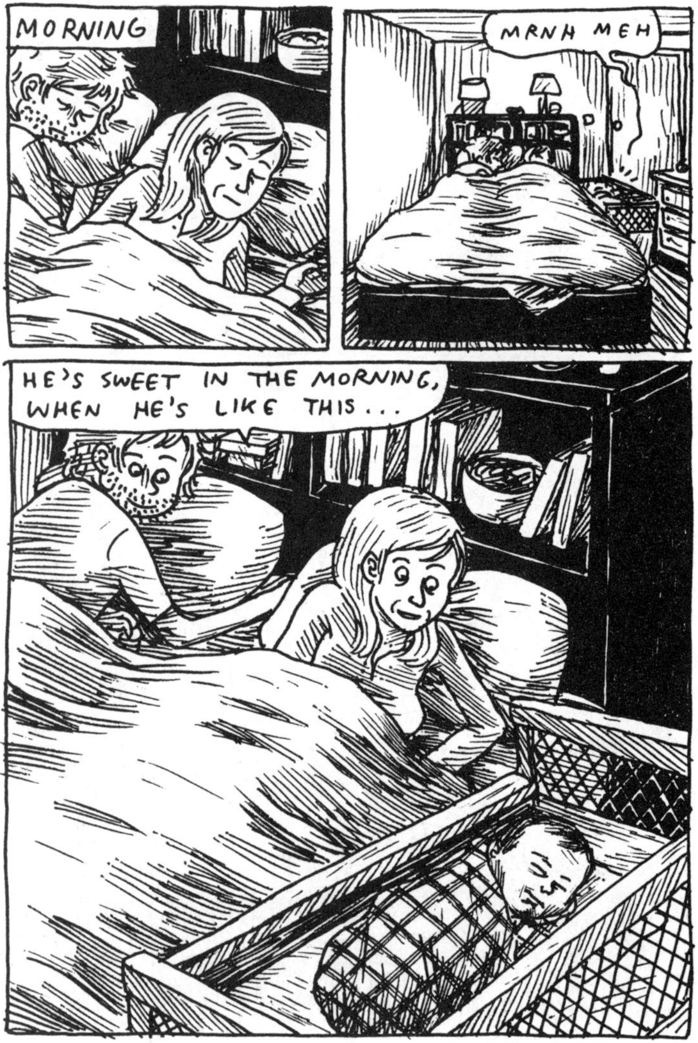
MORNING
MRNH MEH
HE'S SWEET IN THE MORNING, WHEN HE'S LIKE THIS...

CHRONOLOGY AND NOTES

ALTHOUGH THESE STORIES ARE AUTOBIOGRAPHICAL, THEY HAVE NO DOUBT BEEN DISTORTED, BY MEMORY AND MY OWN BIASED PERSPECTIVE, FROM WHAT MAY HAVE ACTUALLY OCCURRED. IN SOME CASES, NAMES HAVE BEEN CHANGED, AND DETAILS HAVE BEEN INADVERTENTLY FUDGED.

A SHORT INTRODUCTION OCCURRED AUGUST 2006, DRAWN APRIL 2007.

THESE THINGS THESE THINGS OCCURRED 2002-2003, DRAWN MARCH THROUGH MAY 2005. VARIOUS ANDREW BIRD LYRICS USED BY PERMISSION: "11:11" LYRICS ©2001 WEGAWAM MUSIC CO., "LULL" LYRICS ©2003 WEGAWAM MUSIC CO., "SOVAY" LYRICS ©2003 WEGAWAM MUSIC CO., "THE NAMING OF THINGS" LYRICS ©2005 WEGAWAM MUSIC CO., "HEADSOAK" LYRICS ©2001 WEGAWAM MUSIC CO.

FOUND IN HIS HOME OCCURRED SOMETIME SUMMER 1992, DRAWN SEPTEMBER 2006.

THAT'S WHAT I WAS AFRAID OF OCCURRED FALL OF 2001, DRAWN AUGUST 2006.

MISSING THE MOUNTAINS OCCURRED FALL 2003, DRAWN JANUARY TO MARCH 2007.

MARIE VERSUS: THE CAR OCCURRED JANUARY 2005, DRAWN JUNE 2006. "ANGOULÊME" REFERS TO THE ANGOULÊME INTERNATIONAL COMICS FESTIVAL HELD ANNUALLY IN THE CITY OF ANGOULÊME IN SOUTHERN FRANCE.

EVERYTHING GETS FUCKED UP BUT OCCASIONALLY GETS REPAIRED OCCURRED JUNE 2005, DRAWN JANUARY 2006.

MEANWHILE... OCCURRED FALL 2005, DRAWN JULY 2006.

THE CALM BEFORE THE STORM OCCURRED OCTOBER 2005, DRAWN JULY 2006.

THE UNPLANNED POTENTIAL OF LIFE OCCURRED FEBRUARY 2006, DRAWN AUGUST 2006.

LITTLE THINGS OCCURRED SPRING THROUGH FALL 2004, DRAWN MAY THROUGH SEPTEMBER 2005.

A TINY PIECE OF MYSELF OCCURRED SPRING THROUGH WINTER 2006, DRAWN MARCH AND APRIL 2007.